T5-AGU-245

Perspectives
in
Experimental Gerontology

Perspectives in Experimental Gerontology

A Festschrift for Doctor F. Verzár

Compiled and Edited by

NATHAN W. SHOCK, Ph.D.

Chief, Gerontology Branch
National Institute of Child Health and Human Development
and
The Baltimore City Hospitals
Baltimore, Maryland

With the assistance of

F. BOURLIERE, M.D.

H. VON HAHN, Ph.D.

D. SCHLETTWEIN-GSELL, M.D.

CHARLES C THOMAS • PUBLISHER
Springfield • Illinois • U.S.A.

ST. PHILIPS COLLEGE LIBRARY

591.3
S559p

Published and Distributed Throughout the World by
CHARLES C THOMAS • PUBLISHER
BANNERSTONE HOUSE
301-327 East Lawrence Avenue, Springfield, Illinois, U.S.A.
NATCHEZ PLANTATION HOUSE
735 North Atlantic Boulevard, Fort Lauderdale, Florida, U.S.A.

This book is protected by copyright. No part of it may be reproduced in any manner without written permission from the publisher.

© *1966, by* CHARLES C THOMAS • PUBLISHER
Library of Congress Catalog Card Number: 66-16822

With THOMAS BOOKS *careful attention is given to all details of manufacturing and design. It is the Publisher's desire to present books that are satisfactory as to their physical qualities and artistic possibilities and appropriate for their particular use.* THOMAS BOOKS *will be true to those laws of quality that assure a good name and good will.*

Printed in the United States of America
B-7

CONTRIBUTORS

Alexanders, Peter, Ph.D., D.Sc.—*Head, Radiobiology Department, Chester Beatty Research Institute, Institute of Cancer Research, Royal Cancer Hospital, London, England*

Balázs, András, N.Sc.—*Institute for Gerontology, Budapest, Hungary.*

Barrows, Charles H., Jr., Sc.D.—*Gerontology Branch, National Institute of Child Health and Human Development, National Institutes of Health and the Baltimore City Hospitals, Baltimore, Maryland.*

Bertolini, A. M., M.D.—*Institute of Gerontology, University of Milan, Milan, Italy.*

Bourliére, François, M.D.—*Centre de Gérontologie et Department de Physiologie, Faculté de Médicine de Paris, Paris, France.*

Brauer, Ralph W., Ph.D.—*U. S. Naval Radiological Defense Laboratory, San Francisco, California.*

Comfort, Alex, D.Sc.—*MRC Gerontology Group, Department of Zoology, University College, London, England.*

Chvapil, Milos, M.D.—*Department of Experimental Biology, Institute of Industrial Hygiene and Occupational Diseases, Prague, Czechoslovakia.*

Curtis, Howard J., Ph.D.—*Biology Department, Brookhaven National Laboratory, Upton, New York.*

Elden, Harry R., Ph.D.—*Gerontology Branch, National Institute of Child Health and Human Development, National Institutes of Health and the Baltimore City Hospitals, Baltimore, Maryland.*

Faris, B., Ph.D.—*Boston University School of Medicine, Boston, Massachusetts.*

Franzblau, C., Ph.D.—*Boston University School of Medicine, Boston, Massachusetts.*

Gordon, Helmut A., M.D.—*Department of Pharmacology, College of Medicine, University of Kentucky, Lexington, Kentucky.*

Hall, David A., Ph.D.—*Department of Medicine, The University of Leeds, Leeds, England.*

Haranghy, László, M.D.—*Institute of Gerontology, Budapest, Hungary.*

Hayflick, Leonard, Ph.D.—*Wistar Institute of Anatomy and Biology, Philadelphia, Pennsylvania.*

23232

Kirk, John E., M.D.—*Division of Gerontology, Washington University School of Medicine, St. Louis, Missouri.*

Medvedev, Zhores A., Ph.D.—*Laboratory of Molecular Radiobiology, Institute of Medical Radiology, Obninsk, USSR.*

Milch, Robert A., M.D.—*The Johns Hopkins University School of Medicine, Baltimore, Maryland.*

Rockstein, Morris, Ph.D.—*Department of Physiology, University of Miami School of Medicine, Miami, Florida.*

Sacher, George, B.S.—*Division of Biological and Medical Research, Argonne National Laboratory, Argonne, Illinois.*

Schaub, M. C., M.D.—*Institute of Experimental Gerontology, Basel, Switzerland.*

Schlettwein-Gsell, Daniela, M.D.—*Institute of Experimental Gerontology, Basel, Switzerland.*

Selye, Hans, M.D., Ph.D.—*Institute of Experimental Medicine, and Surgery, University of Montreal, Montreal, Canada.*

Shock, Nathan W., Ph.D.—*Gerontology Branch, National Institute of Child Health and Human Development, National Institutes of Health and the Baltimore City Hospitals, Baltimore, Maryland.*

Sinex, F. Marott, Ph.D.—*Boston University School of Medicine, Boston, Massachusetts.*

Strehler, Bernard L., Ph.D.—*Gerontology Branch, National Institute of Child Health and Human Development, National Institutes of Health and the Baltimore City Hospitals, Baltimore, Maryland.*

Szent-Györgyi, Albert, M.D., Ph.D.—*Institute for Muscle Research, Marine Biological Laboratory, Woods Hole, Massachusetts.*

Troup, Gary M., M.D.—*Department of Pathology, University of California, School of Medicine, Los Angeles, California.*

von Hahn, Holger P., Ph.D.—*Institute of Experimental Gerontology, Basel, Switzerland.*

Walford, Roy L., M.D.—*Department of Pathology, University of California, School of Medicine, Los Angeles, California.*

Weiss, Paul, Ph.D.—*Graduate School of Biomedical Sciences, The University of Texas at Houston, Houston, Texas.*

Welford, Alan T., Ph.D.—*St. John's College, Cambridge, England.*

Wulff, Verner, Ph.D.—*Masonic Research Laboratories, Utica, New York.*

PREFACE

THIS VOLUME was assembled as a tribute to a great man, Fritz Verzár. In some respects, experimental gerontology represents a second career for Dr. Verzár, a scientist with many recognized accomplishments in the field of physiology. In other respects, Dr. Verzár's many contributions to gerontology represent the extension of his career in physiology. In any event, Dr. Verzár brought to the field of gerontology a critical mind associated with an enthusiastic and imaginative experimental approach. The impact of his work has been so widespread that many investigators in gerontology wished to accord him some special recognition in commemoration of his 80th birthday. This Festschrift is the result.

The goal of the book is to present an overview of ideas in the field of experimental gerontology, with emphasis on "ideas" and "experiments." Therefore, it represents more a collection of essays than a detailed summary of all the factual data on specific problem areas. In fact, authors were urged to avoid detailed presentation of experimental data. They were enjoined to place major emphasis on ideas and to project future developments in as imaginative a manner as possible. This is an unusual and difficult assignment for any scientist, but contributors have followed the instructions of the editor. It is hoped that investigators in all of the biological sciences will be challenged by the ideas presented.

The essays are organized under five general headings: Aging at the Molecular Level, Aging in Tissue, Models of Aging, Environmental Factors in Aging, and Theories of Aging. It is apparent that some important areas of research havt been omitted, such as human physiology and the behavioral and clinical aspects of aging. This omission was forced by space limitations and the emphasis on experimental approaches to the problems of aging.

The selection of contributors to the volume was a difficult task, since every investigator in experimental gerontology should have been included. Had this volume been assembled in 1955 instead of 1965 the task would have been simple, since the number was so few that all could have been included. However, in 1965 the number of competent investigators working on various aspects of experimental gerontology was so large that arbitrary selections had to be made.

I can only extend my thanks to the authors who so graciously responded to the invitation and offer my regrets to the many who should also have been invited, but were not.

To Dr. Verzár, birthday greetings, with special salute as you continue to approach the crest of a career with a long and brilliant trajectory.

N. W. Shock
Baltimore City Hospitals

CONTENTS

SECTION IV
MODELS OF AGING

SECTION V
ENVIRONMENTAL FACTORS IN AGING

SECTION VI
THEORIES OF AGING

SECTION VII
THE FUTURE

Perspectives
in
Experimental Gerontology

Section I

FRITZ VERZÁR

The Man and His Work

Chapter 1

FRITZ VERZÁR; THE MAN AND HIS WORK

FRANÇOIS BOURLIÈRE

One has often debated on the "optimum environment" for artistic and scientific achievements. Many times it has been claimed that eras of political stability and abundance were more productive, intellectually speaking, than periods of political unrest and economic uncertainty. On the other hand, some people maintain that a great many of the major discoveries have taken place in troubled times, and that the lives of most artistic and scientific geniuses are far from being devoid of troubles, crises and even tragedies. It is not my purpose here to discuss again that question. However, the life-history of Fritz Verzár seems to show that, though worries of all kinds can indeed interfere with scientific research, they cannot prevent a creative mind from making significant contributions to man's knowledge.

Fritz Verzár (Fig. 1) was born on September 18, 1886 in Budapest, the eldest of a family of three sons. His father, an Hungarian reformist, was a physician; his mother was the daughter of the famous German theologian, Professor Gottlob Pfleiderer. Interested since boyhood in natural sciences, the young Fritz quite naturally entered the medical school of his home town, where he obtained his entire medical training. As early as 1905 he started working in the anatomical department of the medical faculty, and it was there that he made his first scientific discovery. Having heard that the chick's embryo starts moving rhythmically within the egg shell as early as the fourth or fifth day, at an age when no nerves nor any striated muscles are yet differentiated, Verzár started his own search for an explanation. Very rapidly he discovered the cause of these rhythmic movements: autonomous plain muscle cells forming characteristic "star patterns" in the amnion. This led to his first scientific publication (1907) with Professor M. von Lenhos-

ST. PHILIPS COLLEGE LIBRARY

FIGURE 1. Fritz Verzár.

sék. This finding remained unnoticed for half a century and was "rediscovered" only fifty years later.

During the third and fourth years of his medical curriculum, Verzár's interests shifted from morphology to physiology; he first began working on fat metabolism in Professor G. Mansfeld's pharmacological laboratory, before becoming the research-assistant to Professor F. Tangl in the department of "pathological physiology." Tangl was a great admirer of N. Zuntz and M. Rubner and was therefore mainly interested in energy metabolism. Independently or in collaboration with Tangl, Verzár undertook many respiration experiments on dogs, in which he measured oxygen consumption after the extirpation of various organs (spleen, kidney, liver, pancreas), in order to discover their role in energy production.

It was in Tangl's laboratory that Verzár met Peter Rona, the nephew of Julius Bernstein, then a famous electrophysiologist at Halle a.S., and former assistant of Du Bois Raymond. Having heard that Bernstein was looking for a research assistant, and being attracted by the new and promising field of electrophysiology, Verzár accepted this position and moved to Germany in 1910. There he met Ernest Laqueur, who was to become a famous pharmacologist in Amsterdam, and there also he became aware for the first time of the way politics can interfere with research plans! Not being "persona grata" *vis-à-vis* the local government, old Julius Bernstein was flatly refused the necessary money to buy the then fashionable apparatus—a string galvanometer. That is why Verzár was probably one of the very last physiologists to have worked with the Du Bois Raymond *rheotome,* which Bernstein himself built around 1860! It was also during this stay in Halle that Verzár became familiar with Bernstein's "membrane theory," according to which, excitation is due to a change in membrane permeability. Years later Verzár extended this explanation to the changes in peripheral nerves caused by narcosis.

Bernstein retired during the summer of 1911. Verzár, having been given an Hungarian State Research Fellowship, went to England to spend a year in Cambridge with Joseph Barcroft. For a young man educated in the strongly hierarchized academic atmosphere then (and unfortunately still) prevailing in continental

European countries, to spend a year in a British university was an exciting experience. To quote his own words, he found Cambridge "wonderful, both extremely romantic and friendly." In Barcroft's laboratory Verzár first continued his experiments on the role of various organs in energy metabolism; he became familiar with the technique of estimating an organ's respiration (especially the M. gastrocnemius of the cat) by gas analysis of arterial and venous blood. He also continued his stimulation experiments and found that oxygen consumption follows the contraction during recovery and rest (long rebuilding after-effect following an anoxibiotic contraction). It was in Cambridge that Verzár became acquainted with Keith Lucas who had shortly beforehand constructed a capillary electrometer with which he registered nerve action potentials. Keith Lucas, being an engineer, needed someone to do the animal experiments with him. He was helped by an unpaid student from Trinity College, a thin and rather shy young man whose name was later to become famous: Adrian. In Keith Lucas's laboratory, Verzár started to investigate the effect of nerve excitation on the polarization of nerve membrane. He sent a constant current through a nerve and found indeed that a striking change in the polarizing current took place during the excitation —with a small phase that continued. Greatly excited by this discovery, which was published in *Pflüger's Archiv* in 1913, Verzár left Cambridge with the determination to devote his whole lifetime to electrophysiology. "Man proposes but God disposes." In the autumn of 1912, our young Hungarian physiologist was called back home for military service and Verzár did not resume his scientific work until 1913, when he was appointed Privatdozent of Pathological Physiology in Budapest's University.

The beginning of the first World War was soon to come—and in a most unusual way for Fritz. In the summer of 1914 he was called back to military service and appointed naval medical officer on a ship christened "Franz Ferdinand," which left Trieste for Morocco the very same day the heir of the Austro-Hungarian Empire was murdered in Sarajevo. The Mediterranean cruise therefore did not last long. As soon as the ship reached its home port, war broke out and Verzár was ordered straight to his regiment on the Carpathian front line. After a month he accidentally broke one of his legs and was sent back to Debrecen's hospital—on the top of a coal truck. As soon as he had recovered he was appointed head of the bacteriological laboratory of the military hospital in this very same city, not suspecting that Debrecen was to become the center of his activities for the next sixteen years. In the autumn of 1914, crowds of Russian prisoners of war were brought in with typhus, dysentery and malaria. One day in the next winter Verzár and his assistant, Oscar Weszeczky, found in the stools of a Russian soldier the germs of cholera. Their diagnosis was confirmed a few weeks later by bacteriologists in Vienna, and our young amateur microbiologist was immediately appointed "supervisor of the hospitals for infectious diseases" in that area, where there was a mortality rate of 500 people a week from cholera alone! When the threat of cholera was over, other epidemics came, from typhus to "asiatic influenza." There were not many opportunities left for research in such troubled places and times. Nevertheless Verzár's inquisitive spirit did not stand still during the war years. Using the bulb of a Barcroft apparatus as a respirometer he studied the oxygen uptake and carbon dioxide output of a colony of *Bacterium coli,* at a time when Warburg's apparatus did not exist.

In the summer of 1918, the military situation started deteriorating rapidly for the Central Powers, and the political atmosphere became suddenly quite explosive over all of Central Europe. But in those days, when people of the far-off provinces of the Austrian Empire were kept informed only by a few local newspapers tightly controlled by the government, "mass panic" did not occur frequently, and local administration continued to exercise some initiative apart from the context of the general political situation. That is precisely what happened in Hungary, where the government decided to turn the Debrecen High-school for Theology, Law and Philosophy into a full fledged university—the second in the country. At that time the city, already the second in the Kingdom in population, was nevertheless still a typical country community in the heart of the *Puszta* (which means in Hungarian "the flat country") amidst huge corn and wheat fields, with its thousands of small white-washed houses, with green and brown windows. Fritz Verzár was immediately appointed full Professor of Experimental Pathology in the Medical Faculty, with only three colleagues: J. Vészi (who was to die one month later from asiatic influenza), F. Orsós and J. Kenézy. On October 23, 1918 Emperor Karl, King of Hungary, and Empress Zita came to Debrecen to open officially the new University. It was to be their last public appearance. In the middle of the opening ceremony, the Emperor was suddenly called to the telephone. Revolution had broken out both in Budapest and in Vienna. The imperial couple then left to go directly into exile in Switzerland. The rather simple armchair in worked black timber which was used as an imperial throne during that very last episode of Habsburg history has been salvaged; it stands today in Fritz's study in Arlesheim.

1919 was a very troubled year for Hungary. The Rumanian army occupied part of the country, including Debrecen, and Verzár returned to Budapest—only to find the capital in the midst of Bela Kun's marxist revolution. Unable to find any position there, he moved to Germany and then to Holland, where he worked for some months as assistant to Professor H. Zwaardemaker in the Physiological Laboratory of Utrecht University. But the appeal of the *Puszta* was strong. Having heard that the Rumanians were supposed to leave Hungary soon, Verzár returned to his native land before the end of the year—only to find Debrecen still occupied by foreign troops, the University closed and neither funds nor working possibilities left. During the summer of 1920, W. Storm van Leeuwen, who had just been appointed Professor of Pharmacology in Leiden, offered to Verzár the position of "Conservator" in his laboratory, and Fritz went to Holland for the second time. Then he was offered a chair in Java (Buitenzorg), but again he felt homesick. He gave up his position and lodgings in Leiden to his friend Albert Szent-Györgyi and returned to settle in Debrecen in November 1920.

During the next ten years Verzár became the leading figure of the new medical faculty here, and became its first dean in 1921-22 and its first medical *Rector Magnificus* in 1928-29 (Fig. 2). Everything had to be built up and organized, starting from nothing. The first University building to be completed in 1922 was the Institute of Physiology and Experimental Pathology where the second stage of his scientific career was to take place. Between 1922 and 1929 Verzár's experimental research was mainly centered upon neurophysiology and the study of vitamins. Using the string galvanometer he had bought in 1919, he was able to demonstrate the "rebound" of vagus sensory fibers during heart contraction by magnifying it through a polarizing current. Unfortunately electrophysiology is an expensive type of research and the limited financial means of the Debrecen medical school did not enable its professor of Physiology to buy the apparatuses needed to expand

FIGURE 2. The Medical School, Debrecen.

his pioneer investigations. Verzár then reluctantly decided to try his luck in a field which did not need (at that time) elaborate technical equipment: vitamins and hormones. Between 1922 and 1930 a number of papers were therefore published by the Debrecen group on the action of various endocrine secretions, and some on vitamins. Particular attention was given to the relationship between the adrenal cortex and vitamin B. The working assumption was that vitamins are the precursors of both enzymes and hormones.

It was during his Debrecen years that Verzár became interested in the physiology of intestinal absorption and the movements of intestinal villi. He worked out a technique to show their rhythmic contractions which he succeeded in filming. It was also at that time that he was struck by the selective absorption of certain sugars by the intestinal epithelium, a problem he investigated later with much success.

In addition to his laboratory work, Verzár was extremely active in the field of university organization and administration. Supported by Count Klebelsberg, then Minister of Education of the Bethlen government, the Debrecen Medical Faculty developed

FIGURE 3. Tihany Biological Research Institute.

steadily. Verzár, having been appointed Secretary of the National Research Fund, made ambitious plans for the development of medical research in Hungary. He was also the originator of the Tihany Biological Research Institute (Fig. 3) built on the shores of Lake Balaton—a central European counterpart of the famous biological stations of Naples, Plymouth and Woods Hole. Appointed director of Tihany in 1926, he kept this position until 1938, the time of the "Anschluss."

Despite a "major family disaster" (to use his own words) in 1922, the Debrecen and Tihany years were very happy ones for Verzár. There he was able to train a group of bright assistants, some of whom have left their mark in the history of Hungarian medicine and science: A. Beznák (later Professor of Physiology in

Ottawa), G. Ludány (later Professor of Physiology in Kolozsvár), Esther Kokas (now at Chapel Hill, USA), A. Kúthy (formerly Professor of Biochemistry in Budapest), G. Méhes (now Professor of Pharmacology in Pécs), Pius Koller (now at the Chester Beatty Cancer Research Institute in London) and many others. Every type of honor seemed to be bestowed on him: Honorary City Doctor, Presbyter of the Reformed Church, etc. In 1930 he was even invited by Count Klebelsberg to become Secretary of State for Education in Budapest. Why then did Verzár, at the peak of his career, abruptly decide to emigrate to Switzerland? This is a question to which I have never found an entirely satisfactory answer. Various types of motivation were probably influential in this unexpected decision. Verzár himself stresses the fact that he was tired by too much administrative work, which did not leave enough time for experimental research. Otto Loewi, the Graz pharmacologist and Nobel Prize winner, once emphasized the point that, as *Rector Magnificus* of his University, Verzár had to take serious action against some ultra-nationalistic and anti-Jewish student organizations. The fact remains that the invitation of the University of Basel to join its staff in 1930 was readily accepted, and that the forty-four-year-old physiologist left his beloved native Hungary for the "Western Paradise of Switzerland."

The *Vesalianum* (Fig. 4) in Basel—as the university building in which are located the laboratories of physiology, biochemistry and pharmacology was (and still is) called—was meanwhile far from being an ideal place for research. Erected in 1885 by Friedrich Miescher, the building had none of the facilities one might expect in a dynamic university like Basel. The physiology laboratory was located on the groundfloor; its equipment was mostly out of date and its staff limited. For someone who has held an important position in his own country, to settle, at the age of over forty, in a foreign land is not an easy venture; and the adjustment to the new conditions of life and work does not often go without difficulties. In spite of many handicaps Verzár found compensation in the beauty of the Swiss landscape and his freedom to engage in laboratory research. Having equipped his laboratory and increased his personnel, he resumed his work on intestinal absorption and adrenal secretion, making at that time some of his most important contributions to physiological science. His findings on the mechanism of sugar absorption are so well known that it is useless to describe his experiments at length. Having supposed that phosphorylation occurred in the intestinal epithelium, Verzár inhibited it by iodoacetic acid and other substances and found that the selective absorption of glucose and galactose was prevented. Adrenalectomy had the same result. Turning to fat absorption, he was also

FIGURE 4. The Vesalianum, Basel.

able to show that neutral fats are not synthesized if phosphorylation is inhibited. All these experiments were summarized in the book *Absorption from the Intestine* that Verzár published in 1936 with Jean McDougall—his co-worker since 1933, who was to become his second wife in 1938. In the later thirties the *Vesalianum* team concentrated more and more on adrenal physiology.

It was during these years that Verzár first showed that adrenalectomized cats and rats could be maintained by the administration of desoxycorticosterone (DOCA). Since both electrolyte and carbohydrate metabolism remained normal, the other cortico-steroids which were later isolated must have been produced from desoxycorticosterone. He especially noted that glycogen and potassium and sodium changes during muscle activity were restored by the administration of DOCA. These effects of DOCA were also demonstrated in isolated muscle preparations. Reichstein having then synthesized desoxycorticosterone, Verzár and his co-workers tested its action on sugar absorption in the intestine. They were also able to show that DOCA can keep adrenalectomized cats alive for a year. Most of these findings were summarized in a book on the physiology of the adrenal cortex which very unfortunately came off the press on September 1, 1939—the very same day that World War II started so that much of Dr. Verzár's pioneer work was not known in Europe and the USA until years later.

It was during the war years that Verzár began to show an active interest in various international organizations. As early as 1942 he was approached by the Geneva Office of WHO to take part in a post-war nutrition program; but being "locked in" Switzerland, he was not able to do much until the end of the war. In the meantime he wrote a *Lehrbuch der Inneren Sekretion* which was widely used by generations of students. From January to October 1948 Verzár was in charge of the Human Nutrition Program of FAO, then in Washington. It was his second visit to the USA (the first having taken place in 1929, when the International Congress of Physiology was held in Boston). Many more were to take place during the forthcoming seventeen years! In 1949, the United Nations Secretariat appointed him member of the Commission for the Study of the Coca Problem in Peru and Bolivia, where he spent four months travelling in the Andes. This UN mission resulted in the official UN Coca Report (of which Verzár was responsible for the physiological chapter) and an unpublished short novel entitled *The Cocaco**—a humorous satire on the UN Agencies' usual methods of working—of which I am privileged to own a copy. Latin America obviously impressed Verzár deeply; I suspect he loved the cheerfulness, the colorful way of life and the pride of its people, which subconsciously reminded him of his native Hungary. He was to come back in 1957 to reorganize the preclinical teaching in Caracas and once more in 1964 to take part in the Centennial of the Medical Academy in Mexico.

His work for International Agencies did not prevent Verzár

* *The Cocaco,* A novel by L. Success. 33 pages.

from continuing his experimental research in the *Vesalianum* and at the St Moritz-Bad Mountain Laboratory, where the family spent their summer months after the war. In Basel he was helped by enthusiastic assistants and students: H. Wirtz (now with Geigy A.G. research department), E. Flückiger (now with Sandoz), and many others. During those years Verzár's interests were centered upon two very different topics: the role of the atmospheric condensation nuclei and the nutritional status of mountain people in Switzerland. The first experiments were mainly performed at St Moritz,* where an automatic condensation nuclei counter was constructed and the role of these nuclei on respiration were studied under both normal and pathological conditions. This work is now continued in Germany. Verzár's interest in nutrition obviously originated in his vitamin studies during the Debrecen years, but Barcroft's invitation to take part in the 1946 Postwar Nutrition Conference in Cambridge certainly strengthened it. In 1956, he organized another Nutrition Conference in Basel, which led to the establishment of the International Union of Nutrition Societies. Later the Swiss Federal Government asked him to study the nutrition of mountain folk in Switzerland—a team work which culminated in the publication of the volume entitled *Ernährung und Gesundheitzustand der Bergvölkerung der Schweiz* (1962).

It was after a visit which the great European pioneer of gerontology, V. Korenchevsky, paid him in 1952 that Verzár began to be interested in the biology of aging. Strongly encouraged and supported by his friend K. Miescher, he began at once to set up a rat colony and to study progressive loss of adaptability of the aging organism. His first paper was presented at the London Congress in 1954. When in, 1956, it was time for him to retire from the *Vesalianum,* he moved his rat colony and his laboratory to the anatomical department and continued his experiments. In the same year he organized the International Symposium of Experimental Gerontology which took place in Basel and as a result of which *Gerontologia* was founded in 1957. Next year, with the financial help of the Basel Pharmaceutical Industry, a house was bought at Non-

* With his characteristic enthusiasm, Dr. Verzár established a research laboratory in St Moritz in 1944 to study physiological and especially respiratory factors in the adjustment to high altitude.

nenweg 7 and the *Institut für experimentelle Gerontologie* established (Fig. 5). The detailed story of this venture is given in Chapter 2, but it is worth emphasizing here that the maintenance of this lively research center has been an endless struggle for its director. To run such a laboratory with a small budget is not an easy matter. Many younger scientists would have already given up.

FIGURE 5. Institut für experimentelle Gerontologie, Basel.

One may wonder about the secret of Verzár's incredible enthusiasm and liveliness. No doubt it is due in part to his excellent health. At seventy-nine this stocky, blue eyed man looks definitely younger than most people of his generation. He has nevertheless always been handicapped by an asthma which began when he was five years old. His allergic disorders quite probably explain his life-long interest in bio-climatology—as well as his love for outdoor life. But Fritz is also a remarkably well balanced man. Although interested in almost everything—from music to biophysics—he has always taken the trouble to balance his intellectual activities with some kind of physical exercise. He used to practice rowing on the Danube when he was a student and he began skiing as soon as he arrived in Switzerland in 1930. He continued to do so regularly until 1940 when he had a serious accident which kept him in bed for many months. Even now, when he is in St Moritz, he climbs mountains much more easily than many younger sedentary research workers. For many years Verzár has had an unusually sound schedule of rest and activity which enables him to work efficiently without undue fatigue. Leaving at about 9 A.M. the beautiful village of Arlesheim, 12 kilometers from Basel, where he had lived since 1939 amidst beech woods, orchards and vineyards, he drives to his laboratory where he works until 4 to 4:30 P.M. Then he comes back to his quiet house where he enjoys family life with his wife, son and daughter. After dinner he goes to bed rather early, sleeps seven hours and wakes up around 5 A.M. to spend two to three hours reading in his study. Friends from Europe or overseas are always welcomed in Arlesheim, and it is a delight for the visitor to spend hours with the Verzárs discussing history, biology, philosophy or even world politics! One cannot avoid being amazed by the overwhelming enthusiasm of our old "Boss"; at almost eighty he still enjoys planning new experiments and discussing new ideas. Obviously, research has always been for him an exciting intellectual venture. I remember his remark, a few years ago, during one of the lively afternoon discussions which took place during a symposium in Gatlinburg. When some participants were gravely discussing the meaning of science, Verzár unexpectedly remarked "For me, science means mainly fun for the scientist!" I have the feeling that this never ending delight in unveiling the unknown is the very essence of his Fountain of Youth.

Chapter 2

THE INSTITUTE OF EXPERIMENTAL GERONTOLOGY IN BASEL

DANIELA SCHLETTWEIN-GSELL

VERZÁR'S INTEREST in experimental gerontology dates back to 1952, when—still in the Physiological Institute of Basel University—he started to measure the adaptation capacity of old animals towards cold, heat and oxygen tension. Learning capacity and memory of young and old rats were also tested in this institute by his wife Jean McDougall,[8] and it was in these years that he systematically started to rear a colony of senescent Wistar rats.

In April 1954 he invited the Gerontological Society of Switzerland which until then had mainly been interested in clinical and social problems, to a "Symposium on the possibilities of experimental research on aging." Several institutes of Basel university and members of the chemical and pharmaceutical industry participated. When in 1955 Prof. Dr. F. Bernstein gave a lecture on the relationship between measurements of presbyopia and life-expectation as calculated from data in Göttingen and New York in Verzár's Institute,[1] his ideas found great interest. Still in the same year, Dr. K. Miescher, research director at CIBA AG, together with Verzár initiated a team for longitudinal research on men (*Arbeitsgemeinschaft für Alterns-forschung am Menschen*), which was spontaneously joined by several members of the university (Appendix E). Yearly measurements were to be taken on 100 employees of the CIBA AG. Results of the first ten years' investigations will be presented at the Seventh International Congress of Gerontology in 1966.

The growing interest in problems of the aging process enabled Verzár to invite the Biological and Medical Research Committee of the European Section of the International Association of Gerontology for a "Symposium on experimental gerontology" held in Basel in April 1956. More than forty scientists of ten European countries were invited to the Physiological Institute in Basel which was made possible by the financial support of the Interpharma.* More than 160 participants from all over Europe participated. Proceedings were published in the same year.[2]

In these years, Verzár was elected secretary and later chairman of the Biological Research Committee of the International Association of Gerontology for Europe. In 1956 he also founded *Gerontologia,* a journal exclusively reserved for papers on experimental research in aging, with the S. Karger AG as publishers. With his activity in gerontology still growing Verzár was retired from the university in October 1956 and left the physiological institute.

The Department of Education procured a small laboratory for his use in the Institute of Anatomy, where Verzár without interruption continued to work with the help of a temporary technical assistant. With the support of the CIBA AG he was able to keep his colony of senescent Wistar rats which, by that time, had grown to more than 1,000 animals. It was under these circumstances that Verzár started his basic studies on the changes of the tail tendon during the aging process. He actually never ceased to experiment although during the first months after he had left the university he had to wait, hope and fight for every single facility. When—in the last months of 1956—Dr. D. van Slyke and Dr. K. Mason visited him in his small laboratory they suggested an annual grant in order to assure continuation of the experimental work. The Muscular Dystrophy Association of America since then provides a generous donation for experimental research every year.

With never-ceasing optimism Verzár immediately rented a three room apartment on the fourth floor at Klingelbergstrasse 11, additional to the already existing facilities. One room of the apartment was designed to serve as his office, one room was reserved for experimental psychology. In the third room his growing staff settled down. A centrifuge was installed in the bathroom, a colorimeter set up in the kitchen, equipment was washed in the kitchen sink and the baking-oven of the electric stove served as an autoclave. When, in June 1957 Verzár was asked by the Federal Health

---

* Ciba AG, I. R. Geigy AG, F. Hoffmann-La-Roche & Co. AG, Sandoz AG, and Dr. A. Wander AG.

Office of Switzerland to direct an investigation on the nutritional status of the mountain population of Switzerland, a group of two physicians and a nutritionist were additionally housed in a room under the roof of the same house (Appendix C).

It was in this environment that work went on until September, 1959. In these years Verzár showed the striking differences between the force exerted during thermal shrinkage by young and mature rat tail tendon. "The simplicity and elegance of Verzár's system has stimulated a great deal of study of the tail tendon system" (Sinex, 1964).[3] At the same time all data on the nutritional status of the mountain population of Switzerland were gathered.[4] All those who have collaborated with Verzár during these years will never forget the enthusiasm of this pioneer atmosphere and with special pleasure remember the charm of the temporary, often improvised, always moving, equipment.

In the last months of 1958 Verzár received a grant from the F. Hoffmann-La-Roche & Co. AG which permitted the rental of more spacious laboratories for a period of five years and the assistance of a graduate coworker.

Verzár's conviction that work in experimental gerontology had a most promising future led him to persuade the donors to allow the funds to be used for the acquisition of a building instead of for annual rental. This building was to belong to a *Stiftung für experimentelle Alternsforschung* (Foundation for Experimental Gerontology) organized by Verzár on January 1, 1959 to which members of the university, representatives of the chemical industry and the government were asked to join and serve on the board of control (Appendix A).

On May 1, 1959 the building at Nonnenweg 7 in which the present Institute of Experimental Gerontology is located, was taken over. The building, originally a private house dating back to the late nineteenth century had served as a nurses' residence for more than ten years. Further donations were obtained by Dr. Verzár to finance the most urgent renovations necessary for laboratory research. The outside of the house was not cleaned or modernized until 1963.

On September 1, 1959 work started in all laboratories. A few days later it was possible to transfer the animal colony to the specially prepared quarters in the basement of the building and on October 1, 1959 the official inauguration of the Institute was held to which the chairman of the International Association of Gerontology, delegates of the gerontological societies of Switzerland and the neighbouring countries, the members of the foundation and the press were invited. This is how the Institute of Experimental Gerontology came into existence.

In the seven years which have elapsed, experimental work has been carried out in different fields of interest. In Verzár's personal laboratory—situated on the ground floor of the institute, next to his office, the secretariat and the library—work has centered around the aging of collagen. Thermal denaturation has been measured in tendon and skin of animals and men. Isometric and isotonic as well as chemical methods have been worked out. Radiated animals, hypophysectomized animals as well as animals sensitized with DHT have been studied. The influence of several factors on the physical properties of connective tissue have been studied and attempts have been made to characterize the nature of crosslinkages formed in the collagen molecule. A complete list of Verzár's papers is given in a bibliography of this volume.

The first floor of the building is designed for three graduate assistants. Two spacious laboratories, an office and three smaller rooms reserved for analytical instruments are available. The concept of crosslinkage, as demonstrated in collagen, obviously has implications concerning the state of other insoluble macromolecules of the aging cell: experiments have therefore concentrated on aging of DNA[5] and aging of collagen in different organs.[6] Since the team of the Federal Health Department which under Verzár investigated the nutritional status of the mountain population had revealed some interesting facts on the nutrition of physically active old subjects, nutritional factors are also studied.[7]

In the second floor laboratories for experimental psychology,[8] histology,[9] and photography are installed as well as equipment for the measurement of the action of different drugs in old age.[10] A further room contains Verzár's collection of more than 50,000 alphabetically arranged reprints and a counter for atmospheric nuclei on which Verzár works when he takes a holiday from the Institute.[11]

Thanks to the fact that the building was originally built as a private house it was possible to reserve a room with private bath as a guest room. This has enabled Verzár continuously to invite guest investigators who have stimulated the work of the Institute (Appendix D).

In the basement of the building the old age colony of Wistar-rats which consists of up to 2000 animals is housed. These are all descendants of a couple of rats Verzár had brought along from Hungary in 1930. Animals are kept under standard conditions. Growth, lifespan and causes of death are carefully registered.[12] For a period of more than one year a group of animals was kept with daily physical activity.[13] Besides rats, there have been hamsters and guinea-pigs for special purposes and in the former bathroom of the house an old age colony of South African claw-frogs (xenopus laevis) was reared which contained animals up to fifteen years of age and showed that aging of collagen in poikilotherms follows the same pathway as in mammals.[14]

The staff of the Institute varies between eight and twelve persons (Appendix B), of which three to four are graduate assistants. The salary of two of them has been taken over by the National Foundation for Scientific Research of Switzerland (*Schweizerischer Nationalfonds zur Förderung der wissenschaftlichen Forschung*). This staff has regularly been enlarged by guest investigators (Appendix D) and students working on their dissertation (Appendix H). Cooperation with several other institutes has procured additional working facilities (Appendix F). Regular colloquia are held in the library, with invited lecturers from all over the world, which find growing interest at the university and in the chemical industry (Appendix G).

Meetings of the investigators involved in the longitudinal study of aging in men also take place in the Institute.

In 1964 the European Biological Section of the International Association of Gerontology again met in Basel and held a symposium on experimental gerontology at the Institute from October 23-25, where fifty-six papers were submitted by investigators from fourteen different countries.[15]

Although the Institute still operates on annual grants from a number of sources, it is hoped that some mechanism will be found for long term financing which will assure the continuation of the Institute which has contributed so much to experimental gerontology.

REFERENCES

1. Bernstein, F., and Bernstein, M.: Law of physiologic aging as derived from long range data in refraction of the human eye. *Arch. Ophthal. (Chicago), 34:*378, 1945.
2. Verzár, F. (ed.): *Experimentelle Alternsforschung.* Basel, Birkhäuser, 1956.
3. Sinex, F. M.: Cross-linkage and aging. In: Strehler, B. (ed) *Advances in Gerontology, Vol. I.* New York, Academic Press, 1964, pp. 165-180.
4. Verzár, F., and Gsell, D.: *Ernährungs- und Gesundheitszustand der Bergbevölkerung der Schweiz.* Eidg. Gesundheitsamt, Bern, 1962.
5. Hahn, H. P. von: Age related alterations in the structure of DNA. *Gerontologia (Basel), 10:*174, 1964-65.
6. Schaub, M. C.: The aging of collagen in the striated muscle. *Gerontologia (Basel), 8:*16, 1963.
7. Gsell, D.: Untersuchungen über die Nahrung von alten Menschen. *Gerontologia (Basel), 2:*321, 1958.
8. Verzár-McDougall, E. J.: Studies in learning and memory in aging rats. *Gerontologia (Basel), 1:*65, 1957.
9. Gömöri, Z.: Histologische Veränderungen in der Grosshirnrinde von Ratten mit Verlust des Erinnerungsvermögens im Alter. *Gerontologia (Basel), 3:*288, 1959.
10. Farner, D.: Pharmakologische Wirkungen bei Tieren verschiedenen Alters. *Gerontologia (Basel), 5:*35, 1961.
11. Verzár, F.: Fünfzehn Jahre Höhenklimaforschung der Klimaphysiologischen Station St. Moritz-Bad. *Schweiz. Med. Wschr., 93:*251, 1963.
12. Gsell, D.: Absterbekurven und Wachstumscharakteristika einer "Alterszucht" von Wistar-Ratten. In Weihe, H. (ed) *Die Umwelt der Versuchstiere.* Bern, Huber, 1963.
13. Gsell, D., von Hahn, H. P., and Schaub, M. C.: Serum and muscle creatine in exercised aging rats. *Gerontologia (Basel), 9:*42, 1964.
14. Brocas, J., and Verzár, F.: The aging of *Xenopus laevis. Experientia, 17:*421, 1961.
15. Various: Abstracts of the Symposium. *Excerpta Med.* [XX], *8:*1, 1965.

APPENDIX A

Board of Control of the Foundation for Experimental Gerontology

(Stiftungsrat der Stiftung für experimentelle Alternsforschung)

Chairman: Dr. P. Zschokke, Chief, Department of Education.

Members: Dr. A. Cerletti, Research director, Sandoz AG; Dr. E. Hockenjos, Dr. K. Miescher; Prof. Dr. P. Plattner, Research director, Hoffmann La Roche AG; Prof. Dr. F. Verzár; Prof. Dr. A. Werthemann, Rector of the University.

APPENDIX B

Members of the Institute

Research Staff

E. Jean Verzár-McDougall, Ph.D. 1956-
Vera Freydberg-Lucas, B.Sc. 1956-1957
Z. Gömöri, M.D. 1957-1958
Daniela Schlettwein-Gsell, M.D. 1957-
A. Meyer, Ph.D. 1958-1961
H. Thoenen, M.D. 1959-1962
Dorothee Farner, Ph.D. 1959-1962
Regine Gsell, B.S. 1960-1961
M. C. Schaub, M.D. 1961-
H. P. von Hahn, Ph.D. 1962-
H. Spichtin, B.S. 1965-

Technical Staff

Yvette Kunz 1956-1957
K. Huber 1956-1958
E. Berger 1957-
F. Freuler 1957-1963
Vally John-Vetter 1959-
Christine Mock 1959-
Margrit Wenk-Bürki 1959-1962
Z. Elö 1960-1961
G. Mewis 1961-1961
Franziska Schnetz 1961-1962
Verena Elsässer 1962-1963
Gerda Pfanner 1962-1963
Gertrud Jenny 1962-1963
Adelheid Döbeli-Gehr 1963-1963
W. Gasche 1963-1966
Elvira Fritz 1963-
Lilian Novakovich 1963-1964
J. Schneeberger 1963-1965
Verena Fausch 1964-1965

APPENDIX C

Study Group for the Investigation of the Nutritional Status of the Mountain Population of Switzerland

Chairman: Prof. Dr. F. Verzár
Physicians: Daniela Gsell, M.D., R. Develey, M.D., L. Steinke, M.D.
Nutritionists: Claire Curdy, Verena Gerber, Hedi Indermühle, Brigitt Streuli

APPENDIX D

Guest Investigators

1957. Dr. I. Banga Physiological Institute, University of Budapest (Hungary)	Effect of weak organic acids on collagen
1957/58. Dr. E. Kokas Physiological Institute, University of Budapest (Hungary)	Old age creatinuria
1959. Drs. T. and S. Csáky Pharmacological Institute, University of North Carolina, Chapel Hill, N.C. (U.S.A.)	Blood pressure in old age
1960. Dr. H. Mislin Zoological Institute, University of Mainz (Germany)	Aging of lymphatic tissue
1961. Dr. J. Brocas Physiological Institute, Ecole de Médecine, Paris (France)	Aging of poikilotherms
1961. Dr. H. Gordon Research center on germfree animals, Notre-Dame University, South Bend, Ind. (U.S.A.)	Aging of germ-free animals
1962. Dr. E. Kokas Physiological Institute, University of North Carolina, Chapel Hill N.C. (U.S.A.)	Absorption of glucose in old age
1963. Dr. J. Rigó Physiological Institute, University of Budapest (Hungary)	Influence of magnesium on aging of the aorta
1964. Prof. E. Batschelet Statistical Laboratory, Catholic University of America, Washington, D.C. (U.S.A.)	Statistical evaluation of longitudinal research
1965. Dr. D. Korbuly Radiobiological Clinic, University of Budapest (Hungary)	Resorption of sodium and potassium in old age
1965. Dr. D. Korbuly University of Budapest (Hungary)	Nutritional intake in families of different size and age
1966. Dr. M. Boros Farkas Institute of Pathophysiology, Pécs (Hungary)	Collagen research

APPENDIX E

Study Group for Longitudinal Research in Men

(Arbeitsgemeinschaft für Alternsforschung am Menschen)

Chairman: Prof. Dr. F. Verzár
Secretary: Dr. J. Tripod, CIBA AG
Co-workers: Prof. E. Batschelet, Statistics; Prof. Dr. R. Brückner, Ophthalmology; Prof. Dr. O. Gsell, Internal Medicine; Prof. Dr. M. Monnier, Physiology; Prof. Dr. R. Schuppli, Dermatology
Members: Dr. Dr. h. c. K. Miescher, Dr. A. L. Vischer

APPENDIX F

Cooperation with Other Laboratories

Prof. Dr. A. Árvay Department of Gynaecology, Debrecen, Hungary	Aging of collagen during pregnancy
Dr. S. Bloch Department of Gynaecology, Basel, Switzerland	Aging of endocrine organs
Prof. Dr. M. Brenner Institute of Organic Chemistry, Basel, Switzerland	Chemistry of aging collagen
Dr. I. V. G. A. Durnin Institute of Physiology, Glasgow, Scotland	Oxygen consumption in aging men
Prof. O. Haferkamp Institute of Pathology, Bonn, Germany	Immunoglobulins in old age
Prof. Dr. H. Kraut Max Planck Institute of Nutrition, Dortmund, Germany	Work capacity of old subjects
Prof. Dr. R. Margaria Department of Physiology, Milano, Italy	Work performance and heart rate
Dr. J. Mayer Harvard School of Public Health, Boston, Mass. U.S.A.	Serum-cholesterol in an aging population with high fat intake and high physical activity
Dr. S. Oeriu Academy of the Republic Bucharest, Roumania	Cystine metabolism in collagen
Dr. H. Selye Institute of Experimental Surgery, Montreal, Canada	Calciphylaxis
Prof. Dr. H. Willenegger Department of Surgery, Liestal, BL Switzerland	Collagen in scars

APPENDIX G

Colloquia Held at the Institute

3.11.1959	Dr. B. Exer, Basel	Collagen
6.11.1959	Dr. R. Fricke, Marburg	Methods in collagen research
18.12.1959	Dr. J. Finkelstein, Santiago, Chile	Methods of research
12.1959	Dr. H. Thoenen, Basel	The expedition to the Andes of the Alpine Club of Switzerland
5. 4.1960	Session of the Gerontological Society of Switzerland	
6. 5.1960	Dr. H. Kay, Oxford	Methods of experimental psychology
6.1960	Dr. B. Exer, Basel	Collagen
25.10.1960	Dr. G. Kelemen, Boston	Old age diseases of animals
12.1960	Dr. Goald, New York	Collagen and vitamin C deficiency
24. 1.1961	Dr. A. T. Miller, Scientific Liaison Officer, Embassy of U.S.A., London	The regulation of energy metabolism
13. 3.1961	Prof. F. Hulse, Tuscon, Arizona	Anthropological measurements on Italian-Swiss-people in Switzerland and California
14. 6.1961	Dr. L. Kasprzyk, Poland	Research in Poland
30. 1.1962	Dr. A. L. Vischer, Basel	Husband and wife in old age
9. 7.1962	Dr. S. Balo Banga, Budapest	Collagen
19. 7.1962	Prof. Dr. K. Meyer, New York	Mucopolysaccharides
21. 9.1962	Dr. N. W. Shock, Baltimore	Gerontological research
25. 2.1963	Dr. H. P. von Hahn, Basel	The function of DNA in the aging process
5.11.1963	Dr. M. Staehelin, Basel	Hormonal regulation of protein synthesis
19.11.1963	Dr. R. Lossli, Füllinsdorf/Basel	Influence of genotype and environment on laboratory animals
3.12.1963	Dr. H. Weihe, Bern	Adaptation capacity of rats
15. 2.1964	Dr. S. Rigó, Budapest	Magnesium and arteriosclerosis
10.10.1964	Dr. G. Kelemen, Los Angeles	Pathology of rats
16.10.1964	Dr. H. Selye, Montreal	Calciphylaxis
4.11.1965	Dr. H. P. von Hahn, Basel	The role of histones in the aging of nucleoprotein

APPENDIX H

Doctoral Dissertations at the Institute

1958	Daniela Gsell	Der Nahrungsverbrauch alter Menschen
1959	Z. Gömöri	Histologische Veränderungen in der Grosshirnrinde von Ratten mit Verlust des Erinnerungsvermögens im Alter
1961	Dorothee Farner	Pharmakologische Wirkungen bei Tieren verschiedenen Alters
1962	R. Develey	Über den Kaffeeverbrauch in den Schweizer Bergen
1963	A. Meyer	Chemische Veränderungen am alternden Collagen
1963	M. C. Schaub	The aging of collagen in striated muscle

Chapter 3

A BIBLIOGRAPHY OF F. VERZÁR; 1907-1965

H. P. VON HAHN AND M. C. SCHAUB

THE PUBLISHED WORK of Professor Frederic Verzár covers, up to 1965, a period of fifty-eight years, from his first paper on chick musculature from the University of Budapest in 1907 to the latest comprehensive essay on the biological aspects of aging in the "Handbuch der Praktischen Geriatrie," published in 1965. In this astonishing period of uninterrupted productivity, 472 publications in journals and periodicals have appeared under his name as author or co-author, and he has furthermore been the author or editor of eighteen books or monographs or serial publications. This does not include the several hundred papers published during this period under his direction by his assistants and pupils, but which do not carry his name, and which have regretfully had to be omitted for lack of space.

The major number of Professor Verzár's papers were written in German, with others in Hungarian and English. A few have been published in other languages, French, Italian, Spanish, Portuguese and Dutch. As it would have been impossible to print the original titles as well as their English translations, only the English (translated by the compilers of this bibliography) is given, with the language of the original in brackets. In the first section, books, monographs, and serial publications of which Professor Verzár is author or editor are listed. In the second, all publications in journals and other periodicals, irrespective of their nature, are listed in chronological order. Within each year-group, no special order has been established.

I. BOOKS AND MONOGRAPHS WRITTEN AND EDITED BY F. VERZÁR

1. VERZÁR, F.: *Orvosi Laboratoriumi Munkálatok. (Medical laboratory methods.)* Debrecen, 1921, 262 pp.

2. VERZÁR, F.: *Életröl, Betegségröl és Halálról. (On life, disease, and death.)* Budapest, 1925, 231 pp.
3. VERZÁR, F., AND MCDOUGALL, E. J.: *Absorption from the intestine.* London, Longmans, Green, 1936, 298 pp.
4. VERZÁR, F.: *Die Funktion der Nebennierenrinde. (The function of the adrenal cortex.)* Basel, Verlag Benno Schwabe, 1939, 266 pp.
5. VERZÁR, F.: *Theorie der Muskelkontraktion. (The theory of muscular contraction.)* Basel, Verlag Benno Schwabe, 1943, 107 pp.
6. VERZÁR, F.: *Atlas der Ernährungslehre. (An atlas of nutrition.)* Glattbrugg-Zürich, GESGA Verlag, 1946, 63 pp.
7. VERZÁR, F.: *Lehrbuch der inneren Sekretion. (Textbook of endocrinology.)* Liestal, Verlag Ars Medici Lüdin, 1948, 609 pp.
8. VERZÁR, F., AND GSELL, D.: *Ernährung und Gesundheitszustand der Bergbevölkerung. (Nutrition and health-status of the mountain population of Switzerland.)* Bern, Eidgenössisches Gesundheitsamt, 1962, 521 pp.
9. VERZÁR, F.: *Lectures on experimental gerontology.* Springfield, Thomas, 1963, 129 pp.
10. VERZÁR, F.: *Experimentelle Gerontologie. (Experimental gerontology.)* Stuttgart, Ferdinand Enke Verlag, 1965, 180 pp.
11. VERZÁR, F. (ed.): *A Debreceni Tisza István Tudományos Tarsaság. Orvos-Természettodományi Osztályának munkái. (Proceedings of the Medical and Natural History Section of the Stephen Tisza Society of Debrecen. Volumes I-VI.* Debrecen, 1925-1930.
12. VERZÁR, F. (ed.): *Collected Papers of the Hungarian Biological Research Institute in Tihany. Volumes I-XII.* 1926-1938.
13. VERZÁR, F. (ed.): *Höhenklimaforschungen des Basler Physiologischen Institutes. (Research on high altitude climate of the Institute of Physiology of the University of Basel.)* Volume I, 1945, Volume II, 1948, Volume III, 1952. Basel, Verlag Benno Schwabe.
14. VERZÁR, F. (ed.): *Symposium über Gegenwartsprobleme der Ernährungsforschung. (Symposium on present problems of nutritional research.)* Basel, Birkhäuser Verlag, 1952, 312 pp.
15. VERZÁR, F. (ed.): *Experimentelle Alternsforschung. (Experimental Research on Ageing.)* Symposium of the Biological and Medical Research Committees of the European Section of the International Association of Gerontology, held in Basel, April 1956. Basel, Birkhäuser Verlag, 1956, 290 pp.
16. VERZÁR, F. (ed.): *Gerontologia.* Journal of Experimental Biological and Medical Research on Aging. Volumes 1-10, 1957-1965. Basel and New York, Verlag S. Karger.
17. SPIESS, O., AND VERZÁR, F.: *Über das Leben (de vita). Eine akademische Festrede von Daniel Bernoulli. (On Life (de vita)—An academic address by Daniel Bernoulli.)* Publ. in Proceedings of the Society for Natural Sciences of Switzerland. Basel, Birkhäuser Verlag, 1941, 88 pp.
18. VERZÁR, F. (ed.): *Tisza Memorial Volume. Introduction,* pp. 3-10, Debrecen, 1928.

II. BIBLIOGRAPHY OF F. VERZÁR, 1907-1965

1907

1. VERZÁR, F.: On the pattern of the smooth muscle cells in the amnion of the chick. (German) *Int. Mschr. Anat. Physiol. 24*:292, 1907.

1908

2. Mansfeld, G. (with Hamburger, E., and Verzár, F.): The transport of fat in phosphorus poisoning. (Hungarian) *Magy. Orv. Arch.,* 1908.
3. Mansfeld, G. (with Hamburger, E., and Verzár, F.): The transport of fat during starvation. (Hungarian) *Magy. Orv. Arch.,* 1908.

1909

4. Mansfeld, G. (with Hamburger, E., and Verzár, F.): Studies on the physiology and pathology of fat transport. (German) *Arch. Ges. Physiol., 129:*46, 1909.
5. Verzár, F.: On the effect of methyl and ethyl alcohol on the muscle fibre. (German) *Arch. Ges. Physiol., 128:*398, 1909.
6. Verzár, F.: On the physiological effects of alcohol (Hungarian) *Math. Term. Ert., 27:*68, 1909.

1911

7. Verzár, F.: The effect of intravenous infusions of saline on the respiratory gas exchange. (German) *Biochem. Z., 34:*41, 1911.
8. Verzár, F.: The size of liver activity. (German) *Biochem. Z., 34:*52, 1911.
9. Verzár, F.: Is the liver function essential for the oxidation of carbohydrates? (German) *Biochem. Z., 34:*63, 1911.
10. Verzár, F.: Parenteral starch metabolism. (German) *Biochem. Z., 34:*66, 1911.
11. Verzár, F.: Papers on the "specific-dynamic effect" of nutrients. (Review) (German) *Naturwiss. Rundsch., 26:*536, 1911.
12. Verzár, F.: New publications on muscle fatigue. (Review) (German) *Naturwiss. Rundsch., 26:*508, 1911.
13. Verzár, F.: On the nature of thermal currents in nerves. (German) *Arch. Ges. Physiol., 143:*252, 1911.
14. Verzár, F.: A quick-reading, closed capillary electrometer. (German) *Z. Biol. Technik Methodik, 2:*203, 1911.
15. Laqueur, E., and Verzár, F.: On the specific effect of carbon dioxide on the respiratory center. (German) *Arch. Ges. Physiol., 143:*395, 1911.

1912

16. Verzár, F.: The work of the pancreas and its effect on the oxidation of carbohydrates. (German) *Biochem. Z., 44:*201, 1912.
17. Verzár, F.: Action currents of the nerve in electrotonus. (German) *Zbl. Physiol., 26:*399, 1912.
18. Verzár, F.: The gaseous metabolism of striated muscle in warm-blooded animals, Part I. *J. Physiol., 44:*243, 1912.
19. Verzár, F.: The influence of lack of oxygen on tissue respiration. *J. Physiol., 45:*39, 1912.
20. Verzár, F.: Modern theories of narcosis. (Review) (German) *Naturwiss. Rundsch., 27:*32, 1912.

1913

21. Verzár, F.: The change of polarization of the nerve by excitation. (German) *Arch. Ges. Physiol., 152:*279, 1913.

22. Verzár, F., and Fejér, A. v.: The oxidation of glucose in pancreas diabetes. (German) *Biochem. Z. 53:*140, 1913.
23. Verzár, F.: The size of spleen metabolism. (German) *Biochem. Z. 53:*69, 1913.
24. Verzár, F.: Changes of nerve polarization during excitation. (Hungarian) *Math. Term. Erk.,* 1913.
25. Verzár, F., and Fejer, A. v.: The oxidation of sugar in pancreas diabetes. (Hungarian) *Math. Term. Erk.,* 1913.
26. Igersheimer, and Verzár, F.: The pathogenesis of methyl alcohol and Atoxylamblyopia. (German) *Arch. Augenheilk., 75:*27, 1913.

1914

27. Verzár, F., and Krause, J.: The oxidation of glucose in pancreas diabetes. III. (German) *Biochem. Z., 66:*48, 1914.
28. Verzár, F.: The oxidation of glucose in pancreas diabetes. V. (German) *Biochem. Z. 66:*75, 1914.
29. Verzár, F., and Felter, M.: Investigations on the theory of the so-called Veratrin-contraction. (German) *Arch. Ges. Physiol., 158:*421, 1914.
30. Verzár, F.: On smooth muscle cells with myogenic rhythm (German) *Arch. Ges. Physiol., 158:*419, 1914.

1916

31. Verzár, F.: The gas exchange of muscle. (German) *Ergebn. Physiol., 15:*1, 1916.
32. Verzár, F., and Weszeczky, O.: On carriers in Flexner-dysentery. (German) *München. Med. Wschr., 8:*291, 1916.
33. Verzár, F., and Weszeczky, O.: On the analysis of faeces for typhoid and cholera bacilli. (German) *Deutsch Med. Wschr., 16:*1, 1916.

1917

34. Verzár, F.: Muscular contraction and *rigor mortis.* (Hungarian) *Magy. Orv. Arch.,* 1917.
35. Verzár, F.: The influence of blood supply on oxygen consumption of muscle. (Hungarian) *Magy. Orv. Arch.,* 1917.
36. Verzár, F.: On spontaneously agglutinizing typhoid bacilli. (German) *Zbl. Bakt. (Orig.), 80:*161, 1917.

1918

37. Tangl, F., and Verzár, F.: On the effect of curare and various narcotic drugs on gas exchange. (German) *Biochem. Z., 92:*318, 1918.
38. Verzár, F.: Some epidemiological observations on Koch-Week's conjunctivitis. (German) *Wiener Med. Wschr., 48:*1, 1918.
39. Verzár, F.: Mixed infections with tropica and tertiana? (German) *Deutsch Med. Wschr., 39:*1, 1918.
40. Verzár, F.: Contraction and rigor of striated muscle after investigations with vital dyes. (German) *Biochem. Z. 90:*63, 1918.
41. Verzár, F.: Investigations on the connections between different metabolic processes in *Bacterium coli* commune. (German) *Biochem. Z. 91:*1, 1918.
42. Verzár, F.: What happens in muscle during contraction? (Hungarian) *Természettudományi Közlöny, 709,* 1918.

1920

43. Verzár, F.: Reversal of reflexes (paradoxical reflexes) through fatigue and shock. (German) *Pflügers Arch., 183:*210, 1920.
44. Verzár, F.: The oxygen consumption of muscle with reduced oxygen supply. (German) *Pflügers Arch., 183:*239, 1920.
45. Verzár, F., and Gara, M.: Contributions to the method of gas analysis in blood. (German) *Pflügers Arch., 183:*235, 1920.
46. Verzár, F.: On the demonstration of changes in permeability of nerves during narcosis and excitation. (German) *Biochem. Z. 107:*98, 1920.
47. Verzár, F., and Bögel, J.: Investigations on the effect of accessory nutrients. (German) *Biochem. Z., 108:*185, 1920.
48. Verzár, F., and Beck, R.: Changes in salting-out properties of bacteria of the typhoid group through different conditions. (German) *Biochem. Z., 107:*81, 1920.
49. Verzár, F., and Bögel, J.: Further investigations on the regulations of metabolism in bacteria. (German) *Biochem. Z., 108:*208, 1920.
50. Storm, van Leeuwen, W., and Verzár, F.: Influence of vitamins on drug action. *Vergadering der Natuurkundige Afdeeling,* 27 Nov. 1920, Deel XXIX.

1921

51. Verzár, F., and Weszeczky, O.: Investigations on racial biology with isohemaglutinins. (German) *Biochem. Z. 126:*33, 1921.
52. Storm van Leeuwen, W., and Verzár, F.: The sensitiveness to poisons in avitaminous animals. *J. Pharmacol. Exp. Ther., 18:*293, 1921.

1922

53. Verzár, F.: Investigations on the acid theory of muscular contraction. (German) *Arch. Néerlandaises Physiol. de l'Homme et des Animaux, 7:*68, 1922.
54. Verzár, F., Bögel, J., and Szányi, W.: Tension and stretching properties of muscle in acid and chemical contraction. (German) *Biochem. Z. 132:*64, 1922.
55. Verzár, F., and Szányi, W.: The substitution of potassium by uranium in striated muscle. (German) *Biochem. Z., 132:*54, 1922.
56. Verzár, F.: New investigations on isohemaglutinins. (German) *Klin. Wschr., 1:*929, 1922.
57. Verzár, F.: Racial investigations on blood. (German) *Umschau Nr., 22:*343, 1922.

1923

58. Verzár, F.: Reversal of reflexes (paradoxical reflexes) through central fatigue in warmblooded animals. (German) *Pflügers Arch., 199:*109, 1923.
59. Verzár, F., Nábráczky, J., and Szányi, W.: The metabolic regulation by acid in *Bac. coli* comm. (German) *Biochem. Z., 141:*13, 1923.
60. Verzár, F., and Beznák, A. v.: The function of the adrenals in vitamin B deficiency. (German) *Arb. d. II. Abtlg. der wiss. St. Tisza Ges. in Debreczen, 1:*75, 1923.
61. Verzár, F., and Beznák, A. v.: The function of the adrenals in vitamin B deficiency. (Hungarian) *Arb. d. II. Abtlg. der wiss. St. Tisza Ges. in Debreczen, 1:*73, 1923.

62. Verzár, F., and Keller, F.: The oxygen content of capillary blood. (German) *Biochem. Z., 141:*21, 1923.
63. Verzár, F.: The determination of the pharmacological value of guajacol preparations. (German) *Klin. Wschr., 2:*12, 1923.
64. Verzár, F.: The process of excitation in the nerve. (Hungarian) *Arb. d. II. Abtlg. der wiss. St. Tisza Ges. Debreczen, 1:*29, 1923.
65. Verzár, F.: The importance of the quality of nutrients. (Hungarian) *Orvosképzés, 13:*1, 1923.
66. Verzár, F.: Investigations on the effect of the sympathetics on muscle tone. (German) *Arb. d. II. Abtlg. der wiss. St. Tisza Ges. Debreczen, 1:*45, 1923.
67. Verzár, F.: Reflex Dorsopalpebralis. (Hungarian) *Arb. d. II. Abtlg. der wiss. St. Tisza Ges. Debreczen, 1:*51, 1923.
68. Verzár, F.: Experiments on the effects of the sympathetic system on muscle tone. (Hungarian) *Arb. d. II. Abtlg. der wiss. St. Tisza Ges. in Debreczen, 1:*41, 1923.
69. Verzár, F.: The role of vitamins in human nutrition. (Hungarian) *Természettudományi Közlöny, 55:*193, 1923.
70. Verzár, F.: The treatment of diabetes with insulin. (Hungarian) *Magy. Orv. Arch.,* 1923.

1924

71. Verzár, F., and Péter, F.: The hypertrophy of the adrenal cortex in vitamin B deficiency. (German) *Pflügers Arch., 206:*659, 1924.
72. Verzár, F., Kokas, E., and Árvay, Á.: The binding of cholesterol in the nervous system in vitamin B deficiency. (German) *Pflügers Arch., 206:*666, 1924.
73. Verzár, F., and Vásárhelyi, B.: The function of the thyroid in vitamin B deficiency. (German) *Pflügers Arch., 206:*675, 1924.
74. Verzár, F., and Kokas, E.: The function of the hematopoetic system in avitaminoses, specially in experimental scurvy. (German) *Pflügers Arch., 206:*688, 1924.
75. Verzár, F.: The change in nerve polarization on excitation. (German) *Pflügers Arch., 206:*703, 1924.
76. Verzár, F., and Vásárhelyi, B.: The CO_2 content of capillary blood and its determination. (German) *Biochem. Z., 151:*246, 1924.
77. Verzár, F., and Zih, A.: Further investigations on metabolic regulation in *Bacillus coli.* Comm. III. (German) *Biochem. Z., 151:*254, 1924.
78. Verzár, F.: The alcoholic diagnosis of typhoid and paratyphoid. (German) *Klin. Wschr., 3:*43, 1924.
79. Verzár, F., Vásárhelyi, B., and Szányi, W.: The use of the compensation-manometer for diagnosis in the clinical laboratory. (German) *Klin. Wschr. 3:*1955, 1924.
80. Verzár, F., and Péter, F.: The hypertrophy of the adrenals in vitamin B deficiency. (German) *Arb. d. II. Abtlg. der wiss. St. Tisza Ges. in Debreczen, 1:*69, 1924.
81. Verzár, F.: The central nervous system. (German) *Jahresbericht über die ges. Physiol.,* 1924.

1925

82. Verzár, F., and Péter, F.: The muscular action currents in aldehyde contraction and similar contractions. (German) *Pflügers Arch., 207:*192, 1925.

83. Verzár, F., and Kovács, G.: Action currents in apparent tonic muscular contraction in man. (German) *Pflügers Arch., 207*:204, 1925.

1926

84. Verzár, F.: Depolarization and positive final wave (T-wave) in nerves during excitation. (German) *Pflügers Arch., 211*:1926.
85. Verzár, F.: The electrographic analysis of the excitation process in nerves. (German) *Arb. d. II. Med.-naturwiss. Abtlg. wiss. St. Tisza Ges. in Debreczen, 1*:No. 4-5, 1926.
86. Verzár, F., and Péter, F.: The tonic excitation process in the vagus nerve. (German) *Pflügers Arch., 212*:24, 1926.
87. Verzár, F., and Beznák, A.: The binding of cholesterol in the nervous system in vitamin B deficiency. (German) *Arb. d. II. Med.-naturwiss. Abtlg. wiss. St. Tisza Ges. in Debreczen, 1*:No. 4-5, 1926.
88. Verzár, F.: The tonic excitation process in nerves. (German) *Abstr. of Comm. XII. Int. Physiol. Congr. Stockholm,* August 3-6, 1926; *Skandinav. Archiv, 49*:237, 1926.
89. Verzár, F.: The central nervous system. (Review) (German) *Jahresbericht über die ges. Physiol.,* 1926.

1927

90. Verzár, F., and Kokas, E. v.: The role of intestinal villi in absorption. (German) *Pflügers Arch., 217*:397, 1927.
91. Verzár, F.: The measurement of blood gas exchange in individual organs. (German) *Handbuch der biol. Arbeitsmethoden, Abt. IV, Teil 10*:985, 1927.
92. Verzár, F.: The uncertainties in the nomenclature of the blood groups and their practical consequences. (German) *Klin. Wschr., 6*:1, 1927.
93. Verzár, F., and Fridrik, B.: Determination of thyroid preparations with respiration experiments on the rat. (Hungarian) *Orvosképzés,* 1927.

1928

94. Verzár, F.: Investigations on the depolarization wave in the nerve. V. (German) *Pflügers Arch., 219*:1, 1928.
95. Verzár, F.: The depolarization wave and other polarization phenomena in mollusc nerves. VI. (German) *Pflügers Arch., 219*:19, 1928.
96. Verzár, F.: The influence of diet on the sensitivity to hormones and drugs. (Hungarian) (Lecture given to the Medical Assoc. Debreczen) *Orvosképzés,* 1928.
97. Verzár, F.: Isohemaglutination in the service of anthropology. (German) *Verhandlg. der Ständigen Kommission für Blutgruppenforschung; Ukrainisches Zbl. Blutgruppenforschung, 2*:1, 1928.
98. Verzár, F., and Zih, A.: Bilirubin as a possible hematopoetic hormone. (German) *Klin. Wschr., 7*:1031, 1928.
99. Verzár, F.: The central nervous system. (Review) (German) *Jahresbericht Physiologie,* 1928.
100. Verzár, F.: Count Tisza and the University of Debreczen. (Hungarian) *Tisza-Emlékkönyi, Debreczen,* 1928.

1929

101. Verzár, F., and Kúthy, A. v.: The role of the bile acids in the absorption of fat. (German) *Biochem. Z. 205*:369, 1929.
102. Verzár, F., and Zih, A.: The hematopoetic effect of bilirubin and other hemoglobin derivatives. (German) *Biochem. Z., 205*:388, 1929.
103. Verzár, F., and Kúthy, A. v.: The binding of paired bile acids with fatty acids and their role in fat absorption. II. (German) *Biochem. Z., 210*:265, 1929.
104. Verzár, F.: The measurement of basal metabolism and the specific-dynamic effect in experiments with rats. (German) *Pflügers Arch., 222*:717, 1929.
105. Verzár, F.: The effect of vitamin E on the hypertrophy of female genitalia. (German) *Arb. d. II. Abtlg. der wiss. St. Tisza Ges. in Debreczen, 3*:No. 4, 1929.
106. Verzár, F.: The role of bilirubin in the regulation of the number of red corpuscules. (German) *Z. Ges. Exp. Med., 68*:475, 1929.
107. Verzár, F. and Kúthy, A. v.: The exhaustion of pancreas secretion through carbohydrate overloading. (German) *Arb.d.II.Abtlg. der wiss. St. Tisza Ges. in Debreczen, 3*:No. 4, 1929.
108. Verzár F., and Kúthy, A. v.: The binding of paired bile acids with fatty acids and their role in fat resorption. III. Surface tension. (German) *Biochem. Z., 210*:281, 1929.

1930

109. Verzár, F., and Kúthy, A. v.: The physiological importance of hydrotropy. (German) *Biochem. Z., 225*:267, 1930.
110. Bencsik, F., Gáspár, A., Verzár, F., and Zih, A.: Further investigations on the effect of bilirubin on the erythrocyte count. (German) *Biochem. Z., 225*:278, 1930.
111. Verzár, F., and Kúthy, A. v.: The exhaustion of insulin formation by carbohydrate overloading. (German) *Pflügers Arch., 225*:606, 1930.
112. Verzár, F.: The history of natural sciences in Debreczen. (Hungarian) *Med. Debrecen,* 1930.
113. Verzár, F.: Obituary of Angelo Mosso. (German) *Naturwiss. Rundsch.,* 1930.
114. Verzár, F.: New investigations on the effects of climate at high altitudes. (Review) (German) *Naturwiss. Rundsch.,* 1930.

1931

115. Verzár, F.: Problems and results in the field of intestinal absorption. (Review) (German) *Ergebn. Physiol., 32*:391, 1931.
116. Verzár, F.: The effect of vitamin E on the hypertrophy of the uterus. (German) *Pflügers Arch., 227*:499, 1931.
117. Verzár, F.: Absorption from the intestine. (German) *Klin. Wschr., 10*:1, 1931.
118. Verzár, F.: The effect of vitamin E deficiency on the fur of rats. (German) *Pflügers Arch., 227*:511, 1931.
119. Verzár, F., Árvay, A. v., and Kokas, E. v.: Basal metabolism of rats on a vitamin E-free diet and the compensation of the vitamin E-deficiency with anterior pituitary hormone. (German) *Biochem. Z., 240*:19, 1931.
120. Verzár, F., and Árvay, A. v.: The increase of basal metabolism by ovarian hormone. (German) *Biochem. Z., 240*:28, 1931.

121. Verzár, F., and Wahl, V.: The effect of anterior pituitary hormone on oxygen consumption of guinea pigs. (German) *Biochem. Z., 240:*37, 1931.

122. Árvay, A. v., and Verzár, F.: Gas exchange during muscular work after removal of the adrenals. (German) *Biochem. Z., 234:*186, 1931.

123. Barcroft, J., and Verzár, F.: The effect of exposure to cold on the pulse rate and respiration of man. *J. Physiol., 71:*373, 1931.

124. Verzár, F., and Kúthy, A. v.: The role of paired bile acids for fat absorption. IV. (German) *Biochem. Z., 230:*451, 1931.

125. Verzár, F.: Old Hungarian connections with Basel. (Hungarian) *Debreczeni Szemle,* 1931.

126. Verzár, F.: Communications on early medical students from Hungary in Basel. (Hungarian) *Ungar. ärztl. Wschr., 23:*1, 1931.

1932

127. Verzár, F.: Absorption from the intestine. (German) *Handbuch der normalen und pathologischen Physiologie, Ergänzungsband, 78,* 1932.

128. Verzár, F.: Intestinal movement. (German) *Handbuch der normalen und pathologischen Physiologie, Ergänzungsband, 47,* 1932.

129. Verzár, F.: Vitamin E. (German) *Z. Vitaminforsch. 1:*116, 1932.

130. Verzár, F.: Vitamins and internal secretion. (German) *Schweiz. Med. Wschr., 62:*57, 1932.

131. Verzár, F.: The process of excitation in the nervous system. (German) *Schweiz. Med. Wschr., 62:*556, 1932.

132. Fischer, Elisabeth, and Verzár, F.: The effect of amino acids, anemic serum and liver extract on the number of red corpuscles, compared with the effect of bilirubin. (German) *Z. Ges. Exper. Med., 80:*385, 1932.

133. Verzár, F.: The regulation of lung volume. (German) *Schweiz. Med. Wschr., 62:*265, 1932.

1933

134. Verzár, F.: The changes in vital capacity in high mountains. (German) *Schweiz. Med. Wschr., 63:*17, 1933.

135. Verzár, F.: The regulation of lung volume. (German) *Pflügers Arch., 232:*322, 1933.

136. Verzár, F.: Demonstration of a respirometer. (German) *Schweiz. Med. Wschr., 63:*458, 1933.

137. Verzár, F.: Investigations on the mechanism of the regulation of red corpuscles in high mountains. (German) *Schweiz. Med. Wschr., 63:*460, 1933.

138. Verzár, F., and Ostern, P.: Investigation of intestinal villi in fluorescent light. (German) *Schweiz. Med. Wschr., 63:*1031, 1933.

139. Ludány, G. v., and Verzár, F.: The influence of the spleen on the bilirubin content of serum. Experiments on the effect of splenectomy, splenic contraction, anemia and asphyxia. (German) *Biochem. Z., 257:*130, 1933.

140. Verzár, F.: On the forces of resorption from the intestine. (German) *Klin. Wschr., 12:*489, 1933.

141. Verzár, F., Árvay, A. v., Peter, J., and Scholderer, H.: Serum bilirubin and erythropoesis in high mountains. (German) *Biochem. Z., 257:*113, 1933.

1934

142. Verzár, F., and Laszt, L.: Investigations on the absorption of fatty acids. (German) *Biochem. Z., 270:*24, 1934.
143. Verzár, F., and Laszt, L.: The inhibition of fat absorption by phlorhizin and adrenalectomy. (German) *Verh. Ver. Schweiz. Physiol.,* 1934.
144. Verzár, F., and Laszt, L.: The inhibition of fat absorption by monoiodoacetic acid and phlorhizin. (German) *Biochem. Z., 270:*35, 1949.
145. Süllmann, H., and Verzár, F.: The diffusibility of blood fat. (German) *Biochem. Z., 270:*44, 1934.
146. McDougall, E. J., Verzár, F., Erlenmeyer, H., and Gaertner, H.: Heavy water in the animal body. *Nature, 134:*1006, 1934.
147. Verzár, F.: The increase in lung volume from increased oxygen requirement as "third form" of respiratory regulation. (German) *Schweiz. med. Jahrbuch,* 1934.
148. Verzár, F., Süllmann, H., and Vischer, A.: The differentiation of blood pigments in human serum. (German) *Biochem. Z. 274:*7, 1934.
149. Verzár, F.: Six years of the Hungarian Biological Research Institute in Tihany. (Hungarian) *Orvosképzés,* 1934.
150. Verzár, F., and Laszt, L., The inhibition of fat absorption by phlorhizin and adrenalectomy. (German) *Schweiz. Med. Wschr., 64:*1178, 1934.
151. Verzár, F.: The importance of vitamins in a general biological context. (German) *Ergebn. Biol. 10:*103, 1934.

1935

152. Verzár, F., and Laszt, L.: The inhibition of fat absorption after adrenalectomy. (German) *Biochem. Z., 276:*11, 1935.
153. Verzár, F., and Laszt, L.: The inhibition of fat absorption by phlorhizin. (German) *Biochem. Z., 276:*1, 1935.
154. Verzár, F., and Laszt, L.: Absorption from the intestine of isotonic solutions of glucose and sorbose, compared with sodium sulfate. (German) *Biochem. Z., 276:*28, 1935.
155. Verzár, F.: The activity of the intestinal mucous membrane in absorption. (German) *Schweiz. Med. Wschr., 65:*569, 1935.
156. Verzár, F.: The pathology of intestinal absorption. (German) *Schweiz. Med. Wschr., 65:*1093, 1935.
157. Verzár, F.: Inhibition of fat absorption. *J. Physiol., 84:*410, 1935.
158. Verzár, F.: The role of diffusion and activity of the mucous membrane in the absorption of various sugars from the intestine. (German) *Biochem. Z., 276:*17, 1935.
159. Verzár, F., and Laszt, L.: The adrenal cortex and fat absorption. (German) *Biochem. Z., 278:*396, 1935.
160. Laszt, L., and Verzár, F.: Growth inhibition with monoiodoacetic acid and antagonistic influence by vitamin B and adrenal cortex. (German) *Pflügers Arch., 236:*693, 1935.
161. McDougall, E. J., and Verzár, F.: The absorption of water from saline and sugar solutions. (German) *Pflügers Arch., 236:*321, 1935.
162. Verzár, F. and Haffter, C.: The effect of heavy water (deuterium oxide) on isolated organs. (German) *Pflügers Arch., 236:*714, 1935.

163. Verzár, F., and Laszt, L.: The effect of the suprarenal glands on fat absorption. (German) *Schweiz. Med. Wschr., 65:*732, 1935.

164. Verzár, F.: The absorption of fat. (Russian) *Sechnov J. Physiol. USSR XXI:* No. 5-6, p. 145.

1936

165. Verzár, F., and Jeker, L.: Histological investigations on fat absorption after adrenalectomy. (German) *Pflügers Arch., 237:*13, 1936.

166. Süllmann, H., Szécsényi-Nagy, L., and Verzár, F.: The differentiation of the serum pigments. (German) *Biochem. Z., 283:*263, 1936.

167. Verzár, F.: The activity of the intestinal mucous membrane in absorption and the influence of the suprarenal glands. (German). *Acta Brevia Neerlandica, 6:*No. 3-4, 1936.

168. Verzár, F.: The activity of the intestinal mucous membrane in absorption and the influence of the suprarenal glands. (Dutch) *Nederl. Tijdschrift voor Geneeskunde, 80:*2171, 1936.

169. Verzár, F., and Jeker, L.: An attempt to influence the shape of the intestinal villi by liquid nutrients. (German) *Verh. Ver. Schweiz. Physiol.*, January, 1936.

170. Verzár, F., and Laszt, L.: Sodium and water metabolism in relation to disturbances of carbohydrate metabolism after adrenalectomy. *Nature, 138:*844, 1936.

171. Verzár, F., and Laszt, L.: The connection between vitamin B_2 and the adrenal hormone. (German) *Pflügers Arch., 237:*476, 1936.

172. Verzár, F., and Laszt, L.: The effect of lactoflavin and flavin phosphate on adrenal deficiency and iodoacetic acid poisoning. (German) *Verh. Ver. Schweiz. Physiol.* June, 1936.

173. Verzár, F., and Laszt, L.: The role of lactoflavin and flavin phosphate on adrenal deficiency and iodoacetic acid poisoning. (German) *Z. Vitaminforschung, 5:*265, 1936.

174. Verzár, F., and Laszt, L.: The adrenal cortex and fat transport. (German) *Biochem. Z., 288:*356, 1936.

175. Verzár, F., Szécsényi, L., and Jeker, L.: Investigations on the mechanism of lung volume regulation. (German) *Verh. Ver. Schweiz. Physiol.,* January, 1936.

176. Laszt, L., and Verzár, F.: Vitamin B_2 and the adrenal cortical hormone. (German) *Verh. Ver. Schweiz. Physiol.*, January, 1936.

177. Laszt, L., and Verzár, F.: The adrenal cortex and fat absorption. (German) *Biochem. Z., 288:*351, 1936.

178. Laszt, L., and Verzár, F.: The influence of iodoacetic acid and adrenalectomy on fat transport. (German) *Biochem. Z., 285:*356, 1936.

179. Laszt, L., and Verzár, F.: On chronic iodoacetic acid poisoning and its relation of Gee-Herter's disease. (German) *Pflügers Arch., 237:*483, 1936.

180. Verzár, F.: Johannes Hungarus, a well known Hungarian architect of the Middle Ages. (Hungarian) *Debreczeni Szemle,* Sept. 1, 1936.

181. Verzár, F.: The physician of Erasmus. (Hungarian) *Pesti Naplo,* June 15, 1936.

182. Verzár, F., Szécsényi-Nagy, L., Haffter, C., and Wirz, H.: The tonus of the diaphragm and its relation to the tonus of the smooth musculature of the lung. (German) *Pflügers Arch., 238:*387, 1936.

183. VERZÁR, F., AND JEKER, L.: The physiological atelectasis of the lung. (German) *Pflügers Arch., 238:*379, 1936.
184. ERLENMEYER, H., AND VERZÁR, F.: Does heavy water have an influence on physiological processes? (German) *Z. Biol., 97:*519, 1936.

1937

185. VERZÁR, F.: Vitamin E. *Handb. Biol. Arbeitsmethoden Abt. V.,* Teil *3:*1269, 1937.
186. VERZÁR, F.: The problem of people's nutrition. (German) *Schweiz. Med. Wschr., 67:*377, 1937.
187. VERZÁR, F.: Disturbances of absorption through disease of the adrenal cortex. (German) *Schweiz. Med. Wschr., 67:*823, 1937.
188. VERZÁR, F.: Adrenal cortex and intestinal absorption. *Amer. J. Dig. Dis., 4:*545, 1937.
189. VERZÁR, F., AND LASZT, L.: The connection between the disturbance of carbohydrate metabolism and sodium- and water-metabolism in the adrenalectomized animal. (German) *Verh. Ver. Schweiz. Physiol.,* January, 1937.
190. VERZÁR, F., LASZT, L., AND SCHAEDELI, L.: Vitamin B_2 and adrenal cortical hormone. (German) *Enzymologia, 3:*16, 1937.
191. VERZÁR, F., AND LASKOWSKI, M.: Investigations on bone alterations in chronic iodoacetic acid poisoning. (German) *Biochem. Z., 292:*312, 1937.
192. VERZÁR, F., AND WIRZ, H.: Further investigations on the condition of selective glucose absorption. (German) *Biochem. Z., 292:*174, 1937.
193. VERZÁR, F., HÜBNER, H., AND LASZT, L.: The binding of lactoflavin as lactoflavin phosphate in the body after adrenalectomy. (German). *Biochem. Z., 292:* 152, 1937.
194. VERZÁR, F., AND SÜLLMANN, H.: The binding of phosphoric esters in the intestinal mucous membrane during absorption. (German) *Biochem. Z., 289:*323, 1937.
195. KARRER, P., LASZT, L., AND VERZÁR, F.: The curative effect of natural and synthetic flavin phosphate on the B_6-avitaminosis of the rat (pellagra, acrodynia). (German) *Pflügers Arch., 239:*644, 1937.
196. LASZT, L., AND VERZÁR, F.: The growth effect of flavin phosphate from liver on adrenalectomized and normal rats. (German) *Pflügers Arch., 239:* 653, 1937.
197. LASZT, L., AND VERZÁR, F.: The role of vitamins B_2, B_4 and B_6 in adrenal deficiency (experiments with yeast extracts). (German) *Pflügers Arch., 239:* 136, 1937.
198. LASZT, L., AND VERZÁR, F.: The disturbances of carbohydrate metabolism and their connection with sodium metabolism. (German) *Biochem. Z., 292:*159, 1937.
199. LASZT, L., AND VERZÁR, F.: A new method for the qualitative and quantitative determination of the adrenal cortical hormone. (German) *Verh. Ver. Schweiz. Physiol.,* January, 1937.
200. REICHSTEIN, T., VERZÁR, F., AND LASZT, L.: Activity of corticosteron in the glucose test in rats. *Nature, 139:*331, 1937.
201. JUDOVITS, N., AND VERZÁR, F.: The absorption of various sugars after adrenalectomy (German) *Biochem., Z., 292:*182, 1937.
202. VERZÁR, F.: The movement of intestinal villi in the dog. (German). *Veröffentlichung der Reichsstelle für den Unterrichtsfilm,* 1937.

1938

203. VERZÁR, F.: Fat metabolism. *Ann. Rev. Biochem., 7:*163, 1938.
204. VERZÁR, F.: The function of the adrenal cortex. (German) Kongressbericht I des XVI. Internat. Physiologenkongresses, Zürich, 1938.
205. VERZÁR, F.: On primary and secondary avitaminoses. (German) *Schweiz. Med. Wschr., 68:*975, 1938.
206. LASZT, L., AND VERZÁR, F.: The curative effect of flavin phosphate and the ineffectiveness of nicotinamide on the B_6-avitaminosis of the rat. (German) *Verh. Ver. Schweiz. Physiol.,* January, 1938.
207. LASZT, L., AND VERZÁR, F.: Disturbances of fat absorption and the binding of flavin after adrenalectomy in the cat. (German) *Verh. Ver. Schweiz. Physiol.,* January, 1938.
208. FITZGERALD, O., LASZT, L., AND VERZÁR, F.: The selective absorption of sugar after hypophysectomy and its influencing by the hormone of the adrenal cortex. (German) *Pflügers Arch., 240:*619, 1938.
209. ISSEKUTZ, B. V. AND VERZÁR, F.: The role of the adenohypophysis and the suprarenal gland in fat transport. (German) *Pflügers Arch., 240:*624, 1938.
210. ISSEKUTZ, B. V., LASZT, L., AND VERZÁR, F.: Disturbances of sugar and fat absorption after adrenalectomy. (German) *Pflügers Arch., 240:*612, 1938.
211. HÜBNER, H., AND VERZÁR, F.: Phosphorylation of riboflavin by extracts of intestinal mucous membrane and the effect of iodoacetic acid. (German) *Helv. Chim. Acta., 21:*1006, 1938.
212. VERZÁR, F.: The physiology of the adrenal cortex. (German) Reichsarbeitstagung, Bayreuth, 1938.
213. VERZÁR, F.: Impressions from the 16th International Congress of Physiology. (German) *Basler Nachrichten,* August 30, 1938.

1939

214. VERZÁR, F.: Creatine metabolism in muscular dystrophy caused by vitamin E deficiency and the effect of tocopherol. (German) *Z. Vitaminforsch., 9:*242, 1939.
215. VERZÁR, F.: Creatinuria in vitamin E deficiency and its cure by DL-tocopherol. (German) *Schweiz. Med. Wschr., 69:*738, 1939.
216. DEMOLE, V., AND VERZÁR, F.: Neuromuscular disturbances in rats on a vitamin E free diet. (German) *Verh. Ver. Schweiz. Physiol.,* Bern, February, 1939.
217. PULVER, R., AND VERZÁR, F.: The phosphorylation of riboflavin by the intestinal mucous membrane. (German) *Enzymologia, 6:*333, 1939.
218. VERZÁR, F., AND SOMOGYI, J. C.: Connection between carbohydrate and potassium metabolism in normal and adrenalectomized animals. *Nature, 144:*1014, 1939.
219. VERZÁR, F.: Reports of the Committee on Hygiene of the League of Nations on problems of nutrition of the population. (German) *Schweiz. Med. Wschr., 69:*1248, 1939.
220. VERZÁR, F.: Obituary of Professor Te. S. London. (German) *Schweiz. Med. Wschr., 69:*1314, 1939.
221. FITZGERALD, O., AND VERZÁR, F.: The effect of adrenal cortical hormone on the glycogen content of the liver of hypophysectomized rats. (German) *Pflügers Arch., 242:*30, 1939.
222. VERZÁR, F.: Report on activities. (German) *Le Rotarien Suisse, XIV:*623, Dec. 1939.

223. VERZÁR, F.: A Hungarian tomcat in Scheffel's "Trompeter von Säckingen". (Hungarian) *Hungarica,* 1939.

1940

224. MINIBECK, H., AND VERZÁR, F.: The selective uptake of various sugars into the tissues of normal and adrenalectomized animals. (German) *Helv. Med. Acta., 7,* Suppl. V:7, 1940.
225. SOMOGYI, J. C., AND VERZÁR, F.: The effect of an intravenous injection of sugar on serum potassium in normal and adrenalectomized animals. (German) *Helv. Med. Acta, 7,* Suppl. V:20, 1940.
226. SOMOGYI, J. C., AND VERZÁR, F.: The relation between selective sugar absorption and potassium. (German) *Helv. Med. Acta, 7,* Suppl. V:30, 1940.
227. FITZGERALD, O., MASON, M., AND VERZÁR, F.: The changes in serum bilirubin and red cell count in high mountains. (German) *Helv. Med. Acta, 7,* Suppl. V:50, 1940.
228. VERZÁR, F.: Investigations on the function of the smooth musculature of the lung (experiments on frog lung.) (German) *Helv. Med. Acta, 7,* Suppl. V:58, 1940.
229. MINIBECK, H., AND VERZÁR, F.: The effect of muscular work on the flavin content of the liver. (German) *Z. Vitaminforsch., 10:*79, 1940.
230. VERZÁR, F.: The relation between carbohydrate- and potassium-metabolism in normal and adrenalectomized animals. (German) *Verh. Ver. Schweiz. Physiol.,* January, 1940.
231. VERZÁR, F., AND SOMOGYI, J. C.: Liberation of potassium from muscle by acetyl choline and muscle contraction and its absence after adrenalectomy. *Nature, 145:*781, 1940.
232. VERZÁR, F.: The smooth musculature of the frog lung. (German) *Verh. Ver. Schweiz. Physiol.,* January 1940.
233. PULVER, R., AND VERZÁR, F.: Connection between carbohydrate and potassium metabolism in the yeast cell. *Nature, 145:*823, 1940.
234. PULVER, R., AND VERZÁR, F.: The relation between potassium- and carbohydrate-metabolism in yeast. (German) *Helv. Chim. Acta, 23:*1087, 1940.
235. VERZÁR, F.: The treatment of Addison's disease with adrenal cortical hormones. (German) *Schweiz. Med. Wschr., 70:*1229, 1940.
236. VERZÁR, F.: The relation between carbohydrate and potassium metabolism and the effect of the adrenal cortex. (German) *Verh. Schweiz. Naturf. Ges.,* Locarno, 1940, p. 200.

1941

237. VERZÁR, F.: Desoxycorticosterone as a hormone of the adrenal cortex. (German) *Verh. Ver. Schweiz. Physiol.,* January, 1941.
238. SOMOGYI, J. C., AND VERZÁR, F.: Potassium delivery in muscular contraction after adrenalectomy. (German) *Arch. Int. Pharmacodyn., 65:*17, 1941.
239. SOMOGYI, J. C., AND VERZÁR, F.: The effect of acetylcholine on potassium in striated muscle in normal and adrenalectomized animals. (German) *Arch. Int. Pharmacodyn. 65:*221, 1941.
240. VERZÁR, F., BUCHER, R., SOMOGYI, J. C., AND WIRZ, H.: Investigations on adrenalectomized cats treated with desoxycorticosterone. (German) *Helv. Med. Acta, 7,* Suppl. VI:58, 1941.

241. Somogyi, J. C., and Verzár, F.: The delivery of potassium from muscle after adrenalectomy and after poisoning with monoiodacetic acid in the frog (German) *Helv. Med. Acta, 7,* Suppl. VI:81, 1941.

242. Somogyi, J. C., Wirz, H., and Verzár, F.: Changes in total blood and plasma volumes in high altitude. (German) *Helv. Med. Acta, 7,* Suppl., VI:44, 1941.

243. Verzár, F.: Growth potential after caloric deficiency. (German) *Helv. Med. Acta, 7,* Suppl. VI: 7, 1941.

244. Verzár, F.: The function of the adrenal cortex. (German) *Vitamine Hormone, 1:*85, 1941.

245. Verzár, F.: Desoxycorticosterone as a hormone of the adrenal cortex. (German) *Schweiz. Med. Wschr., 71:*411, 1941.

246. Pulver, R., and Verzár, F.: Potassium and carbohydrate metabolism of leucocytes. (German) *Helv. Chim. Acta, 24:*272, 1941.

247. Verzár, F.: The relation between carbohydrate and potassium metabolism and the effect of the adrenal cortex. (German) *Schweiz. Med. Wschr., 71:*878, 1941.

248. Verzár, F., and Somogyi, J. C.: The effect of adrenalin on plasma potassium and blood sugar in normal and adrenalectomized animals. (German) *Verh. Ver. Schweiz. Physiol.,* July, 1941.

249. Verzár, F.: The adrenal cortex and sexual hormones. (German) *Schweiz. Med. Wschr., 71:*1329, 1941.

250. Verzár, F., and Montigel, C.: The demonstration of disturbances in phos-Phorylation after adrenalectomy. (German) *Schweiz. Med. Wschr., 71:*101, 1941.

251. Verzár, F.: The suprarenal gland and muscle fatigue. (German) *Verh. Schweiz. Naturf. Ges.,* 1941, Basel.

252. Verzár, F., and Somogyi, J. C.: The effect of adrenalin on plasma potassium and blood sugar in the normal and adrenalectomized animal. (German) *Pflügers Arch., 245:*398, 1941.

1942

253. Verzár, F., and Montigel, C.: The influence of the adrenal cortex on the phosphorylation of glycogen in muscle. (German) *Helv. Chim. Acta, 25:*9, 1942.

254. Verzár, F., and Montigel, C.: The influence of the adrenal cortex on the phosphorylation of glycogen in muscle. II. The effect of desoxycorticosterone. (German) *Helv. Chim. Acta, 25:*22, 1942.

255. Montigel, C., and Verzár, F.: The restitution of reduced phosphorylation of glycogen *in vitro* by desoxycorticosterone. (German) *Verh. Ver. Schweiz. Physiol.,* January, 1942.

256. Verzár, F.: Muscular fatigue and the suprarenal gland. (German) *Schweiz. Med. Wschr., 72:*661, 1942.

257. Verzár, F., and Montigel, C.: Decrease in glycogen phosphorylation in muscles *in vitro* after adrenalectomy and restoration with desoxycorticosterone. *Nature, 149:*49, 1942.

258. Verzár, F.: The relation between carbohydrate and potassium metabolism and the effect of the adrenal cortex. (A reply to the remarks by Druckrey). (German) *Schweiz. Med. Wschr., 72:*597, 1942.

259. Verzár, F.: A calculator for red cell counts. (German) *Verh. Ver. Schweiz. Physiol.,* June, 1942.

260. Wirz, H., and Verzár, F.: Demonstration of adrenalectomized cats. (German) *Verh. Ver. Schweiz. Physiol.,* June, 1942.

261. Schweizer, W., and Verzár, F.: The effect of oxygen deficiency on lung volume. (German) *Verh. Ver. Schweiz. Physiol.,* June, 1942.

1943

262. Verzár, F.: Calcium metabolism on white and brown bread diets. (German) *Schweiz. Med. Wschr., 73:*80, 1943.

263. Verzár, F.: A model to a theory of muscular contraction. (German) *Verh. Ver. Schweiz. Physiol. Pharmakologen* Zürich, January 30, 1943 *Helv. Physiol. Acta, 1:*8, 1943.

264. Verzár, F.: The adrenal cortex and the thyroid gland. (German) *Schweiz. Med. Wschr., 73:*25, 1943.

265. Montigel, C., and Verzár, F.: Investigations on the carbohydrate metabolism after adrenalectomy. I. Decrease of glycogen phosphorylation in adrenalectomized cats and dogs and restitution by desoxycorticosterone and other steroid hormones. (German) *Helv. Physiol. Acta 1:*115, 1943.

266. Montigel, C., and Verzár, F.: Investigations on carbohydrate metabolism after adrenalectomy. II. The formation of glycogen under the influence of desoxycorticosterone. (German) *Helv. Physiol. Acta,* 1:137, 1943.

267. Montigel, C., and Verzár, F.: Investigations on the carbohydrate metabolism after adrenalectomy. III. The analysis of serum. (German) *Helv. Physiol. Acta 1:*143, 1943.

268. Verzár, F.: The Institute of Physiology. (German) Geschichte der Universität Basel, 1943.

269. Verzár, F.: Desoxycorticosterone and sexual function. (German) *Helv. Physiol. Acta, 1:*389, 1943.

1944

270. Verzár, F., and Vögtli, W.: The oxygen saturation of arterial and capillary blood in medium altitudes. (German) *Helv. Physiol. Acta, 2:*c-22, 1944.

271. Verzár, F.: The mechanism of action of the adrenal cortical hormone. (German) *Schweiz. Med. Wschr., 74:*253, 1944.

272. Verzár, F.: Andreas Vesalius in Basel. On the 400th anniversary of the publication of his "Fabrica Corporis Humani" in 1543. (German) *Verh. Naturf. Ges. Basel, 55:*178, 1944.

273. Verzár, F.: Friedrich Miescher as physiologist. (German) *Helv. Physiol. Acta, 2,* Suppl. II:19 1944.

274. Verzár, F.: Toxicity experiments with desoxycorticosterone. (German) *Helv. Physiol. Acta, 2:*c-55, 1944.

275. Verzár, F.: Obituary of the Nobel Prize winner Alexis Carrel. (German) Basler Nachrichten, September 12, 1944.

276. Verzár, F.: Obituary of Professor Steinach. (German) *Basler Nachrichten,* May 16, 1944.

1945

277. Verzár, F.: The water uptake of muscles in potassium chloride after adrenalectomy. (German) *Helv. Physiol. Acta, 3:*c-16, 1945.

278. Doetsch, R., Vögtli, W., and Verzár, F.: Basal metabolism at medium altitudes (5,600 feet above sea level). (German) *Helv. Physiol. Acta, 3:*c-8, 1945.

279. Vögtli, W., Doetsch, R., and Verzár, F.: The red cell count at medium altitudes (5,600 feet a.s.) (German) *Helv. Physiol. Acta, 3*:c-17, 1945.
280. Vögtli, W., and Verzár, F.: The influencing of vital capacity and respiration in patients with asthma bronchiale and normal man by a broncholytic spray. (German) *Schweiz. Med. Wschr., 75*:457, 1945.
281. Wirz, H., Doetsch, R., and Verzár, F.: The basal metabolism of normal, thyroidectomized, adrenalectomized, and both thyroidectomized and adrenalectomized cats. (German) *Helv. Physiol. Acta, 3*:c-18, 1945.
282. Doetsch, R., Verzár, F., and Wirz, H.: The adrenal cortex and the thyroid gland. (German) *Helv. Physiol. Acta, 3*:565, 1945.

1946

283. Vögtli, W., and Verzár, F.: The destruction of erythrocytes at the beginning of a stay in high mountains. (German) *Helv. Physiol. Acta, 4*:c-32, 1946.
284. Verzár, F., and Vögtli, W.: The determination of O_2 and CO_2 tensions in tissues on ascension to high altitudes. (German) *Helv. Physiol. Acta, 4*:c-29, 1946.
285. Gutzwiller, N., and Verzár, F.: The influence of the number of condensation nuclei on the precipitation of atmospheric impurities during adiabatic expansion. (German) *Helv. Physiol. Acta, 4*:c-15, 1946.
286. Verzár, F.: Post-war conference on nutrition of the Nutrition Society in London. (German) *Schweiz. Med. Wschr., 76*:996, 1946.
287. Verzár, F.: The regulation of the lung volume and its disturbances. *Schweiz. Med. Wschr. 76*:932, 1946.

1947

288. Verzár, F.: The regulation of erythrocyte count at high altitudes. (German) *Schweiz. Med. Wschr., 77*:15, 1947.
289. Verzár, F.: Obituary of Sir Joseph Barcroft. (German) *Experientia, 3*:298, 1947.
290. Demole, V., and Verzár, F.: The effect of adrenalectomy and treatment with desoxycorticosterone on ascorbinemia and ascorbinuria of the cat. (German) *Experientia, 3*:419, 1947.
291. Verzár, F., and Wenner, V.: The effect of desoxycorticosterone and insulin on the breakdown and synthesis of glycogen. (French) *Bull. Soc. Chim. Biol. (Paris) 29*:304, 1947.
292. Verzár, F.: Professor Emil Abderhalden on his 70th birthday. (German) *Nationalzeitung Basel,* March 8, 1947.
293. Verzár, F., and Vögtli, W.: The O_2 and CO_2 contents of arterial blood in asthma bronchiale and its influencing by a broncholytic spray. (German) *Schweiz. Med. Wschr., 77*:980, 1947.
294. Tissières, A., Vogt, O., and Verzár, F.: The influence of thymectomy on the sensitivity of rats towards vitamin A and D deficiencies and towards proteins. (German) *Helv. Physiol. Acta, 5*:c-54, 1947.
295. Sass-Kortsák, A., Peyser, E., and Verzár, F.: O_2 and CO_2 in respired air as regulators of lung volume. (German) *Helv. Physiol. Acta, 5*:c-46, 1947.
296. Stutz, V., and Verzár, F.: Nucleic acid content of liver after thymectomy. (German) *Helv. Physiol. Acta, 5*:c-52, 1947.
297. Verzár, F.: Switzerland's contribution to war-time food research. *Proc. Nutr. Soc., 5*:311, 1947.

1948

298. Verzár, F., and Wenner, V.: The influence *in vitro* of desoxycorticosterone on glycogen formation in muscle. *Biochem. J., 42*:35, 1948.
299. Verzár, F., and Wenner, V.: Glycogen production from glucose-1-phospate by liver and muscle of normal and adrenalectomized animals. *Biochem. J., 42*:42 1948.
300. Verzár, F., and Wenner, V.: The action of steroids on glycogen breakdown in surviving muscle. *Biochem. J., 42*:48, 1948.
301. Vogt, O., Tissières, A., and Verzár, F.: The influence of thymectomy on the sensitivity of rats towards vitamin A and D deficiencies and low protein diets. (German) *Int. Z. Vitaminforsch 20*:44, 1948.
302. Mentha, J., Vögtli, W., and Verzár, F.: The influence of desoxycorticosterone on glycogen metabolism during working of the isolated diaphragm of normal and adrenalectomized rats. (German) *Helv. Physiol. Acta, 6*:853, 1948.
303. Verzár, F.: Food for the family of nations. (Lecture 18.3.1948. Community Service Society, New York.)
304. Verzár, F.: Influence of internal secretion on fat absorption and transport. *Arch. Sci. Physiol., II*:43 1948.

1949

305. Leupin, E. and Verzár, F.: Influence of desoxycorticosterone on glycogen formation and glucose uptake of isolated muscle. *Nature, 163*:836, 1949.
306. Verzár, F.: Demonstration of a counter for activity of the surviving rat diaphragm. (German) *Helv. Physiol. Acta, 7*:c-3, 1949.
307. Leupin, E., Vögtli, W., and Verzár, F.: The effect of adrenal cortical steroids on carbohydrate metabolism of the isolated mammalian muscle. (German) *Helv. Physiol. Acta, 7*:c-13, 1949.
308. Sass-Kortsák, A., Wang, F. C., and Verzár, F.: Comparative investigations on the formation of glycogen in liver and muscle by desoxycorticosterone, 17-hydroxy-11-dehydrocorticosterone and complete extract, in adrenalectomized rats. (German) *Helv. Physiol. Acta, 7*:c-18, 1949.
309. Wang, S. I., and Verzár, F.: Erythropoesis at 6,170 feet altitude in normal and thyroidectomized rabbits. (German) *Schweiz. Med. Wschr., 79*:713, 1949.
310. Sass-Kortsák, A., Wang, F. C., and Verzár, F.: Influence of desoxycorticosterone acetate on liver and muscle glycogen of adrenalectomized animals. *Amer. J. Physiol., 159*:256, 1949.
311. Wang, F. C., and Verzár, F.: Comparison between glycogenetic property of desoxycorticosterone, 11-dehydro-17-hydroxycorticosterone (Compound E) and adrenal cortical extract. *Amer. J. Physiol. 159*:263, 1949.
312. Bozovic, L., Leupin, E., and Verzár, F.: The influence of desoxycorticosterone and adrenalin on carbohydrate metabolism of muscle *in vitro*. (German) *Helv. Physiol. Acta, 7*:328, 1949.

1950

313. Verzár, F., and Wang, F. C.: Reversal of glycogenetic to glycogenolytic action of desoxycorticosterone in rats. *Nature, 165*:114, 1950.
314. Verzár, F.: Metabolic effects of adrenal cortical hormone. (German) *Schweiz. Med. Wschr., 80*:468, 1950.

315. Leupin, E., and Verzár, F.: Glycogen formation and glucose uptake of isolated muscle with 11-deoxycorticosterone and 11-dehydro-17-hydroxycorticosterone. *Biochem. J., 46:*562, 1950.

316. Leupin, E., and Verzár, F.: Potassium and carbohydrate metabolism in surviving muscle. (German) *Helv. Physiol. Acta, 8:*c-27, 1950.

317. Peyser, E., Sass-Kortsák, A., and Verzár, F.: Influence of O_2 content of inspired air on total lung volume. *Amer. Physiol., 163:*111, 1950.

318. Sailer, E., and Verzár, F.: The excretion of corticosteroids at rest, during muscular work and at altitude. (German) *Helv. Physiol. Acta, 8:*c-72, 1950.

319. Sailer, E., and Verzár, F.: The function of the thyroid gland at reduced atmospheric pressure. (German) *Helv. Physiol. Acta, 8:*c-74, 1950.

320. Verzár, F.: The point of attack of cortin in carbohydrate and electrolyte metabolism. (German) In "Conferenze di Endocrinologia", Soc. Ed. Universitaria, Firenze, 1950.

1951

321. Verzár, F.: Permanent acclimatization to high altitude. (German) *Bull. Schweiz. Akad. Med. Wiss. 7:*26, 1951.

322. Bühlmann, A., Wang, S. I., Wirz, H., and Verzár, F.: The erythrocyte count at medium altitudes. (German) *Schweiz. Med. Wschr., 81:*80, 1951.

323. Wang, S. I., Wirz, H., and Verzár, F.: The oxygen saturation of arterial blood in man and rabbit at 6,100 feet, and its relation to the increased erythrocyte count. (German) *Schweiz. Med. Wschr., 81:*82, 1951.

324. Verzár, F.: The "third form" of respiratory regulation during the climb to high altitudes and in the high altitude populations of the Andes. (German) *Bull. Schweiz. Akad. Med. Wiss., 7:*201, 1951.

325. Verzár, F., and Vidovic, V.: The effect of adrenal cortical hormone on the function of the thyroid, investigated with I^{131}. (German) *Helv. Physiol. Acta, 9:*214, 1951.

326. Verzár, F., and Vidovic, V.: Inhibition of thyroid function by strong supercooling. (German) *Helv. Physiol. Acta, 9:*c-13, 1951.

327. Verzár, F.: The "third form" of respiratory regulation. (Spanish) *Cienca Investigación, 7:*303, 1951.

328. Verzár, F.: *In vitro* influences of corticosteroids on phosphorylating enzymes. *Ann. N.Y. Acad. Sci. 54:*716, 1951.

1952

329. Verzár, F.: The counts of lymphocytes and eosinophil leucocytes at 6,100 and 11,320 feet. (German) *Schweiz. Med. Wschr., 82:*324, 1952.

330. Verzár, F., and Sailer, E.: Glucose absorption and alkaline phosphatase of the small intestine after adrenalectomy, in animals treated with NaCl. (German) *Helv. Physiol. Acta, 10:*247, 1952.

331. Verzár, F., Sailer, E., and Richterich, R.: The influence of the adrenal cortex on alkaline phosphatase in the intestinal mucous membrane. (German) *Helv. Physiol. Acta, 10:*231, 1952.

332. Flückiger, E., and Verzár, F.: The influence of the thyroid gland, the adrenal cortex and the pituitary gland on decrease and recovery of body temperature at low atmospheric pressure. (German) *Helv. Physiol. Acta, 10:*c-15, 1952.

333. Leupin, E., and Verzár, F.: The absorption of olive oil and paraffin oil from the intestine of the rat. (German) *Helv. Physiol. Acta, 10:*c-17, 1952.

334. Flückiger, E., and Verzár, F.: Decrease and recovery of body temperature at low atmospheric pressure and the influence of the thyroid gland, the pituitary gland, and the adrenal cortex. (German) *Helv. Physiol. Acta, 10:*349, 1952.

335. Verzár, F., and Vidovic, V.: The action of thyrotrophic hormone and cortisone on the uptake of I^{131} by the thyroid gland. *J. Endocr., 8:*321, 1952.

336. Verzár, F., Sailer, E., and Vidovic, V.: Changes in thyroid activity at low atmospheric pressures and at high altitudes, as tested with I^{131}. *J. Endocr. 8:*308, 1952.

337. Verzár, F.: The influence of corticoids on enzymes of carbohydrate metabolism. *Vitamins & Hormones, 10:*297, 1952.

338. Verzár, F.: The nature of the adrenal cortical secretion. In: "The Suprarenal Cortex", 5th Symp. Colston Res. Soc., Bristol 1952, p. 39.

339. Verzár, F.: Phosphorylation. (Italian) *Enciclopedia Medica Italiana, 4:*1403, 1952.

340. Verzár, F.: The connection of carbohydrate and potassium metabolism, in relation to the adrenal cortex. *Ciba Found. Coll. Endocr., 2:*439, 1952.

341. Verzár, F.: The influence of corticosteroids on carbohydrate and electrolyte metabolism *in vitro. Ciba Found. Coll. Endocr. 2:*418, 1952.

342. Verzár, F.: The inadequacy of biological differentiation of so-called "mineralo- and carbohydrate-corticoids". *Ciba Found. Coll. Endocr., 2:*179, 1952.

343. Granados, H., and Verzár, F.: The influence of pantothenic acid and other B-vitamins on the adrenalectomized rat. *Int. Rev. Vitamin Res., 24:*403, 1952.

1953

344. Verzár, F.: A counter for condensation nuclei with automatic registration. (German) *Archiv Meterologie Geophysik, 5:*372, 1953.

345. Flückiger, E., and Verzár, F.: Lasting adaptation to low atmospheric pressure, demonstrated on heat regulation. (German) *Helv. Physiol. Acta, 11:*69, 1953.

346. Flückiger, E., and Verzár, F.: The effect of adrenalin and noradrenalin on the function of the thyroid gland. (German) *Arch. Exp. Path. Pharmakol., 219:*160, 1953.

347. Verzár, F.: The activity of the thyroid gland under the influence of the adrenal cortex, the adrenal medulla, the pituitary gland, and oxygen deficiency. (German) *Bull. Schweiz. Akad. Med. Wiss., 9:*121, 1953.

348. Verzár, F., Keith, J., and Parchet, V.: Temperature and humidity of air in the respiratory tract. (German) *Pflügers Arch., 257:*400, 1953.

349. Flückiger, E., and Verzár, F.: The influence of sugar metabolism on Na^{24} uptake into muscle and the effect of adrenal cortical hormone. (German) *Schweiz. Med. Wschr., 83:*849, 1953.

350. Lüthy, E., and Verzár, F.: Hexokinase and adenosinetriphosphatase in the epithelium of the intestinal mucous membrane of normal and adrenalectomized animals. (German) *Schweiz. Med. Wschr., 83:*850, 1953.

351. Verzár, F.: The control of thyroid activity with I^{131} in the rat. *Radioisotope Techniques, 1:*264, 1953.

352. Bider, M., and Verzár, F.: Continuous counting of atmospheric condensation nuclei (preliminary results with the registering counter in Basel). (German) *Geofis. Pura Appl., Milano, 26*:127, 1953.

353. Verzár, F., Vidovic, V., and Hajdukovic, S.: The influence of hypothermia on the uptake of I^{131} by the thyroid. *J. Endocr., 10*:46, 1953.

354. Bitterli, H., and Verzár, F.: Experiences with the automatic counter for condensation nuclei. (German) *Arch. Meteor. 6*:211, 1953.

1954

355. Flückiger, E., and Verzár, F.: The effect of corticosteroids on the Na^{24}- and K^{42}-exchange of surviving muscle. (German) *Helv. Physiol. Acta, 12*:57, 1954.

356. Flückiger, E., and Verzár, F.: The influence of carbohydrate metabolism on the sodium and potassium exchange of surviving muscle. (German) *Helv. Physiol. Acta, 12*:50, 1954.

357. Lüthy, E., and Verzár, F.: Adenosinetriphosphatase and hexokinase in the epithelium of the small intestine in normal and adrenalectomized rats. *Biochem. J., 57*:316, 1954.

358. Verzár, F.: Our present views on the place of action of adrenal cortical hormones and the relation with the other endocrine organs. (German) *Moderne Probleme der Pädiatrie, 1*:198, 1954.

359. Verzár, F.: Demonstration of an automatic counter for condensation nuclei, with registering hygrometer and thermometer. (German) *Helv. Physiol. Acta, 12*:c-8, 1954.

360. Flückiger, E., and Verzár, F.: The effect of aldosterone ("electrocortin") on sodium, potassium and glycogen metabolism of isolated muscle. (German) *Experientia, 10*:259, 1954.

361. Verzár, F.: Compensatory hypertrophy of kidney and adrenal in the lifespan of rats. IIIrd Congress International Association of Gerontology, London. 1954, p. 139.

362. Verzár, F.: Adaptation in old age: Compensatory hypertrophy of kidney and adrenal. IIIrd Congress International Association of Gerontology, London. 1954, p. 263.

363. Verzár, F., and Flückiger, E.: Lack of adaptation to low oxygen pressure in aged animals. IIIrd Congress International Association of Gerontology, London. 1954, p. 524.

364. Verzár, F., and Flückiger, E.: Adaptation to low atmospheric pressure. IIIrd Congress International Association of Gerontology, London. 1954, p. 263.

365. Verzár, F., and Flückiger, E.: Adaptation to low atmospheric pressure in old animals. (German) *Schweiz. Med. Wschr., 84*:1324, 1954.

366. Ackermann, P., Bider, M., and Verzár, F.: Continuous counting of atmospheric condensation nuclei. (German) *Geofis. Pura Appl., Milano, 29*:167, 1954.

367. Flückiger, E., and Verzár, F.: Influence of adrenalectomy on sodium and potassium exchange in muscle. *Acta Endocr., 17*:80, 1954.

368. Verzár, F.: Continuous counting of atmospheric condensation nuclei in St. Moritz. (German) *Verh. Schweiz. Naturf. Ges.* 1954, p. 116.

369. Verzár, F.: The retention of atmospheric condensation nuclei in the respiratory tract. (German) *Verh. Schweiz. Naturf. Ges.* 1954, p. 117.

370. Verzár, F.: Complete diet as a means to combat an addiction. (German) *Int. Z. Vitaminforschung, 25*:303, 1954.

371. Verzár, F.: The influence of dietary factors on endocrine disturbances of the adrenal cortex (German) *Int. Z. Vitaminforschung, 25:*304, 1954.
372. Verzár, F.: The retention of atmospheric condensation nuclei in the respiratory tract. (German) *Helv. Physiol. Acta, 12:*c-92, 1954.

1955

373. Verzár, F.: Nutrition as a factor against addiction. *Voeding, 16:*461, 1955.
374. Verzár, F.: Alterations in thermoelastic contraction of skin and nerves in aging animals. (German) *Experientia, 11:*230, 1955.
376. Verzár, F., Hügin, F., and Massion, W.: Retention of atmospheric condensation nuclei in the respiratory tract. (German) *Pflügers Arch., 261:*219, 1955.
376. Verzár, F., Hügin, F., and Massion, W.: Retention of atmospheric condensation nuclei in the respiratory tract. (German) *Pflügers Arch., 261:*219, 1955.
377. Flückiger, E., and Verzár, F.: Lack of adaptation to low oxygen pressure in aged animals. *J. Geront., 10:*306, 1955.
378. Verzár, F., and Hügin, F.: Functional hypertrophy in old age. (German) *Schweiz. Med. Wschr., 85:*686, 1955.
379. Verzár, F., and Flückiger, E.: The function of the thyroid gland after adrenalectomy. (German) *Schweiz. Med. Wschr., 85:*660, 1955.
380. Verzár, F.: Nutrition as a factor against addiction. *Amer. J. Clin. Nutr., 3:*363, 1955.
381. Flückiger, E., and Verzár, F.: Thyroid function after adrenalectomy. *J. Endocr.,* 13:39, 1955.
382. Verzár, F.: Continuous record of atmospheric condensation nuclei and of their retention in the respiratory tract. *Geofis. Pura Appl., Milano, 31:*183, 1955.
383. Verzár, F.: Alterations of the thermoelastic contraction of tendon fibres in old age. (German) *Helv. Physiol. Acta, 13:*c-64, 1955.
384. Verzár, F.: An automatic counter for condensation nuclei. (German) *Ber. Deutsch. Wetterdienstes Nr. 22,* 1955.

1956

385. Verzár, F., and Freydberg, V.: Changes of thyroid activity in the rat in old age. *J. Geront., 11:*53, 1956.
386. Hügin, F., and Verzár, F.: Investigations on the hypertrophy through overstrain of the heart in young and old rats. (German) *Pflügers Arch., 262:*181, 1956.
387. Verzár, F.: Experimental results for a theory of the point of action of vitamin E. (German) III. Int. Vitamin E Congress, Venezia, 1955; Ed. Valdonega Verona, 1956.
388. Verzár, F.: The aging of collagen. (German) *Helv. Physiol. Acta, 14:*207, 1956.
389. Hügin, F., Keith, J., Verzár, F., and Wirz, H.: Alterations in the vegetative-autonomous excitability in a high altitude climate. (German) *Schweiz. Med. Wschr., 86:*650, 1956.
390. Hügin, F., and Verzár, F.: Failure of heat regulation at low temperatures as a phenomenon of aging. (German) In Verzár, F. (ed): *Symposium über exp. Alternsforschung,* Basel, Birkhäuser, 1956, p. 96.
391. Verzár, F.: The aging of collagen. In Verzár, F. (ed): *Symposium über exp. Alternsforschung,* Basel, Birkhäuser, 1956, p. 35.

392. Freydberg, V., and Verzár, F.: Turnover of Ca^{45} in young and old animals. In Verzár, F. (ed): *Symposium über exp. Alternsforschung,* Basel, Birkhäuser, 1956, p. 88.

393. Flückiger, E., and Verzár, F.: The effect of cortisol and cortexone on glycogen metabolism. (German) *Schweiz. Med. Wschr., 86:*1263, 1956.

394. Brückner, R., Gsell, O., Hügin, F., Batschelet, E., and Verzár, F.: Continuous measurement of the aging process—comparative investigations on the eye and other organs. (German) In Verzár, F. (ed): *Symposium über exp. Alternsforschung,* Basel, Birkhäuser, 1956, p. 279.

395. Verzár, F.: The suprarenal glands. (Italian) *Enciclopedia Medica Italiana,* 1956, p. 150.

1957

396. Herpertz, E., and Verzár, F.: An attempt to characterize atmospheric condensation nuclei by coagulation measurements and at different expansions. (German) *Geofis. Pura Appl., Milano, 36:*149, 1957.

397. Bider, M., and Verzár, F.: Registration of the number of condensation nuclei at St. Moritz for several years. (German) *Geofis. Pura Appl., 36:*110, 1957.

398. Herpertz, E., Israel, H., and Verzár, F.: A comparison of measurements of atmospheric electricity and condensation nuclei on the Jungfraujoch (11,740 feet). (German) *Geofis. Pura Appl., 36:*218, 1957.

399. Verzár, F.: Studies on adaptation processes as a method of research in aging. *Ciba Found. Coll. on Aging, 3:*60, 1957.

400. Verzár, F., and Huber, K.: The influence of vitamin E (tocopherol) on creatine metabolism of normal rats and rats with muscular dystrophy. (German) *Int. Z. Vitaminforschung 27:*394, 1957.

401. Hügin, F., and Verzár, F.: Failure of heat regulation in old animals. (German) *Gerontologia, 1:*91, 1957.

402. Flückiger, E., and Verzár, F.: Glycogen, sodium and potassium metabolism of the surviving muscle under successive or simultaneous influence of corticosteroids. (German) *Helv. Physiol. Acta. 15:*304, 1957.

403. Flückiger, E., and Verzár, F.: The effects of corticosteroids on muscle preparations. (German) *Helv. Physiol. Acta, 15:*293, 1957.

404. Verzár, F.: Atmospheric condensation nuclei as a measure of air pollution. (German) *Nat. Zeitung, Basel,* 1957, No. 406 and 410.

405. Verzár, F., and Hügin, F.: The effect of old age on the development of hypertrophy through overstrain of organs. (German) *Acta Anat. 30:*918, 1957.

406. Freydberg-Lucas, V., and Verzár, F.: The calcium metabolism of different organs in young and old animals. (German) *Gerontologia, 1:*195, 1957.

407. Verzár, F., and Kunz, Y.: Production of atmospheric condensation nuclei by solar radiation. *Geofis. Pura Appl., 38:*215, 1957.

408. Verzár, F.: The aging of connective tissue. *Gerontologia, 1:*363, 1957.

409. Verzár, F.: Why experimental gerontology? (German) In: *Der Weg ins Alter,* Basel, Birkhäuser, 1957, p. 138.

1958

410. Verzár, F: Problems of general biology of aging. *J. Geront., 13,* Suppl. *1:*6, 1958.

411. Verzár, F., and Freydberg-Lucas, V.: Ca^{45} uptake and turnover of tendon fibres as influenced by thermic contraction and age. *Gerontologia, 2:*11, 1958.

412. Verzár, F., and Huber, K.: The structure of the tendon fibre. (German) *Acta Anatom., 33*:215, 1958.
413. Verzár, F., and Huber, K.: Thermic contraction of single tendon fibres from animals of different age after treatment with formaldehyde, urethane, glycerol, acetic acid and other substances. *Gerontologia, 2*:81, 1958.
414. Verzár, F., and Huber, K.: The affinity of collagen fibres for radio-isotopes Ca^{45}, Na^{24}, K^{42} and I^{131} during thermic contraction. *Gerontologia, 2*:113, 1958.
415. Verzár, F.: Biologic effects of low level radiation. (Discussion) *Bull. Swiss Acad. Med. Sci., 14*:479, 1958.
416. Verzár, F.: Biological problems of experimental gerontology. (German) *Triangel, 3*:253, 1958.
417. Verzár, F.: The adaptation of man to high altitudes. (German) *Ciba Sympos., 6*:142, 1958.

1959

418. Verzár, F.: Muscular dystrophy in old age. *Geront. Clin., 1*:41, 1959.
419. Verzár, F.: Trends in gerontological literature. *Excerpta Med. (XX), 2*:97, 1959.
420. Verzár, F., and Evans, D. A.: Production of atmospheric condensation nuclei by sunrays. *Geofis. Pura Appl., 43*:259, 1959.
421. Verzár, F.: The discovery of atmospheric condensation nuclei by Paul-Jean Coulier in 1875. *Experientia, 15*:362, 1959.
422. Verzár, F.: Influence of ionizing radiation on the age reaction of collagen fibres. *Gerontologia, 3*:163, 1959.
423. Verzár, F.: Experiments on the influencing of old age creatinuria by alpha-tocopherol acetate and selenium. (German) *Gerontologia, 3*:232, 1959.
424. Meyer, A., and Verzár, F.: Age-changes of the hydroxyproline release during thermic contraction of collagen fibres. (German) *Gerontologia, 3*:184, 1959.
425. Gsell, D., and Verzár, F.: On an attempt to cure a polyvalent vitamin deficiency in children in a mountain valley. (German) *Int. Z. Vitaminforsch., 30*:217, 1959.
426. Verzár, F.: The aging of connective tissue. (German) In W. Doberauer (ed): *Aktuelle Geriatrie,* Wien, Bergland-Druckerei, 1959, p. 27.
427. Verzár, F.: Note on the influence of procain (Novocain), para-aminobenzoic acid and diethylethanolamine on the aging of rats. *Gerontologia, 3*:351, 1959.

1960

428. Verzár, F.: Physiology of the adrenal cortical hormones. (German) In: Ammon, R., and Dirscherl, W. (eds): *Fermente, Hormone, Vitamine. Band II,* Stuttgart, George Thieme Verlag, 1960, p. 450.
429. Verzár, F.: Muscular dystrophy in old age. (German) In W. Doberauer (ed): *Geriatrie und Fortbildung,* Wien, Bergland-Druckerei, 1960, p. 27.
430. Verzár, F.: Increased binding of hydroxyproline in skin collagen with increasing age. (German) *Gerontologia, 4*:104, 1960.
431. Verzár, F., and Thoenen, H.: The effect of electrolytes on the thermic contraction of collagen fibers. (German) *Gerontologia, 4*:112, 1960.
432. Verzár, F., and Farner, D.: Investigations on the effects of drugs on animals of different ages. (German) *Gerontologia, 4*:143, 1960.

433. Verzár, F.: Adaptation to environmental changes at different ages. *Amer. Inst. Biol. Sci.* Sympos. No. 6, 1960.

1961

434. Verzár, F.: The age of the individual as one of the parameters of pharmacological action. *Acta Physiol. Acad. Sci. Hung., 19:*313, 1961.
435. Verzár, F.: Pathology and physiology of senescence. (French) In Pacaud, S. (ed).: *Le vieillissement des fonctions psychologiques et psychophysiologiques.* Ed. du centre national de la recherche scientifique, Paris 1961, p. 175.
436. Verzár, F., and Meyer, A.: Chemical changes in collagen fibres during thermic contraction. (German) *Gerontologia, 5:*163, 1961.
437. Brocas, J., and Verzár, F.: The aging of *Xenopus laevis. Experientia, 17:*421, 1961.
438. Farner, D., and Verzár, F.: The age parameter of pharmacological activity. *Experientia, 17:*421, 1961.
439. Verzár, F., and Willenegger, H.: The aging of collagen in the skin and in scars. (German) *Schweiz. Med. Wschr., 91:*1234, 1961.
440. Verzár, F.: Biology of aging. (Italian) *Gazz. Sanit.,* 1961, 390.
441. Brocas, J., and Verzár, F.: The aging of *Xenopus laevis,* a South African frog. *Gerontologia, 5:*22, 1961.
442. Brocas, J., and Verzár, F.: Measurement of isometric tension during thermic contraction as criterion of the biological age of collagen fibres. *Gerontologia, 5:*223, 1961.
443. Verzár, F.: The determination of the biological age of collagen in tendons and in corium (isometric, isotonic and hydroxyproline methods). (German) *Helv. Physiol. Acta, 19:*c-46, 1961.
444. Weber, R., Meyer, A., Brenner, M., and Verzár, F.: Chemical investigations on the problem of the thermic contraction of tendon collagen (German) *Helv. Physiol. Acta 19:*c-116, 1961.

1962

445. Verzár, F.: The aging of the central nervous system, and the altered effects of drugs due to it. (German) In W. Doberauer (ed): *Diagnostik und Therapie im Alter,* Wien, 1962, p. 11.
446. Verzár, F.: Biology of aging. (German) *Ophtalmologica, 143:*243, 1962.
447. Verzár, F.: Liberation of mechanical tension by heating of collagen fibres. *Experientia, 18:*310, 1962.
448. Verzár, F.: Biology of aging. (German) *Schweiz. Med. Wschr., 92:*1449, 1962.
449. Verzár, F.: Methods of experimental gerontology. (German) In Kaiser, H. (ed): *Der Mensch im Alter.* Schriftenreihe d. med. pharm. Studiengesellschaft, Frankfurt a.M., 1962, p. 52.
450. Verzár, F.: Internal tensions in the collagen macromolecule and their changes with aging. *Experientia, 18:*474, 1962.
451. Verzár, F.: Aging of newly formed collagen. *Experientia, 18:*473, 1962.
452. Verzár, F.: Biology of aging. (Portuguese) *Gazz. Sanit.,* No. 3/4, 3, 1962.
453. Verzár, F.: Problems of experimental gerontology and geriatric therapy. (German) In: *Scriptum Geriatricum 1962,* W. Doberauer (ed), Wien, 1962, p. 37.

1963

454. VERZÁR, F.: Fifteen years of research on high altitude climate at the Station for Climate Physiology in St. Moritz-Bad. (German) *Schweiz. Med. Wschr. 93*:251, 1963.
455. VON HAHN, H. P., AND VERZÁR, F.: Age-dependent thermal denaturation of DNA from bovine thymus. *Gerontologia, 7*:105, 1963.
456. VERZÁR, F., AND GORDON, H. A.: Effects of aging on the reaction of stretched and unstretched collagen fiber to heat and formaldehyde treatment. *Gerontologia, 7*:85, 1963.
457. ÁRVAY, A., TAKACS, J., AND VERZÁR, F.: The influence of pregnancy on the aging of collagen (experiments on rats). (German) *Gerontologia, 7*:77, 1963.
458. VERZÁR, F.: The aging of collagen. *Sci. Amer. 208*:4, 104, 1963.
459. VERZÁR, F., AND GSELL, D.: The nutritional status of mountain populations in Switzerland. In: *World Reviews of Nutrition and Dietetics 4,* pp. 40-51, Pitman Medical, London, 1963.
460. VERZÁR, F.: Molecular alterations of collagen in aging and diseases. (German) *Schweiz. Med. Wschr., 93*:1036, 1963.
461. VERZÁR, F.: Differentiation of different crosslinks in collagen by tension measurements. (German) *Z. Physiol. Chem., 355*:38, 1963.
462. OERIU, S., AND VERZÁR, F.: The influence of cysteine on collagen fibres. *Gerontologia, 8*:242, 1963.
463. VERZÁR, F.: New results of experimental gerontology. (German) In: W. DOBERAUER, (ed): *Scriptum Geriatricum 1963,* Wien, 1963, p. 51.

1964

464. VERZÁR, F.: On the 10th anniversary of the Swiss Nutrition Society, 26 April 1963 in Basel. (German) *Int. Z. Vitaminforschung, 34*:47, 1964.
465. VERZÁR, F.: Results of experimental gerontology. (German) In: O. GSELL, (ed): *Krankheit der über 70-jährigen,* Bern, Verlag Huber, 1964, p. 11.
466. VERZÁR, F.: Aging of the collagen fiber. In D. A. Hall (ed): *Int. Rev. Connect. Tissue Res., 2*:243, 1964.
467. VERZÁR, F.: Intrinsic factors of aging. In: P. FROM HANSEN, (ed): *Age with a Future,* Copenhagen, Munksgaard, 1964, p. 22.
468. VERZÁR, F.: Aging of connective tissue. *G. Geront., 12*:915, 1964.
469. VERZÁR, F.: Factors which influence the age-reaction of collagen in the skin. *Gerontologia, 9*:209, 1964.

1965

470. VERZÁR, F.: Biology of aging. (German) In: W. DOBERAUER, A. HILTMAIR, R. NISSEN UND F. H. SCHULZ (eds): *Handbuch der praktischen Geriatrie,* Stuttgart, F. Enke Verlag, 1965, p. 101.
471. VERZÁR, F.: Obituary of Dr. Theo Oettli. (German) *Schweiz. Med. Wschr., 95*:748, 1965.
472. VERZÁR, F.: Problems of experimental gerontology. (German) In: *International Conference on Gerontology,* publ. by Akadémiai Kiadó, Budapest, 1965, p. 25.
473. VERZÁR, F., SPICHTIN, H., AND GASCHE, W.: Renaturation of collagen fibers after different methods of denaturation. *Gerontologia, 11*:226, 1965.

Section II

AGING AT THE MOLECULAR LEVEL

Chapter 4

AGING IN MOLECULES–DNA

HOLGER P. VON HAHN

FOUR RECENT REVIEWS, each covering the subject of the role of DNA in the aging process from a different point of view, have given an extensive coverage of the literature on DNA and aging (Blumenthal and Berns, 1964; Clark, 1964; Medvedev, 1964; von Hahn, 1965). The reader is therefore referred to these articles for detailed lists of references on this subject.

The purpose of the present article is, first, to attempt to assemble a picture of our present understanding of "aging" as applied to the DNA molecule, and of the possible mechanisms leading to such "aging"; second, to draw some conclusions as to what the major problems appear to be and what could be done to resolve them. It is inevitable that both the picture presented and the conclusions drawn from it reflect the personal view of the writer and are therefore necessarily biased, and certainly incomplete. If they should stimulate others to complete the picture and correct the conclusions, their purpose will have been well served.

All considerations of the "aging" of DNA must be based on the structure and the function of the DNA molecule in the cell. The primary purpose of research into the "aging" of DNA is to determine whether DNA is involved in—the cause of—age-related alterations in cellular metabolism. This presumes that DNA does in fact have a functional relationship with the rest of the cell. As is generally believed today, this function is that of primary informational matrix for protein synthesis, by virtue of the "genetic code." According to the present views of DNA as an informational macromolecule, the linear sequence of the four nucleotides along one strand of the Watson-Crick double helix contains the information, encoded in triplets of nucleotides, for a co-linear polypeptide chain. The "information" is "read out" by an intermediary carrier, "messenger"-RNA. The key to our following discussion is the "read-out" mechanism: the double helix must be "un-twined" locally, at the beginning of a structural gene (under the direction of an immediately adjacent operator). In the open loop thus formed, the RNA-polymerase enzyme system is fixed, and free nucleotide triphosphates are attached to their corresponding base-partners on the DNA "coding-strand" by H-bonds (and possibly other, stronger types of bonds). The RNA polymerase forms a lengthening RNA chain as it moves along the DNA strand together with the "loop." Ribosomes then attach to the free end of the newly-formed messenger-RNA and detach it from the DNA. Two points in this mechanism appear to be of importance for our subject:

1) The code, as far as is known, is "read out" in a definite direction: the triplets do not contain the same information if read "backwards." If a single nucleotide base in a triplet is changed (that is, if the substituents on the purine or pyrimidine rings are changed) the "message" of the entire triplet will be changed to give either another amino acid, or nonsense—in which case the read-out will stop at this point, giving an incomplete peptide. This is the molecular basis of what is generally known as "point mutation." This mechanism predicts the appearance of altered proteins, containing one or more changed amino acids, and also of shortened peptide chains. In both cases, the function of the product will be more or less altered, depending on the place of the mutation along the gene (along the peptide chain).

2) The "read-out" requires the local unwinding of the DNA double helix. The Watson-Crick structure is held together by hydrogen bonds between the complementary nucleotide pairs, and further types of bonds not yet entirely elucidated, such as energy released by the "stacking" of the bases within the helix, so-called "hydrophobic" bonds, and water molecules attached in an ordered pattern. These are all weak types of bonds when compared to the normal covalent bond, and thus the two strands of a double helix separate and reform easily. Any changes or additions to the amount of bonding between the two strands will interfere with the read-out process. Such interference is assumed to be involved in the normal regulation of gene expression, "repression" or "in-

duction." In the operon model of gene regulation as formulated by F. Jacob and J. Monod, in 1961, the normal state of a gene is the repressed one, in which a "repressor" is bound to it. "Induction" involves inactivation of the "repressor" by small specific molecules called "inducers." There has been much speculation on the nature of the repressors, and some evidence has pointed to their being of a protein nature. Since the discovery of the repressor function of histones on DNA-dependent RNA synthesis *in vitro* it has been postulated that these basic proteins, which are attached to DNA by ionic bonds in the native nucleoprotein complex, are the natural regulators of gene expression. The problem of the specificity of such a regulation with the limited number of different histone types available need not concern us here. What appears important is that the "read-out" is blocked at the DNA level by the attachment of these basic proteins to the nucleic acid. The effect might be due to interference with the unwinding of the double helix. This sensitive point in the regulation mechanism is also subject to interference by other specific reactions, such as for example the selective binding of Actinomycin to DNA. The result of a permanent blocking of this mechanism would be the complete, irreversible repression of the affected gene or gene-section, with a consequent loss of genetic information for the cell, and the loss of the synthesis of certain proteins.

On a much larger scale, chromosome damage in the form of deletions occurring during mitosis would also lead to a loss of genetic information. The hypothesis of Szilard (1959) also postulates the inactivation of large chromosome segments, even entire chromosomes, by random radiation "hits."

Mutations and Aging

In considering the role that point mutations may play in aging, we are not considering genetic factors in the sense of hereditary transmittance of traits concerned with a species-specific pattern of lifespan and aging. What we are interested in here is the possibility that the accumulation of point mutations in cells of somatic organs during the lifetime of the individual may adversely affect the physiological function of the organ by a progressive loss of fully functional cells. Lethal mutations, which eliminate the cell within a short time, while adding to the overall loss of functional cells, do not burden the organ as cells bearing sublethal, deleterious mutations do, which can exert a damaging influence over the entire remaining lifespan of the individual. If the damage to the DNA is such as not to impair mitosis, the mutation may be carried over several generations of daughter cells, unless it is "repaired" by reinsertion of the correct nucleotide during DNA reduplication, in organs with appreciable mitotic rates. In other cases, the damage may result in abnormal mitoses giving pictures of chromosome abnormalities, and leading either to immediate death because of incomplete separation of the daughter cells, or to cells with abnormal chromosome complements. Such cells, too, are not likely to survive (cancerous cells appear to be exceptional in this respect). Since many parenchymal organs (unless artificially stimulated), and especially muscle and central nervous system, have very small, or even unmeasurable mitotic rates during adult life, mutations can be considered to be restricted to the cell in which they first occur.

The "somatic mutation theory" of aging (Danielli, 1956; Curtis, 1964) maintains that aging can be satisfactorily explained as the consequence of the accumulation of mutations in somatic cells. The evidence concerning this theory has been widely discussed in recent years (Alexander, 1963; Blumenthal and Berns, 1964; Clark, 1964; Curtis, 1964; Strehler, 1964), but it has not yet led to an agreement between those who support this concept and those who do not consider somatic mutations an important factor in aging. One important point under discussion concerns the rate of spontaneous mutation in somatic cells. There is as yet no direct way of determining mutation rates in somatic cells, such as the breeding methods used for determing genetic mutations. Various indirect methods described (such as chromosome abnormalities in metaphase in regenerating liver, or the "auto-immunity" hypothesis) have been challenged as not giving a true measure of somatic mutations or as not being necessarily only the result of such mutations.

Estimates of mutation rates in somatic organs vary widely (Maynard Smith and Lamb, 1964; Curtis, 1964; Failla, 1960) and do not as yet provide an objective basis for judgment. Another important point is raised by Strehler (1964), who discusses the fact that radiation appears to both shorten lifespan as well as increase the number of chromosome abnormalities: the fact that a single variable (radiation) causes an effect in two dependent variables (life span and chromosome damage) does not necessarily show that the one effect (mutation) is the cause of the other (shortened life span). It still remains to be demonstrated that aging is caused by, rather than accompanied by, somatic mutations or chromosome abnormalities. This does not, of course, affect the undoubted fact that mutations do occur in somatic cells and that they will be (with exceedingly rare exceptions) deleterious to the cell, if they occur in the functional part of the genome, which in highly differentiated cells has been estimated as less than one percent of the total gene material.

It would appear that the argument about the role of somatic mutations as a cause of aging will not be advanced before precise experimental methods are available for determining qualitatively and quantitatively the occurrence of such events in somatic cells, and their rate of accumulation. This, from the strictly chemical point of view, should ideally involve the complete elucidation of nucleotide sequences in the DNA of all chromosomes and the assignment of definite subsequences for each gene. Mutations could then be clearly defined by alterations in the sequences. Although the first completely known nucleotide sequence in a nucleic acid (alanine transfer RNA) has just been published, it is a large step from the seventy-seven nucleotides in this small molecule to the thousands of nucleotides in DNA strands of molecular weights measured in millions. Thus this ideal method is not practical at present.

But there exists a tool for identifying nucleotide sequences by precise chemical and physical methods: the reformation of the double helix of DNA from isolated complementary single strands. The double helix will only reform completely if the correct two complementary strands meet. Partial formation of helical structure is possible by matching regions from two different DNA single strands. This method has recently been used with notable success to demonstrate the evolutionary relationship of selected animal species: the closer related the species, the longer the matching sequences in DNA, and thus the longer the regions of helical hybrid structure formed. This is of course just the reverse of what is expected when mutations accumulate: the more mutations, i.e., the more changed bases on one DNA strand, the less helical regions it will form with unmutated ("young") DNA. An attack on the problem of somatic mutations and aging along these lines is being undertaken at present (F. M. Sinex, personal communication).

An extremely sensitive method for detecting small changes in protein structure is the testing of immunologic properties. In the classical example of insulin from various animal species, the alteration of a single amino acid leads to a detectable change in immune properties. Blumenthal and Berns (1964) have recently discussed in great detail the hypothesis that somatic mutations may lead to altered proteins which then could give rise to autoimmune reactions, and that a number of degenerative diseases and other nonclinical age-related phenomena may be due to such reactions. Alterations of DNA base sequence are of course not the only origin of altered protein structure: the entire "reading" and "translating" apparatus as well as the still unknown mechanism for the formation of the highly specific secondary and tertiary structures of proteins are equally liable to damage, as has been pointed out by Medvedev (1961) and Orgel (1963). But if a single amino acid change can be pinpointed in a protein of known sequence, this can with very great probability be attributed to an alteration in base-sequence in DNA. As the "codons" become known with more precision, and the possible chemical mechanisms of substituent changes on the purine and pyrimidine ring systems are elucidated, it will become possible to predict with accuracy whether a detected exchange of one amino acid for another can be due to a "point mutation" on DNA. The techniques of immunology and immunochemistry will detect the altered proteins, amino acid analysis and sequence determination will give the protein primary structure, and after an amino acid exchange has been pinpointed, the chemistry of nucleotide substitutions will say whether a, and what type of, point mutation is involved.

Interference with the "Read-out" Mechanism

The second aspect of structural aging in DNA we are considering is the possibility that with advancing age there may occur an increasing amount of interference with the intricate "read-out" mechanism, as described above. Since such events would interfere with strand separation, they would also interfere with DNA reduplication and thus with mitosis, and while a certain amount of repair is possible, as demonstrated by Curtis, one would not in general expect cells with a considerable amount of such damage to survive mitosis. We are thus again most interested in postmitotic cells which will not reach another division. These are also the cells where the time factor will increasingly be in favour of such randomly occurring events, because of the absence of DNA breakdown during interphase. If, as Szilard (1959) pointed out, the probability of injury to the genetic material remains constant per unit time during life, then the number of injuries per unit genetic material will increase with the age of the molecule (in the absence of turnover).

There is very little precise chemical theory as to the possible nature of damage to the "read-out" mechanism, for the good reason that the details of that mechanism are only now beginning to be understood. DNA is a linear macromolecule of defined helical structure. In this, it resembles fibrous proteins, such as the helically arranged collagen. This structural similarity, and the fact that both substances show negligible turnover in adult tissues, led F. Verzár (1962) and F. Marott Sinex (1957) to postulate "structural aging" of DNA in analogy to the well-known structural aging in collagen as demonstrated by Verzár with the thermic contraction test. While Sinex considered irreversible denaturation processes as causes of aging, Verzár considered the accumulation of stable crosslinks, as in collagen. Both denaturation and crosslinking are well-known chemical reactions in DNA *in vitro,* and both could certainly interfere with the normal "unwinding" process. In the mammalian cell, DNA is associated with histones in a complex of defined structure. These histones are strong protectors of DNA against thermal denaturation (strand separation), as has been shown experimentally. Most of the histone is easily removed by high electrolyte concentrations, but all DNA preparations from mammalian sources contain some residual, very tightly bound protein. While part of this is certainly histone, some of it is neutral or acidic protein of as yet poorly defined nature. Its function is not yet understood, but it may play an important role in maintaining DNA structure.

Investigation of the thermal stability of DNA from aged animals has indicated that there may occur an increasing amount of irreversible binding of protein to DNA, inhibiting denaturation (von Hahn and Verzár, 1963; von Hahn 1964/65). The chemical nature of this process is not yet known, but the formation of stable crosslinks between functional groups of proteins and DNA is chemically quite feasible, either by direct bond formation or with the help of small bifunctional molecules. In contrast, during this investigation no evidence for direct DNA-DNA interstrand crosslinking was found (von Hahn, 1964/65).

If such a process does indeed take place, and if it impairs the "availability" of genetic information, then it should be possible to test for this in an *in vitro* system. DNA-dependent cellfree RNA- and protein-synthesizing systems have been assembled with defined components from different sources. These systems synthesize DNA, RNA or protein only when a DNA "primer" is present. It should be possible with such a system, by careful analysis of the reaction products, to demonstrate that DNA from aged cells is a poorer primer than "young" DNA. Ideally, it might become possible to select certain regions of the genome, coding for specific proteins, and look for the loss of synthesizing ability for one of these proteins, either with immunochemical methods or by fractionation and identification of the reaction products.

Besides this functional approach, the structural analysis of DNA from aged cells should be pursued with the sensitive physicochemical methods now available. Density gradient centrifugation might show bands of small amounts of otherwise undetectable crosslinked aggregates. Gel-filtration of histones permits the isolation of DNA firmly bound to histones. Comparative biochemistry of DNA from postmitotic organs and from those with high mitotic rates would serve to confirm the idea that only DNA without turnover ages.

Experimental work on this general approach to the problem of DNA and aging is only at its very beginning. One major difficulty is the isolation and purification of native DNA from those organs with the desired irreversibly postmitotic cells—such as central nervous system and muscle. These organs have low DNA content and large proportions of contaminating RNA and other substances, from which DNA is difficult to separate without considerable losses in yield.

Several important questions have not been satisfactorily answered so far: What are the primary causes of damage to the DNA molecule, and which of the chemically possible mechanisms of damage probably occur *in vivo*? Is the rate of spontaneous mutation or of structural damage to the DNA molecule *in vivo* sufficient to account for the observed loss of functional cells in aging organs? What proportion of the functional cells of an organ can be damaged by any type of injury before the function of that organ is seriously impaired? These questions must find precise answers before it will be possible to judge whether or not DNA has an important role in the aging process.

REFERENCES

ALEXANDER, P., AND CONNELL, D. I.: Do somatic mutations influence the life span of mice? VIth Int. Congress Geront., Excerp. Med. Int. Congr. Series No. 57, Abstr. 68, 1963.

BLUMENTHAL, H. T., AND BERNS, A. W.: Autoimmunity and aging. *Advances Geront. Res., 1*:289, 1964.

CLARK, A. M.: Genetic factors associated with aging. *Advances Geront. Res., 1*:207, 1964.

CURTIS, H. J.: Cellular processes involved in aging. *Fed. Proc., 23*:662, 1964.

DANIELLI, J. F.: On the aging of cells in tissues. *Experientia,* Suppl. No. 4, 55-59, 1956.

FAILLA, G.: The aging process and somatic mutations. In: *The Biology of Aging.* B. L. Strehler, ed., A.I.B.S., 170, 1960.

MAYNARD SMITH, J., AND LAMB, M. J.: Radiation and aging in insects. *Exp. Geront., 1*:11, 1964.

MEDVEDEV, ZH. A.: Aging of the organism at the molecular level. *Usp. Sovr. Biol. 51*:299, 1961.

MEDVEDEV, ZH. A.: The nucleic acids in development and aging. *Advances Geront. Res., 1*:181, 1964.

ORGEL, L. E.: The maintenance of the accuracy of protein synthesis and its relevance to aging. *Proc. Nat. Acad. Sci. U.S.A., 49*:517, 1963.

SINEX, F. M.: Aging and the lability of irreplaceable molecules. *J. Geront., 12*:190, 1957.

Strehler, B. L.: Studies on the comparative physiology of aging. III. Effects of X-radiation dosage on age-specific mortality rates of *Drosophila melanogaster* and *Campanularia flexuosa. J. Geront., 19:*83, 1964.

Szilard, L.: On the nature of the aging process. *Proc. Nat. Acad. Sci. USA, 45:*30, 1959.

Verzár, F.: Biologie des Alterns. *Schweiz. Med. Wschr., 92:*1449, 1962.

von Hahn, H. P.: Age-related alterations in the structure of DNA. II. The role of histones. *Gerontologia (Basel), 10:*174, 1964/65.

von Hahn, H. P.: *Nucleinsäuren und Nucleoproteine in Zellen alternder Organe.* Habilitationsschrift, Basel und Bern, 1965.

von Hahn, H. P., and Verzár, F.: Age-dependent thermal denaturation of DNA from bovine thymus. Preliminary communication. *Gerontologia (Basel), 7:*104, 1963.

Chapter 5

AGE-ASSOCIATED CHANGES IN THE METABOLISM OF RIBONUCLEIC ACID*

V. J. WULFF

INTRODUCTION

THERE is considerable evidence to support the concept that the nuclei of cells play a crucial role in the control of cellular activity. (Goldstein and Micou, 1959; Brachet, 1960; Suskind and Yanofsky, 1961; Zalokar, 1961; Cavalieri and Rosenberg, 1963; Harris, 1963; Spiegelman, 1963; Prescott, 1964; Markert, 1964; Schneiderman and Gilbert, 1964; Clever, 1964; McCarthy and Hoyer, 1964). The hypothesis—that nuclear control of cell activity resides in the deoxyribonucleic acid (DNA) of the genome and is mediated by the DNA-directed synthesis of ribonucleic acid (RNA) which, in turn, controls the synthesis of specific proteins that function to regulate the chemical activity of cells—is widely accepted.

The results of investigations in this laboratory during the past five years indicate the existence of measurable differences in the metabolism of RNA in young and old adult mice and rats. The observations indicate a more rapid turnover of RNA in the cells of certain tissues of old animals compared to young animals. It is suggested that this observed increase in turnover of RNA may be the manifestation of age-related changes that have occurred and accumulated in nuclear deoxyribonucleic acid. The evidence which provides the basis for these statements, the inferences drawn and speculation indulged in are detailed below.

* This work was aided by grant HD00056 of the National Institute of Child Health and Human Development, National Institutes of Health, Public Health Service, Dept. of Health, Education and Welfare and by contract AT(30-1)3518 between the U. S. Atomic Energy Commission and the Masonic Foundation for Medical Research and Human Welfare.

OBSERVATIONS ON RNA METABOLISM

Autoradiographic Studies

Our investigation of RNA metabolism in relation to age began with experiments to find reasons for the rather dramatic reduction in RNA content of certain cells and tissues of rats and mice between birth and the young adult stage of life (Dawbarn, 1932; Wulff and Freshman, 1961; Wulff, Piekielniak and Wayner, 1963). Autoradiography was employed to estimate the incorporation of H^3-cytidine into several tissues of weanling and young, middle-aged and old adult mice. The amount of label in liver, kidney, ventricular and skeletal muscle six hours after a single intraperitoneal injection of H^3-cytidine varied with age of the mice (Wulff, Quastler and Sherman, 1961, 1962, 1964); kidney cortex exhibited increased labeling with increasing age from fifteen to 542 days; the other tissues showed minimal labeling at sixty-nine days of age and increased labeling both in younger (fifteen days) mice and older (260 and 542 days) mice. The loss of most of the label after exposure of tissues to ribonuclease (Wulff *et al.*, 1964) indicated that the measured radioactivity was chiefly associated with nuclear and cytoplasmic ribonucleic acid. Subsequent experiments in which the time-course of labeling and the influence of precursor specific activity on labeling were investigated (Wulff *et al.*, 1964; Wulff, Quastler, Sherman and Samis, 1965) in young and old adult mice confirmed the earlier results.

Extraction and Characterization of Nuclear RNA

Specific Activity

The autoradiographic detection of an age-related increase in the labeling of RNA of liver (and other tissues) gave no information as to the relationship between the amount of RNA and radioactivity. To determine this relationship it was necessary to adapt and develop techniques to harvest liver nuclei in large yield and to extract, purify and measure the amount and radioactivity of nuclear RNA (Georgiev, 1961; Georgiev and Mant'eva, 1962a,b; Samis, Wulff and Falzone, 1964). These experiments were performed on liver of young (110-120 days) and old (822 to 894 days) rats labeled *in vivo* with H^3-cytidine and killed at various intervals after intraperitoneal injection, usually sixty minutes. The results of these experiments demonstrate: 1) that RNA extracted from liver nuclei of old rats exhibits a higher specific activity (ratio of radioactivity and amount) than RNA extracted from liver nucli of young rats (Samis *et al.*, 1964; Wulff *et al.*, 1966); 2) that the specific activity of cytidylic acid recovered from nuclear RNA of old rat liver is about twice that obtained from nuclear RNA of young rat liver (Wulff *et al.*, 1966), and 3) that the amount of RNA extracted per unit DNA (the RNA/DNA ratio) is the same for liver nuclei of old and young rats (Wulff *et al.*, 1966). The results of experiments performed on kidney and heart of young (95-127 days) and old (756-876 days) rats (Perry, 1965) were similar to the data obtained from liver; the RNA extracted from kidney and heart nuclei of old rats had a higher specific activity than that obtained from young rats. The results of the experiments in which labeled RNA was extracted and measured confirm and extend the earlier autoradiographic findings. They indicate that the incorporation of labeled H^3-cytidine into RNA of liver, kidney and heart nuclei is greater in old than in young rats and, in liver, this increased incorporation is known to occur in the absence of a net increase in nuclear RNA.

To circumvent the complexities associated with the incorporation of labeled precursors into nuclear RNA (i.e., pool size differences—Mandel, 1964; flow of label through various compartments—Russell, 1958), the rate of loss of labeled nuclear RNA was measured in liver of old (812-827 days) and young (124-125 days) rats (Wulff *et al.*, 1966). These experiments were performed under *in vitro* conditions which permitted continued RNA synthesis in the absence of labeled precursor, with the result that labeled RNA disappeared appreciably faster from old rat liver nuclei than from young rat liver nuclei. These data indicate a rapid replacement of nuclear RNA in liver, a replacement which is more rapid in liver of old than young rats (50 per cent of the initial radioactivity in old liver remained after thirteen to fifteen minutes incubation; in young after twenty-one to twenty-three minutes).

Composition and Sedimentation

The observations considered thus far suggest that the turnover of RNA, i.e., synthesis and loss, is appreciably higher in "old" nuclei than in "young" liver nuclei. To obtain some insight into the meaning of these observations, it is necessary to know whether the increased turnover is characteristic of all RNA's, i.e., ribosomal, messenger and transfer, or whether it can be attributed more to one type than to others.

At present, this question can only be partially resolved. The fractionation procedures employed in the extraction of nuclear RNA (Samis *et al.*, 1964) permit the differential extraction of nuclear RNA of relatively low specific activity at temperatures of 50° C. and lower and the extraction of nuclear RNA of relatively high specific activity at temperatures of 65° C. or higher (Georgiev, 1961; Georgiev and Mant'eva, 1962a,b; Georgiev *et al.*, 1963; Samis *et al.*, 1964). Both these fractions of nuclear RNA are rapidly labeled in young rats; the 50° C. fraction reaches its maximum specific activity between 15 minutes and 25 minutes after intraperitoneal injection of a single dose of H^3-cytidine and a fraction extracted at 75° C. exhibits its maximum specific activity between 25 minutes and 30 minutes after injection of the label (Wulff, *et al.*, 1966).

Liver nuclear RNA extracted at low (50° C. and lower) temperatures has been characterized as ribosomal RNA by Georgiev and co-workers (1961, 1962, 1963) and that extracted at higher (55° C. and above) temperatures has been characterized as messenger RNA. This characterization is based upon the rapidity of labeling and upon the determination of the nucleotide composition of the RNA fractions: the low temperature fraction is relatively rich in cytidlyic and guanylic acid and, in this respect, resembles cytoplasmic ribosomal RNA; the higher temperature fraction has a lower cytidylic and guanylic acid content and is richer in adenylic and uridylic acid resembling, in this respect, the nucleotide composition of rat DNA except that, in the latter, uridylic acid is replaced by thymidylic acid. The analysis of the composition of the RNA fractions obtained in our experiments (Wulff *et al.*, 1966) yielded results essentially similar to those obtained by Georgiev and co-workers (1961, 1962, 1963).

The characterization of the low and high specific activity RNA fractions by centrifugation in a 5 to 20 per cent sucrose density gradient (Wulff *et al.,* 1966) indicates a surprising absence of correlation between ultraviolet absorption (i.e., amount of RNA) and radioactivity. The 50° C. and 65° C. RNA extracts both exhibit broadly dispersed radioactivity profiles, which indicates that the radioactivity is chiefly associated with a relatively small population of RNA molecules exhibiting values from 10 to 45 Svedberg units. Two features of the sedimentation profiles are of particular interest: 1) the radioactivity is not associated with ribosomal RNA, as had been assumed for the 50° C. fraction; and 2) the radioactivity is associated with a small heterogenous population of RNA molecules that sediment over a broad region of the profile, i.e., the radioactivity is associated with a polydispersed component. Heterogeneity, as demonstrated by sucrose density gradient centrifugation, has been one of the characteristics attributed to messenger RNA (Hiatt, 1962; Spiegelman and Hayashi, 1963; Kidson and Kirby 1963; Brawerman *et al.,* 1963; Penman *et al.,* 1963; DiGirolamo *et al.,* 1964; Revel and Hiatt, 1964).

Although the nucleotide composition and sedimentation characteristics described above suggest that the high specific activity is associated with a polydispersed component which may be messenger RNA, these indications must be considered tentative. No one of the criteria of messenger RNA, i.e., rapid turnover, nucleotide composition similar to DNA (except that UMP is substituted for TMP), heterogeneity, ability to stimulate amino acid incorporation in *in vitro* protein synthesizing systems, nor any combination of these criteria represents a definitive identification of messenger RNA. A definitive definition can be achieved by isolating one specific messenger RNA and demonstrating the synthesis of a specific enzyme protein by this messenger in an *in vitro* system. Such an identification has not yet been achieved for mammalian nor for bacterial or viral RNA (Guttman and Novick, 1963; Attardi *et al.,* 1963; Novelli and Eisenstadt, 1963; Reich *et al.,* 1963). Therefore, although it is tempting to suggest that the age-associated increase in turnover of rat liver nuclear RNA is chiefly in messenger RNA, this suggestion is, at present, in the realm of speculation.

THEORETICAL CONSIDERATIONS

The autoradiographically determined age-related increase in H^3-cytidine incorporation into RNA of liver and other tissues of mice led to the formulation of a theory (Wulff *et al.*, 1962) to account for the observed results. This hypothesis suggested that the intranuclear genetic sites of RNA synthesis sustain changes or "damage" with repeated use and produce defective messenger RNA which, in turn, produces protein that is enzymatically defective or inactive. To compensate for the production of faulty messenger RNA, the theory predicted an increase in RNA synthesis to insure an adequate production of enzymatically active protein. On the basis of this theory, the RNA content of nuclei in cells of old animals should be greater than in those from young animals. Since this is not the case in the old and young adult rat liver nuclei used in our experiments, the hypothesis must be revised.

The fact that labeled cytidine is incorporated more rapidly into nuclear RNA in liver of old than young rats and the fact that labeled RNA is displaced more rapidly from liver nuclei of old rats relative to young rats indicates an increase in rate of RNA synthesis in the old animals, an increase that is presumably mediated by an increased activity of RNA polymerase. A number of observations have been recently published which point to the conclusion that RNA polymerase activity is quite labile in mammalian tissues. It has been shown (Tata, 1964) that thyroid hormone administration to thyroidectomized rats produces an increase in rate of RNA synthesis long before general metabolism is elevated and that this increase in rate of RNA synthesis may be attributed to stimulation of an RNA polymerase (Widnell and Tata, 1963) whose product is RNA of the ribosomal type (Widnell and Tata, 1964; Widnell, 1965). Forty-two hours after hormone administration, the time when an elevated BMR is first measurable, a modest (25 per cent) increase in the activity of an apparently different RNA polymerase can be demonstrated, a polymerase whose product is an RNA the base composition of which resembles DNA more than it does ribosomal RNA (Widnell, 1965).

In addition, the activity of liver RNA polymerase and the rate of RNA synthesis has been shown to be significantly increased by injection of small amounts of 0.15 M NaCl into the hepatic portal vein (Lieberman *et al.*,1965), and the fact that withdrawal of food from rats increases RNA synthesis in twenty-four hours (Kidson and Kirby, 1964) implies that starvation stimulates the liver RNA polymerase system. In addition to the effect of thyroxine described above, several other hormones have been shown to have a marked effect on liver RNA synthesis (Feigelson *et al.*,1962; Kenney and Kull, 1963; Korner, 1963; Barnabei and Sereni, 1964; Barnabei *et al.*, 1965; Weber *et al.*, 1965). These observations suggest that the age-associated increase of RNA turnover in rat liver (and other tissues) could be mediated by a hormone-controlled mechanism.

From the point of view of cellular economy, an undesirable feature of the age-associated and apparently generalized increase of RNA turnover is the implied lack of specificity. If randomly occurring changes in the DNA of cell populations are responsible for the observed increase of RNA turnover this would be, at best, an inefficient compensation, for it would affect the product of normal and altered structural genes equally. However, the specificity necessary to improve the efficiency of a compensatory general increase in RNA turnover may be imposed by controlled degradation of proteins (Schimke, 1964; Shimke *et al.*, 1964) rather than by mechanisms similar to those known to operate in microoroganisms (Jacob and Monod, 1961). Schimke and co-workers (1964) have shown that the level of liver arginase and tryptophan pyrrolase at any time is the resultant of two processes; synthesis and degradation. These authors suggest that the rate of synthesis is hormone-controlled and the rate of degradation is substrate-controlled, high substrate levels decreasing the rate of degradation and low substrate levels increasing the rate of degradation.

This mechanism provides the specificity inherent in the model of regulation of protein synthesis proposed by Jacob and Monod (1961), a specificity which is essential for efficient regulation of cell metabolism, but the specificity is manifest at the end of the chain of events, rather than at the beginning.

An obvious consequence of the two processes proposed—increase in turnover of nuclear RNA and regulation of enzyme levels by substrate-controlled rate of degradation—implies an increase in rate of protein turnover in tissues of old organisms. Evidence exists which does, indeed, support this contention. Barrows and Roeder (1961) have found a significant increase in cathepsin activity in liver and kidney of old (twenty-four months) rats compared to younger (one, three, five and twelve months old) rats and a slight but consistent increase in the rate of disappearance of S^{35}-methionine from liver, heart, kidney and skeletal muscle of old (twenty-four months) rats compared to young (twelve months) rats. The incorporation of C^{14}-leucine into liver protein (microsomal, soluble and total protein) is about 70 per cent greater in old (815-817 days) than young (116-118 days) rats 15 minutes and 30 minutes after injection of the labeled precursor (Wulff *et al.*, 1966). Perry (1965) found a significant increase in rate of incorporation of C^{14}-leucine into proteins of kidney and heart of old (815-817 days) compared to young (116-118 days) rats. These observations suggest that protein turnover in tissues of old rats may exceed that of young rats.

Quite independent of the mechanism producing the increased turnover of liver nuclear RNA in old rats is the question as to why the observed age-associated changes in RNA metabolism are necessary. It is tempting to suggest, as others have already suggested (Failla, 1957, 1960; Henshaw, 1957; Szilard, 1959; Sacher, 1959; Clarke and Maynard Smith, 1961; Strehler, 1962; Medvedev, 1962, 1964; Wulff *et al.*, 1962, 1964; Curtis, 1963; Curtis and Crowley, 1963) that age-related changes in the genome of cells may be responsible for aging of multicellular organisms and for the observed changes in RNA metabolism.

Although the manifestation of these alterations in DNA are ultimately responsible for aging, senescence and death of multicellular organisms, these changes occur only when several compensatory processes have ceased to be active or effective. One of these compensatory processes is cell division or mitosis, which tends to dilute out those cells carrying alterations by cells not so altered. A second compensatory process is the increased rate of RNA synthesis already discussed, which increases to provide altered cells with an adequate complement of enzymatically active protein. A third compensatory process is a low-level, but gradually increasing, turnover of DNA with increasing age of the animal, a turnover which may be the sign of a process that repairs altered DNA. This DNA repair concept is based upon observations of an age-related increase in the incorporation of H^3-thymidine into rat liver DNA, an increase which occurs in the face of a decreasing mitotic index with increasing age of rats (Post and Hoffman, 1964; Pelc, 1964) and in the absence of a net increase in DNA per cell (Wulff *et al.*, 1966).

It is noteworthy that the increasing incidence of autoimmune reactions with increasing age of organisms has been incriminated in the aging process (Walford, 1962; Blumenthal and Berns, 1964) and evidence for a two-phase aging process, one temperature independent and one temperature dependent, has been presented (Clarke and Maynard Smith, 1961; Maynard Smith, 1962). Both of these concepts are relevant to this presentation. The occurrence and accumulation of alterations in the DNA of cell populations could result in the synthesis of altered polyribonucleotides and polypeptides which could be antigenically active (Seaman *et al.*, 1965). The two phases of the aging process (Maynard Smith, 1962) may be attributed to an "irreversible decay of the protein synthetic mechanisms" which occurs at a rate independent of temperature and takes place early in the life of adult *Drosophila subobscura* and a temperature-dependent phase which occurs later in life of the fruit flies and may be attributed to a rate of destruction of proteins that exceeds their rate of synthesis (Maynard Smith, 1962). Both these ideas are compatible with the observations and inferences presented above.

CONCLUSION

The thesis that the age-associated increase in turnover of RNA is a manifestation of changes or "errors" in the genetic code of cell populations, which serves to provide altered cells with an adequate complement of enzymatically active protein, is subject to criticism. Classical notions regarding the stability of genetic material suggest that it is unlikely that a sufficient number of alterations would occur during the life span of an individual to effect physiological changes. However, observations reported from several laboratories (Pelc, 1964; Feigelson *et al.*, 1962) which indicate a turnover in the thymidylic acid residues of DNA in non-dividing tissues in the absence of increasing ploidy (Wulff *et al.*, 1966) suggest a lability of DNA which heretofore had not been suspected. It is conceivable, however, that the observed increased turnover of RNA may be the consequence of changes at the cellular level, as suggested by Maynard Smith (1962), "which have similar physiological effects . . . as those caused by somatic mutations."

The possibility that the observed increased RNA turnover may be the result of changes in an aging individual other than alterations in DNA, cannot be excluded. Factors which may affect the rate of incorporation of labeled precursor into RNA, such as differences in RNA cytidylic acid precursor pool size, differences in cytidine kinase activity, differences in compartment kinetics and perhaps others, are effectively ruled out by the observations that labeled RNA in old rat liver nuclei is replaced more rapidly by unlabeled RNA than in young rat liver nuclei. However, the apparent lability of the RNA polymerase system in liver (and perhaps in other organs and tissues) necessitates precise control and knowledge of those factors in the test animals which may affect RNA polymerase activity. For instance, withdrawal of food (starvation), which is known to influence RNA synthesis (Kidson and Kirby, 1964) and protein synthesis (Schimke, 1962, 1964) may produce effects at different rates in old and young adult rats. Since, in our experiments, most of the animals were deprived of food sixteen hours prior to injection, the induced starvation may possibly be a factor in shaping the results obtained. However, the results of a limited number of experiments on young and old rats not deprived of food prior to injection were similar to those obtained with food-deprived rats. The influence of possible variations in circadian rhythm in young and old rats may also have influenced our results, although labeling experiments in our laboratory were routinely carried out between 8:00 and 10:00 hours (Barnum *et al.*, 1958; Ehret, 1960; Schweiger *et al.*, 1964). The known effects of various hormones on RNA metabolism raises the question as to whether the observed age-associated changes in RNA metabolism may be the result of a changed hormonal balance in old rats and mice. The results of investigations of endocrine function in relation to age (Rubin *et al.*, 1955; Korenchevsky, 1961) indicate a change in hormonal balance does occur. In many cases studied, some endocrines do exhibit an age-associated regression (e.g., gonads, thyroid, thymus) whereas others do not (e.g., adenohypophysis, adrenal cortex, islands of Langerhans).

Since these criticisms, and possibly others, cannot be answered at this time, the significance of the finding reported here must be couched in terms of a theory—a theory which serves to define the observed age-related increase in turnover of nuclear RNA as a compensatory process that permits multicellular organisms an extended life as adults and which suggests that senescence and death occur when this compensation is no longer effective.

REFERENCES

Attardi, G., Naono, A., Rouviere, J., Jacob, F., and Gros, F.: Production of messenger RNA and regulation of protein synthesis. *Cold Spring Harb. Symp. Quant. Biol., 28:*363, 1963.

Barnabei, O., Romano, B., and Di Bitonto, G.: Early effect of cortisone on the activity of nuclear ribonucleic acid polymerase of rat liver. *Arch. Biochem. Biophys., 109:*266, 1965.

Barnabei, O., and Sereni, F.: Cortisol-induced increase of tyrosine-α ketoglutarate transaminase in the isolated perfused rat liver and its relation to ribonucleic acid synthesis. *Biochim. Biophys. Acta, 91:*239, 1964.

Barnum, C. P., Jardetzky, C. D., and Halberg, F.: Time relations among metabolic and morphologic 24-hour changes in mouse liver. *Amer. J. Physiol., 195:*301, 1958.

Barrows, C. H., Jr., and Roeder, L. M.: Effect of age on protein synthesis in rats. *J. Geront., 16:*321, 1961.

Blumenthal, H. T., and Berns, A. W.: Autoimmunity and aging. *Advances Geront. Res., 1:*289, 1964.

Brachet, J.: Ribonucleic acids and the synthesis of cellular proteins. *Nature (London), 186:*194, 1960.

Brawerman, G., Gold, L., and Eisenstadt, J.: A ribonucleic acid from rat liver with template activity. *Proc. Nat. Acad. Sci. USA, 50:*630, 1963.

Cavalieri, L. F., and Rosenberg, B. H.: Nucleic acids and information transfer. *Progress in Nucleic Acid Research and Molecular Biology, 2:*1, New York, Academic Press, 1963.

Clarke, J. M., and Maynard Smith, J.: Two phases of aging in *Drosophila subobscura. J. Exp. Biol., 38:*679, 1961.

Clever, U.: Actinomycin and puromycin: Effects on sequential gene activation by ecdysone. *Science, 146:*794, 1964.

Curtis, H. J.: Biological mechanisms underlying the aging process. *Science, 141:*686, 1963.

CURTIS, H., AND CROWLEY, C.: Chromosome aberrations in liver cells in relation to the somatic mutation theory of aging. *Radiat. Res., 19:*337, 1963.

DAWBARN, M. C.: The nucleo-cytoplasmic ratio of the white mouse and its variation with age. *Aust. J. Exp. Biol. Med. Sci., 9:*213, 1932.

DIGIROLAMO, A., HENSHAW, E. C., AND HIATT, H. H.: Messenger ribonucleic acid in rat liver nuclei and cytoplasm. *J. Molec. Biol., 8:*479, 1964.

EHRET, C. F.: Action spectra and nucleic acid metabolism in circadian rhythms at the cellular level. *Cold Spring Harb. Symp. Quant. Biol., 25:*149, 1960.

FAILLA, G.: Considerations bearing on permissible accumulated radiation doses for occupational exposure. The aging process and cancerogenesis. *Radiology, 69:*23, 1957.

FAILLA, G.: The aging process and somatic mutations. *The Biology of Aging. A.I.B.S.,* Pub. *6:*170, 1960.

FEIGELSON, M., GROSS, P. R., FEILGELSON, P.: Early effects of cortisone on nucleic acid and protein metabolism of rat liver. *Biochim. Biophys. Acta, 55:*495, 1962.

GEORGIEV, G. P.: Ribonucleic acid of the chromosomal-nucleolar apparatus. *Biokhimiia, 26:*1095, 1961.

GEORGIEV, G. P., AND MANT'EVA, V. L.: The isolation of DNA-like RNA and ribosomal RNA from the nucleolo-chromosomal apparatus of mammalian cells. *Biochim. Biophys. Acta, 61:*153, 1962a.

GEORGIEV, G. P., AND MANT'EVA, V. L.: Methods of separation and nucleotide composition of informational and ribosomal ribonucleic acids of the chromosomal-nucleolar apparatus. *Biokhimia, 27:*949, 1962b.

GEORGIEV, G. P., SAMARINA, O. P., LERMAN, M. I., AND SMIRNOV, M. N.: Biosynthesis of messenger and ribosomal ribonucleic acids in the nucleolo-chromosomal apparatus of animal cells. *Nature (London), 200:*1291, 1963.

GOLDSTEIN, L., AND MICOU, J.: On the primary site of nuclear RNA synthesis. *J. Biophys. Biochem. Cytol., 6:*301, 1959.

GUTTMAN, B. S., AND NOVICK, A.: A messenger RNA for β-galactosidase in *Escherichia coli. Cold Spring Harb. Symp. Quant. Biol., 28:*373, 1963.

HARRIS, H.: Nuclear ribonucleic acid. *Progress in Nucleic Acid Research, 2:*19, New York, Academic Press, 1963.

HENSHAW, P. S.: Genetic transition as a determinant of physiologic and radiologic aging and other conditions. *Radiology, 69:*30, 1957.

HIATT, H. H.: A rapidly labeled RNA in rat liver nuclei. *J. Molec. Biol., 5:*217, 1962.

JACOB, F., AND MONOD, J.: Genetic regulatory mechanisms in the synthesis of proteins. *J. Molec. Biol., 3:*318, 1961.

KENNEY, F. T., AND KULL, F. J.: Hydrocortisone-stimulated synthesis of nuclear RNA in enzyme induction. *Proc. Nat. Acad. Sci. USA, 50:*493, 1963.

KIDSON, C., AND KIRBY, K. S.: Selective alterations of mammalian messenger RNA synthesis: Evidence for differential action of hormones on gene transcription. *Nature (London) 203:*599, 1964.

KIDSON, C., KIRBY, K. S., AND RALPH, R. K.: Isolation characteristics of rapidly labelled RNA from normal rat liver. *J. Molec. Biol., 7:*312, 1963.

KORENCHEVSKY, V.: *Physiological and Pathological Aging.* New York, Hafner, 1961.

KORNER, A.: Growth hormone control of messenger RNA synthesis. *Biochem. Biophys. Res. Commun., 13:*386, 1963.

LIEBERMAN, I., KANE, P., AND SHORT, J.: The portal vein and the control of liver ribonucleic acid metabolism. *J. Biol. Chem., 240:*3140, 1965.

Mandel, P.: Free nucleotides in animal tissues. *Progress in Nucleic Acid Research and Molecular Biology, 3*:299, New York, Academic Press, 1964.

Markert, C. L.: The role of chromosomes in development. *The Role of Chromosomes in Development.* New York, Academic Press, 1964.

Maynard Smith, J.: Review lectures on senescence. I. The causes of aging. *Proc. Roy. Soc. Biol., 157*:115, 1962.

McCarthy, B. J., and Hoyer, B. H.: Identity of DNA and diversity of messenger RNA molecules in normal mouse tissues. *Proc. Nat. Acad. Sci. USA, 52*:915, 1964.

Medvedev, Zh. A.: Aging at the molecular level and some speculations concerning maintaining the functioning of systems for replicating specific macromolecules. *Biological Aspects of Aging.* New York, Columbia Univ. Press, 1962.

Medvedev, Zh. A.: The nucleic acids in development and aging. *Advances Geront. Res. 1*:181, 1964.

Novelli, G. D., and Eisenstadt, J. M.: Specific template RNA for β-galactosidase. *Informational Macromolecules.* New York, Academic Press, 1963.

Pelc, S. R.: Labelling of DNA and cell division in so called nondividing tissues. *J. Cell. Biol., 22*:21, 1964.

Penman, S., Scherrer, K., Becker, Y., and Darnell, J. E.: Polyribosomes in normal and poliovirus-infected Hela cells and their relationship to messenger RNA. *Proc. Nat. Acad. Sci. USA, 49*:654, 1963.

Perry, K. W.: *Age-associated studies on nucleic acids and proteins in rat kidneys and hearts.* Ph.D. dissertation, Syracuse University, Syracuse, New York, 1965.

Post, J., and Hoffman, J.: Changes in the replication times and patterns of the liver cell during the life of the rat. *Exp. Cell Res., 36*:111, 1964.

Prescott, D. M.: Cellular sites of RNA synthesis. *Progress in Nucleic Acid Research and Molecular Biology, 3*:33, New York, Academic Press, 1964.

Reich, E., Acs, B., Mach, B., and Tatum, E. L.: Some properties of RNA metabolism in mammalian and bacterial cells. *Informational Macromolecules.* New York, Academic Press, 1963.

Revel, M., and Hiatt, H. H.: The stability of liver messenger RNA. *Proc. Nat. Acad. Sci. USA, 51*:810, 1964.

Rubin, B. L., Dorfman, R. I., and Pincus, G.: 17-ketosteroid excretion in aging subjects. *Ciba Foundation Colloquia on Aging, 1*:126, Boston, Little, Brown, 1955.

Russell, J. A.: The use of isotopic tracers in estimating rates of metabolic reactions. *Perspect. Biol. Med., 1*:138, 1958.

Sacher, G. A.: Relation of lifespan to brain weight and body weight in mammals. *Ciba Foundation Colloquia on Aging, 5*:115, Boston, Little, Brown, 1959.

Samis, H. V., Jr., Wulff, V. J., and Falzone, J. A., Jr.: The incorporation of H^3-cytidine into ribonucleic acid of liver nuclei of young and old rats. *Biochim. Biophys. Acta, 91*:223, 1964.

Schimke, R. T.: Differential effects of fasting and protein-free diets on levels of urea cycle enzymes in rat liver. *J. Biol. Chem., 237*:1921, 1962.

Schimke, R. T.: The importance of both synthesis and degradation in the control of arginase levels in rat liver. *J. Biol. Chem., 239*:3808, 1964.

Schimke, R. T., Sweeney, E. W., and Berlin, C. M.: An analysis of the kinetics of rat liver tryptophan pyrrolase induction: The significance of both enzyme synthesis and degradation. *Biochem. Biophys. Res. Comm., 15*:214, 1964.

Schneiderman, H. A., and Gilbert, L. I.: Control of growth and development in insects. *Science, 143:*325, 1964.

Schweiger, E., Wallraff, H. G., and Schweiger, H. G.: Endogenous circadian rhythm in cytoplasm of *Acetabularia:* Influence of the nucleus. *Science, 146:*658, 1964.

Seaman, E., Van Vunakis, H., and Levine, L.: Antigenicity of polynucleotides. *Biochemistry (Wash.), 4:*1312, 1965.

Spiegelman, S.: Information transfer from the genome. *Fed. Proc., 22:*36, 1963.

Spiegelman, S., and Hayashi, M.: The present status of the transfer of genetic information and its control. *Cold Spring Harb. Symp. Quant. Biol., 28:*161, 1963.

Strehler, B. L.: *Time, Cells and Aging*. New York, Academic Press, 1962.

Suskind, S. R., and Yanofsky, C.: Genetic control of enzyme structure. *Control Mechanisms in Cellular Processes*. New York, Ronald Press, 1961.

Szilard, L.: On the nature of the aging process. *Proc. Nat. Acad. Sci. USA, 45:*30, 1959.

Tata, J. R.: Accelerated synthesis and turnover of nuclear and cytoplasmic RNA during the latent period of action of thyroid hormone. *Biochim. Biophys. Acta, 87:*528, 1964.

Walford, R. L.: Auto-immunity and aging. *J. Geront., 17:*281, 1962.

Weber, G., Srivastava, S. K., and Singhal, R. L.: Role of enzymes in homeostasis. VII. Early effects of corticosteroid hormones on hepatic gluconeogenic enzymes, ribonucleic acid metabolism and amino acid level. *J. Biol. Chem., 240:*750, 1965.

Widnell, C. C.: Characterization of the product of the RNA polymerase of isolated rat liver nuclei. *Biochem. J., 95:*42, 1965.

Widnell, C. C., and Tata, J. R.: Stimulation of nuclear RNA polymerase during the latent period of action of thyroid hormone. *Biochim. Biophys. Acta, 72:*506, 1963.

Widnell, C. C., and Tata, J. R.: Evidence for two DNA-dependent RNA polymerase activities in isolated rat-liver nuclei. *Biochim. Biophys. Acta, 87:*531, 1964.

Wulff, V. J., and Freshman, M.: Age-related reduction of the RNA content of rat cardiac muscle and cerebellum. *Arch. Biochem. 95:*181, 1961.

Wulff, V. J., Piekielniak, M., and Wayner, M. J., Jr.: The ribonucleic acid content of tissues of rats of different ages. *J. Geront. 18:*322, 1963.

Wulff, V. J., Quastler, H., and Sherman, F. G.: The incorporation of H^3-cytidine in mice of different ages. *Arch. Biochem. 95:*548, 1961.

Wulff, V. J., Quastler, H., and Sherman, F. G.: An hypothesis concerning RNA metabolism and aging. *Proc. Nat. Acad. Sci., USA, 48:*1373, 1962.

Wulff, V. J., Quastler, H., and Sherman, F. G.: The incorporation of H^3-cytidine into some viscera and skeletal muscle of young and old mice. *J. Geront., 19:* 294, 1964.

Wulff, V. J., Quastler, H., Sherman, F. G., and Samis, H. V., Jr.: The effect of specific activity of H^3-cytidine on its incorporation into tissues of young and old mice. *J. Geront. 20:*34, 1965.

Wulff, V. J., Samis, H. V., Jr., and Falzone, J. A., Jr.: The metabolism of ribonucleic acid in young and old rodents. *Advances in Gerontological Research, Vol. 2*. New York, Academic Press, 1966.

Zalokar, M.: Ribonucleic acid and the control of cellular processes. *Control Mechanisms in Cellular Processes*. New York, Ronald Press, 1961.

Chapter 6

AGING IN COLLAGEN

HARRY R. ELDEN, PH.D.

THIS ANALYSIS of molecular aging of collagen concerns itself with changes that occur within and between molecules of tropocollagen. Emphasis on tropocollagen at the outset restricts one to the small soluble fraction of total collagen in tissues. In order to examine the more abundant insoluble fraction, it is necessary to deal with highly aggregated collagen; or, one must proceed to disperse these aggregates into soluble units. Accumulation of insoluble aggregates is the most obvious response of connective tissue to aging. Therefore, it is essential for the future progress of gerontological research in this field that the *centrifugate* of collagen solutions be studied as thoroughly as has the *supernate.*

Investigations of molecular collagen provide considerable insight into stability of connective tissue. However, it is relevant to inquire whether or not molecular alterations of connective tissue are deleterious to the physiological status of an organism. The molecular changes in aging collagen become increasingly relevant to physiological aging when one can describe the inter-relationships between these greatly different structural levels. It is shown herein that elasticity of aging collagen in blood vessels may depend upon the structure, stability, and aggregation of tropocollagen at the molecular level of organization. This is less true for tendon and skin. Thus, a bridge does exist wherein gross physiological properties may be determined by events taking place at the molecular level.

CRYSTALLINE TROPOCOLLAGEN

The molecular structure of tropocollagen constrains three polypeptide chains into a coiled-coil helical configuration. A high degree of crystallinity is maintained by the proline-hydroxyproline amino acid sequence. The melting temperature (T_M) at which the ordered crystalline state is destroyed is related linearly to the content of proline + hydroxyproline in collagen of different species (Josse and Harrington, 1964). Thus, measurement of T_M in a particular species would reflect changes (with aging) in the intramolecular crystallinity of tropocollagen. A pronounced contraction of the macromolecule attends the destruction of crystallinity, and it is reflected at the macroscopic level by shrinkage of oriented connective tissue structures such as tendons. Evaluation of T_M by thermal shrinkage tests is not without complications, so one should identify the melting point so evaluated as the thermal shrinkage temperature (T_S). Several investigators (Hall and Reed, 1957; Brown, Consden and Glynn, 1958; Lawson, 1963; Chvapil and Jensovsky, 1963; Radhakrushnan, Ramanathan, and Nayudamma, 1964; and Elden, 1965) have reported the values of T_S for collagen as a function of age. It is important to emphasize how little T_S changes with aging (Table I), in spite of the many attempts to assert otherwise. It must be admitted that a rise of about 5° can

TABLE I

INVARIANT SHRINKAGE TEMPERATURE OF AGING CONNECTIVE TISSUE

Source	*Age*	*T_S* °C	*Range* °C	*Reference*
Human	7, 9 years 89 years		(65–69) (62–68)	Hall and Reed, 1957
Human	0–14 years 45–88 years	63.9 67.0	(61–67) (66–68)	Brown, Consden and Glynn, 1958
Rat Tail Tendon	1–18 months	55		Lawson, 1963
	60 days 240 days 950 days	62.5 63.0 65.5	(±0.5) (±0.62) (±0.25)	Chvapil and Jensovsky, 1963
	6 months 24 months	59.8 64		Radhakrushnan, Ramanathan and Nayudamma, 1964
	2 months 18 months	56 56	(0.6) (±0.6)	Elden, 1965

be established by these and other data. However, a report by Cadavid and Paladini (1964) on changes with aging in collagen amino acids suggests only a low increase in the ratio of proline to hydroxyproline; generally, the amino acid composition is independent of age. Since the melting temperature is governed by the sum of proline and hydroxyproline, future work along the line of hydrothermal shrinkage stability would profitably accept the fact that melting temperature and crystallinity (proline + hydroxyproline) change but little with aging.

The nearly constant values of T_S for collagen that ages *in vivo* raises questions about the design and interpretation of certain experiments. One can not use elevation of T_S attending the interaction of collagen with biochemical metabolites (Milch, 1963) as a logical means to find age-promoting substances. Because of the results described above, one would have to select those metabolites which did not change T_S rather than those which raised it.

On the other hand, it has been shown (Gross, 1964) that the denaturation temperature of freshly reconstituted collagen increases about 5° from an initial value of 52° in 375 days of *in vitro* incubation at 37° C. The final value of 57° C. compares favorably with 59° for tendons incubated along with the gels of reconstituted collagen. In contrast there was a progressive and marked reduction in the amount of collagen gel which re-dissolved upon periodic cooling. Consequently, it is not necessary to have great changes in T_S for collagen to become insoluble as it does in natural aging. This point can not be over-emphasized; its acceptance immediately directs one's attention to those measurements which detect subtle alterations in tropocollagen rather than extensive remodelling of its molecular structure.

TRANSIENT AGGREGATION OF COLLAGEN

The early studies on molecular weight of tropocollagen yielded values that ranged from $15\text{-}20 \times 10^6$ down to $1 \times 10^{3-4}$. It is now realized that these were high molecular weight aggregates and depolymerization products, respectively. The mechanism of aggregation is not known, and certainly the functional groups responsible for the increase in molecular weight are known even less. However, it appears that those involved are few in number by the above-mentioned data on the invariance of amino acid composition with aging. Experiments by Gross (1964) on the reversible association of collagen prove that reactions of the tertiary structure level can reduce the solubility. Undoubtedly, this is accompanied by an increase in three-dimensional space of the collagen matrix. It follows from the increased aggregation of collagen with aging, that some functional groups might be totally lost, or partially buried (slow reacting), or weakly shielded (faster reacting), while others remain free (instantly reactive). Attempts have been made to find these lost functional groups, e.g., by cleavage of ester-like bonds with hydroxyl amine and hydrazine (Gallop and Seifter, 1962); digestion with collagenase followed by separation of fragments (Grassman, Hormann, and Norwig, 1962); and the degradation, separation, and identification of multiple chain segments of tropocollagen (Lewis and Piez, 1964). These procedures lead further to the identification of permanent inter- and intra-molecular attachments. Subtle modes of interaction, however, are destroyed by the degradation, digestion and separation methods. Transient modes of inter-molecular attachment can be studied by certain techniques which are experimentally feasible and applicable to the study of molecular aging of collagen.

Measurement of water sorption and swelling of tissues can be used to study the surface of collagen fibers in aging connective tissue. The absorption isotherm for water on collagen is sigmoid in shape and conforms to the B.E.T. theory except at very low and high water vapor pressure (Bull, 1944). Raising the temperature (20 to 70°) causes the progressive desorption of water and the reduction of the area covered by a monolayer of water. Sufficient measurements have been made to demonstrate that monolayer area is greatly influenced by alteration of side chain functional groups and destruction of the crystalline phase. In addition, heats of immersion are particularly sensitive to alterations in side chain amino, hydroxy and carboxy groups. The pH sensitivity of tissue swelling in water also depends upon the availability of titratable acid and base groups. It would be very interesting to know what one finds when these tests are applied to tropocollagen, insoluble aggregates, and whole connective tissue obtained from aging animals.

The above techniques are applicable to collagen in non-aqueous systems as well as water. There is good reason to believe from protein studies in general (Wishnia and Pinder, 1964) that weakly polar alcohols and nonpolar hydrocarbons can be adsorbed. This would give surface area measurements considerably less than those obtained with water. Interaction between collagen and probing molecules depends upon the number of hydrophilic and hydrophobic collagen sites and the choice of sorbents. Thus, it is possible theoretically to titrate the gradation of polarity of collagen fibers without totally dispersing or solubilizing them. Loss of capacity of aging collagen to sorb a particular molecule would suggest the disappearance of reaction functionality. In this way, one conceivably would pursue the transient modes of inter- and intra-molecular aggregation of aging collagen.

Acid and base functional groups of purified collagen and hide have been thoroughly investigated by pH-titration (Bowes and Kenten, 1948). Measurements invariably have been conducted at equilibrium, while the transient uptake of acids and bases has been ignored. Masked ionic residues are present in collagen (Kern, 1960), and the ionic charge on collagen regulates the alignment of tropocollagen during the reconstitution process (Martin, Mergenhagen and Scott, 1961). Consequently, if there are labile acid-base groups, they will be severed during equilibration and escape detection. A slow rate of uptake could be detected just as different rates of H-D exchange are detectable from buried and free functional H groups in collagen (Bensusan and Nielsen, 1964).

Finally, to conclude this series of proposals for detecting transient modes of aggregation, dye binding experiments should be considered as potentially important approaches to elucidating the surface of aging collagen fibers. Veis and Cohen (1954) pointed out that amino acid composition and titration of purified collagen, hide powder or gelatin are essentially unchanged with aging. They proceeded to demonstrate, however, that modification of dye binding techniques permits one to measure the extent of modified side chain groups in partially degraded collagen. Even though the maximum number of bound dye molecules is the same for native and denatured collagen, the concentration dependence of binding parallels the extent of degradation. This technique should be applied to the study of aging collagen; hopefully, one would elucidate the degree of interaction of ionic residues in a series of fractions of the insoluble collagen of aging connective tissue.

PERMANENT AGGREGATION OF COLLAGEN

Wiederhorn and Reardon (1952) presented biophysical evidence for the existence of permanent inter- or intra-molecular bonding, i.e., crosslinks in collagen. They showed that the stress-strain curve of thermally denatured tendons followed a thermodynamic function derived for amorphous crosslinked polymers, *viz.*, equation 1:

$$1)\qquad F = -T(dS/dL)_T = \frac{RT}{M_C} V_2^{1/3} \left[(L/L_O) - (L/L_O)^{-2}\right]$$

The molecular weight between crosslinks of melted tendon (M_C) was about 50,000, and it could be reduced considerably by introducing further crosslinks with formaldehyde treatment. Then Crewther and Dowling (1958) showed that a postulation of series inter-digitation of amorphous and crystalline collagen segments gives a kinetic mechanism that satisfactorily agrees with data; see equation 2:

$$2)\qquad C \xrightarrow[\text{cryst}]{} C \xrightarrow[\text{amorph}]{} ;\quad F = F_{cryst} = F_{amorph}$$

Furthermore, Donnan-Proctor-Wilson analysis of the mechanism of the pH-dependence of osmotic swelling of collagen (Hill and Nursten, 1964) requires the postulation of an elastic restraint that opposes imbibition of solution during swelling; equation 3:

$$3)\qquad \text{Swelling Volume} = (\text{Elastic Constant}) \times (\text{Concentration of Diffusible Ions})$$

The rate of uptake of water (dW/dt) by rat tail tendon, and acetic acid by collagen, decrease with time so rapidly that an elastic restraining factor (BW) must be postulated in addition to a gradient term (A/W) to account for the kinetic data (Elden, 1963a); see equation 4:

$$4)\qquad dW/dt = K(A/W - BW)$$

Further evidence was provided by Veis and Cohen (1958) to support the presence of crosslinks in collagen by studying the degradation of hide collagen to gelatin. Alcohol coacervates of solubilized collagen exhibited discrete molecular weight ranges of fragments; also, the magnitude for entropy of dissolution required that large quantities of water be immobilized. This was accomplished, presumably by restricting the water in a cage of amorphous polypeptide chains of melted collagen that necessarily had to be crosslinked periodically. Later Veis, Anesey, and Cohen (1962) demonstrated the production of three components, i.e., alpha, beta and gamma collagen, as the main constituents of the various coacervates. Needless to say, this has been expanded considerably by others working simultaneously and consecutively to where it is now established that collagen is permanently aggregated by intra- and inter-molecular linkages. In the words of Jackson (1959) as cited by Veis *et al.* (1962), "following the synthesis of the collagen molecule increasingly larger and more firmly cross-linked aggregates of these molecules are found requiring more and more drastic methods of extraction." The increased aggregation of collagen with aging, therefore, directs the attention of investigators to methods for studying macromolecular aggregates in the "bulk." Experiments by Kohn and Rollerson (1959) demonstrate a way in which this had already been done.

Human diaphragm tendons were exposed to various combinations of acid (pH 2.5), heating at 56° C., and time of reaction (fifteen, thirty and sixty minutes). Uptake of water attending or following the particular treatment was measured as a function of age from 0 to 90 years. A differential analysis of the over-lapping and accumulated swelling functions of age suggested that a serial transformation of collagen occurs by equation 5:

5) $$C_A \rightarrow C_B \rightarrow C_C \rightarrow C_D$$

Therefore, tendon collagen is progressively aggregated in the transformation of A to D. At any time the tissue contains an assortment of A to D components. The Kohn-Rollerson type of experiment should be encouraged because it helps to establish the fact that aging has had an influence on a particular substance or system.

Now it is a privilege to recognize the pioneering work of Prof. Verzár (1964) and his studies on the thermal degradation of aging tendons. He has shown with utmost simplicity yet unquestionable fidelity that so-called "inert" collagen is markedly changed by the aging process. Few, if any, other macromolecular substances have had their biological senescence so amply demonstrated experimentally. His basic observation has stimulated research activities throughout the world.

Analysis of transient shrinkage phenomena at the melting point is based implicitly on the thermoelastic properties of crosslinked amorphous networks. The extent of contraction at constant load, or the force required to maintain constant extension are functional variables related to each other by equation 1. The two methods used by Verzár, i.e., force needed to prevent contraction and force of tendons melted at constant length, should be interrelated by equation 1 if conditions of thermodynamic equilibrium prevail. This is more likely to exist for old tendons than for young, because higher aggregation prevents "creeping" or stress-relaxation, of the highly stressed melted phase. Except for the carefully planned thermodynamic studies of Flory and Garrett (1958) and Lawson (1963) a state of equilibrium has not been demonstrated explicitly in the tendon experiments reported. Furthermore, since these tests are conducted at constant melting temperature, they do not indicate changes in T_S with aging.

A valuable aspect of thermal degradation is the retardation in rate at which aging tendons undergo transformation. The early work of Banga, Balo and Szabo (1956) showed that tendons melted in 40% KI contracted more and relaxed less with advancing age. Weir (1949) conducted a thermodynamic analysis of the rate of shrinkage and showed that it has a very high activation energy, but he did not study the relaxation process. Several kinetic models have been proposed and mathematically expressed, but one can show from empirical analysis of data that a two-step mechanism exists (Elden, 1963b). A two-step mechanism of thermal degradation of collagen in solution has been demonstrated by Engel (1962); *viz.,* optical rotation changes rapidly which indicates that crystallites depolymerize first, then viscosity declines more slowly as the amorphous chains separate. Molecular aggregation of collagen in aging tendons is demonstrated by the reduced rate of relaxation. If relaxation is considered in a rheological sense as a function of the size of a kinetic unit, then higher viscosity and lower rate of terminal relaxation imply an increase in size of kinetic units. Since tropocollagen is a fundamental unit of structure in the aged collagenous tissue, it must have become aggregated or crosslinked in order for it to become larger and more viscous in a rheological sense.

PHYSIOLOGIC RELATIONS OF MOLECULAR COLLAGEN

Finally, in this essay one should attempt to place the molecular aging of collagen in relation to the physiological functions of connective tissue. Blood vessels, skin and tendon are restrained from ultimate deformation or they are made capable of transmitting tension and compression by their collagen and elastin structures. Macroscopic tissue elasticity is a property which extends over the hierarchy of structural elements between molecular and physiological levels. Elasticity, or stiffness, of tissues is frequently associated with a description of their aging, but it has not been clearly defined.

Stress vs. strain of crystalline collagen was measured by Rigby, Hirai, Spikes and Eyring (1959) in rat tail tendon and it is clearly nonlinear. This can be explained by proposing that elastic modulus (K) increases linearly with increments of strain, *viz.*, equation 6.

6) $\text{Stress/strain} = d(F/W_O)/d(L/L_O) = K' = K_C(L - L_O)/L_O$

Integration between limits of F, F_o, and L, L_o gives equation 7 which agrees very well with experimental data; see Figure 1.

7) $F/W_O = K_C(L/L_O - 1)^2$; W_O is proportional to cross-sectional area.

Evaluation of K_C by equation 7 is complicated by the fact that K_C decreases logarithmically with increasing W_O. After proper consideration of W_O, shown in Figure 2, it is then seen that aging does not markedly change the elastic modulus K_C. This is disconcerting, because stiffness of connective tissue has traditionally been associated with aging. The exact definition of stiffness in a complex tissue, obviously, needs to be examined further.

Analysis of elasticity of aging human abdominal skin by Jansen and Rottier (1958) also indicates that stiffness does not change with aging. Experiments by Fry, Harkness, and Harkness (1964) on ringlets of rat skin show that tensile strength per mm^2 of surface collagen is independent of strain required to rupture the tissue.

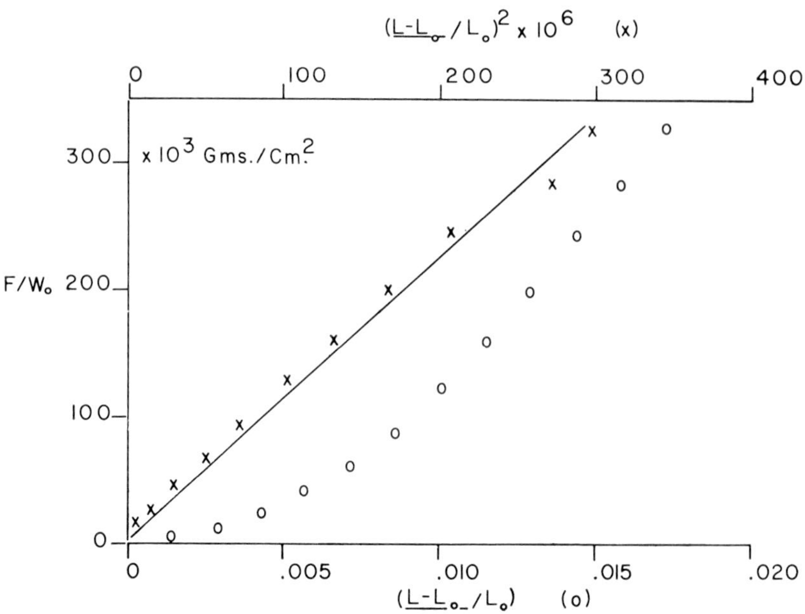

FIGURE 1. Stress (F/W_0) on the y-axis is plotted *vs.* strain—1 on the lower x-axis (o), whereas (strain—1)^2 is plotted on the upper x-axis (x). The latter graphical presentation agrees with the theory underlying equation 7. The slope of this graph, however, depends upon tendon thickness W_0.

The ratio of tensile strength/tensile strain increased with aging, but so does the amount of collagen used to transmit the strain (in their system). The extensibility of skin as defined by Fry *et al.* (1964) is a rate of stretching under constant load which diminishes with age as the collagen increases. This extensibility function is not comparable to that used above. It is correct by a first approximation, therefore, that intrinsic elasticity is independent of age when the amount of collagen or sample size is appropriately considered.

Biophysical analysis of the mechanism of stress *vs.* strain in blood vessels (Elden, unpublished data) proposes that pressure-volume data of Roach and Burton (1959) obey the following equations:

8)
$$F = K_E(L/L_O) + K_C(L_C/L_{O,C} - 1) \quad ; \quad L > L_{O,C}$$
$$F = K_E(L/L_O) + \quad 0 \quad ; \quad L < L_{O,C}$$
$$L_C = L - L_{O,C}$$

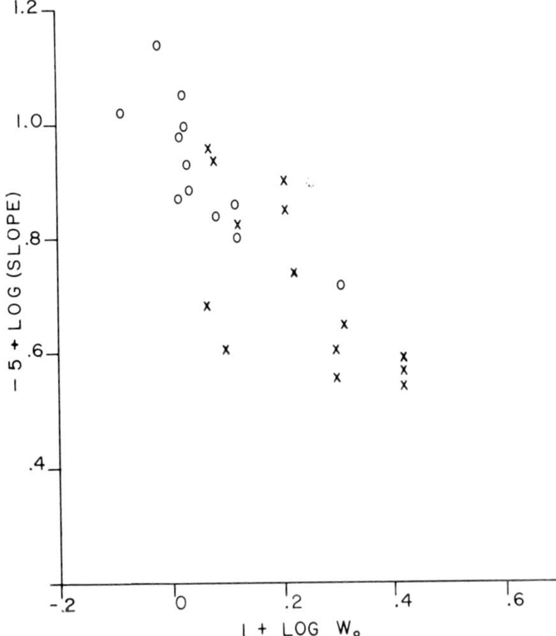

FIGURE 2. The log of the slope of the elasticity function (determined from the linear plots of x as in Fig. 1) plotted against tendon diameter (W_o). x = males; o = females. Thus larger tendons are less stiff than small ones.

Figure 3 illustrates the physical mechanism of equation 8. The collagen critical strain, defined as ($L_{o,\,c}/L_o$) is a measurement of the "slack" of collagen fibers in the vessel wall, whereas elastin fibers have no slack but stretch continuously from original sample length (L_o). Interpretation of data (twenty to ninety years) reveals that $L_{o,c}/L_o$ decreases with aging often an abrupt rise at twenty years; the nonlinear stiffness factor of collagen (K_C) increases at twenty years but remains constant until after the ninth decade; while collagen content of blood vessels does not change in proportion. These facts are illustrated in Figures 4 and 5. Therefore, it appears that contiguity of fibers rapidly increases with aging while their inherent stiffness remains constant until late in life. The late increase in K_C may also be a reflection of accumulated collagen. Increased stiffness of arterial connective tissue may then be due to

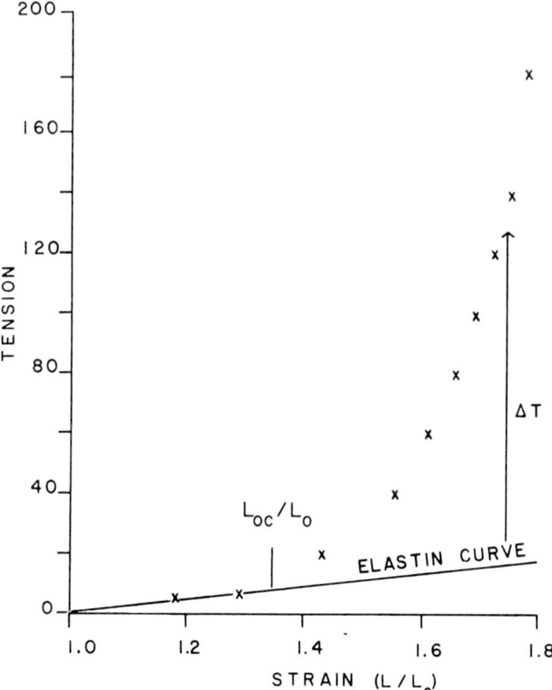

FIGURE 3. Separation of collagen and elastin contribution to tension-circumference data of expanded human iliac artery. Data are taken from Roach and Burton (1959) in order to test the new theory of elasticity. The abrupt increase in nonlinear stress at $L_{0,c}/L_0$ depends upon reaction of collagen fibers as their "slack" is reduced.

more frequent fiber-to-fiber contacts or attachments which occur at or near the physiological level of macromolecular organization. Physiological aging may be enhanced by this alteration of vessels, if blood flow in small arterioles is diminished. Collapse of vessels is possible because their walls conceivably undergo progressive elevation of circumferential tension as $L_{0,c}/L_0$ decreases. It is obvious, therefore that relationships between elasticity of connective tissue at the physiologic level must be examined at the molecular level to further explain the age-promoted mechanism of fiber-fiber contiguity, aggregation and crosslinking.

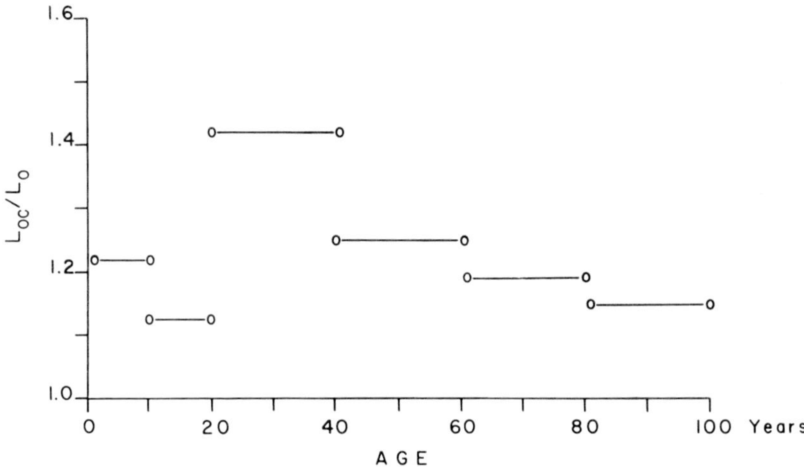

FIGURE 4. Dependence on age of critical strain ratio ($L_{0,C}/L_0$ where collagen fibers begin to carry load during arterial dilation.

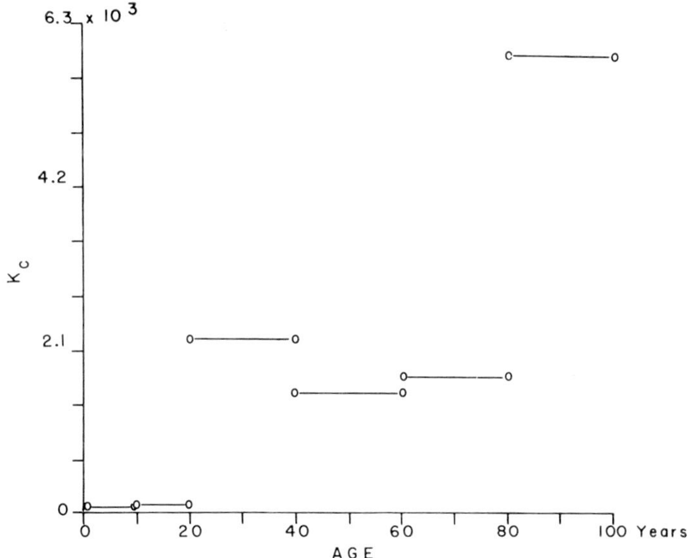

FIGURE 5. Dependence on age of intrinsic stiffening constant K_C of equation 7 for collagen fibers. The contribution of elastin to arterial elasticity has been delineated by subtracting the linearly extrapolated portion of initial data shown in Figure 3.

REFERENCES

BANGA, I., BALÓ, J., AND SZABÓ, D.: The structure, aging, and rejuvenation of collagen fibres. *Experientia,* Suppl. *IV*:28, 1956.

BENSUSAN, H. B., AND NIELSEN, S. O.: The deuterium exchange of peptide group hydrogen atoms during the gelatin-collagen fold transition. *Biochemistry, 3:*1367, 1964.

BOWES, J. H., AND KENTEN, R. H.: The amino acid composition and titration curve of collagen. *Biochem. J., 43:*358, 1948.

BROWN, P. C., AND CONSDEN, R.: Variation with age of shrinkage temperature of human collagen. *Nature, 181:*349, 1958.

BULL, H. B.: Adsorption of water vapor by proteins. *J. Amer. Chem. Soc., 66:*1499, 1944.

CADAVID, N. G., AND PALADINI, A. C.: Amino acid composition of dermal collagen fractions in rats of different ages. *Biochem. J., 92:*436, 1964.

CHVAPIL, M., AND JENSOVSKY, L.: The shrinkage temperature of collagen fibers isolated from the tail tendon of rats of various ages and from different places of the same tendon. *Gerontologia (Basel), 7:*18, 1963.

CREWTHER, W. G., AND DOWLING, L. M.: The thermal shrinkage of collagen in solutions of electrolytes. *J. Phys. Chem., 62:*678, 1958.

ELDEN, H. R.: A kinetic analysis of swelling of rat tail tendon. *J. Polymer Sci., 1A:*23, 1963a.

ELDEN, H. R.: The interaction of connective tissue with aqueous urea. I. Reversible and irreversible effects. *Biochim. Biophys. Acta, 75:*37, 1963b.

ELDEN, H. R.: Biophysical aspects of aging in connective tissue. *Adv. Biol. Skin, 6:*229, 1965.

ENGEL, J.: Investigation of the denaturation and renaturation of soluble collagen by light scattering. *Arch. Biochem. Biophys., 97:*150, 1962.

FLORY, P. J., AND GARRETT, R. R.: Phase transitions in collagen and gelatin systems. *J. Amer. Chem. Soc., 80:*4836, 1958.

FRY, P., HARKNESS, L. R., AND HARKNESS, R. D.: Mechanical properties of the collagenous framework of skin in rats of different ages. *Amer. J. Physiol., 206:*1425, 1964.

GALLOP, P. M., AND SEIFTER, S.: Features of primary structure and unusual linkages in the collagen molecule. *Collagen Seminar,* N. Ramanathan, Ed., New York, Wiley, (Interscience Publishers), 1962, p. 249.

GRASSMAN, W., HORMANN, H., AND NORWIG, A.: Degradation of collagen with collagenase: Structure of the non-polar regions of the collagen fibers. *Collagen Seminar,* N. Ramanathan, Ed., New York, Wiley, (Interscience Publishers), 1962, p. 263.

GROSS J.: Thermal denaturation of collagen in the dispersed and solid state. *Science, 143:*960, 1964.

HALL, D. A., AND REED, R.: Hydroxyproline and thermal stability of collagen. *Nature, 180:*243, 1957.

HILL, T., AND NURSTEN, H. E.: The swelling of hide powder in hydrochloric acid solution. *J. Soc. Leather Trades' Chem., 48:*321, 1964.

JACKSON, D. S.: *Connective tissue, thrombosis, and atherosclerosis.* I. H. Page, Ed., New York, Academic Press, 1959, p. 67.

JANSEN, L. H., AND ROTTIER, P. B.: Some mechanical properties of human abdominal skin measured in excised strips. *Dermatologica, 117:*65, 1958.

JOSSE, J., AND HARRINGTON, W. F.: Role of pyrrolidine residues in the structure and stabilization of collagen. *J. Mol. Biol., 9:*269, 1964.

KERN, H. L.: Masked condition of ionic residues in collagen. *Biochim. Biophys. Acta, 42:*345, 1960.

KOHN, R. B., AND ROLLERSON, E. J.: Studies on the effect of heat and age in decreasing ability of human collagen to swell in acid. *J. Gerontol., 14:*11, 1959.

LAWSON, N. W.: Hydrothermal shrinkage of rat tail tendon. *Texas Repts. Biol. Med., 21:*461, 1963.

LEWIS, M. S., AND PIEZ, K. A.: Sedimentation equilibrium studies of the molecular weight of single and double chains from rat skin collagen. *Biochemistry, 3:*1126, 1964.

MARTIN, G. R., MERGENHAGEN, S. E., AND SCOTT, D. B.: Relation of ionizing groups to the structure of the collagen fibril. *Biochim. Biophys. Acta, 49:*245, 1961.

MILCH, R. A.: Studies of collagen tissue aging: Interaction of certain intermediary metabolites with collagen. *Gerontologia (Basel), 7:*129, 1963.

RADHAKRUSHNAN, V. M., RAMANTHAN, N., AND NAYUDAMMA, Y.: A note on the effect of age and sex on the shrinkage temperature of tendon collagen. *Leather Sci., 11:*102, 1964.

RIGBY, B. J., HIRAI, N., SPIKES, J. D., AND EYRING, H.: The mechanical properties of rat tail tendon. *J. Gen. Physiol., 43:*265, 1959.

ROACH, M. R., AND BURTON, A. C.: The effect of age on the elasticity of human iliac arteries. *Gen. J. Biochem. Physiol., 37:*557, 1959.

VEIS, A., AND COHEN, J.: The degradation of collagen: A method for the characterization of native collagen. *J. Am. Chem Soc., 76:*2476, 1954.

VEIS, A., AND COHEN, J.: The role of cross-linkages in the solubilization of insoluble collagen. *J. Phys. Chem., 62:*459, 1958.

VEIS, A., ANESEY, J., AND COHEN, J.: The characterization of the gamma-component of gelatin. *Arch. Biochem. Biophys., 98:*104, 1962.

VERZÁR, F.: Aging of the collagen fiber. *Int. Rev. Con. Tiss. Res., 2:*244, 1964.

WEIR, L. F.: Rate of shrinkage of tendon collagen. *J. Res. Natl. Bur. Stands., 42:*17, 1949; *44:*599, 1950.

WIEDERHORN, N. W., AND REARDON, G. V.: Studies concerned with the structure of collagen II. Stress-strain behavior of thermally contracted collagen. *J. Polymer Sci., IX:*315, 1952.

WISHNIA, A., AND PINDER, T.: Hydrophobic interactions in proteins: Conformation changes in bovine serum albumin below pH 5. *Biochemistry, 3:*1377, 1964.

Chapter 7

CHEMISTRY AND MATURATION OF ELASTIN

C. FRANZBLAU
F. M. SINEX
B. FARIS

INTRODUCTION

At the present time, there are relatively few investigations concerned with the chemistry of elastin. Yet, all are agreed that this element of connective tissue must be understood if one is to understand in full the physiology and chemical pathology of the larger blood vessels in addition to the development, aging and repair of other tissues such as lung and elastic ligaments. The elastic properties of elastin which are so important to the proper functioning of blood vessels and ligaments must be related to the content of crosslinkages in that protein. In considering the changes which occur in connective tissue proteins during maturation and aging, a knowledge of the chemistry of the crosslinkages in such proteins appears to be a prerequisite for any meaningful study. In contrast to collagen, the introduction of relatively few covalent crosslinkages will radically alter the physical chemical characteristics of elastin since other types of interchain bonds (such as hydrogen and ionic) appear to be minimal in elastin. The lack of hydrogen bonds and ionic bonds may contribute an inherent instability, which in turn may lead to an apparent increase in the pigmentation and fluorescence observed in the elastin of older animals.

CHEMISTRY OF THE CROSSLINKAGES

Work in our laboratory was directed toward the elucidation and characterization of the unusual ultraviolet absorbing materials contained in elastin. As reported previously, we isolated

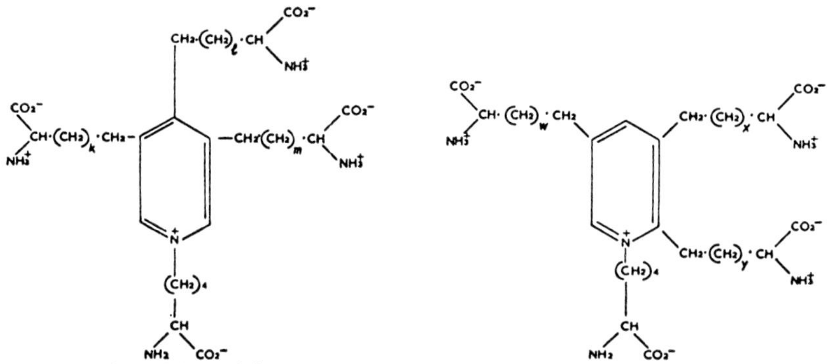

FIGURE 1. Structure of desmosine and isodesmosine according to Thomas *et al.*[2]

two components which from our data appeared to be polyfunctional aromatic amino acids. They were not present in any other protein we examined, but were found in significant amounts in all elastin preparations we studied. While our work was in progress, Partridge *et al.*[1] described these same two amino acids in peptides isolated from enzymatic hydrolysates of elastin. Subsequently the group in Cambridge showed that these two amino acids contained a pyridine ring alkylated in four positions including the ring nitrogen. In this communication, Thomas *et al.*[2] suggested the structures for the two isomers shown in Figure 1. They were named desmosine and isodesmosine. From the structure of these two substances and from the nature of the peptide in which they were contained, Partridge[3] proposed that these two amino acids were involved in the crosslinkages of elastin. The question remains, however, how many peptide chains are crosslinked by these unusual amino acids. From the structure of the desmosine, it is evident that two, three or four chains may be crosslinked. In order to gain more insight into the nature of these new amino acids and what role they played in the protein crosslinkages, we attempted to isolate peptides from various proteolytic digests of elastin which were enriched in their concentration of desmosine and isodesmosine. In the course of this study, we observed that such peptides could be obtained but that they contained yet another hitherto undescribed ninhydrin positive substance, which we designated as X_4.[4]

X_4 was isolated from a total acid hydrolysate of elastin by the usual chromatographic techniques.[4] The purified material did not absorb ultraviolet light in contrast to the desmosine. The infrared spectrum was typical of an amino acid. Dinitrophenylation studies, potentiometric titrations in the presence of formaldehyde, NMR spectra and electrophoretic mobility of X_4 suggested the presence of two primary amine groups and one secondary amine. These data together with manometric ninhydrin-CO_2 determinations (α-amino groups), nitrous acid-nitrogen determinations (total amino groups), Kjeldahl determinations (total nitrogen) and total carbon determinations by combustion have led us to propose the following structure for X_4:

$$\begin{array}{l} COO^- \\ \cdot \\ CH - NH_3^+ \\ \cdot \\ (CH_2)_x \\ \cdot \\ CH_2 \\ \cdot \\ NH_2^+ \\ \cdot \\ CH_2 \\ \cdot \\ (CH_2)_y \\ \cdot \\ CH - NH_3^+ \\ \cdot \\ COO^- \end{array}$$

The above mentioned data indicate that $x + y = 6$, and the simplest assumption one can make is that $x = 3$ and $y = 3$. This yields the new amino acid N^{ϵ}-(5-amino 5-carboxypentanyl)-lysine.

Final proof of structure of any compound lies in its synthesis. By treating α-acetyl lysine with an oxidizing agent such as N-bromosuccinimide, one forms the α-amino adipic semi-aldehyde derivative. This compound, when treated with an equal concentration of unreacted α-acetyl lysine followed by reduction with hydrogen over palladium, yields a product which, when hydrolyzed in 6N HCl behaved exactly the same as X_4 both electrophoretically and chromatographically on ion exchange resins. We concluded from these data that X_4 is in fact N^{ϵ}-(5-amino 5-carboxypentanyl)-lysine. We now suggest the trivial name lysinonorleucine for this new amino acid.[5]

In our original note,[4] we suggested that there were at least four possible reasons for the presence of X_4 in hydrolysates of elastin. The first would be that X_4 is a hitherto undescribed amino acid present in the polypeptide backbone *per se* of elastin molecules. The second that X_4 is a discrete amino acid involved in the crosslinking of several polypeptide chains of elastin. A third suggestion is that X_4 together with desmosine and isodesmosine are degradation products of the true crosslinking substance present in elastin before hydrolysis with acid, and the fourth that X_4 is a degradation product of another substance unrelated to the desmosines.

We feel that to distinguish between these possibilities, we ultimately have to isolate a pure peptide or peptides which contain X_4. We are attempting to purify further the desmosine and X_4 enriched peptides obtained from the various enzymatic digests described previously. If, for instance, we found peptides rich in the desmosines and not in X_4 or *vice versa,* we could probably eliminate the third possibility.

BIOSYNTHESIS OF THE CROSSLINKAGES IN ELASTIN

Partridge *et al.*[6] and Miller *et al.*[7] have shown that during development of the chick embryo, the concentrations of desmosine and isodesmosine in the aortic elastin increase while the lysine concentration in the elastin decreases. This suggests lysine as the precursor of the desmosines. This was borne out by studies in tissue culture with radioactive lysine which showed that four lysines are indeed incorporated into one desmosine or one isodesmosine molecule.

Since our original data with the desmosine-enriched peptides suggested a possible relationship of X_4 to the desmosines, we decided to repeat the experiments of Miller *et al.*,[7] and concentrated our efforts primarily on the formation of X_4 in the aortic elastin of developing chick embryos.

Our findings confirm those of Miller *et al.*[7] and Partridge *et al.*,[6] and show that, with time, there was an increase in concentration of the desmosines with a concomitant decrease in the lysine concentration. In addition, our data indicate that X_4 appears to be synthesized in the elastin at the same rate as the desmosines.

Partridge *et al.*[6] suggested that the synthesis of desmosine takes place in the following manner. Three residues of bound lysine, deaminated at the ε-amino group, together with one intact lysine residue are condensed, probably enzymatically, to form the desmosines. The ε-amino group of the fourth lysine serves as the pyridine ring nitrogen in the desmosines.

We feel that the synthesis of lysinonorleucine occurs in a similar manner. The first step is probably a deamination of an ε-amino group of a lysine residue located in a peptide chain. This first step may be catalyzed by a pyridoxal-requiring enzyme system and may in fact be the same enzyme involved in the desmosine biosynthesis. Second, the resulting α-amino adipic semialdehyde residue combines with an ε-amino group of a lysine residue in another peptide chain to form a Schiff base. This complex is then reduced possibly by a pyridine nucleotide requiring enzyme. This biosynthetic scheme is illustrated in Figure 2.

OTHER COMPONENTS OF ELASTIN

Elastin *in situ* shows a strong fluorescence and appears somewhat yellow in color. The fluorescence is broad with an emission maximum around 450 mμ. When solubilized by acid, enzymes, or base, the resulting solution is clearly yellow, resembling the color of urine. This color is most pronounced after acid hydrolysis and in solutions of peptides prepared from the elastin of older blood vessels. In addition to desmosine and isodesmosine, there are a number of other ultraviolet absorbing components. We have noted that there is a complex of compounds emerging from the amino acid analyzer in the vicinity of phenylalanine and tyrosine, which show an absorption maximum of 268 mμ, and another substance or substances emerging with the basic amino

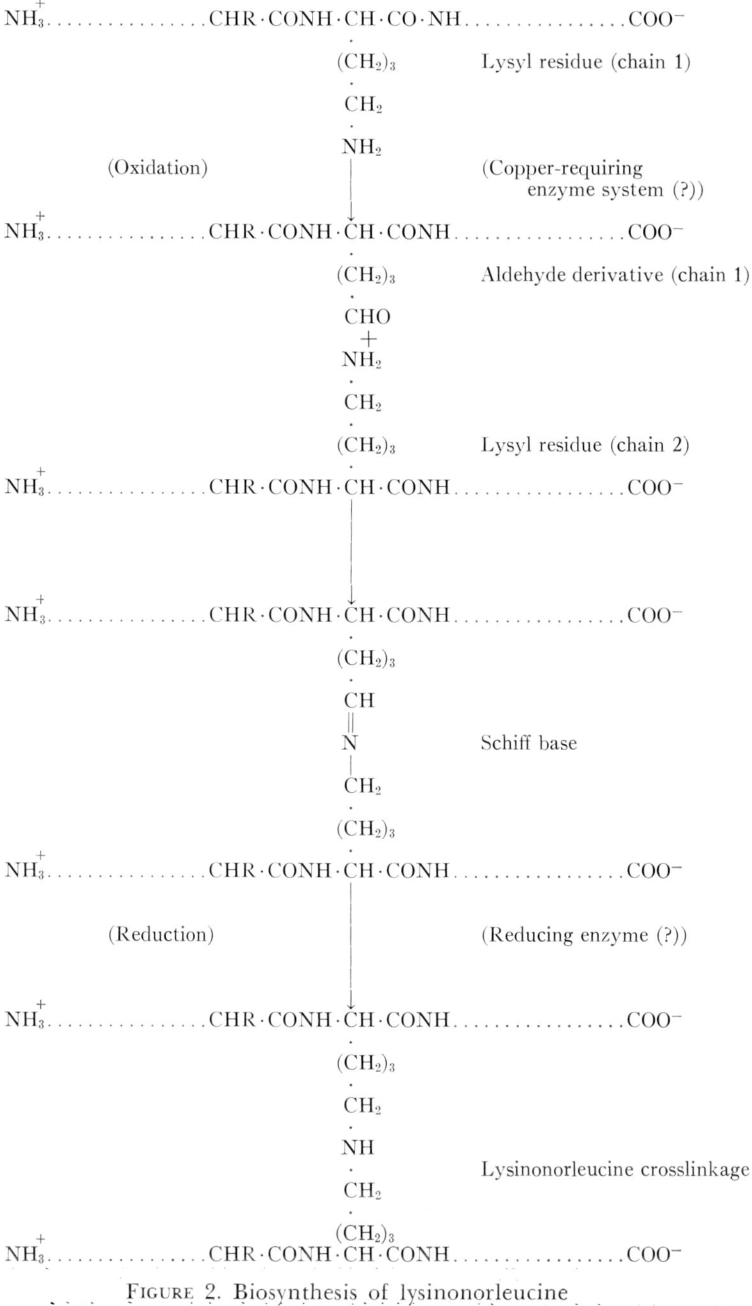

FIGURE 2. Biosynthesis of lysinonorleucine

acids which show a maximum at 285 mμ.[8,9] These do not appear to be phenolic on the basis of shifting to short rather than long wave lengths in alkali. The fluorescence of peptide fractions from enzymatic digests of elastin and acid hydrolysates thereof show 340 mμ activation and 405 mμ emission. This material appears to be associated with the 285 mμ absorbing fraction. The yellow pigments which emerge from cation exchange columns under strong acid conditions are not fluorescent. They are not, however, artifacts which arise from the resin itself.

ELASTIN AND AGING

The assumption that chemical changes occur, with time, in elastin, which contribute to aging, is based on several observations. Large blood vessels become less stretchable with time Elastin largely determines the elastic properties of normal blood vessels in the range of physiological pressures. The internal elastic intima in older blood vessels often appears frayed with duplication of parts of the intima. Older elastin is reported to be more fluorescent and yellower than younger elastin. Finally, since the concentrations of desmosine, isodesmosine and lysinonorleucine increase during maturation, it may be postulated that one or all of these crosslinkages continue to increase throughout the life span. A recent report by Cleary and Jackson[10] suggests that in the elastin of bovine *ligamentum nuchae,* X_4 (lysinonorleucine) increases with age while the desmosines remain at a constant concentration.

None of these observations can be considered conclusive at this time. The extensibility of blood vessels may change for other reasons. The viscosity of the medium through which the free chain segments of elastin move may be increased, or the space filled by other substances. Since the elasticity of a rubber-like polymer depends upon such thermal movement, the stretchability of the wall may be profoundly altered without chemical changes in elastin.

The duplication of intima may be the result of some other type of stimulus. The changes in fluorescence and pigmentation have not actually been shown to have functional significance and studies are not complete concerning the concentration of desmosine, isodesmosine and lysinonorleucine during senescence.

Nevertheless, this protein seems well adapted for studies to test the hypothesis that aging is the result of chemical changes in irreplaceable molecules.

SUMMARY

The maturation of elastin is accompanied by the appearance of three unusual crosslinking structures—desmosine, isodesmosine and lysinonorleucine. In addition, other aromatic structures are present. The significance of these unusual compounds in aging is not well established but possible implications have been discussed. The relative ease with which the concentration of desmosine, isodesmosine and lysinonorleucine can be determined should lead to a considerable clarification of their role in maturation and aging in the near future.

REFERENCES

1. Thomas, J., Elsden, D. F., and Partridge, S. M.: Constitution of the cross-linkages in elastin. *Nature (London), 197*:1297, 1963.
2. Partridge, S. M., Elsden, D. F., and Thomas, J.: Partial structure of two major degradation products from the cross-linkages in elastin. *Nature (London), 200*:651, 1963.
3. Partridge, S. M.: Elastin. *Advances in Protein Chemistry, 17*:227, 1962.
4. Franzblau, C., Sinex, F. M., and Faris, B.: Isolation of an unknown component from hydrolysates of elastin. *Nature (London), 205*:802, 1965.
5. Franzblau, C., Sinex, F. M., Faris, B., and Lampidis, R.: Identification of a new cross-linking amino acid in elastin. *Biochem. Biophys. Res. Comm., 21*:575, 1965.
6. Partridge, S. M., Elsden, D. F., Thomas, J., Dorfman, A., Telser, A., and Ho, P.-L.: Biosynthesis of the desmosine and isodesmosine cross-bridges in elastin. *Biochem. J., 93*:30c, 1964.
7. Miller, E. J., Martin, G. R., and Piez, K. A.: The utilization of lysine in the biosynthesis of elastin crosslinks. *Biochem. Biophys. Res. Comm., 17*:248, 1964.
8. Sinex, F. M.: The chemical basis of the absorption and emission spectra of elastin. *Fed. Proc., 2*:656, 1965.
9. Sinex, F. M., Franzblau, C., and Faris, B.: Isolation of an unusual ultraviolet absorbing component of elastin. *Fed. Proc.,* in press, 1966.
10. Cleary, E. G., and Jackson, D. S.: Changes in amino acid composition of bovine ligament elastin with aging. Abstract from International Symposium on the Biochemistry and Physiology of Connective Tissue, Lyon, 1965.

Section III

AGING IN TISSUES

Chapter 8

AGING OF CONNECTIVE TISSUES*

ROBERT AUSTIN MILCH

A VERY CONSIDERABLE and rapidly expanding body of information exists with respect to the physical-chemical properties and structural organization of variably isolated and "purified" components of native connective tissues (e.g., collagen, elastin and ground substance protein-polysaccharides). Relatively little is known, however, about their actual network structures, aggregation states or mutual interactions *in vivo*. Also, considerably more is known about collagen than about any of the other components of connective tissue.

What has been learned about collagen, furthermore, has basically come from highly refined physical-chemical, x-ray diffraction and electron-microscopic analyses of that very small fraction (usually amounting to no more than about 1-2 per cent of the total dry tissue mass, even in young tissues) which can be solubilized *in vitro* by neutral salts, weak organic acids and guanidine. Far less is certain about the residual "insoluble," or more highly crosslinked collagen structures other than the fact that they seem to be proportionately increased *in vivo* during the course of natural aging phenomena, be they in skin, tendon, cartilage, aorta or any of the other "supporting" tissues.

Indeed, the demonstration that such chemical events apparently do occur biologically has in large part given rise to the crosslinking hypothesis of connective tissue aging, which has derived so much of its current acceptance from the numerous elegant studies of Professor Verzár and his school. The hypothesis states, in substance, that the aging process is characterized by the progressive

* Aided, in part, by a gift from the Alan Wurtzburger Memorial Fund of the Johns Hopkins Hospital and by grants from the National Institute of Arthritis and Metabolic Diseases (AM-02642) and the American Cancer Society (IN-11F).

introduction of inter-chain crossbonds between polypeptide subunits of the constituent fibrous proteins and that these, in turn, alter the physical and chemical properties of the respective matrices so as to render them relatively more stable and less soluble.

Some additional support for the hypothesis has perhaps been provided by studies on the genetically determined alcaptonuria syndrome in man. Abnormal retention of an otherwise normal metabolic intermediate (homogentisic acid) in this disorder seems to account for the later development of the specific pathological states which are constantly observed in affected individuals; namely, ochronosis and alcaptonuric arthritis and arteriosclerosis.[1] This observation naturally led to a systematic search for other compounds of dietary or metabolic origin which could serve as crosslinking agents for whole native tissues and isolated connective tissue components.

Two rather remarkable general facts were subsequently discovered. First, it was found that only a few compounds amongst known major metabolites could behave in this manner. All of these were low molecular weight aliphatic aldehydes which adhered to a "three-carbon" selection rule and existed in solution in the hydrated (gem-dihydroxy or aldol) rather than the free carbonyl form (Fig. 1).[2]

Secondly, it was found that these aldehydes (which are present in abundant amounts in smoking tobacco and in most occidental diets) bound to both collagen and elastin chains,[3,4] had a tendency to localize rather selectively in the aortic wall when administered parenterally[5] and were capable of inducing certain "degenerative" morphological lesions[6] in experimental animals.

More recently, it has also been discovered that other oxidation products, derived *in vitro* from the periodate oxidation of certain ground-substance polysaccharides or their structural analogues, such as dialdehyde starch, can similarly act as crosslinking agents for collagen, and for elastin structures as well, and that these, too, are hydrated (gem-dihydroxy form) aldehydes.[7] Such compounds, interestingly, do not possess any of the polymer-diluent, or *plasticizer* effects of their unoxidized analogues, which appear to be capable, at least *in vitro*, of uniquely determining the tensile, swelling and thermal shrinkage properties of any given collagen or elastin

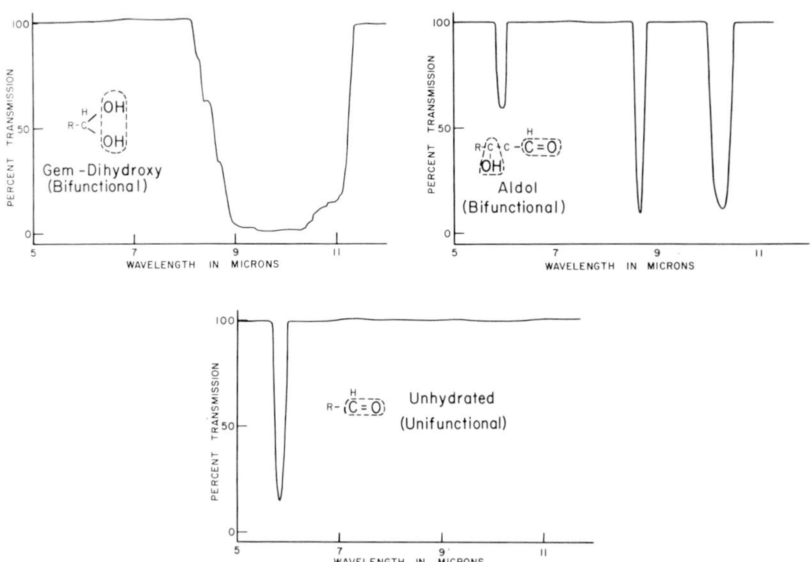

FIGURE 1. Characteristic infrared absorption bands of aqueous aldehyde solutions. Compounds which exist in the gem-dihydroxy form show broad absorption in the 8.3-11.0 micron region, due to coupled C-C and C-O stretching vibrations and coupled C-H bending and C-O stretching vibrations. Compounds which exist in the unhydrated, or free carbonyl form show the characteristic C=O stretching vibration at about 5.9 microns, whereas those which exist in the β-hydroxy-carbonyl (aldol) form show both the carbonyl stretching vibration and two sharp bands in the 8.3-11.0 micron region. Gem-dihydroxy and aldol form compounds both possess two reactive groups per molecule (bifunctional) and can act as *inter*chain crosslinking agents for collagen and elastin networks. On the other hand, those which exist in the unhydrated form possess only one group per molecule (unifunctional) and, as a consequence, are capable only of forming *intra*chain linkages of the Schiff base type with amino residues which possess freely rotatable nitrogen atoms. The structures of such compounds are distinctly different from that of homogentisic acid oxidation polymers, in which crosslinking reactions can theoretically occur via Schiff base formation at multiple sites.

matrix[8] (Fig. 2) and of forming soluble complexes with lipid materials.[9,10]

Electrophoretic observations on dichloracetic acid-solubilized native tissues agree in some respects with these and earlier isolation studies.[11] They support the conclusion, also, that more than one fundamental process may perhaps characterize the aged con-

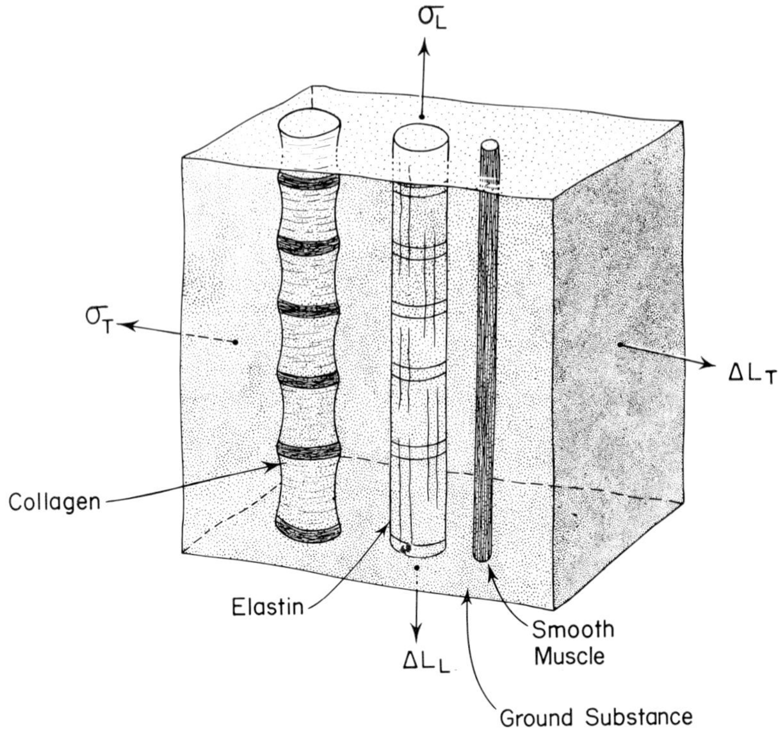

FIGURE 2. Diagrammatic representation of the structural elements involved in determining the "bulk polymer" properties of native connective tissues. Collagen, elastin and smooth muscle networks are considered to exist independently of one another (though it is known that, in arterial walls, there are many interconnections between elastin lamellae and smooth muscle fibers). Since little reliable information is currently available on the properties of smooth muscle networks and since such structures are of only minor importance in most connective tissue matrices other than some arterial walls, the ultimate tensile and equilibrium swelling properties of the bulk connective tissue "polymer" are considered primarily to be some integral function of the respective properties of the constituent collagen and elastin networks and, especially, the degree to which each is diluted, or plasticized by ground-substance protein-polysaccharides. Mechanical properties, such as nominal tensile stress-at-break (σ) and elongation (ΔL) also vary with the helical distribution pattern of the fiber bundles (gross fabric structures), being characteristically different along the transverse (T) and longitudinal (L) axes of any tissue (anisotropy). Removal of the ground substance phase or its "depolymerization" by disruption of the sulfate and/or the peptide and/or the backbone carbohydrate moieties or by oxidation to the corresponding hydrated aldehyde forms results in an increased number of effective load-bearing network strands

nective tissue. Specifically, it appears that in tissues other than the aorta (which seems to be a special case involving concurrent and very profound *regenerative* as well as *degenerative* processes) fibrous protein crosslinking phenomena occur simultaneously with phenomena which produce apparently decreased contents and degrees of polymerization of ground-substance polysaccharides (Fig. 3).[12,13]

An age-dependent loss of the plasticizing function of the constituent carbohydrate polymers, perhaps mediated by lysosomal or other enzymes, theoretically could alone result in relatively increased elastic moduli and decreased swelling volumes of fibrous protein matrices. This is observed *in vitro* with both native and "purified" collagen tissues[8] and corresponds almost exactly with what has been repeatedly observed *in vivo* in naturally aged soft tissues, such as skin and tendon.

It is also conceivable that the characteristic loss or diminution of the carbohydrate content of connective tissues during aging is more apparent than real. Inter-chain binding of polysaccharides through their oxidized dialdehyde derivatives in both collagen and elastin subunits could prevent the compounds from reacting with the usual chemical and histochemical reagents and, hence, would appear to be decreased in amount. Moreover, it is also possible that covalent inter-chain crosslinkages can be formed by exogenously derived aldehydes not only between collagen and elastin chains, but also between these chains and those of the repeating peptide units[11,15] (glycine-glutamic acid-proline-serine) of ground-substance protein-polysaccharide complexes. Such interactions would similarly prevent detection of the latter by routine analytical techniques and would account for both the quantitative and the types of electrophoretic patterns which have been observed

---

per unit volume and, hence, an increase in the measured nominal tensile stress-at-break, an increase in the apparent elastic modulus and a decrease in both the swelling properties and mechanical extensibility, such as would be observed in chronologically "old" tissues. Conversely, addition of a compatible ground-substance diluent to otherwise unmodified collagen and/or elastin networks would result in exactly opposite effects, such as are observed in chronologically "young" or "immature" connective tissues. (See aso Figure 3).

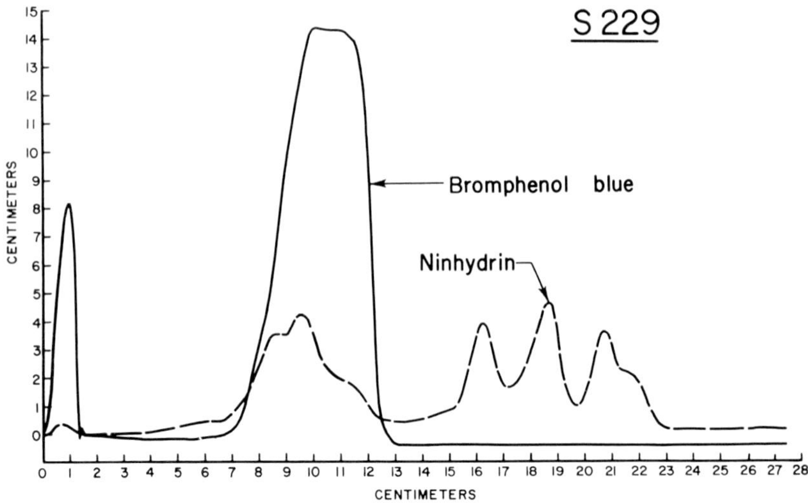

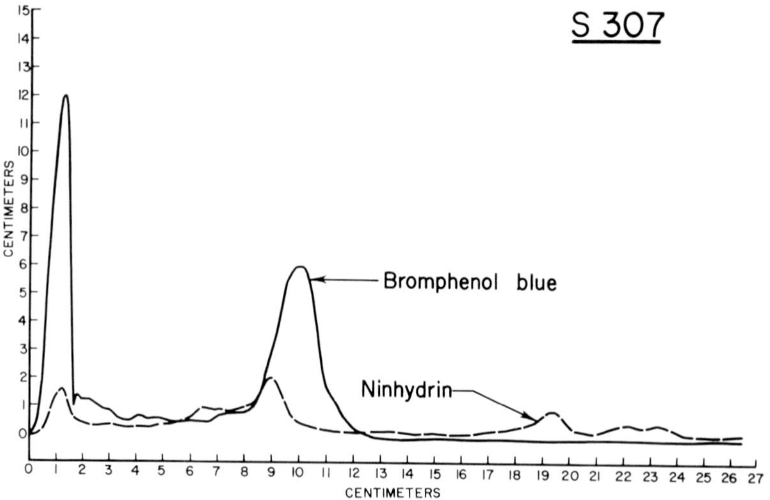

FIGURE 3. Densitometric traces of paper electrophoretic patterns of dichloracetic acid-solubilized human skin samples. (S229) = abdominal skin obtained at autopsy of a stillborn white male five fetal months of age; (S307) = abdominal skin obtained at autopsy of a seventy-eight-year-old colored female dead of arteriosclerotic cardiovascular disease. Note that the *non-migrating* bromphenol blue-positive band at the point of sample application (which

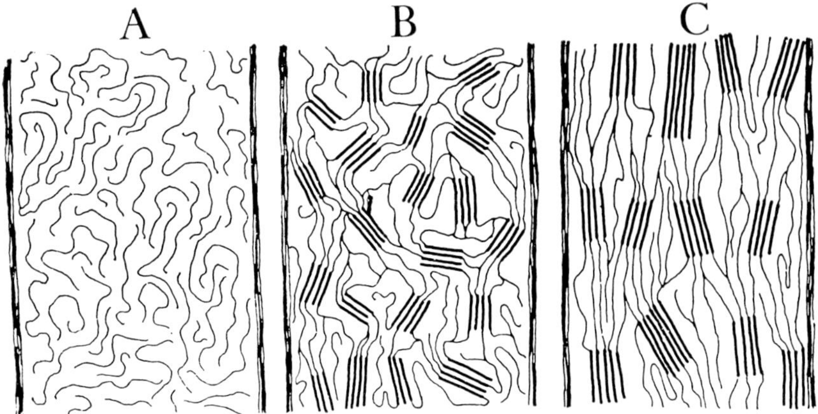

FIGURE 4. Diagrammatic representation of states of aggregation of hypothetical polymers consisting of the same backbone configuration: (A) randomly coiled amorphous structures; (B) partially crystalline (laterally ordered); (C) ordered and oriented crystalline structure.

(Fig. 3). Specific aldehydes may, in certain instances, also actually split-off loosely bound carbohydrates and carbohydrate-protein complexes from collagen and elastin subunits as a consequence of ion-ion or ion-dipole interactions.

No decision can be made for the moment between any of these potential mechanisms. In terms of polymer structure, each would be expected to yield a fibrous protein structure which would behave as if it were more laterally ordered ("crystalline") and more "insoluble" than the corresponding unoriented and amorphous structures of similar backbone composition (Fig. 4). Furthermore, each would be predicted to be characterized by the "locking-in" of dipoles normally present along the respective polypeptide chains

---

represents a highly crosslinked fraction consisting primarily of collagen structures) is the predominant fraction in the "old-type" skin sample, whereas the *migrating* (cationic in dichloracetic acid and representing a similar, though less highly crosslinked fraction) is the predominant component in the "young-type" skin. Also, note that the remaining migrating bands, which are ninhydrin-positive but fail to stain with bromphenol blue (and which contain abundant amounts of glucose, galactose and, to a lesser extent, of fucose) are markedly diminished in intensity and amount in the more mature, chronologically "older" skin.

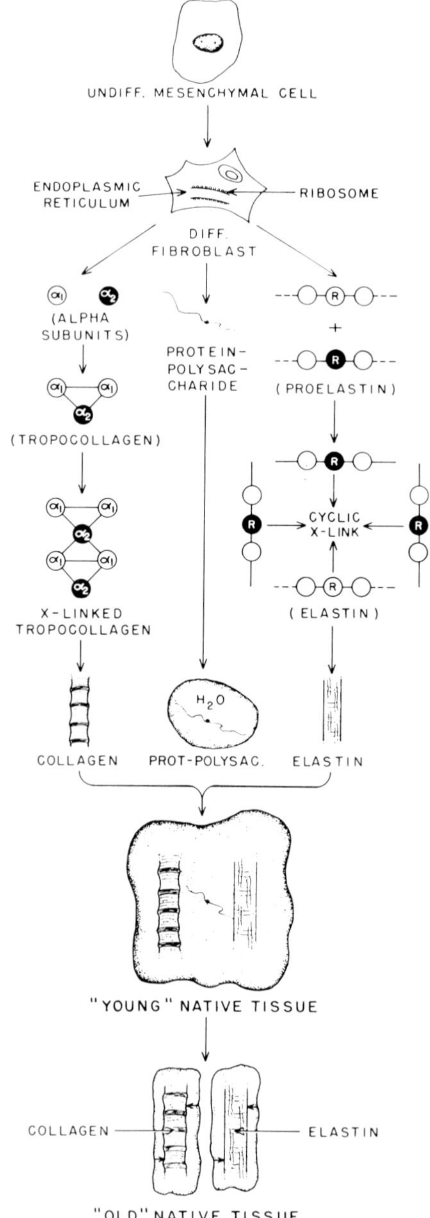

FIGURE 5. Diagrammatic representation of biosynthesis, maturation and aging phenomena in native connective tissues. Differentiation of reticulum cells into fibroblasts is followed by elaboration (in a currently unknown temporal

and would possess axial contraction (shrinkage), as well as chemical extractability and mechanical properties which would be displaced in the direction expected of structures with correspondingly lower entropy contents. This is exactly what has been observed *in vivo* in Verzár's hydroxyproline and mechanical tension tests of biological age[16] and, experimentally, in both aldehyde-crosslinked[17] and "de-plasticized"[18] connective tissue matrices.

An entirely new concept of connective tissue aging phenomena may thus be suggested (Fig. 5). This hypothecates that age-dependent changes in the content and states of aggregation and/or oxidation of ground-substance protein-polysaccharide complexes (which are exquisitely sensitive to genetic, immunochemical, hormonal and enzymic influences) are critical determinants both of the polymer-diluent (plasticizer) and the steric volume-exclusion[19] effects on, and hence the physical properties of, the associated collagen and elastin networks. Apparently increased ("pathological") crosslinking of the latter structures with advancing age, as well as their relatively enhanced tendency to mineralization and their relatively decreased degree of hydration may thus be considered to be principally, if not exclusively, consequences of oxidative dis-aggregation, or "de-polymerization of ground-substance complexes.

In this as in other views, the biosynthesis and maturation of connective tissue matrices are thought to derive from the metabolic activity of differentiated fibroblastic cells, which alone seem

---

sequence, but one which appears to be strongly influenced by external factors such as tension and the partial pressures of O_2 and CO_2) of all three major components of native tissues; collagen, elastin and ground-substance protein-polysaccharide complexes. Collagen and elastin monomers are crosslinked extracellularly to yield soluble tropocollagen and proelastin units, which are further crosslinked to yield insoluble collagen and elastin networks. Polysaccharides are principally involved, in this view, at a relatively later stage in fiberogenesis, after considerable crosslinking has occurred. It is proposed that the age-dependent loss of ground-substance materials, whether a consequence of direct crosslinking by oxidized ground-substance materials or of additional factors mediated by hormonal or enzymic reactions, is primarily responsible for the observed properties of native tissues and that these are explicable in terms of the "bulk polymer" concept outlined in Figure 2.

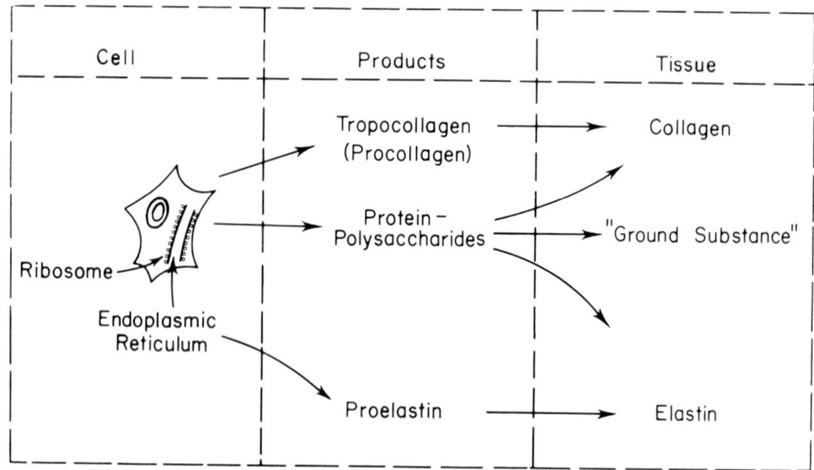

FIGURE 6. Products of fibroblastic cell function. Each of the three major constituents of native connective tissues are thought to be synthesized on ribosomal particles and elaborated into the extracellular "space" via the endoplasmic reticulum.

capable of elaborating all three major components (i.e., collagen, elastin and ground-substance) of native connective tissues (Fig. 6).

Soluble tropocollagen and proelastin elastin chains are envisaged as being secreted via the endoplasmic reticulum into the extracellular space where they undergo specific crosslinking interactions.[20] Hydrogen-bonded tropocollagen helices, consisting of a succession of two α_1- and one α_2- subunits or of dissimilar α_1, α_2 and α_3 subunits (representing the *alkali- and salt-extractable* monomers) are thought to be covalently crosslinked at a later time to form the corresponding β- components of *acid-extractable* tropocollagens as well as larger subunits, including γ- compounds with all three chains linked together.

For elastin, the assumption is that the side chains of three lysine residues lying close together in the amino acid sequence of soluble proelastin chains are first deaminated and oxidized to their corresponding semi-aldehyde derivatives. The site of insoluble "fiber" formation presumably is the point at which three such residues are brought into apposition with a fourth unmodified lysine side chain with the formation of the cyclic crosslinks desmosine and isodesmosine.[21]

There is little direct evidence currently available which demonstrates that progressive crosslinking actually occurs in either collagen or elastin *chains* with advancing age. However, there is little question but that native connective *tissues,* including the arterial wall,[22] do act in this manner.[16,22-26] So far as is known, moreover, from the many reported studies on the relative insolubility of *mature* collagen and elastin in aqueous and organic solvents and of their extremely slow rates of metabolic turnover, collagen and elastin structures (with the exception of the post-partum uterus and of certain soft tissues and bone during active resorptive processes), when once fully formed, remain essentially inert throughout the lifetime of the organism.

A major question is then raised as to possible micromorphologic sites in fibrous protein structures where subtle chemical changes can induce rather major alterations in the physical properties of tissues. One might propose, especially in the light of recent data by Bornstein and Piez,[27] Petruska and Hodge,[28] Harding,[29] Smith[30] and Stevens[31] for collagen and by Gotte *et al.*[32,33] for elastin, somewhat different three-dimensional models of native connective tissue structures than have been described heretofore which could provide these sites.

Elastin might be considered to exist much as described in either Lansing's or Hall's model; namely, as an intertwined or cabled network of interconnecting, fine fibrils embedded in and both chemically and physically ("entanglements") bound at many different points to the protein-polysaccharide ground-substance matrix.

Collagen, on the other hand, could be thought of as a linear array of tropocollagen monomers (perhaps existing either as two α_1—chains with repeating sequences of 5 identical subunits and a single α_2 strand of 7 identical subunits, or as some more complex structure with dissimilar α_1, α_2 and α_3 polypeptide chains) packed end-to-end in such a fashion that only about two-thirds to three-quarters of their total number are in the typical quarter-overlapped arrangement. The "holes" produced in the protein structure by nonalignment of tropocollagen polymers in their quarter-overlapped "crystalline" regions, with the remaining polymers in the non-overlapped, unoriented or "amorphous" regions, might serve as the site of polysaccharide localization within collagen "fibers" (Fig. 7). These presumably also represent the regions of the tyrosine–containing telopeptides and of the aldehydes, which may link the collagen in an insoluble complex with carbohydrates of the ground-substance. Additional sites may also occur along the surface of the protein structure, so that a continuous layer of polysaccharide could conceivably exist as a protein-polysaccharide "sheath" both around and within the collagen protein structure, much as proposed for the elastin structure.

Argyrophilic "reticulum" fibers might then be considered, as suggested earlier by others, either to be very young collagen fibrils or a "branch line" of the fiber which possesses an abundant polysaccharide sheath both about and within the central protein structure. "Immature" and "young" collagen fibers could be thought of as those which possess relatively smaller "sheaths," while "mature" and "old" fibers could be construed to be those in which there are still smaller and/or disaggregated polysaccharide phases associated with the protein, which itself possesses both a relatively higher internal cross-link density and a relatively lower degree of initial dilution (or, hydration).

The nature of the various crosslinks involved in these interactions has not as yet been completely established. Carbohydrates are almost certainly involved, at least in part, in the formation of both collagen[29] and elastin[32,33] fibers and undergo unequivocal changes during aging. One might reasonably predict, therefore, that a correlation could be made between the content and degree of polymerization of extractable carbohydrates, on the one hand, and the equilibrium swelling and ultimate tensile properties of any given tissue, on the other hand; also, that this relationship might be a direct function of chronological age. Current observations in this laboratory suggest that this is in fact, generally the case, at least so far as native skin samples are concerned.

Considerably more information is obviously required to validate—or even to explore adequately—what might be termed this "plasticizer" concept of connective tissue aging processes. The concept does have the merit, however, not only of reconciling a number of the apparently inconsistent hypotheses outlined heretofore, but also of being in concert with the enlarging body of evidence supporting the likely importance both of crosslinking

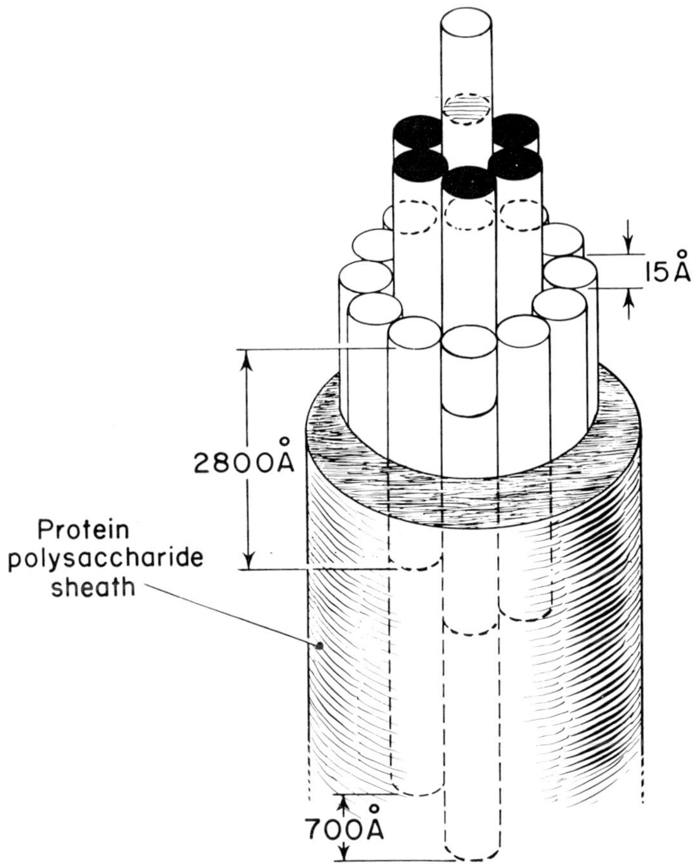

FIGURE 7. Postulated molecular structure of an hypothetical collagen "fiber." Linear tropocollagen monomers, measuring 15 × 2800 Å, are believed to be clustered about a central monomer in rings composed of multiples of six tropocollagen monomers each. The first and second rings (shown here) possess 6 and 12 tropocollagen monomers, respectively; additional rings can contain up to 78 molecules per ring. In addition, the tropocollagen monomers are packed end-to-end in such a manner that only about ¾ (in small fibers of 45 Å diameter) to ⅔ (in large fibers with diameters of approximately 400 Å) are in the typical quarter-overlapped (700 Å) arrangement. The entire fiber is thought to be surrounded by an electron-transparent (in ordinary preparations) protein-polysaccharide "sheath," which also occupies the "holes" present in the non-overlapped, amorphous regions of the fiber. These possibly represent the regions in which chemical and physical interactions occur between tropocollagen structures and ground substance polysaccharides. In mineralizable collagens, they may also represent the regions of the "nucleation sites" for apatite crystal formation.

mechanisms[16,34,35] and of the ground-substance materials[11,12,36,37] in aging processes. It has, too, in contradistinction to virtually all previous hypotheses, the very decided advantages of taking all known connective tissue elements into consideration and of being amenable to direct experimental observations and analysis in terms of rather straight forward polymer chemistry.[38]

A systematic analysis of the physical properties of aging native tissues, notably skin, aorta and articular cartilage, and the relationship of these properties to the physical-chemical properties of the respectively isolated collagen, elastin and protein-polysaccharide phases are currently engaging the full attention of this laboratory. The results, while far from even partially complete, are encouraging and suggest not only that the proposed working model may represent a fairly accurate estimate of the actual state of biological affairs, but also that relatively simple oxidation of ground-substance polysaccharides to their corresponding hydrated dialdehyde foms may account for the crosslinking phenomena, the loss of detectable ground-substance materials and the "inelasticity" which has been described as characteristic features of naturally aging connective tissues.*

REFERENCES

1. Milch, R. A.: Biochemical studies on the pathogenesis of collagen tissue changes in alcaptonuria. *Clin. Orthop., 24:*213, 1962.
2. Milch, R. A.: Aqueous solution infrared spectra of collagen-reactive aldehydes. *Biochim. Biophys. Acta, 93:*45, 1964.
3. Milch, R. A.: (a) Thermal shrinkage of aldehyde-treated goatskins, *J. Amer. Leather Chems. Assn., 57:*581, 1962; (b) Studies of collagen tissue aging: Interaction of certain intermediary metabolites with collagen. *Gerontologia (Basel), 7:*129-152, 1963; (c) Reaction of certain aliphatic aldehydes with gelatin, *Gerontologia (Basel), 10:*117, 1965.
4. Milch, R. A., and Clifford, R. C.: Binding of aldehydes to collagen and elastin networks, Submitted for publication.
5. Kincaid, D. T., Baker, L. D., Jr., and Milch, R. A.: Tissue distribution and aortic binding of dl-glyceraldehyde-C-14. *J. Surg. Res., 5:*120, 1965.
6. Milch, R. A., Jude, J. R., and Knaack, J.: Effects of collagen-reactive aldehyde metabolites on the structure of the canine aortic wall and their possible role in atherogenesis. *Surgery, 54:*104, 1963.

* Dedicated to the memory of Dr. Henry Milch, a distinguished and imaginative orthopaedic surgeon of New York, who died suddenly and most unexpectedly from complications of the connective tissue aging processes which are of concern here.

7. MILCH, R. A., AND MURRAY, R. A.: Infrared spectra of aqueous dialdehyde starch solutions. *J. Amer. Leather Chems. Ass., 59*:310, 1964.
8. MILCH, R. A.: (a) Polymer-diluent and certain other effects of solvent environment on the thermal shrinkage (contraction) and tensile strength properties of native calfskins, *Biorheology*. In press. (b) Some topological properties of carbohydrate-plasticized collagen matrices. Proceedings of International Symposium on Connective Tissue. Lyon, France, September 1-2, 1965.
9. KLASSEN, G. A., AND MILCH, R. A.: Surface extraction of aortic lipids by high molecular weight dextrans. *J. Surg. Res.*, in press, 1966.
10. JARADO, M., AND NISHIDA, T.: Interaction of dextran sulfate with low-density lipoproteins of plasma. *J. Lipid Res., 6*:331, 1965.
11. STIDWORTHY, G., MASTERS, Y. F., AND SHEPLAR, M. R.: The effects of aging on mucopolysaccharide composition of human costal cartilage as measured by hexosamine and uronic acid content. *J. Geront., 13*:10, 1958.
12. MILCH, R. A., GEY, G. O., AND NAUGHTON, M. A.: Subunit patterns of rapidly proliferating connective tissues. *Biochim. Biophys. Acta, 100*:623, 1965.
13. MILCH, R. A., AND NAUGHTON, M. A.: Fractionation of human skin components by paper electrophoresis in dichloracetic acid. *Gerontologia (Basel), 11*:153, 1965.
14. MUIR, H.: The nature of the link between protein and carbohydrate of a chondroitin sulfate complex from hyaline cartilage. *Biochem. J., 69*:195, 1958.
15. ANDERSON, B., HOFFMAN, P., AND MEYER, K.: The o-serine linkage in peptides of chondroitin 4- or 6-sulfate. *J. Biol. Chem., 240*:156-167, 1965.
16. VERZAR, F.: (a) The aging of collagen. *Sci. Amer., 208*:104-113, 1963; (b) Aging of the collagen fiber, *in*, Hall, D. A. (Ed.), *International Review of Connective Tissue Research.* New York, Academic Press, 1964, Vol. 2, pp. 243-300.
17. MILCH, R. A.: FRISCO, L. J., AND SZYMKOWIAK, E. A.: Solid-state dielectric properties of aldehyde-treated goatskin collagen. *Biorheology, 3*:9, 1965.
18. PARTINGTON, F. R., AND WOOD, G. C.: The role of non-collagen components in the mechanical behaviour of tendon fibres. *Biochim. Biophys. Acta, 69*:485, 1963.
19. GERBER, B. R., AND SCHUBERT, M.: The exclusion of large solutes by cartilage proteinpolysaccharide. *Biopolymers, 2*:259, 1964.
20. GROSS, J.: The behavior of collagen units as a model in morphogenesis. *J. Biophys. Biochem. Cytol., 2:* (Suppl.), 261, 1956.
21. PARTRIDGE, S. M., ELSDEN, D. F., THOMAS, J., DORFMAN, A., TELSER, A., AND HO, P. L., Biosynthesis of the desmosine and isodesmosine cross-bridges in elastin. *Biochem. J., 93*:30C, 1964.
22. ROACH, M. R., AND BURTON, A. C.: (a) The reason for the shape of the distensibility curves of arteries. *Canad. J. Biochem. Physiol., 35*:681, 1957; (b) The effect of age on the elasticity of human iliac arteries. *Canad. J. Biochem. Physiol., 37*:557, 1959.
23. BANFIELD, W. G.: (a) The solubility and swelling of collagen in dilute acid with age variations in man. *Anat. Rec., 114*:157, 1952; (b) Age changes in the swelling capacity of human Achilles tendon. *J. Geront., 11*:372, 1956; (c) Age changes in the acetic acid-soluble collagen in human skin. *Arch. Path.* (Chicago) *68*:680, 1959.

24. Brown, P. C., and Consden, R.: Variation with age of shrinkage temperature of human collagen. *Nature (London) 181*:349, 1958.

25. Kohn, R. R., and Rollerson, E. J.: (a) Studies on the effect of heat and age in decreasing ability of human collagen to swell in acid. *J. Geront., 14*:11, 1959; (b) Aging of human collagen in relation to susceptibility to the action of collagenase. *J. Geront., 15*:10, 1960.

26. Bakerman, S.: Quantitative extraction of acid-soluble human skin collagen with age. *Nature (London) 196*:375, 1962.

27. Bornstein, P., and Piez, K. A.: A biochemical study of human skin collagen and the relation between intra- and intermolecular cross-linking. *J. Clin. Invest., 43*:1813, 1964.

28. Petruska, J. A., and Hodge, A. J.: A subunit model for the tropocollagen macromolecule. *Proc. Nat. Acad. Sci. USA, 51*:871, 1964.

29. Harding, J. J.: The unusual links and cross-links of collagen. *Advances Protein Chem., 20*:109-190, 1965.

30. Smith, J. W.: Packing arrangement of tropocollagen molecules. *Nature (London) 205*:356, 1965.

31. Stevens, F. S.: The cleavage of tyrosyl peptides by pepsin from collagen solubilized by the Nishihara technique. *Biochem. Biophys. Acta, 97*:465, 1965.

32. Gotte, L., Stern, P., and Partridge, S. M.: The chemistry of connective tissues. 8. The composition of elastin from three bovine tissues. *Biochem. J., 87*:344, 1963.

33. Moret, V., Serafini-Fracassini, A., and Gotte, L.: The carbohydrate composition of the NaCl-soluble fraction from autoclaved elastin. *J. Atheroscler. Res., 4*:184, 1964.

34. Gustavson, K. H.: *The Chemistry of Tanning Processes.* New York, Academic Press, 1956, pp. 345-372.

35. Milch, R. A.: Possible role of aldehyde metabolites in the aging processes of connective tissue. *Southern Med. J., 58*:153, 1965.

36. Sobel, H., and Marmorston, J.: The possible role of the gel-fiber ratio of connective tissue in the aging process, *J. Geront., 11*:2, 1956.

37. Sobel, H., Masserman, R., and Parsa, K.: Effect of age on the transvascular passage of I^{131}-labeled albumin in hearts of dogs. *J. Geront., 19*:501, 1964.

38. Flory, P. J.: Theory of elastic mechanisms in fibrous proteins. *J. Amer. Chem. Soc., 78*:5222, 1956.

Chapter 9

CONNECTIVE TISSUE—ITS ROLE IN THE AGING PROCESS

DAVID A. HALL

IT IS A GREAT HONOUR to contribute to this volume in commemoration of Professor Verzár's eightieth birthday, and even more so to have as my responsibility one of the chapters on connective tissue. If, during the past twenty years, any one person has demonstrated that connective tissues deserve more detailed study, it is Professor Verzár himself. Over the years I have been privileged to watch the growth of the Basel school and to assess its observations as they have impinged on the field in which I have been engaged, and I accept my task with a deep sense of gratitude for the farsightedness and consideration which Professor Verzár has always brought to the many discussions which we have had on our mutual interest.

Other chapters in this volume deal specifically with the aging of the two major connective tissue components, collagen and elastin, at the molecular level. Here I hope to present the problem as it affects the integrated system of which these two form a part.

Experimental gerontology, by its very definition, aims at a solution of the problems of aging by a consideration of the effects of certain artificial stimuli which it is assumed may simulate, at least in part, the overall aging process. Normally the application of scientific methods to a problem of this nature would necessitate the examination of the aging process as it affects the individual components, followed by the formulation of hypotheses relating to the composite system in which these components play their part in conjunction with one another. Unfortunately it has not proved possible to develop the study of connective tissue aging along these classical lines. As the importance of such tissues has become apparent, empirical data relative to the complete system have been amassed, and in many cases this has preceded more fundamental studies, not only on the aging, but also on the structure and function of the individual components themselves. The ultimate aim of connective tissue gerontology must be to demonstrate how age changes in these structures of the body may affect other organs and hence in the final analysis the functioning of the body as a whole, and to this end quite an arbitrary choice of materials and methods has had to be made.

The term connective tissue covers a highly diverse group of structures which demonstrate an equally diverse range of aging effects. They differ from one another in the distribution of the normal tissue components, namely cells, fibres and ground substance, and it is only to be expected that their response to age will vary both in degree and in time of onset. Thus any attempt to lay down hard and fast rules to cover connective tissue in all its forms must of necessity fail dismally. Although the logical type of tissue to study would appear at first sight to be a poorly differentiated one, from which it should be possible to extrapolate to more highly specialised ones, the very simplicity of such tissues, especially with regard to function, renders difficult the assessment of age changes in their properties. The easiest tissues to study are those which are most specialised in their function. In these cases the choice of parameter is much easier. Incidentally, of course, changes in the function of specialised tissues often result in far-reaching reactions in the body as a whole. Thus calcification of vascular tissue will have a far more profound effect than similar alterations of sheets of fascia. Because of this disproportionate importance of certain tissues, the majority of studies on connective tissue aging have been restricted to a very few structures, namely tendons, skin, the vascular system and to a lesser extent the lungs. Much of the evidence which will be considered below, therefore, refers to tissues which cannot to regarded as typical, but if due allowance is made for the fact that differences do exist between the structure and composition of various tissues these atypical studies may serve as a basis for the development of tentative hypotheses to explain the processes of aging in connective tissue as a whole.

Cellular Aging in Connective Tissue

The major difference between connective tissues from various sites lies in the relative amounts of the three elements which together make up their structure; namely, cells, fibrous tissue and ground substance. In foetal tissues there is a higher concentration of cellular material than in the adult, and it has been suggested that the whole aging process may be attributed to a failure to replace these cells as death progressively reduces their number throughout life. This might explain age changes in certain tissues, but in others marked cellular activity can be observed even in advanced age.

Vascular tissue may be taken as an example, even though it is particularly difficult to differentiate between those effects directly associated with the physiological processes of aging and those due to pathological atherosclerotic changes. One aspect of the overall change in the artery wall is an apparent increase in the activity of those fibroblasts responsible for the production of new elastic fibres in the region of the intimal membrane, and of collagen fibres in and around the atherosclerotic plaques. It has not yet been ascertained whether this apparent surge of activity represents an attenuated relic of the fibroblastic activity which in foetal life resulted in the initial laying down of the tissues, or is in fact due to the activation of a completely new set of cells. Branwood has suggested (1963) that this late fibroblastic activity follows the differentiation of the endothelial cells, and that this can be retarded by the deposition of lipid in the endothelial layer. Other workers have attributed the appearance of fine elastic fibres in the region of the intimal membrane to the activity of the smooth muscle cells which migrate from the inner layers of the media. Whichever is the case it would not appear likely that cell death plays an important role throughout the whole aging process in the vascular tissue, although in very advanced age, where intimal and medial degeneration may occur, a decrease in cell numbers may be significant.

Changes in Fibre Distribution

When one considers the data which have been reported regarding changes in the relative concentration of the fibrous proteins, elastin and collagen, in connective tissues, one is struck by two rather disturbing facts. Firstly, again taking vascular tissue as an example, considerable differences can be observed between the results reported by different groups of workers. Thus Lansing

(1951) reported a slight reduction (48 per cent to 42.5 per cent) over the range < twenty years to > sixty years. Faber and Møller-Hou (1952) and Myers and Lang (1945) however reported a larger drop (35 per cent to 22-27 per cent) over the same age range. Bertolini (1958) observed a drop of 40 per cent but recorded that the effect is greatest above an age of forty-five to fifty, whilst Scarcelli (1961) claimed that there is in fact a marked increase in elastin (250 per cent) during the first twenty years, followed by an even greater drop (50 per cent) than that observed by other workers. Secondly, and this is even more apparent from studies of aging skin, there is a very low correlation between the amount of elastin present in aging tissue as deduced by an assessment of stained histological sections and the amount determined by chemical means (*cf.* Hall, 1964 for a more detailed discussion).

It would appear that much of the confusion, may be laid at the door of the sampling and extraction procedures employed. Many analytical studies appear to have been carried out with a fine disregard for the structures being analysed. Most workers employing aortic tissue remove the adventitia, but little care is taken to determine how much media is removed at the same time, with the result that the ratio of intima to media can vary considerably. Similarly in sampling skin tissue, little regard is taken of the fact that, especially in aging skin, the distribution of elastica staining material is anything but uniform. The methods of preparation also leave much to be desired. Analyses of elastin content usually depend on the specific removal of collagen and ground substance by treatment with solvents believed to be without effect on elastin. Unfortunately there is still little proof that methods designed to remove all the collagen (Partridge and Davis, 1955; Hall, 1955; Balo and Banga, 1950) are without effect on elastin, nor that methods designed to leave the elastin intact (Fitzpatrick and Hospelhorn, 1960; Czerkawski, 1962) remove all the collagen and ground substance. This results in marked variations in the published values for elastin/collagen ratios in aging tissues especially since the relative solubilities of the tissue components in solvents or enzyme solutions can be shown to vary so greatly with age. For instance Felsher (1961) has shown that so-called "elastotically degenerate" elastica staining fibres in dermis, such as appear in great numbers in senile skin, are far more readly attacked by decinormal alkali than are young intact elastic fibres. Until such time as sampling, extraction and analysis can be carried out in a truly defined fashion, all assessment of the elastin content of connective tissues will be open to doubt. One observation which could easily be made, and which might in the future assist in the interpretation of the results, is the simultaneous estimation of the collagen and ground substance content of the tissues along with elastin levels. These two additional values could be determined by a measurement of the hydroxyproline and hexosamine content of the solubilised fraction of the tissue and together with the elastin values would indicate the true distribution of the solid constituents of the tissue.

Pseudoelastin and Age

The existence of elastica staining material in aging connective tissues which is not accounted for in analytical figures for the true elastin content of the tissue, raises the question of the existence of pseudoelastin.

Some years ago our group in Leeds suggested that elastin and collagen might originate in the same fibroblast, the ultimate structure and chemical composition depending on the environment. (Hall *et al.,* 1955; Burton *et al.,* 1955). The hypothesis was also advanced that an appreciable amount of the material staining as elastin, especially in aging connective tissue, might originate in collagen fibres which had become degraded with age. These early observations were based in the main on morphological studies, as was the subsequent work of Keech and Reed (1957) but later chemical and biochemical studies (Hall, 1956, 1957) provided support for the concept, and demonstrated that under experimental conditions the production of material having many of the physical and tinctorial properties of elastin was accompanied by the removal from the collagen molecule of those amino acids the abstraction of which would be necessary to convert the structure of collagen into one more closely resembling that of elastin.

Unfortunately, in spite of the care taken at the time to disassociate ourselves from any claim that true elastin could be derived from collagen, this suggestion was attributed to us and drew down on us a considerable amount of criticism. Our hypothesis depended on a number of important assumptions. Some of these still remain assumptions, but a number have been justified in the period since 1955.

A considerable amount of work has been done recently to ascertain the exact intracellular locus of synthesis of the collagen molecule. Although material with the composition of collagen has been isolated from the microsomes of fibroblasts (Lowther, Green and Chapman, 1961), the earlier stages in the synthesis, in which smaller subunits of the structure are formed have not been clarified. Recent studies on the nature and amino acid composition of these subunits should shortly lead to the development of methods for their identification inside the fibroblast. It may then be possible to demonstrate that differing environmental conditions result in the synthesis of different proteins.

The discovery of the subunits in collagen has led to the justification of one of the assumptions made ten years ago. On the basis of the fact that treatment of collagen with phthalate buffer results in the extraction of a protein fraction which is exceptionally rich in hydroxyproline (Hall, 1957) it appeared logical to assume that the constitution of collagen could not be represented by the triad structure suggested by Astbury, nor by the tetrad structure suggested by Schroeder *et al.* (1954). On the basis of x-ray diffraction studies, Cowan *et al.*, (1955) had suggested that one of the three protein chains of the collagen molecule must differ from the other two. Recent identification and characterisation of the α-subunits of collagen has indicated that in fact all three such subunits differ from one another (Piez, 1964). Previously it has been suggested that two of the units were identical (Piez, Eigner and Lewis, 1963), but even at this stage there was considerable evidence that the amino acid composition of these different subunits of the collagen molecule differed markedly from one another.

Since further analyses will be necessary to determine the individual composition of the three distinct α-subunits, detailed discussion of the results so far reported would be of little significance. Suffice it to say that certain specific amino acids, notably valine, by which collagen and elastin differ so markedly, show similar trends in the subunits. The discovery of pairs of ester linkages joining segments of the subunits together indicates that analytical studies at an even finer level of separation will be necessary.

It would appear appropriate to make yet another assumption, namely that one or more of these ester-linked units will be shown to contain the major portion of the valine and others most of the hydroxyproline. The biosynthesis of collagen can therefore be assumed to require the linkage of a selection of fragments including the hydroxyproline-rich ones, whereas the biosynthesis of elastin will be accomplished from a selection including the fragments rich in valine.

During the next few years we may hope that a study of the soluble proteins extractable from the neighbourhood of the aging fibrous proteins of connective tissue will lead to the identification of individual subunit fragments. From this it should be possible to determine whether the elastica staining material which appears in increasing amounts in aging tissue is derived from degraded collagen or from degraded elastin. Recent gross analytical studies on senile dermis, in which the enzyme elastase has been employed to microdisect elastica staining material from the tissues, carried out by my colleague, Miss R. S. Slater, have shown that at least part of the elastica staining material in senile skin is derived from the elastic tissue originally present and consists possibly of collagen fibres to which the degradation products of these elastin fibres have become attached. Further analytical studies on the possible fragments of elastin and collagen will permit the origin of these pseudoelastic masses to be determined exactly.

Similar studies will enable us to determine whether the elastic fibres which provide the duplicated and triplicated intimal membranes in aging aortae originate in the endothelial cells or in the smooth muscle cells, since the day should not be far off when it will be possible to identify individual subunit fractions within these cells and possibly even to identify the ribosome nucleic acid particles responsible for their initial synthesis and subsequent polymerisation to form the intact protein molecule.

Our discussion of connective tissue aging has therefore come a full circle and we are back to the cell again. Future studies on connective tissue, and studies of its age change are only a part of a greater whole, and must ultimately reduce to a study of the products of cellular activity and more deeply to a study of the processes which control such synthesis. The logical approach would be to identify and characterise these systems first and then proceed to a study of the hormonal factors which can influence the synthesis in the body as a whole. Connective tissue research will however, I am sure, continue to develop in the illogical way that has characterised it in the past and there are already signs that studies on the nature of the hormonal control of connective tissue synthesis are getting ahead of the more fundamental work. This only serves to make the topic even more fascinating than it might be if the logical approach were adhered to strictly.

REFERENCES

Balo, J., and Banga, I.: Elastolytic activity of pancreas extracts. *Biochem. J., 46:*384, 1950.

Bertolini, A.: Quantitative changes of the elastic component of human aorta and pulmonary artery during growth and senescence. *Chir. Pat. Sper., 6:*240, 1958.

Branwood, A. W. The fibroblast. In: *Internat. Rev. Connective Tissue Res.* ed. Hall, D. A. New York, Academic Press, 1963.

Burton, D., Hall, D. A., Keech, M. K., Reed, R., Saxl, H., Tunbridge, R. E., and Wood, M. J.: Apparent transformation of collagen fibrils into 'elastin.' *Nature (London) 176:*966, 1955.

Cowan, P. M., McGavin, J., and North, A. C. T.: The polypeptic chain configuration of collagen. *Nature (London), 176:*1062, 1955.

Czerkawski, J. W.: Elastin, a sialoprotein. *Nature (London), 194:*869, 1962.

Faber, M., and Møller-Hou, G.: The human aorta. V. Collagen and elastin in the normal and hypertensive aorta. *Acta Path. Microbiol. Scand., 31:*377, 1952.

Felsher, Z.: Observations on senile elastosis. *J. Invest. Derm., 37:*163, 1961.

Fitzpatrick, M. J., and Hospelhorn, V. D.: Biochemical properties of different elastins. *J. Lab. Clin. Med., 56:*812, 1960.

Hall, D. A.: The reaction between elastase and elastic tissue. I. The substrate. *Biochem. J., 59:*459, 1955.

Hall, D. A.: Chemical studies on the relationship between collagen and elastin. *Experientia Suppl. 4:*19, 1956.

Hall, D. A.: Collagen and elastin, the effect of age on their relationship. *Gerontologia, 1:*347, 1957.

Hall, D. A.: *Elastolysis and Aging.* Springfield, Thomas, 1964.

Hall, D. A., Keech, M. K., Reed, R., Tunbridge, R. E., Saxl, H., and Wood, M. J.: Collagen and elastin in connective tissue. *J. Geront., 10:*388, 1955.

Keech, M. K., and Reed, R.: Enzymic elucidation of the relationship between collagen and elastin: an electron microscope study. *Ann. Rheum. Dis., 16:*35, 1957.

Lansing, A. I., Roberts, E., Ramasarma, G. B., Rosenthal, T. B., and Alex, M.: Changes with age in amino acid compositions of arterial elastin. *Proc. Soc. Exp. Biol. Med., 76:*714, 1951.

LOWTHER, D. A., GREEN, N. M., AND CHAPMAN, J. A.: Metabolic activity of collagen associated with subcellular fractions of guinea pig granulomata. *J. Biophys. Biochem. Cytol., 10*:373, 1961.

MYERS, V. C., AND LANG, W. W.: Some changes in the human thoracic aorta accompanying the aging process. *J. Geront., 1*:141, 1945.

PARTRIDGE, S. M., AND DAVIS, H. F.: Composition of the soluble proteins from elastin. *Biochem. J., 61*:21, 1955.

PIEZ, K. A.: Nonidentity of the three chains in codfish skin collagen. *J. Biol. Chem., 239*:C4315, 1964.

PIEZ, K. A., EIGNER, E. A., AND LEWIS, M. S.: The chromatographic separation and amino acid composition of the subunits of collagen. *Biochemistry (Wash.) 2*:58, 1963.

SCARSELLI, V.: Increase in the elastin content of the human aorta during growth. *Nature (London), 191*:710, 1961.

SCHROEDER, W. A., KAY, L. M., LEGETTE, I., HONEN, L., AND GREEN, F. C.: Gelatin; separation and estimation of peptides in partial hydrolysates. *J. Amer. Chem. Soc., 76*:3556, 1954.

Chapter 10

CONNECTIVE TISSUE

M. CHVAPIL

WHEN REVIEWING the huge amount of literature dealing with changes in composition and reactivity of connective tissue during aging one feels that the experimental evidence of a steady stabilisation of "reactivity" of this important tissue component is far away from reality in human beings. The most pleasant example of this statement is the unceasing activity of two outstanding members of the world collagentsia—Prof. K. H. Gustavson in the field of chemical reactivity and Prof. F. Verzár in the research of biological reactivity of collagen. Thus, the influence of the psychic tone upon biochemical reactions is so far not within our experimental efforts, however it should be stressed before other factors controlling connective tissue reactivity.

I do not wish to review here all the literature on the aging of connective tissue. My intention is to give my own opinion on this topic.

INTRODUCTION

Just as I am convinced that all three components of connective tissue (cells, ground substance of mucopolysaccharides and fibrillar structures form a structural as well as functional unity, I believe that connective tissue changes during development should be evaluated for all three components without separating them from one another. Thus all studies on the aging of collagen describe more or less a stabilisation of structure, which takes place in the molecule.

Collagen has been selected for gerontologic studies because it is easily available; its structure is fairly well known, and also because it forms an essential portion of the protein of the body. It is certainly helpful that the methods of molecular biology have been applied so frequently in the study of the aging of collagen. Collagen has only one disadvantage; it is evidently not the factor which limits aging. In much of the experimental literature "maturation" and "aging" of connective tissue are considered as synonymous; but the "aging" of the connective tissue should be characterized by a sudden change in composition or reactivity. To find out when connective tissue is mature and when the aging begins is the problem. Certain changes in old age, often connected with deterioration of the functions of individual organs, meet the above-mentioned requirement for differentiating between maturing and aging of connective tissue.

CHANGES OF FUNCTIONS OF CONNECTIVE TISSUE DURING AGING

Functional changes will be decisive in discussing the changes of connective tissue reactivity during aging. The following main functions of connective tissue should be distinguished (Chvapil 1966).

Physical Functions

1. Mechanical structural stability (tensile strength and elasticity).
2. Connective tissue supporting function in organs.

Physico-chemical Functions

1. Physico-chemical structural stability.
2. Transportive function.
3. Depository function.

Biological Functions

1. Metabolic-synthesizing.
2. Repair.
3. Defensive.

Since this classification of individual functions of connective tissue is based on the process which determines the reaction (analogous to principles of reaction kinetics) whether it be of physical or physical-chemical nature, it is possible to classify the structural stability of collagen molecules aggregates into four

TABLE I

CLASSIFICATION OF THE STRUCTURAL STABILITIES OF CONNECTIVE TISSUE FIBRES

Type of Structural Stability	*Factors Determining Stability*	*Method of Determination*	*Unit of Measurement*
Mechanical or Physical	Ultrastructure of fibres, content of ground substance	tensile strength elasticity	breaking load in g/fibre elongation in % of the original fibre length
Physico-chemical	intra- and inter-molecular cohesive linkages	thermal shrinkage chemical contraction relaxation	°C causing shrinkage shrinkage to % of the original fibre length; velocity constant of the process
		swelling	water binding capacity in g/100g of the protein at a certain pH
		solubility	% of extractable share
Metabolic	complex	size and velocity of the course of incorporation of labelled amino acid into connective tissue protein	specific activity indicated f.e. in cpm/μM of a labelled amino acid, collagen protein or calculation of rate of metabolic turn-over
Hydrolytic	peptide bonds	splitting by proteolytic enzymes and collagenase	

groups as shown in Table I. Each group is characterized by distinct factors, is studied by special methods, and demonstrates the well known steady increase of stabilisation during aging (for details see Verzár, 1964).

The regulating mechanisms controlling the multifold functions of connective tissue in dynamic equilibrium which form a sort of superintegration must be discussed. Let us now consider the effect of aging in these individual functions of connective tissue.

Physical Mechanical Functions

It is clear that connective tissue in organs and tissues, in addition to serving the supporting mechanical functions also influence the course of vessels and nerves and thus the nutrition and trophic balance of tissues. The role of basement membranes for the regulation of the transfer of water, electrolytes and other materials between the blood and cells must also be considered, etc. Let us concentrate on the facts that (1) the density of connective tissue in organs increases during aging, and (2) the metabolically labile forms of connective tissue components (soluble forms of collagenous proteins, hyaluronic acid, chondroitin-sulfuric acid) are substituted by metabolically stabile forms (insoluble collagen, keratosulphate) with increasing age.

Supporting Stroma in Organs During Aging

It is possible to find in the literature at least five different sources of the increase of connective tissue density (predominantly the collagen component). It should be mentioned, however, that until the period of the progressive phase of development a gradual increase of connective tissue density (similar to exponential growth) takes place in all organs and tissues (Harkness, 1961). In the regressive phase of the development of the organism, there is then a dissociation of the growth of the actual functional parenchyma and connective tissue stroma which being less metabolically active degradates more slowly than the functional parenchyma (Schaub, 1963; Chvapil and Deyl, 1965). Thus, the above-mentioned, more extensive accumulation of collagen structures takes place in this period, and it can be presumed that from the functional point of view just this phase of aging is decisive for the function of the respective organ. From Figure 1 it is evident that, although the process of the growth of collagen density has a similar appearance, each organ or tissue maintains its specificity in the velocity of the changes. These concern not only the quantity of connective tissue (or the relation between the individual fractions of collagens, collagen to elastin, individual forms of mucopolysaccharides) but also the changes of structural stability of the individual components and changes of their mutual interactions.

The generality of the gradual increase in density and stabilization of connective tissue in organs as a natural consequence of aging must be examined rather critically, since there is evidence

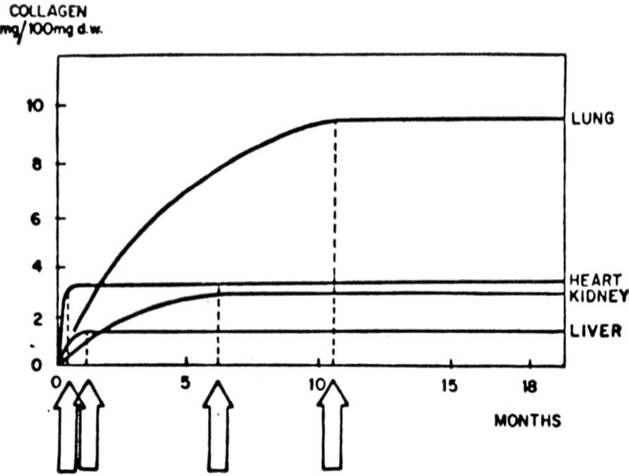

FIGURE 1. Course of concentration of the collagen in different organs during aging. The individual curves show that constant concentration has been reached in different organs at different moments. (From Chvapil and Deyl, 1965.)

that in wild species no great change in the density of collagen occur in various organs with increasing age. Furthermore the reactivity of collagenous structures related to changes in cohesive forces which result in lower structural stability of collagen is less in wild animals than in domesticated controls of the same age (Holečková and Chvapil, 1965).

Factors Controlling the Amount of Connective Tissue in Organs

This brings us to the principal question: what are the factors controlling the amount of connective tissue constituents in organs during aging? It should be mentioned that the influence of domestication upon the content of connective tissue components in the organs includes a complex of factors such as the change in movement, the change in the rhythm of intake and composition of food and the change in the stimulation in the central nervous system. It is obvious that there occurs not only a change in the organ connective tissue but also an influence upon the general reactivity of the organism and chemical composition of the body in general. These factors can be determined experimentally by two methods: by comparing the chemical composition of organs and tissues in domesticated and wild animals of the same line, or by studying the influence of these stimuli (movement, food, rhythm) upon domesticated laboratory animals (Holečková and Chvapil, 1965).

The second approach involves alterations in the rhythm of feeding in domesticated animals which will simulate the eating habits of wild animals. It has been shown that wild animals eat intermittently: days of forced fasting alternate with days of overfeeding. Nevertheless, long-term adaptation of domesticated animals to intermittent feeding[1] does not lead to a change in the composition of organ connective tissue until a slowing down of the aging process takes place in these animals, which can be proved by examining the physico-chemical structural stability of collagen fibres.

Another factor to be considered is the influence of physical load which is so different in wild and domesticated rats. Increased activity on the treadmill decreases markedly the calcium/collagen ratio. On the contrary, it can be shown that with the decreasing motility of the animal during aging an increase of the Ca/collagen quotient occurs (Table II).

The fibroplasia-stimulating effect of mechanical factors has also been shown in tissue cultures. In the uterus and lung the mechanical factor probably causes the steady increase in connective tissue.

As has been shown by Harkness (1964), the mechanical extension of the pregnant rat uterus is the actual stimulus for increased formation of collagen in the uterine wall. Hormonal influences are insignificant (Harkness, 1964). With parenchymatous organs this factor was not considered although for examples in lungs, which contain the highest concentration of connective tissue (approximately 10 per cent dry substance) of all the parenchymatous organs, this dependence is evident (emphysema in glass-blowers).

Repeated pregnancies shorten the life span in rats and speed

---

[1] Interrupted or intermittent fasting is an experimental method in which the animal is fed three times weekly and after adaptation to this type of feeding only twice weekly. The total caloric intake per week is the same as in normally fed animals.

TABLE II

THE INFLUENCE OF VARIOUS EXPERIMENTAL CONDITIONS ON THE CHEMICAL COMPOSITION OF RAT FEMUR

	Growth Changes in Domesticated Rats Before Sexual Maturation	*After Sexual Maturation*	*Growth Changes in Wild Rats*	*Adaptation to Chronic Load*
Bone weight	+++	+	++	++
Dry substance weight		+	++	+
% hydration	−−	−	−	++
% calcium	++	+	+	0
% collagen	+	−	0	0
% citrate	++	−	0	−−
% lactate	−−	−	+−	−
Ca/collagen	+−	++	+	−−
Cit/collagen	+	+−	0	−
Ca/Cit	0	++	+	++

A schematic indication of the changes in the composition of the femur in a group of wild rats (*Rattus Norvegicus*) and white Wistar rats which were studied during ontogeny and after adaptation to chronic physical load (gradually increased speed and duration of the run in the treadmill for thirty-eight months).

According to Vostál, Chvapil, Komárková (1961).

up the aging of the reactivity of connective tissue (Árvay, Takács and Verzár, 1963). Verzár believes that the changed collagen reactivity shortens the life span.

The stable concentration of connective tissue in the various organs of wild rats may be compared with the chemistry of diploid fibroblasts during several recultivations. It is known, that these cells produce in the stationary phase of the growth the same amount of collagenous proteins up to the 35th passage. Then a functional collapse occurs in which the collagen content in cells decreases (Figure 2). Thus I wish to emphasize that during the whole stationary phase, i.e., during the actual functional period of the cells, their composition does not change (Macek, Chvapil and Hurych, 1966).

The studies with tissue cultures show that aging as well as death are inherent to all animal cells. It makes no difference whether these cells remain in the body where they are subjected

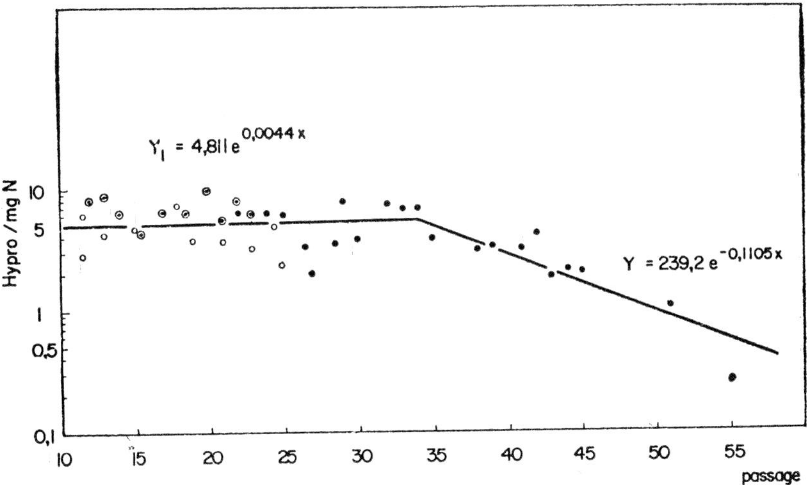

FIGURE 2. The effect of the number of passages on the collagen content in diploid fibroblasts. Starting from the thirty-fourth recultivation the decrease of the concentration of total hydroxyproline in fibroblasts is significant. (From Macek, Chvapil and Hurych, 1966.)

to various body regulations and mutual relations of the whole organism or are isolated from the animal and cultivated under controlled conditions. Because they die off even under these isolated conditions, the reason for their death must be found in the cells themselves.

Morphological Problems with the Increase of Collagen in Tissues

The increase in the content of collagen proteins in a certain tissue is clearly explained biochemically as the result of dynamic equilibrium of the synthesis and degradation processes of metabolism. Morphologically this can occur either as an increase in the number of fibres or an increase in the diameter of the fibres. Newly formed fibres are thin and, during their development in a majority of organs, their diameter increases.

Schwarz (1957) observed that the changes in the diameter of the fibres as well as the changes in the qualitative properties ceased in the period when the function of the intercellular substances of a certain organ reached its optimum. The diameter of the fibre did not, however, remain the same during the entire lifetime.

After reaching its maximum the diameter decreased again in early senescence so that three phases in the development of connective tissue structures were distinguished:

Prefunctional phase—with a rapidly increasing diameter.
Functional phase—with minimal changes.
Regressive phase—with a decreasing diameter.

Changes of Physical Structural Stability During Aging

An interesting finding in the mechanical properties of connective tissue during aging is the steady increase of the tensile strength of collagen fibers. The elasticity, however, of these structures was greatest during the so called "young adult period." Later on (Fig. 3) it declined. The maximum extensibility of the human Achilles tendon was between the ages of twenty-five and thirty years (Rollhäuser, 1951a,b). In animals we obtained a similar result in skin, tendon and isolated collagen fibers (Chvapil and Hrůza, 1962; Hrůza and Chvapil, 1962). It is evident from this that the problem of tissue elasticity can not be reduced to the problem of connective tissue or collagen elasticity under any circumstances. Although the fibrillar proteins are the main supporting mechanism for the size and shape of tissues other tissue components also participate in this function.

Changes in the Physico-chemical Functions of the Connective Tissue During Aging

Physico-chemical functions of connective tissue are represented by those reactions which are dependent on the binding capacities and interactions of the particular mucopolysaccharides of ground substance with collagenous and elastic fibres and with inorganic or organic substances. The degree of organization (polymerization, crystallinity) of mucopolysaccharides and fibrillar structure changes dynamically in the organism and depends on a number of endogenous and exogenous factors. The reactivity of these components of connective tissue is determined mainly by the character and amount of intra- and intermolecular binding forces. It is a credit to Verzár and Bjorksten that the concept of the participation of cross-linkages in macromolecules and especially in

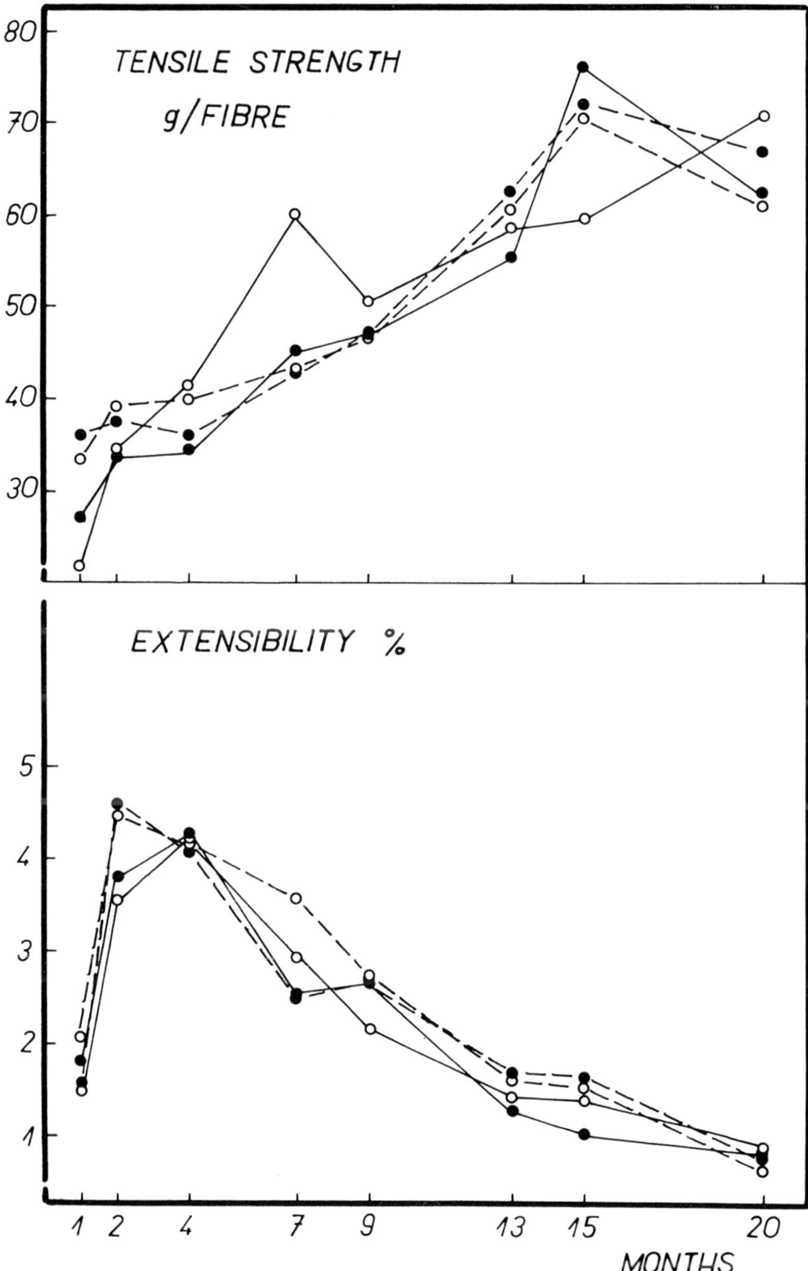

FIGURE 3. The effect of age on the tensile strength and elasticity of collagen fibres from the mouse tail tendon. The individual curves represent data for males and females, hybrid and inbred mice. Neither sexual nor genetic differences were found in the studied parameters. (From Hrůza and Chvapil, 1962.)

TABLE III

Survey of the Linkages Participating in the Stabilization of Collagen Structure

Type of Linkage	*Characteristics of the Linkage*
1. Steric rigidity	Is given by a small free rotation around the peptide bond, in which proline of hydroxyproline participates.
2. Lyophobe contacts	Amongst the side chains of aminoacids.
3. Hydrogen bridges	Between CO^- and HN^+ on the tropocollagen molecule.
4. Cross linkages	Ionic (COO^- and NH^+) or covalent (amide, ester, glycoside) are either intramolecular or intermolecular.
5. Structurally bound water	This is a periodically repeated water linkage to the individual tropocollagen molecules, intermolecularly in continuous chains.

linear proteins during the aging process has been elaborated in such detail.

Cohesive Forces in Collagen Molecules

It is well known that there exist several forms of linkages between collagen polypeptide chains and collagen molecules, and that the popular concept of "cross-linkages" refers solely to the changes in covalent bonds (Table III).

The relation of the various binding forces and a certain kind of collagen is apparent from Hörmann's survey (1963) (Table IV).

The problem of physico-chemical structural stability of collagen has been recently summarized by Verzár (1964) in a very thoughtful way. This enables us to deal in this paper directly with exogenous factors controlling the physico-chemical structural stability which have to be considered in the process of aging.

Factors Controlling the Physico-chemical Functions of Connective Tissue

The study of the physico-chemical structural stability of collagen molecules is connected with the endeavour to identify substances which can be present in the organism under physiological

TABLE IV

LINKAGES STABILIZING THE INDIVIDUAL STAGES OF COLLAGEN MATURATION

	Intramolecular		*Intermolecular*	
	H-bridge	*Covalent Bonds*	*Ionic Bonds*	*Covalent Bonds*
Collagen soluble in neutral medium (solution)	+	−	−	−
Collagen soluble in acid medium (newly formed fibres)	+	+	+	−
Collagen soluble after denaturation of collagen fibres (fibres)	+	+	++*	−
Insoluble collagen (fibres)	+	+	++*	+

(According to Hörmann, 1963).

* Ionic bonds are stronger owing to the interaction of mucopolysaccharides; in addition some intermolecular hydrogen bridges and van der Waals forces participate.

conditions and which can react with protein to form the abovementioned linkages.

Milch (1963) evaluated experimentally the idea that products of intermediary metabolism which normally occur in animals can act as substances inducing in macromolecules the formation of cross-linkages and thus take part in the pathogenesis of the aging process. These states of the reactivity of the connective tissue are manifested chiefly by a decreased water content, fragmentation, pigmentation and calcification of elastic fibres by thickening and strengthening the collagen bundles, and a decrease in the total quantity of mucopolysaccharides. Milch came to the conclusion that only a few low molecular weight aliphatic aldehydes exist which are the product of metabolism and are able to tan collagen and to change its reactivity to that which exists in collagen of old organisms. Other substances, products of the metabolism of carbohydrates, fats and proteins, did not tan collagen *in vitro*.

Under *in vivo* conditions, cross-linkages in collagen structure form owing to the effect of various drugs. As an example, sodium gold thiosulphate increases the degree of cross-linking of collagen because Au binds directly to the collagen structure in the same way as zinc, lead, silver ions, etc. Under *in vivo* conditions these metals can react with collagen. Other drugs such as resorcin, phenylbutazone, salicilates and others also influence the final structural stability of collagen in a way which, however, is not entirely known. The practical significance of these findings is evident because they are mostly antirheumatoid drugs changing the reactivity of collagen structures (Adam, Bartl, Deyl and Rosmus, 1964).

The temperature of the organism and the temperature of the environment are factors which are presumed to direct the course of aging in collagen structures. But since these factors do not exert an isolated effect in the biological system but are always accompanied by other factors which modify the aging of collagen fibres, it cannot be decided in this system which share can be attributed to the organism's temperature. In this connection it is necessary to point out the shrinkage temperature range which can be expected in mammals and possibly in man under physiological as well as pathological conditions. Sinex (1957) has expressed the hypothesis that collagen aging *in vivo* is caused by body temperature. In this connection it would be interesting to know how the shrinkage temperature in the collagen structure changes in organisms which live alternately in higher and lower temperatures. This refers specifically to fish in cold and warm waters, and possibly to the comparison of the properties in the skin collagen of Eskimos living in warm and possibly arctic climate.

Boucek, Noble, Kao and Elden (1958) mentioned a certain difference in the collagen reactivity in the skin of these races, and they found a difference in the degree of extraction of collagen. Since extraction, along with swelling, shrinkage temperature, contraction and relaxation in some electrolytes are indicators of the degree of netting of the collagen structure, a certain similarity can also be expected in the change of the shrinkage temperature. At present there exists, however, sufficient proof that, for example, collagen proteins age under *in vitro* conditions, i.e., they increase their structural stability. Collagen, whether in solution or in the dry state, in the form of a collagen sponge (Chvapil, Holuša and Šafář, 1966) or membrane, gradually increases its structural stability, whilst the rapidity of this change decreases with a decrease in temperature (Fig. 4).

Radiation is another external factor which alters the process of connective tissue aging. Recently changes caused by gamma rays

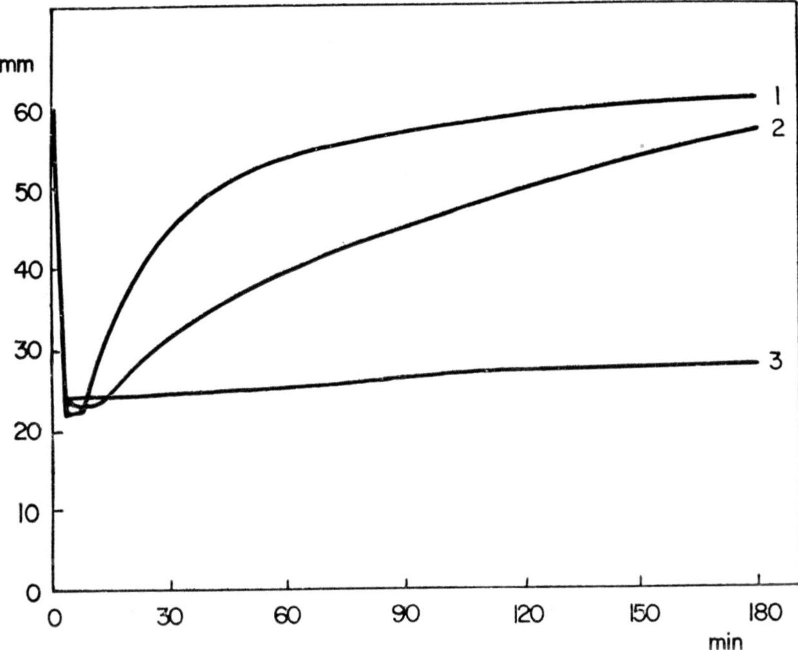

FIGURE 4. Aging of collagen fibre in vitro. The contraction and relaxation phenomenon in 2.5 M sodium perchlorate was studied in collagen fibres isolated from tail tendon in two-month-old rats. The determinations were carried out on fibres immediately after isolation (*curve 1*) and on fibres kept for fourteen (*curve 2*) and 120 days (*curve 3*) in dry state in the tube at 20°. (From Bartoš, 1965.)

which are analogous to age changes have been studied. It has been found that it is possible to bring about the reconstitution of collagen solution by gamma irradiation. Collagen gels are formed, considerably resistant toward swelling and thermal influences, which have no precise shrinkage temperature but rather a range of shrinking temperatures. Their structural stability is very high, but as evident from the above mentioned fact, in some respects it appears to differ from the structural stability of old collagen. The amino acid analysis of these irradiated collagens treated with doses of 0.5 Mrad. do not show the presence of anomalous amino acids. It would seem, therefore, that cross linkages are formed, probably by a free radical mechanism.

Darden, Bradley and Upton (1963) suggested that these cross

TABLE V

CHANGES IN HUMAN DERMIS FROM AGING AND EXPOSURE TO SUNLIGHT

	Aging	*Sun Damage*
Collagen	Increases, less soluble	Decreases, more soluble
Elastin	No change	Increases
Acid mucopolysaccharide	Decreases	Increases
Hexosamine	Decreases	Increases in upper dermis Decreases in lower dermis
Nonfibrous protein	Decreases	Increases

According to Flesch (1964).

linkages are not an integral part of the aging of collagen after observing an identical rise of shrinkage temperature in rat tail tendon collagen from irradiated as well as from non-irradiated rats during the course of aging.

In the course of aging of the collagen structure, cross linkages are formed in the telopeptides and possibly in the polar regions, whereas in the course of irradiation, new cross-linkages may also be formed in nonpolar regions, and with an increasing dose a splitting of the peptide linkage also takes a place. Because the change in T_s has recently been considered to be a manifestation of crystallinity and helix content of the structure, we can take the course of shrinkage in relation to temperature as proportional to the helix content of the structure. The finding that collagen structures irradiated by gamma rays do not show a rapid transition and do not exhibit a great shrinkage velocity evokes the opinion that, in the course of irradiation, the structure retains or even increases its structural stability, but that probably the helix is partly damaged in the sense of helix random coil transition.

The effect of **ultraviolet radiation** has been most closely studied in the skin and there has been a tendency to ascribe all cutaneous manifestation of the aging process to the effect of sunlight. No doubt in the skin parts exposed to sunlight a number of changes in the connective tissue components (and probably also in the nonfibrous components) do occur, but they are very different from the changes occurring during aging, as evident from experiments (Table V).

TABLE VI

INCORPORATION OF C^{14}-HYDROXYPROLINE AND C^{14}-PROLINE INTO SOLUBLE AND INSOLUBLE COLLAGENOUS AND NON-COLLAGENOUS PROTEINS

10^{-4}×Specific Activity (counts/min/μmol)		*Ratio of Collagen to Non-collagen Activity*
Collagenous Hydroxyproline	*Non-collagenous Proline*	
Insoluble proteins		
1.91	8.32	1:4
Soluble proteins		
134.1	12.0	10:1
Ratio of insoluble to soluble protein activity		
1:70	1:1.2	

According to Hurych and Chvapil (1965).
The incorporation studies were carried out in chick embryo skin slices.

Changes in Biological Functions of Connective Tissue During Aging

Among biological functions those phenomena are included that are too complex to permit at present their description with the aid of chemical reactions. Considerations on connective tissue metabolism, the repair process and the formation of antibodies, etc. also belong here. These questions too will probably be worked out in the future by a method similar to the two preceding groups.

Metabolic Synthetic Function

There is a substantial decay in metabolic turnover of collagen proteins in various organs during aging. This represents a striking difference to the metabolism of globular proteins as shown in (Table VI). In collagens isolated from the same tissue, their turnover is related to their extractibility—newly formed collagen extractable in 0.14 M NaCl has a halftime of the same order of magnitude as serum proteins (days), insoluble collagen has a substantially longer halftime (several months). Globular proteins have the same specific activity in spite of their extractibility. Furthermore, the metabolic turnover in collagenous proteins decreases proportionally with age, whereas the metabolic turnover of globular proteins does not substantially change (Hurych and Chvapil, 1965). In this connection it should be mentioned that the activity of RNA, as measured by the incorporation of labeled uracil, is the same in young and old fibroblasts, and that the quantity of RNA in relation to the cell decreases during aging of these cells proportionally with the decrease in collagen synthesis (Woessner, 1962). This proves the different mechanisms of aging of globular and fibrillar connective tissue proteins, and simultaneously presents evidence that the synthesized fibrillar protein ages and not the protein synthesizing system. This statement is also proved by experiments studying the velocity of aging of newly formed collagen in granulation tissue in young and old animals. Collagenous proteins in old animals mature more rapidly (Banfield and Brindley, 1959; Koblet and Frieden, 1960; Verzár and Willenegger, 1961; Hrůza and Hlaváčková, 1963). An experimental gerontologic research of fibroblast functions based on a modern concept would certainly deserve greater attention.

Repair Processes

All considerations of changes in composition and reactivity of connective tissue formed up to now which occur in the course of the lifespan during physiological fibroplasia are repeated in a shortened form during the development of fibroproductive inflammation in the repair process.

Experimentally produced wounds heal more quickly in young animals than in old (Hunt, 1959). Nevertheless it is known that old individuals form, in total, a larger quantity of collagenous structures than young (Boucek, Nobel, Kao and Elden, 1958). Wounds in old animals contain more cells, more blood vessels, and the scars are better and firmer organized than wounds and scars in young rats (Houck and Jacob, 1964). It therefore appears essential to distinguish between the rate of the process and the quantitative aspect of the reaction (Fig. 5).

In several sudies Doberauer (1962, 1963) dealt with the influence of aging upon granulation tissue. He arrived at the conclusion that the three main processes in wound healing, i.e., wound contraction, epithelization and formation of granulation tissue,

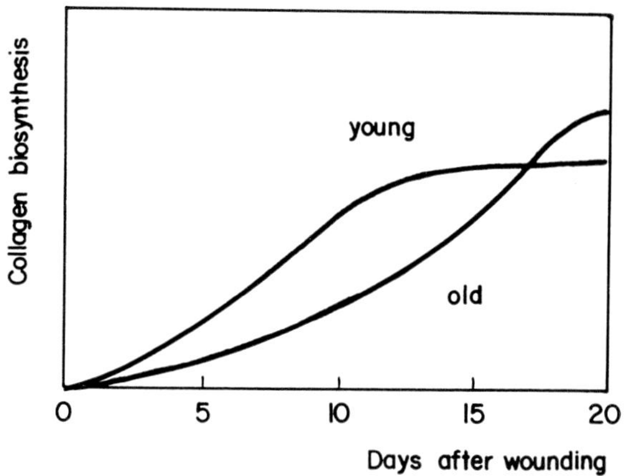

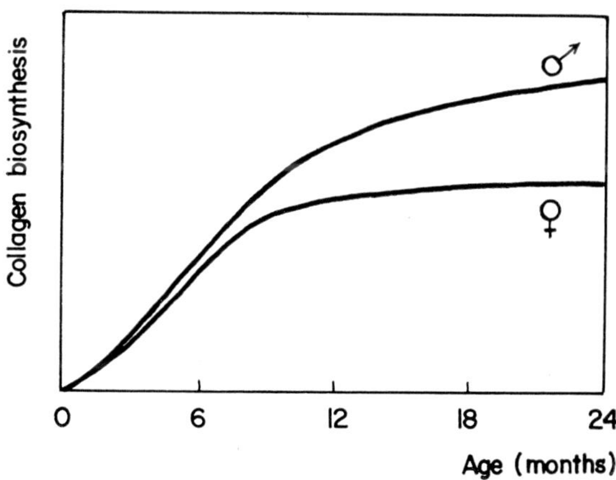

FIGURE 5. Scheme of the effect of the age and sex on the collagen formation capacity during the fibroproductive inflammation. Collagen biosynthesis can be considered in arbitrary units, and the time plot—days after wounding—refers to collagen in granulation tissue. The patterns of collagen reactivity in age and sex relate to every model of fibroproductive inflammation. (From Chvapil and Budínský, 1965.)

change during aging and especially between young and old, whilst between old and very old animals these differences disappear. Doberauer attributed the increased formation of granulation tissue in old and very old animals to the fact that certain systems (of hormonal nature), which limit and control the course of healing, deteriorate.

Forscher and Cecil (1958) found that in adult animals (twelve-month-old rats) the course of healing was slower, and that more frequently degenerative changes in the lesion took place than in younger rats (three-month-old).

The well-known experience of clinicians that in younger individuals symptoms of lung fibrosis appear earlier and the disease takes a quicker course than in the aged has been experimentally confirmed by Ostrovskaja's (1959) extensive data on rats. This observation is connected with the discovery that the connective tissue in young individuals is generally more reactive than that in old, and that the metabolism of collagenous proteins as well as of mucopolysaccharides of the ground substance is quicker in young than in adults or old animals (Neuberger *et al.*, 1955).

Autoregulative Function of the Enzyme-substrate Interaction

Dynamic balance among the individual connective tissue components presumes the existence of enzymatic systems which control the structure and the function of certain components. As an example of such interaction between enzyme and substrate we mention the thoroughly studied influence of the elastase system on the function of connective tissue. Hall (1964) sums up numerous works on the changes in the elastolytic system during aging in the development of arteriosclerosis. In young individuals the elastase as well as the elastolipoproteinase are adsorbed from the plasma into the elastic structure. As in this age elastase inhibitors are present in the plasma and polysaccharides inhibiting elastolysis are in the tissues, no splitting of elastin occurs. As aging proceeds along with the decrease of elastase tissue inhibitor (Yu and Blumenthal, 1958), the first degenerative signs appear in the elastic tissue, but they are always mitigated by the presence of the plasmatic inhibitor. In the final phase of the arteriosclerosis syndrome, there first occurs lipolysis and the binding of the lipids with a large amount of cholesterol, and there is a massive splitting of the elastic tissue in the medium.

Defensive Functions

Another function of connective tissue which I classify as biologic is the *defensive function* with consideration of the antigenicity of connective tissue. From the general point of the biologic reactivity of macromolecules, it would be possible to suppose that antigenicity is connected with the lability of macromolecules and with the reactivity of certain functional groups of the molecule. Because, during aging, the reactivity of macromolecules is generally believed to decrease, however, it is difficult to explain the finding by Heller, Yakulis and Zimmerman (1959) that connective tissue in older animals is a stronger antigen than the tissue in young individuals. Ćervinka, Krajíček, Liška and Vrubel (1964) and Houba and Chvapil (1964) actually proved that the antigenicity of collagen prepared from cattle skin is indirectly proportional to its degree of cross-linking.

There are no data to prove the influence of aging on the composition and reactivity of connective tissue; but still no information is available on how the structure of a tissue (including connective tissue) must be changed so as to cause a change in the function of an organ, and what the interrelation between the dynamics of connective tissue changes and the function of the investigated tissue is.

REFERENCES

ADAM, M., BARTL, P., DEYL, Z., AND ROSMUS, J.: Reaction of gold with collagen *in vivo*. *Experientia, 20*:203, 1964.

ÁRVAY, A., TAKÁCS, J., AND VERZÁR, F.: The effect of pregnancy on the aging of collagen (experiments with rats). *Gerontologia (Basel), 7*:77, 1963.

BANFIELD, W. G., AND BRINDLEY, D. C.: Acetic acid-soluble collagen in human scars. *Surg. Gynec. Obstet., 109*:367, 1959.

BARTOŠ, F.: Changes in some physical-chemical properties of collagen fibres during aging (in Czech.). Ph.D. dissertation, Prague, 1965.

BOUCEK, R. J., NOBLE, N. L., KAO, K. T., AND ELDEN, H. R.: The effects of age, sex and race upon the acetic acid fractions of collagen (human biopsy-connective tissue). *J. Geront., 13*:2, 1958.

CERVINKA, F., KRAJÍČEK, M., LISKA, M., AND VRUBEL, J.: Notes on the question of the antigenicity of collagen. *Folia Biol., 10*:94, 1964.

CHVAPIL, M.: *Physiology of Connective Tissue.* London, Butterworth Sci. Publ., 1966.

CHVAPIL, M., AND BUDÍNSKY, J.: Importance of study of reactivity of connective tissue for obstetrics and gynecology (in Czech). *Čs. Gynek., 30:*428, 1965.

CHVAPIL, M., AND DEYL, Z.: Some theoretical considerations on the aging of collagen. *Gerontologia (Basel), 10:*199, 1965.

CHVAPIL, M., AND HRŮZA, Z.: Sexual differences in the amount and reactivity of connective tissue following an atherogenic diet. *Physiol. Bohemoslov., 11:*430, 1962.

CHVAPIL, M., AND ROTH, Z.: Connective tissue changes in wild and domesticated rats. *J. Geront., 19:*414, 1964.

CHVAPIL, M., HOLUŠA, R., AND ŠAFÁŘ, S.: Experimental and clinical experiences with the collagen sponge as hemostaticum and tampon. *J. Surg. Res.,* 1966. (in press).

CHVAPIL, M., RAKUŠAN, K., WACHTLOVÁ, M., AND POUPA, O.: Collagen content in heart septum in wild and domesticated animals. *Gerontologia (Basel),* 1966 (in press).

DARDEN, E. B., BRADLEY, M., AND UPTON, A. C.: *Influence of early sublethal heterogenous implantation and of breading status on thermal aging of collagen fibers in the mouse.* Proc. of 11th Ann. Meeting of the Rad. Res. Soc., Milwaukee, 1963.

DOBERAUER, W. (Editor): *Scriptum Geriatricum 1962. Vorträge des siebenten Österreichischen Fortbildungskurses für Geriatrie.* Wien, Gesellschaft f. Geriatrie, 1962.

DOBERAUER, W.: Zum Einfluss des Lebensalters auf die Heilung künstlicher Hautdefekte. *Klin. Med., 18:*199, 1963.

FLESCH, P.: Some chemical aspects of aging skin. *Proc. Sci. Sect. Toilet Goods Ass., 41:*23, 1964.

FORSCHER, S. K., AND CECIL, H. C.: Some effects of age on the biochemistry of acute inflammation. *Gerontologia (Basel), 2:*174, 1958.

HALL, D. A.: *Elastolysis and Aging.* Springfield, Thomas, 1964.

HARKNESS, R. D.: Biological functions of collagen. *Biol. Rev., 36:*399, 1961.

HARKNESS, R. D.: The physiology of connective tissue of the reproductive tract. *International Review of Connective Tissue Research, Vol. 2.* New York and London, Academic Press, 1964.

HELLER, P., YAKULIS, V. J., AND ZIMMERMAN, H. J.: Antigenicity of connective tissue extracts. *Proc. Soc. Exp. Biol. Med., 101:*509, 1959.

HOLEČKOVÁ, E., AND CHVAPIL, M.: Effect of domestication on biological age in the rat. *Gerontologia (Basel), 11:*96, 1965.

HÖRMANN, H.: Zur biologischen Entwicklung des Kollogens: Einfluss der zunehmenden Verfestigun auf das physikalische, chemische und biochemische Verhalten des Kollagens. *Beitr. Silikose-Forschung. S.-Bd.* Grundfragen der Silikoseforschung, *5:*205, 1963.

HOUBA, V., AND CHVAPIL, M.: *Die Veränderungen der Antigenizität von Kollagen durch Stabilisierung der Struktur.* Lecture at Symposium on Experimental Gerontology, Basel, 1964.

HOUCK, J. C., AND JACOB, R. A.: Connective tissue. XI Chemical pathology of necrotic wounds. *Proc. Soc. Exp. Biol. Med., 116:*1041, 1964.

HRŮZA, Z., AND CHVAPIL, M.: Collagen characteristics in the skin, tail tendon and lungs in experimental atherosclerosis in the rat. *Physiol. Bohemoslov, 11:*423, 1962.

HRŮZA, Z., AND HLAVÁČKOVÁ, V.: The characteristics of newly formed collagen during aging. *Gerontologia, 7*:221, 1963.

HUNT, A. H.: Wound healing. *Proc. Roy. Soc. Med., 53*:41, 1959.

HURYCH, J., AND CHVAPIL, M.: The role of free hydroxyproline in the biosynthesis of collagen. *Biochim. Biophys. Acta, 107*:91, 1965.

KOBLET, H., AND FRIEDEN, E. H.: Uptake of glycine-1-C^{14} by connective tissue. III. Effects of adrenal hormones and aging. *Proc. Soc. Exp. Biol. Med., 104*:624, 1960.

MACEK, M., CHVAPIL, M., AND HURYCH, J.: Collagen in diploid fibroblasts. *Exptl. Cell Research,* 1966. (in press).

MILCH, R. A.: Studies of collagen tissue aging: Interaction of certain intermediary metabolites with collagen. *Gerontologia (Basel), 7*:129, 1963.

NEUBERGER, A.: Metabolism of collagen under normal conditions. In: *Fibrous Proteins and their Biological Significance.* Symposia Soc. Experiment. Biol., *9*:72, 1955.

OSTROVSKAJA, I. S.: In: Materialy XI. plenuma respublikanskoj komisiji po borbje s silikozom. Izd. AN USSR, Kiev, 1959.

ROLLHÄUSER, H.: Konstitutions -und Altersunterschiede in Festigkeit kollagener Fibrillen. *Jahrbuch f. Morphol. u. mikrosk. Anat., 90*:157, 1951a.

ROLLHÄUSER, H.: Die Festigkeit menschlicher Sehnen nach Quellung und Trocknung in Abhängigkeit vom Lebensalter. *Jahrbuch f. Morphol. u. mikrosk. Anat., 90*:180, 1951b.

SCHAUB, M. C.: Qualitative and quantitative changes of collagen in parenchymatous organs of the rat during aging. *Gerontologia (Basel), 8*:114, 1963.

SCHWARZ, W.: Morphology and differentiation of the connective tissue fibres. *Connective Tissue Symposium, 1957.* Oxford. Blackwell Sci. Publ., 1957.

SINEX, F. M.: Aging and the stability of irreplaceable molecules. *J. Geront., 12*:190, 1957.

VERZÁR, F.: Aging of the collagen fibre. *International Review of Connective Tissue Research, Vol. 2,* New York and London, Academic Press, 1964.

VERZÁR, F., AND WILLENEGGER, H.: Aging of the collagen in skin and scars. *Schweiz. Med. Wschr., 91*:1234, 1961.

VOSTÁL, J., CHVAPIL, M., AND KOMÁRKOVÁ, A.: Biochemical composition of bones in domesticated and wild rats (Czech). *Čs. fysiol., 10*:296, 1961.

WOESSNER, J. F.: Catabolism of collagen and non-collagen protein in the rat uterus during post-partum involution. *Biochem. J., 83*:304, 1962.

YU, S. Y., AND BLUMENTHAL, H. T.: The functional significance of mucopolysaccharide obtained from cattle aorta. *J. Geront., 13*:366, 1958.

Chapter 11

AGING IN RED CELLS

A. M. BERTOLINI

WE HAVE BEEN carrying out for the last few years, at this Institute, a study on the changes of the enzyme systems of human red cells induced by aging. As is well known, enzymatic reaction rates are strongly related to the formation of an enzyme-substrate complex. These reaction rates are, therefore, subject to considerable changes owing to the various causes which interfere in the formation of such enzyme-substrate complexes.

Recently Weber[1] has shed some light on this matter and has classified in two groups the factors which can modify enzyme activities *in vivo* (Fig. 1).

1) First, a certain amount of enzyme must be present, which is actually dependent on the equilibrium existing between the enzyme synthesizing and destroying processes.

2) In the second place, other factors have been proven to be important. Enzymatic reaction rates are, in fact, dependent also on the physical and chemical conditions of the medium (pH range, osmotic pressure, temperature, tension of respiratory gases) as well as on the concentrations of substrates, coenzymes and cofactors which take part in the reaction. Consequently, a study of the enzymatic activities in red cells necessarily involves a parallel investigation of the concentrations of substrates, cofactors and coenzymes as they are found to be present in human red cells under normal conditions.

RESULTS

Enzyme Population in the Aged Erythrocyte

Various enzymes contained in the red cells of young and aged people were tested under the same conditions of pH, ionic strength, incubation temperature and substrate concentrations.

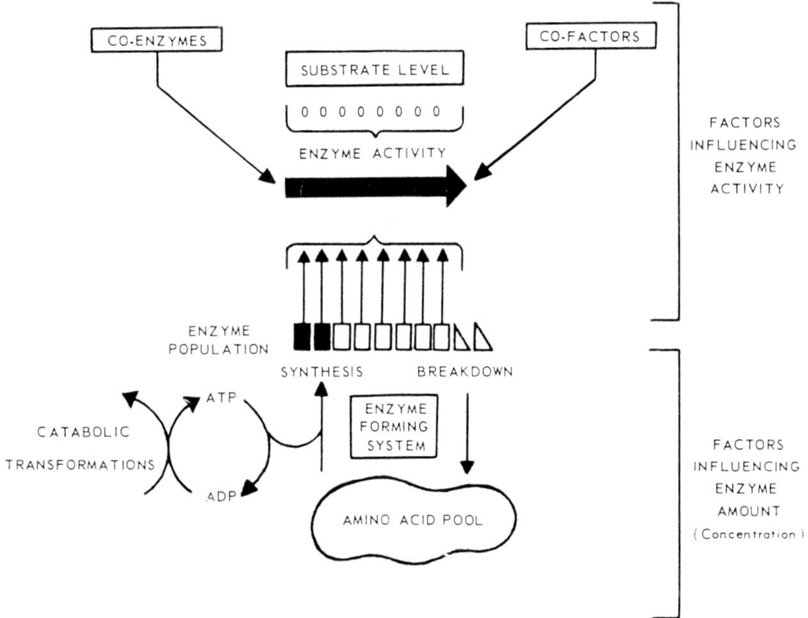

FIGURE 1

Our experiments considered various enzymatic activities, which are subject to change during senility, as described in Table I. From the analysis of the data it can be observed that while some activities, such as the glucose-6-phosphate-dehydrogenase activity,[2] lactic-dehydrogenase activity,[3] catalase activity,[2] and alkaline-phosphatase activity[4] do not show any change with aging, other activities show a departure from normal values of adults. Aldolase activity is reduced about 16 per cent in the aged,[5] glutamic-oxaloacetic-transaminase activity is reduced about 25 per cent,[6] acid phosphatase activity about 33 per cent,[4] and choline esterase activity about the same.[7] On this particular subject it must be pointed out that some authors are of the opinion that the last two activities which we have just mentioned play an important rôle, the former regulating the transport of the phosphate ions to the cells,[8,9] the latter more generally regulating the membrane permeability.[10,11,12] That these negative alterations result in a decrease of enzymatic activities does not surprise us. On the contrary, it suggests some attractive starting points for the interpretation of cellular involution phe-

TABLE I

VARIATIONS OBSERVED IN ELEVEN ERYTHROCYTE ENZYME ACTIVITIES, IN RELATION TO AGE

N.	*Erythrocyte Enzymes*	*Source*	*Activities in Aged Subjects*
1	glucose-6-phosphate-dehydrogenase	hemolysate	
2	lactic-dehydrogenase	stroma	unaltered
3	alkaline-phosphatase	hemolysate	
4	catalase	hemolysate	
5	aldolase	stroma	
6	SGOT	stroma	
7	SGPT	stroma	decreased
8	true choline-esterase	stroma	
9	acid phosphatase	hemolysate	
10	pyrophosphatase	hemolysate	increased
11	diaphorase 1st (NAD dependent)	hemolysate	

nomena in the aged. Furthermore other activities in aged subjects tend to be enhanced, perhaps as an effect of compensation, or perhaps as a more complex phenomenon of the disorganization of the protein-enzyme biosynthesis, which forms the active basis of cell metabolism. In fact, as it is shown in Table I, the pyrophosphatase activity increases about 35 per cent[4] in the aged, and the NAD diaphorase increases accordingly about 30 per cent.[2]

Factors Influencing Enzyme Activity in the Aged Erythrocyte

We did not take into consideration the changes in the physical and chemical characteristics of the erythrocyte medium induced by aging although some alterations are likely to occur also at this level. We examined instead the concentration of coenzymes, cofactors and free substrate in the aged erythrocytes.

Concentration of Coenzymes in the Aged Erythrocytes

The structural requirements for the complete development of an enzyme catalyzed reaction include not only optimal quantities of the enzyme and substrate for the reaction itself, but also of other substances called coenzymes. We limited our study to two aspects of such a complex problem. We observed the change with aging of the total nucleotides, which in the erythrocyte function primarily as phosphate-receptors at high potential, with the adenine nucleotides prevailing among them. We also observed the changes with aging of the nicotinic nucleotides, which quantitatively represent a small fraction of total nucleotides, but actually are very important for their electrontransport function and remarkably useful for the oxidation-reduction processes.

From the results obtained from our experiments, we can state that the erythrocyte content in total nucleotides is subject to only slight variations.

There seems to be only a tendency to an increase of these compounds with age.[13] Since the content of phosphorus with high energy-potential does not show remarkable changes with aging, we can reasonably assume that in an aged erythrocyte there must be an increase of incompletely phosphorylized ADP and AMP nucleotides, which probably indicates an insufficient synthesis of phosphoric esters with high energy-potential, or a slowing down in carbohydrate metabolism.

In regard to the changes with aging of the nicotinic nucleotides contained in the erythrocytes, the data obtained are much more interesting. In the young and adult subjects the concentration of these compounds in erythrocytes remains unaltered up to the sixtieth year of age.[14] After this age a progressive increase of such compounds occurs, while after seventy they decrease approximately 40 per cent. This finding is very constant and we noted it in almost all subjects included in that group.[14]

Concentration of Cofactors in the Aged Erythrocyte

Glutathione is a tripeptide, made up of glutamic acid, cysteine and glycine, which is involved in oxidations and reductions. In these processes it becomes oxidized glutathione, or in other words is converted from GSH into GS-SG. The concentration of synthetized glutathione has been indirectly obtained by determining the sulphydryl groups present in erythrocytes. The mean concentration in reduced sulphydryl groups in erythrocytes was found to be about 70 mg/100 ml of erythrocytes.[15] This value, however, tends to increase 20-30 per cent with aging (see Table II).[16]

Concentration of Free Substrates in the Aged Erythrocyte

Free pentoses have been determined in aged erythrocytes. Such compounds, derived from aerobic glycolysis via the pentose cycle,

TABLE II

VARIATIONS WITH AGING OF FREE SH GROUPS CONCENTRATION IN ERYTHROCYTES
(The values are expressed in mg of reduced glutathione for 100 ml of erythrocytes.)

Groups of Subjects	*GSH mg%*
Average concentration in 123 healthy subjects from 10 to 90 years of age	68.25±14
Average concentration in 32 healthy subjects under 30 years of age	59±20
Average concentration in 54 healthy subjects over 60 years of age	70±21
% variation between the two groups	+30.77%

are found in a very low concentration in the erythrocytes of adults. Over the age of fifty this concentration tends to increase progressively and may even double its value in old age.[13]

DISCUSSION

Normal Erythrocyte Metabolism

The principal function of erythrocytes is to transfer respiratory gases from the pulmonary alveoli to the tissues and *vice-versa*. Practically, the whole amount of O_2 and part of CO_2 is transferred in chemical combination with hemoglobin. Hence, it is necessary to prevent inactivation of this pigment and especially its oxidation to methemoglobin.

The mechanism by which methemoglobin is reduced to hemoglobin is not yet well known in detail. Anyhow, it is associated with the metabolism of glucose[17,18] and depends on $NADPH_2$ and $NADH_2$.[19]
The $NADH_2$ dependent reaction may be summarized as follows:

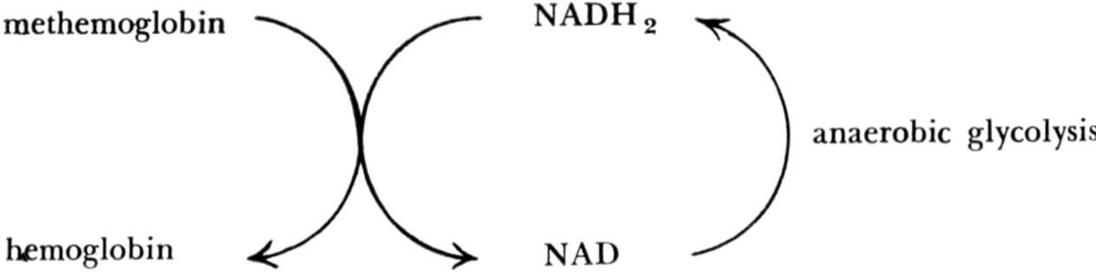

This reaction is catalyzed by a methemoglobin reductase[20] and the $NADH_2$ is supplied by glucose anaerobic utilization. It must be pointed out that the hereditary methemoglobin is associated with lack of this enzyme.[21,22] The reduction of methemoglobin $NADPH_2$ dependent is mediated by glutathione; the reduced glutathione effects directly the methemoglobin reduction through a nonenzymatic reaction, and it is restored by $NADPH_2$ in the presence of a glutathione reductase $NADPH_2$ dependent. As we can see from the following scheme, this mechanism of reduction is, in the end, strongly associated with the pentose shunt:

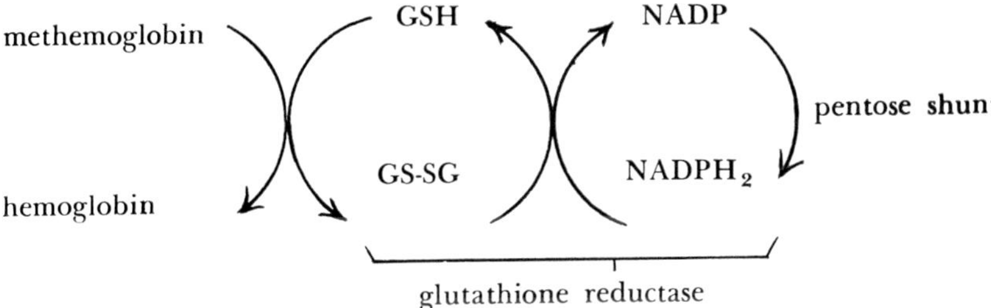

Recently Strömme and Eldjarn[23] have confirmed these experiments on methemoglobin reduction and have demonstrated that two thirds of it are linked to the Embden-Meyerhof pathway of glycolysis ($NADH_2$ regeneration) and the remaining ⅓ to the pentose cycle ($NADPH_2$ regeneration).

Aged Erythrocyte Metabolism

Our results allow us to state that the mechanism of methemoglobin reduction is altered at two different levels: 1) At the level of the $NADPH_2$ regenerating system, otherwise a pentose pool would not occur. It is well known, in fact, that under normal conditions there is no pool of the intermediate metabolites owing to the high enzyme content. 2) At the level of the system responsible for the pyridine coenzyme biosynthesis. These results, in our opinion, provide a biochemical explanation of the experiments performed by Jalavisto;[24] in fact, by nitrifying erythrocytes and changing the whole amount of hemoglobin into methemoglobin, and then observing the slow restoration of hemoglobin from the

TABLE III

BEHAVIOUR OF GLUTATHIONE STABILITY IN RELATION TO AGE, AND EFFECT OF GLUCOSE IN THE INCUBATION MEDIUM

(Buffer of phosphates M/15, pH 7.6, glucose 50 mg per ml of erythrocytes; incubation at 37° C. for 2 hours.) (The values indicate the average per cent variations of GSH concentrations recorded before incubation.)

Groups of Subjects	*N. of Cases*	*Buffer Only*	*Buffer + Glucose*
		Per cent	*Per cent*
Healthy subjects under 30 years of age	39	+ 5.07 ± 0.83	+18.00 ± 2.50
Healthy subjects over 70 years of age	74	−18.2 ± 2.4	− 3.42 ± 1.16

oxidized to the reduced form through the reducing systems of the same erythrocyte put in glucose solution, Jalavisto noticed a slower restoration to normal in the aged than in young erythrocytes.

The aged erythrocyte makes up for this deficiency in part with an abnormal increase of the reduced glutathione pool. The various experiments which we have performed enable us to confirm this statement. By incubating for two hours in a buffer of phosphate M/15 at pH 7.6, the erythrocytes taken from young and aged subjects, we have observed that in the erythrocytes from young

TABLE IV

BEHAVIOUR OF GLUTATHIONE STABILITY IN RELATION TO AGE AND THE EFFECT OF INOSINE ON THE INCUBATION MEDIUM

(Buffer of phosphates M/15, pH 7.6, glucose 50 mg per ml of erythrocytes; incubation at 37° C. for two hours.) (The values indicate the average per cent variations of GSH concentrations recorded before incubation.)

Groups of Subjects	*N. of Cases*	*Buffer Only*	*Buffer + Inosine*
		Per cent	*Per cent*
Healthy subjects under 30 years of age	39	+ 5.07 ± 0.83	− 2.30 ± 1.10
Healthy subjects over 70 years of age	74	−18.2 ± 2.4	−21.10 ± 2.01

subjects there are no significant modifications. On the contrary, in the erythrocytes from the aged there is a breakdown of about 20 per cent in the reduced glutathione concentration.[25] If we add glucose to the medium we observe in the young an increase of 15-20 per cent in the reduced glutathione content. In the aged, instead, the values remain almost unaltered. Inosine added to the incubation medium does not significantly modify the concentration of reduced glutathione in erythrocytes of young or aged sub-

TABLE V

BEHAVIOUR OF GLUTATHIONE STABILITY IN RELATION TO AGE, AND THE EFFECT OF GLUCOSE ON THE INCUBATION MEDIUM

(Buffer of phosphates M/15, pH 7.6, acetylphenylhydrazine 5 mg, glucose 50 mg per ml of erythrocytes; incubation at 37° C. for 2 hours.) (The values indicate the average per cent variations of GSH concentration recorded before incubation.)

Groups of Subjects	*N. of Cases*	*Buffer + APH*	*Buffer + APH + Glucose*
		Per cent	*Per cent*
Healthy subjects under 30 years of age	51	−21.06 ± 2.29	+16.91 ± 2.20
Healthy subjects over 70 years of age	70	−40.77 ± 1.34	−16.90 ± 2.12

jects. Inosine is also unable to prevent the decrease in concentration of reduced glutathione which occurs when the aged erythrocytes are incubated in buffer solution.[25] If erythrocytes are treated with acetylphenylhydrazine, an oxidating drug which stimulates the oxidation of glucose in the erythrocytes via pentophosphates and which tends to transform hemoglobin into methemoglobin, we then observe that in the erythrocytes of healthy subjects there is a decrease of about 20 per cent in the concentration of reduced glutathione. No decrease occurs when glucose and inosine are present in the incubation medium. On the contrary, the aged erythrocytes have a quite different behaviour.[26] In fact, the erythrocytes incubated in a buffer containing acetylphenylhydrazine show a decrease in the concentration of reduced glutathione which is twice as much as under normal conditions, since their values decrease about 40 per cent.[26] This decrease, however, is scarcely modified by adding glucose to the incubation medium and even

TABLE VI

BEHAVIOUR OF GLUTATHIONE STABILITY IN RELATION TO AGE, AND THE EFFECT OF INOSINE ON THE INCUBATION MEDIUM

(Buffer of phosphates M/15, pH 7.6, acetylphenylhydrazine 5 mg, inosine 5 mg per ml of erythrocytes; incubation at 37° C. for two hours.) (The values indicate the average per cent variations of GSH concentration recorded before incubation.)

Groups of Subjects	*N. of Cases*	*Buffer + APH*	*Buffer + Glucose + APH*
		Per cent	*Per cent*
Healthy subjects under 30 years of age	51	−21.06 ± 2.29	− 1.30 ± 0.88
Healthy subjects over 70 years of age	70	−40.77 ± 1.34	−21.71 ± 2.54

less by the addition of inosine. The results of these experiments are summarized in Tables III, IV, V, VI.

Finally, if after an incubation in a medium identical to the previous one (containing glucose and acetylphenylhydrazine), we examine erythrocytes for Heinz bodies[1] we find that aged erythrocytes do not really differ from younger erythrocytes. In the aged, however, there is a slightly larger number of erythrocytes containing more than two inclusions.[27]

Therefore, we can state that in the erythrocytes of the aged, owing to an altered glucose metabolism and to the nicotinic nucleotides reduction, there is a profound adjustment of the reducing mechanism for methemoglobin, partially compensated by an abnormal increase of the reduced glutathione pool. This particular biochemical condition of the aged erythrocyte shows some analogies with other highly interesting hematologic conditions. For instance, in the newly born and during the first week of life there is an increase in the reduced glutathione content,[28] which is accompanied by a very high instability in the presence of oxidating substances, such as phenylhydrazine and acetylphenylhydrazine.[29,30] This behaviour is restored to normal by addition of glu-

[1] Intraerythrocytic inclusions deriving from the oxidative degradation of hemoglobin, converted under these conditions to methemoglobin, sulphohemoglobin, choleglobin and then precipitated with formation of particles of completely denatured hemoglobin.

cose to the incubation medium.[29] Characteristic of this condition is a normal level of glucose-6-phosphate-dehydrogenase[29,30] and an extreme reduction in the nicotinic nucleotides biosynthesis in the erythrocyte, which becomes normal within the second month of life.[31] In primaquine-sensitive subjects and in favism, instead, there is a normal content of reduced erythrocyte glutathione.[15] However, it definitely decreases during hemolytic crises.[32,33] When erythrocytes are incubated *in vitro* with acetylphenylhydrazine, the reduced glutathione stability is very low as its values decrease 75-90 per cent. The addition of glucose may only slightly modify such a condition, while there is a large number (over 50 per cent) of erythrocytes containing five or more Heinz bodies.[34,35] In this pathological condition there is a characteristic absence or extreme reduction of glucose-6-phosphate-dehydrogenase, so that glucose oxidative metabolism is much reduced or almost absent.[36,37] It is therefore evident that in the presence of substances such as the previous ones, which increase the requirement of reducing groups and consequently stimulate the glucose oxidative metabolism, the erythrocyte so altered is unable to supply the $NADPH_2$ and, of course, the reduced glutathione which are required. A massive denaturation of the hemoglobin is the result.

A comparison of the characteristics of the two conditions shows that the aged erythrocyte occupies an intermediate position. It approaches the erythrocyte of a newly born in its normal glucose-6-phosphate-dehydrogenase content, higher basal levels of reduced glutathione and low nicotinic nucleotides content. It also approaches the erythrocyte of primaquine-sensitive subjects in its weak response to the addition of glucose. In aged erythrocytes the biochemical lesion takes place at different levels. Therefore, the metabolic damage is not monocentric but pluricentric.

CONCLUSIONS

The inability to reduce methemoglobin to hemoglobin, under particular experimental conditions, is one of the most characteristic aspects of the aged erythrocyte. Information on this matter is not hard to find. In our opinion the aged erythrocyte holds an intermediate position between that of the newly born—as to the glucose-6-phosphate-dehydrogenase normal content, the higher levels of reduced glutathione and the extreme reduction of nicotinic nucleotides—and the erythrocyte of a primaquine-sensitive subject—as to the difficulty in oxidizing glucose.

It is necessary to know the biochemical lesions which are typical of the aged erythrocyte, in order to start a therapeutic trial. For this reason, the results which we have obtained and those previously reported in the literature may elucidate the behaviour of aged red blood cells as to their low capacity to reduce methemoglobin and on the other hand may provide modern suggestions for substitutive therapy on a coenzyme basis. It is worth remembering, in this regard, that some of the attempts which we made *in vitro* to increase erythrocyte content of nicotinic nucleotides by incubating aged erythrocytes in a medium high in vitamin PP were particularly successful.[38]

In regard to other aspects of the erythrocyte metabolism it is hard to venture ideas, because of the lack of knowledge of aged red blood cells. A systematic, preliminary investigation is therefore required.

REFERENCES

1. Weber, G.: Study and evaluation of regulation of enzyme activity and synthesis in mammalian liver. *Adv. Enzyme Regulation, 1:*1, 1963.
2. Bertolini, A. M., Quarto di Palo, F. M., and Gastaldi, L.: Diaphorase I, catalase and glucose-6-phosphate dehydrogenase activity in the erythrocytes of aged subjects. *Gerontologia (Basel), 10:*167, 1964/65.
3. Bertolini, A. M., Massari, N., and Civardi, F.: L'attività latticodeidrogenasica degli stromi eritrocitari nella senescenza globulare. Nota III. *G. Geront., 9:*547, 1961.
4. Bertolini, A. M., Quarto di Palo, F. M., and Gastaldi, L.: Le variazioni della fosfatasi alcalina, acida e della pirofosfatasi eritrocitarie durante l'invecchiamento fisiologico dell'emazia e l'invecchiamento dell'organismo. *Acta Geront. 12:*81, 1962.
5. Bertolini, A. M., Massari, N., Civardi, F., and Tenconi, L.: L'attività aldolasica degli stromi eritrocitari nella senescenza globulare. Nota IV. *G. Geront., 9:*551, 1961.
6. Bertolini, A. M., Massari, N., and Civardi, F.: L'attività transaminasica degli stromi eritrocitari nella senescenza globulare. Nota I. *G. Geront., 9:*537, 1961.
7. Bertolini, A. M., Massari, N., and Guardamagna, C.: L'attività colinesterasica vera degli stromi eritrocitari nella senescenza globulare. Nota II. *G. Geront., 9:*543, 1961.
8. Prankerd, T. A. J., and Altman, K. I.: A study of the metabolism of phosphorus in mammalian red cells. *Biochem. J., 58:*622, 1954.

9. Prankerd, T. A. J., and Altman, K. I.: The effect of adenosine on the phosphate exchange in mammalian red blood cells. *Biochim. Biophys. Acta., 15:*158, 1954.

10. Goodman, J. R., Marrone, L. M., and Squire, M. C.: Effect of *in vivo* inhibition of cholinesterase on potassium diffusion from the red cell *Amer. J. Physiol., 180:*118, 1955.

11. Lindvig, P. E., Greig, M. E., and Peterson, S. W.: Studies on permeability. V. The effect of acetylcholine and physostigmine on the permeability of human erytrocytes to sodium and potassium. *Arch. Biochem., 30:*41, 1951.

12. Greig, M. E., Faulkner, J. S., and Mayberry, T. C.: Studies on permeability. IX. Replacement of potassium in erythrocytes during cholinesterase activity. *Arch. Biochem., 43:*39, 1954.

13. Bertolini, A. M., Quarto di Palo, F. M., and Spinnler, H. R.: Modificazioni del contenuto in nucleotidi ed in pentosi liberi del globulo rosso nelle varie età della vita e nel corso dell'invecchiamento fisiologico eritrocitario. *Acta Gerontol., 12:*31, 1962.

14. Bertolini, A. M., Quarto di Palo, F. M., and Gastaldi, L.: Il contenuto eritrocitario in nucleotidi piridinici e le sue variazioni con l'età ed in alcune condizioni patologiche. *Acta Gerontol., 12:*44, 1962.

15. Carcassi, U.: *Eritroenzimopatie ed anemie emolitiche.* Pisa, Omnia Medica, 1959.

16. Bertolini, A. M., Quarto di Palo, F. M., and Spinnler, H. R.: Le variazioni in rapporto all'età dell'individuo e durante l'invecchiamento fisiologico dell'emazia del contenuto eritrocitario in gruppi—SH. *Acta Gerontol., 12:* 160, 1962.

17. Wendel, W. B.: Oxidation of lactate by methemoglobin in erythrocytes with regeneration of hemoglobin. *Soc. Exp. Biol. N.Y., 28:*401, 1930.

18. Kiese, M.: Die reduktion des Hämiglobins. *Biochem. Z., 316:264,* 1944.

19. Gutmann, H. R., Jandorf, B. J., and Bodansky, O.: The role of pyridine nucleotides in the reduction of methemoglobin. *J. Biol. Chem., 169:*145, 1947.

20. Gibson, Q. H.: The reduction of methaemoglobin in red blood cells and studies on the cause of idiopatic methaemoglobinaemia. *Biochem. J., 42:*13, 1948.

21. Scott, E. M., and Griffith, I. V.: The enzymic defect of hereditary methemoglobinemia: diaphorase. *Biochim. Biophys. Acta., 34:*584, 1959.

22. Scott, E. M.: The relation of diaphorase of human erythrocytes to inheritance of methemoglobinemia. *J. Clin. Invest., 39:*1176, 1960.

23. Strömme, J. H., and Eldjarn, L.: The role of the pentose phosphate pathway in the reduction of methaemoglobin in human erythrocytes. *Biochem. J., 84:*406, 1962.

24. Jalavisto, E., Salmela, H.: Red cell methemoglobin reduction rate in blood donors, geriatric patients and patients with various clinical conditions. *Ann. Acad. Sci. Fenn.* A5, *75:*1, 1961.

25. Bertolini, A. M., Quarto di Palo, F. M., and Spinnler, H. R.: Variazioni della concentrazione dei gruppi—SH negli eritrociti umani incubati con glucosio od inosina a seconda della età e del sesso dell'individuo. *Atti Accad. Med. Lombard., 17:*127, 1962.

26. Bertolini, A. M., Quarto di Palo, F. M., and Spinnler, H. R.: Le variazioni della stabilità del glutatione eritrocitario in rapporto all'età ed al sesso dell'individuo. *Acta Gerontol., 17:*166, 1962.

27. Quarto di Palo, F. M., and Ciconali, M.: Effetto dell'età del soggetto donatore sulla comparsa di corpi di Heinz nelle emazie incubate *in vitro* con acetilfenilidrazina. *Atti Accad. Med. Lombard., 17*:389, 1962.

28. Szeinberg, A., Ramot, B., Sheba, C., Adam, A., Halbrecht, I., Rikover, M., Wishnievsky, S., and Rabau, E.: Glutathione metabolism in cord and newborn infant blood. *J. Clin. Invest., 37*:1436, 1958.

29. Zinkham, W. H.: An *in vitro* abnormality of glutathione metabolism in erythrocytes from normal newborns: mechanism and clinical significance. *Pediatrics, 23*:18, 1959.

30. Gross, R. T., and Hurwitz, R. E.: The pentose phosphate pathway in human erythrocytes; relationship between the age of the subject and enzyme activity. *Pediatrics, 22*:453, 1958.

31. Habermann, V., and Habermannová, S.: Age difference in nicotinamide mononucleotide synthesis by human erythrocytes. *Nature (London), 186*:389, 1960.

32. Beutler, E.: *In vitro* studies of the stability of red cell glutathione: a new test for drug sensitivity. *J. Clin. Invest., 35*:690, 1956.

33. Beutler, E.: The glutathione instability of drug-sensitive red cells. A new method for the *in vivo* detection of drug sensitivity. *J. Lab. Clin. Med., 49*:84, 1957.

34. Beutler, E., Dern, R. J., and Alving, A. S.: The hemolytic effect of primaquine. VI. An *in vivo* test for sensitivity of erythrocytes to primaquine. *J. Lab. Clin. Med., 45*:40, 1955.

35. Larizza, P., Brunetti, P., Grignani, F., and Ventura, S.: L'individualità bioenzimatica dell'eritrocito "fabico". Sopra alcune anomalie biochimiche ed enzimatiche delle emazie nei pazienti affetti da favismo e nei loro familiari. *Haematologia (Pavia), 43*:205, 1958.

36. Gross, R. T., Hurwitz, R. E., and Marks, P. A.: An hereditary enzymatic defect in erythrocyte metabolism: glucose-6-phosphate dehydrogenase deficiency. *J. Clin. Invest., 37*:1176, 1958.

37. Waller, H. D., Löhr, G. W., and Tabatabai, M.: Hämolyse und Fehen von glucose-6-phosphat-dehydrogenase in roten Blutzellen (Eine Fermentanomalie der Erythrocyten). *Klin. Wschr., 35*:1022, 1957.

38. Bertolini, A. M., Quarto di Palo, F. M., and Gastaldi, L.: Le variazioni con l'età dell'individuo nella biosintesi eritrocitaria dei nucleotidi nicotinici. *Acta. Geront., 12*:156, 1962.

Chapter 12

ENZYMES IN THE STUDY OF BIOLOGICAL AGING

CHARLES H. BARROWS, JR.

INTRODUCTION

THE CONCEPT of program has been proposed to account for the orderly sequence of events which takes place throughout the life span of an organism. Although little detailed information is available to either define or describe this program, it is logical to assume that the sites of control are the individual cells of the organism. Furthermore, the ultimate information source would seem to reside in the genetic material of the cell. It has been proposed that the DNA molecules are the sites of coded information which is transmitted to messenger RNA and used in the formation of protein molecules. These proteins include enzymes which regulate the reactions which are necessary for cellular maintenance and function. It is obvious that the total information needed by the organism must be contained originally within the fertilized ovum. However, it would seem that the information transmitted during embryogenesis must differ from that transmitted during later life in order to account for mechanisms such as cellular differentiation which appear to be associated with initial development. In addition, the physiological and biochemical events which accompany growth are different from those associated with middle and old age. This suggests other changes in the transmission of information during the life span. Nevertheless, in the study of aging, the continuity of the program should not be excluded since the influence of events during early life on those of later periods is unknown. Most gerontologists, however, have been concerned with that portion of the program associated with the interval from the cessation of growth until death.

CHANGES IN ENZYMATIC ACTIVITIES ASSOCIATED WITH SENESCENCE

The enzymatic activities of tissues have been used to define that portion of the program associated with senescence. Age changes in enzymatic activities may be used as expressions of alterations in regulatory mechanisms of physiological functions, cellular particulates and protein synthesis.

Regulatory Mechanisms of Physiological Functions

It has been proposed that those tissues whose cells retain regenerative capacity exhibit little change with senescence, whereas those which contain the so-called fixed postmitotic cells, which are highly differentiated, such as muscle and nerve tissue, show marked alterations with age. This concept is generally accepted by most gerontologists since it appears to explain the age-associated loss of or impairment in physiological functions which have been observed in muscle and nerve but not in liver or intestinal epithelium. Furthermore, it would seem that age changes, if they occur in the latter type of tissue, may be reversed or compensated for by cellular replication with a preferential loss of those cells affected by age. Thus, it seems likely that age changes in enzymes, which regulate the rates of various biochemical reactions which are necessary for physiological functions, are more likely to be detected in the fixed postmitotic cells than in those which retain regenerative capacity. In general, this concept appears to agree with experimental fact. For example, Schmukler and Barrows (1966) reported that a senescent decrement in lactic dehydrogenase activity occurred in skeletal muscle but not in liver of female rats. The activity of ATPase has been shown to decline with age in the flight muscle of houseflies (Rockstein and Brandt, 1963) and in the skeletal muscle of rats (Rockstein and Brandt, 1961) but not in rat liver (Ross and Ely, 1954).

Similar differences in the effect of age on enzymatic activities have been observed between kidney and liver tissue. The activity of renal but not hepatic succinoxidase decreased significantly with senescence in the rat (Barrows, Yiengst and Shock, 1958; Barrows, Falzone and Shock, 1960). Franklin (1962) showed that the total acid phosphatase per unit of tissue nitrogen as well as the per cent activation by Triton X-100 were significantly lower in the kidneys of twenty-three to twenty-five-month-old rats than in twelve to fourteen-month-old animals. No senescent change occurred in either variable in liver tissue.

The tissues which contain highly differentiated cells exhibit age changes not only in those metabolic pathways which they have in common with other types of tissue, but also in their highly specialized functions. For example, Adams and Barrows (1963) and Beauchene, Fanestil and Barrows (1965) showed that the ability of renal cells of rats to perform work as estimated by the active transport of para-aminohippurate (PAH) was markedly reduced with age. Furthermore, a similar impairment was observed in the transport of alpha aminoisobutyrate (AIB), a compound which involves a different biochemical pathway. The activity of Na^+ + K^+-stimulated-ATPase, an enzyme shown to be necessary for the active transport of a variety of substances, was determined in the kidney tissue of these same animals. A striking age decrement in this enzymatic activity accompanied the senescent decreases in PAH and AIB uptakes. Thus the age-dependent impairment in active transport was correlated with a decrement in the activity of an enzyme which is involved in the utilization of energy for this physiological function. On the other hand, Calingaert and Zorzoli (1965) showed that the accumulation of 6-deoxy-D-glucose per unit wet weight by the intestines of mice was not diminished with age. Therefore taken as a whole these data support the concept that age-associated impairments in biochemical systems are most likely to be found in those which regulate specialized physiological functions of highly differentiated cells.

Cellular Particulates

Within the cells are various morphologically identifiable particles which may be isolated by means of differential centrifugation. Present knowledge indicates that these particulates carry out specific cellular functions. For example, the nuclei contain the genetic material which may serve as the information source of the cell; mitochondria provide energy for various cellular functions; microsomes or polysomes are the sites of protein synthesis, and lysosomes may provide the mechanisms for the hydrolysis of intracellular material. Some of the problems inherent in studies of particulates include: 1) the degree to which an enzymatic activity is associated with various particulates, 2) the extent of loss or damage of the particulate during isolation procedures as well as age differences in their fragility and 3) the difficulty of obtaining total enzymatic activity of certain preparations. Nevertheless, it is important to determine whether or not aging affects the quantity and/or quality of the various subcellular particulates.

Barrows, Falzone and Shock (1960) investigated the effect of age on mitochondrial systems in the livers and kidneys of rats. In whole homogenates prepared from renal tissue, senescent decrements in succinoxidase activity as well as in the rates of succinate-stimulated oxidative phosphorylation were observed. No change in the number of cells per unit wet weight of kidney, estimated by the concentration of deoxyribonucleic acid (DNA) occurred. No age-dependent decrements in the succinoxidase activity, based on the protein-nitrogen content of mitochondria isolated from kidney cortical tissue, were established. Comparisons of the protein nitrogen content of mitochondria from young and old rats, based on the turbidimetric estimation of the number of particles within the suspension, also failed to demonstrate any differences. No age-associated alterations were found in liver tissue. These findings were interpreted as indicating a loss of mitochondria from renal but not hepatic cells with senescence. However, there was no evidence for an age-associated biochemical change in the existing mitochondria.

A similar conclusion may be drawn from the data of Rockstein who showed that the number of mitochondria declined with age in the flight muscles of house flies (Rockstein and Bhatnagar, 1965) and that the cytochrome oxidase activity of this tissue decreases proportionally with senescence (Clark and Rockstein, 1964). Calculation of the ratio of enzymatic activity per particulate indicates that the enzyme content of the existing mitochondria remained relatively stable from adulthood (eight days) through senescence (nineteen days).

Lysosomes, first described by de Duve, Pressman, Gianetto, Wattiaux and Applemans (1955), seem to be the intracellular sites of activity of a number of hydrolytic enzymes including phosphatases, cathepsins and RNase. The role proposed for these particulates and the enzymes which they contain is still obscure. Apparently the hydrolytic enzymes are held within the normally impermeable membrane so that uncontrolled degradation of cell constituents cannot take place. However, Bourne (1957) has suggested that an increase in the enzymatic activities of these particulates in tissues of senescent organisms through the loss of some as yet unidentified inhibitory control may help to explain the progressive inefficiency and degeneration of tissues as they age.

Data have been reported which showed a marked increase with senescence in the catheptic activity of liver (Barrows and Roeder, 1961; Barrows, Roeder and Falzone, 1962). On the other hand, the acid phosphatase activity of this tissue did not change with age (Barrows and Roeder, 1961; Franklin, 1962; Ross and Ely, 1954). In addition, although an age-dependent increment in catheptic activity was shown to occur in renal tissue of rats (Barrows and Roeder, 1961), Franklin (1962) reported that the total acid phosphatase activity in the rat kidney declined with age. Therefore, the differential effects of age on these lysosomal enzymes indicates that although senescence may be associated with changes in the number of lysosomes per cell, it must also be accompanied by biochemical alterations in these particles.

Protein Synthesis

It has often been stated that among the various cellular constituents, proteins may be considered the most important because they perform a great number of physiological functions. For example, proteins include: enzymes which control the rates of chemical reactions of the body, hypophyseal hormones which regulate the secretion of other endocrine glands and therefore affect cellular metabolism, antibodies and complement which play key roles in the resistance to infections, and contractile muscle tissue upon which the motility of the organism depends. Many of the concepts of aging have included the inability of senescent organisms to maintain one or a number of these various tissue components. It is therefore important to determine the effect of age on the ability to synthesize protein molecules.

The techniques available for estimating protein synthesis include nitrogen balance measurements, determination of rates of incorporation of labeled amino acids and measurement of specific tissue proteins. Among these proteins are the various enzymes and determination of their activities during protein depletion and repletion provides an estimation of the ability of the tissue to synthesize these molecules. Employing this technique, Barrows and Roeder (1961) failed to demonstrate any age differences in the loss of activities during depletion or the increment during repletion of seven enzymes in various tissues of female rats. In addition, Gregerman (1959) found no age-dependent differences in the adaptive responses of tryptophan peroxidase and tyrosine transaminase to substrate or hydrocortisone administration in the livers of rats. These data provide no evidence to support the concept that there is an impairment in protein synthesis during senescence.

Research Projections

One of the most pressing needs in gerontological research is a more detailed description of the program during the latter part of life. Additional information is needed to evaluate age-associated changes in subcellular particulates. With the development of improved isolation procedures, the age-dependent changes in the biochemical characteristics of lysosomes, including the role of cathepsin, should be established. The inter-relationships among the different particulates may provide key information in this regard. For example, cathepsin may be involved in over-all protein turnover through the hydrolysis of large molecules for resynthesis. Incorporation studies in microsomes, as well as identification and measurement of the specific enzymes involved in protein synthesis in these particles, should therefore be carried out. Extension of studies on adaptive enzymes as an estimate of protein-synthesizing capacity should include tissues such as kidney, brain and muscle since it seems evident that senescent changes are more likely to occur in these tissues than in those which retain regenerative capacity such as liver. The specialized functions of fixed post-mitotic cells also appear to be highly susceptible to the influence of age and warrant more extensive investigation. For example, the effect of senescence on the transmission of nerve impulses should be examined by measuring the activities of cholinesterase and $Na^+ + K^+$-stimulated-ATPase in brain and specific neural tissues.

The physiological and biochemical changes which have been shown to occur during the late period of the life cycle have stimulated gerontologists to propose that senescence is an expression of alterations in the program which have affected the transmission of its information during the latter part of life. One of the current theories of aging, proposed by Medvedev (1962) and Wulff, Quastler and Sherman (1962), attempts to explain the occurrence of such changes and is referred to as the "Error Theory." Although the term "error" seems to imply an accident, it should be pointed out that such changes may be a built-in part of the total program. In either event, this hypothesis proposes that with senescence alterations occur in the structure of the deoxyribonucleic acid (DNA) molecule. This error is transmitted to messenger ribonucleic acid (RNA) and ultimately to newly synthesized enzymes. These defective enzymes may be inactive, and therefore an accumulation of substrates within the cell may take place. This accumulation may stimulate an increase in RNA and enzyme synthesis to compensate for the defective enzymes. If the production of inactive enzymes proceeds to the point that increased synthesis cannot compensate for the error, death of the cell and ultimately of the organism would result.

Although this theory proposes increased rates of synthesis of RNA and protein with age, little or no senescent changes in the concentration of total proteins in tissues have been found (Barrows, Yiengst and Shock, 1958; Barrows, Falzone and Shock, 1960), and age-associated increases in the concentration of RNA have not been a consistent finding (Barrows, Roeder and Falzone, 1962; Wulff, Piekielniak and Wayner, 1963). Thus, if the cells of older organisms maintain constant levels of these components in the presence of the proposed compensatory mechanisms, the hypothesis would be valid only if increased rates of catabolism as well as anabolism of both the protein and nucleic acid occurred in the presence of errors. Therefore, one would predict increases in the activities of enzymes involved in such metabolic pathways. For example, increments in the activities of cathepsin to account for increased protein catabolism and of RNase and specific nucleotidases to carry out increased metabolism of the nucleic acid should occur during the proposed process. Although the specific enzymes involved in the anabolism of these components are not fully known, it should be possible to demonstrate increases in the incorporations of amino acids and nucleotides into protein and RNA respectively under these conditions. At the present time, only fragmentary data are available to support this concept. Age-associated increases in the catheptic activity of liver and in the rate of disappearance of S^{35}-methionine from liver proteins indicated a greater protein catabolism in old than in young rats (Barrows and Roeder, 1961). Studies on the incorporation of H^{3}-cytidine into nuclear RNA of rat liver (Wulff, Quastler and Sherman, 1964) suggested an increased nucleic acid synthesis with age. It must be pointed out that conclusive proof of the validity of the theory must include demonstration that the proposed changes take place when errors are known to be present. Experiments should be carried out in which errors are experimentally introduced into protein and RNA molecules of laboratory animals by feeding analogs of amino acids and nucleotides and the tissues then examined for the predicted biochemical alterations. In addition, studies must be conducted to show that aging is accompanied by these same changes. Other techniques which may prove useful in demonstrating the presence of errors in the tissues of senescent organisms include determination of the specific activity of isolated enzymes. A decrement with age would suggest that a portion of the isolated protein is in an inactive form. In addition, since it is possible that errors of a certain type could be incorporated without inactivation of the enzyme, the effect of age on the qualitative and quantitative patterns of isozymes, which are structurally different forms of a given enzyme, should be investigated.

CHANGES IN ENZYMATIC ACTIVITIES ASSOCIATED WITH ALTERED LIFE SPAN

Another approach to the problem of biological aging would be to determine the deviations in the program which are brought about by those experimental conditions which alter life span. An alteration in program may take place as 1) a change in the rate of transmission of information of the total program; 2) a change in the rate of transmission of information only in certain portions of the program, or 3) the transmission of information which differs from that normally in the program. The pattern of change of most enzymatic activities throughout the life span was characterized by an increase in activity during early life, a period of relatively stable values during adulthood, and a decrease in activity during senescence (Barrows, 1956; Barrows and Roeder, 1961). Investigations were recently carried out to determine whether the program as expressed by this pattern of enzymatic activity was influenced by certain experimental conditions which would affect life span. In the rotifer it was shown that life span can be altered through nutrition (Fanestil and Barrows, 1965). For example, the mean life span of rotifers transferred to fresh pond water daily and given algae (Group A) was 34.0 days, whereas that of animals deprived of algae (Group B) was 45.3 days. Rotifers deprived of algae and transferred to fresh pond water only on Mondays, Wednesdays and Fridays (Group C) lived for 54.7 days. Although the normal age-associated pattern of change in the activities of malic dehydrogenase (MDH) and lactic dehydrogenase (LDH) was observed under all three dietary regimens, restriction delayed the time of occurrence of the changes. In order to minimize the influence of changes in body mass on the changes in the enzymatic activities, the ratio MDH/LDH was calculated in individual animals. In control rotifers this ratio decreased markedly at the age of thirteen days. Reduced dietary intake (Group C) delayed this decrement until the thirty-third day of life. The displacement of the age changes in enzymatic activities towards later life found in rotifers whose life span was increased by dietary restriction is similar to that described by Ross (1959) for various enzymatic activities in the livers of rats. Thus, these data support the concept that changes in the activities of enzymes may be used as expressions of alterations in the program associated with experimental changes in life span. In order to add assurance that the observed biochemical changes reflected alterations in the program, attempts were made to relate the changes in enzymatic activities with a physiological function, *viz.*, egg production in the rotifer. Although no difference was observed in the total number of eggs produced by the animals, the end of the period of fertility occurred at twelve, twenty-two, and thirty days in Groups A, B and C, respectively. Since egg laying started on the fourth day in all groups, the increase in life span due to dietary restriction was accompanied by an increase in the length of the egg-producing period. Thus, the data indicate that the information of the program for enzymatic activities is intimately associated with that for fecundity.

In contrast to the marked influence of dietary restriction in delaying the biochemical and physiological changes which occur during early life, this experimental variable had little or no effect on the time lived after the cessation of egg production or drop in MDH to LDH ratio. The latter finding was supported by data obtained on rats whose life span could not be prolonged if dietary restriction was initiated in late life, that is, at the ages of twelve or nineteen months (Barrows and Roeder, 1965). These findings suggested that there may be two discrete parts of the program, one associated with early life and influenced by nutrition and a second associated with late life which is not altered by dietary intake. Since rotifers are poikilothermic animals, it was possible to investigate this concept further by varying the environmental temperature. Increases in environmental temperature markedly decreased the life span of the rotifer (Fanestil and Barrows, 1965) However, this resulted from a shortening of that period of life from the end of fertility (or drop in MDH to LDH ratio) to death. This finding gave additional support to the proposal that there are two discrete parts of the program and indicated that they are preferentially affected by different experimental conditions. The transmission of information during early life was delayed by undernutrition but unaffected by temperature, whereas that during later life was influenced by temperature and not by nutrition.

In contrast, data are available which indicate that the transmission of information which differs from that normally in the program may be associated with altered life span under certain experimental conditions. For example, the displacement of age changes in enzymatic activity towards later life associated with increased longevity in the studies of Ross (1959) was brought about by feeding the rats a low (8 per cent) protein diet *ad lib*. It is also possible to increase longevity in this species by feeding restricted amounts of an adequate protein diet (Berg and Simms, 1960). However, the data of Barrows and Roeder (1963) showed that this latter type of restriction was not associated with a retardation of the normal pattern of age-dependent changes in enzymatic activities. In contrast, the levels of activity of certain enzymes were higher in restricted rats than those attained by normal animals at any age. Thus, the data suggested that this experimental condition resulted in the transmission of information which differed from that in normal animals. A similar conclusion may be drawn from the finding of Ingle, Wood and Banta (1937) that dietary restriction decreased the total number of young produced by *Daphnia*.

It would be more satisfying if a universal law applied with respect to the impact of experimental manipulations which alter life span on the program. It is possible that discrepancies are apparent because of the choice of variables used to express the program. Thus, future studies must include examinations of additional variables with the goal of identifying those processes in the life cycle which are sensitive indices of the program. On the basis of observations by Hayflick (1965) that fibroblasts grown in tissue culture could not be maintained following approximately fifty cell divisions, it may be proposed that cells are programmed to undergo a finite number of replications during the life span of an organism. The possibility that a slower rate of replication in the tissues of restricted animals accounts for their increased longevity must be examined. The rates of mitoses in various tissues could be estimated by measuring the incorporation of radioactive thymidine by biochemical and radioautographic techniques. Such studies should be carried out on animals subjected to a variety of experimental conditions which affect life span. Undernutrition can be used to alter longevity in numerous species whereas decreased environmental temperature will lengthen life span only in poikilotherms. However, cold temperature as well as noise and bacterial infections could be employed as stress conditions to decrease longevity in homeotherms.

REFERENCES

Adams, J. R., and Barrows, C. H., Jr.: Effect of age on PAH accumulation by kidney slices of female rats. *J. Geront.*, *18*:37, 1963.

Barrows, C. H., Jr.: Cellular metabolism and aging. *Fed. Proc., Baltimore, 15*:954, 1956.

Barrows, C. H., Jr., Falzone, J. A., Jr., and Shock, N. W.: Age differences in the succinoxidase activity of homogenates and mitochondria from the livers and kidneys of rats. *J. Geront. 15*:130, 1960.

Barrows, C. H., Jr., and Roeder, L. M.: Effect of age on protein synthesis in rats. *J. Geront., 16:*321, 1961.

Barrows, C. H., Jr., and Roeder, L. M.: Effects of reduced dietary intake on the activities of various enzymes in the livers and kidneys of growing male rats. *J. Geront., 18:*135, 1963.

Barrows, C. H., Jr., and Roeder, L. M.: The effect of reduced dietary intake on enzymatic activities and life span of rats. *J. Geront., 20:*69, 1965.

Barrows, C. H., Jr., Roeder, L. M., and Falzone, J. A., Jr.: Effect of age on activities of enzymes and concentrations of nucleic acids in tissues of female wild rats. *J. Geront., 17:*144, 1962.

Barrows, C. H., Jr., Yiengst, M. J., and Shock, N. W.: Senescence and the metabolism of various tissues of rats. *J. Geront., 13:*351, 1958.

Beauchene, R. E., Fanestil, D. D., and Barrows, C. H., Jr.: The effect of age on active transport and sodium-potassium-activated ATPase activity in renal tissue of rats. *J. Geront., 20:*306, 1965.

Berg, B. N., and Simms, H. S.: Nutrition and longevity in the rat. II. Longevity and onset of disease with different levels of food intake. *J. Nutrit., 71:*255, 1960.

Bourne, G. H.: The aging of mammalian cells. *In:* W. B. Yapp and G. H. Bourne (Eds.), *The Biology of Aging.* New York, Hafner, 1957, pp. 35-46.

Calingaert, A., and Zorzoli, A.: The influence of age on 6-deoxy-D-glucose accumulation by mouse intestine. *J. Geront., 20:*211, 1965.

Clark, A. M., and Rockstein, M.: Aging in insects. In: *Physiology of Insecta,* I, New York, Academic Press, 1964, pp. 227-281.

DeDuve, C., Pressman, B. C., Gianetto, R., Wattiaux, R., and Appelmans, F.: Tissue fractionation studies. 6. Intracellular distribution patterns of enzymes in rat liver tissue. *Biochem. J., 60:*604, 1955.

Fanestil, D. D., and Barrows, C. H., Jr.: Aging in the rotifer. *J. Geront., 20:*000, 1965.

Franklin, T. J.: The influence of age on the activities of some acid hydrolases in the rat liver and kidney. *Biochem. J., 82:*118, 1962.

Gregerman, R. I.: Adaptive enzyme responses in the senescent rat: Tryptophan peroxidase and tyrosine transaminase. *Amer. J. Physiol., 197:*63, 1959.

Hayflick, L.: The limited *in vitro* lifetime of human diploid cells strains. *Exptl. Cell Res., 37:*614, 1965.

Ingle, L., Wood, T. R., and Banta, A. M.: A study of longevity, growth, reproduction and heart rate in *Daphnia longispina* as influenced by limitations in quantity of food. *J. exp. Zool., 76:*325, 1937.

Medvedev, Zh. A.: Aging at the molecular level and some speculations concerning maintaining the functioning of systems for replicating specific macromolecules. In: N. W. Shock (Ed), *Biological Aspects of Aging.* New York and London, Columbia University Press, 1962, pp. 255-266.

Rockstein, M., and Bhatnagar, P. L.: Age changes in size and number of the giant mitochondria in the flight muscle of the common housefly *(Musca domestica L.). J. Ins. Physiol., 11:*481, 1965.

Rockstein, M., and Brandt, K. F.: Changes in phosphorus metabolism of the gastrocnemius muscle in aging white rats. *Proc. Soc. exp. Biol., N.Y., 107:*377, 1961.

Rockstein, M., and Brandt, K. F.: Enzyme changes in flight muscle correlated with aging and flight ability in the male housefly. *Science, 139:*1049, 1963.

Ross, M. H.: Protein, calories and life expectancy. *Fed. Proc. Baltimore, 18:*1190, 1959.

Ross, M. H., and Ely, J. O.: Aging and enzyme activity. *J. Franklin Inst. 258:*63, 1954.

Schmukler, M., and Barrows, C. H., Jr.: Age differences in lactic and malic dehydrogenase in the rat. *J. Geront., 21:*000, 1966.

Wulff, V. J., Piekielniak, M., and Wayner, M. J., Jr.: The ribonucleic acid content of tissues of rats of different ages. *J. Geront., 18:*322, 1963.

Wulff, V. J., Quastler, H., and Sherman, F. G.: An hypothesis concerning RNA metabolism and aging. *Proc. Nat. Acad. Sci., Wash., 48:*1373, 1962.

Chapter 13

AGING IN ENZYME ACTIVITIES OF HUMAN ARTERIAL TISSUE*

JOHN ESBEN KIRK

THE APPROPRIATE FUNCTIONING of cellular enzymes is an essential role for the process of living. For that reason, quantitative biochemical investigations on changes with age in enzyme activities of tissues constitute an important field in gerontological research. Although one cannot at the present stage of knowledge conclude whether observed enzymic changes are the cause or the result of aging, the acquisition of information about variation with age in tissue enzyme concentrations may prove to be of definite value. In addition, measurements of cofactor concentrations should also be conducted because these compounds are closely related to the functioning of several enzymes and may be rate-limiting factors in some processes of intermediary cellular metabolism.

As yet, not many systematic studies have been reported on age variations in enzyme activities of human organs. Rather extensive research has, however, been made in the author's department on enzyme activities in arterial tissue derived from individuals of various ages. In the present paper, a brief review will be made of age-associated changes in normal arterial tissue; this survey includes assays of forty enzymes and seven coenzymes in samples of the descending thoracic aorta and pulmonary artery. The human aorta is particularly susceptible to pathological age changes which makes enzymic studies on this vascular species of distinct interest. The fact that the pulmonary artery rarely is the site of severe pathology in elderly persons justifies a special consideration of the metabolic behavior of that blood vessel, since such acquired information may be of comparative significance. Investigations on the correlation

* The investigations performed by the author have been supported by a grant from the National Institutes of Health, Public Health Service (HE-00891).

between arteriosclerosis and tissue enzyme activities have previously been reviewed (Kirk, 1963) which have shown that the various enzymes are differently affected by pathological changes; interpretation of the findings with regard to atherogenesis is not as yet possible.

The enzyme studies performed by the author and his associates were carried out on homogenates of intima-media layers of arterial samples obtained fresh at autopsy. The activity assays were made at optimal pH, in the presence of required cofactors and usually at a substrate concentration permitting a zero order reaction; techniques were employed which eliminated interference by other enzymes.

It is generally agreed that quantitative determinations of enzyme activities under such optimal conditions afford a reliable measurement of the enzyme concentrations present in the tissue. However, because the substrate and coenzyme concentrations used for *in vitro* enzymic assays undoubtedly are considerably higher than those present in the tissue, it is not certain to what extent the recorded values correspond to activities exhibited by the tissue *in vivo.* It should further be mentioned that preparation of homogenates involves destruction of cells for extraction of enzymes. For that reason, the observed activities merely represent average enzyme concentrations of the contained cells and do not reveal differences between various types of cells; nor does the technique supply direct information about changes occurring in special intracellular fractions. In spite of these limitations to interpret *in vitro* performed enzyme measurement on homogenates, studies on the variation with age in tissue enzyme concentrations may be an important approach to the physiological basis of aging.

The concentrations of many enzymes in tissues are often greatly in excess of the quantities required for their specific substrates. However, in any sequential series of enzymic reactions, a relatively low concentration of an enzyme catalyzing one reaction of the series may exert a rate-limiting influence on the capacity of the cell to conduct completely and efficiently the entire sequence of transformations. This fact makes it advisable to conduct systematic studies on the effect of age on all enzymes in the main metabolic pathways.

The observed variations with age in enzyme activities and coenzyme concentrations of the aorta and pulmonary artery are presented in Table I. It was considered appropriate to express mean values of fresh arterial tissue recorded for middle-aged (forty to fifty-nine years) and elderly persons (sixty to eighty-nine years) in percentages of those observed for young adults (twenty to thirty-nine-year old individuals). For comparative purposes, data for birth to nine-year old children have also been listed. In addition, coefficients of correlation between age and enzyme and coenzyme values are reported. Since there is often a considerable difference between values found for vascular samples from children and from adults, these statistical calculations were purposely made on analytical data obtained from arterial tissue of adults (twenty to eighty-nine-year old subjects). The calculations were performed both on the basis of wet arterial weight and tissue nitrogen content.

The variety of patterns of enzymic changes which occur with age in the arterial wall is evident from the data presented in the table. Several of the enzymes do not exhibit statistically significant correlation with age, but many display a notable increase from a low concentration in childhood to a higher level at adulthood which is maintained essentially unchanged for some decades after which the activity gradually decreases. A consistent and pronounced decrement from early adulthood to old age has been found for fumarase and creatine phosphokinase in both aortic and pulmonary artery tissue, and a conspicuous increase was observed for beta-glucuronidase. These diverse age-associated changes suggest that the enzymic alterations in the vascular tissue cannot be accounted for solely by a decrease in the number of cells.

Biochemical studies have not as yet been performed on the localization of enzymes in particulate fractions of human arterial cells. Several reviews have been made (Schneider, 1953; Bertolini *et al.*, 1962; Dixon and Webb, 1964) of the distribution of enzymes in cellular particles of some animal tissues; although the available literature is not completely consistent, it was considered of interest to compare the recorded age variations in arterial enzyme activities with their assumed intracellular localization.

Among the cytoplasmic enzymes, a moderate age-associated decrease was displayed in aortic tissue by malic dehydrogenase, glyoxalase I, glycogen phosphorylase, phosphoglucomutase, adenylpy-

TABLE I

VARIATION WITH AGE IN ENZYME ACTIVITIES AND COENZYME CONCENTRATIONS OF HUMAN ARTERIAL TISSUE

	Percentage Values of Fresh Arterial Tissue Expressed on the Basis of Data Recorded for 20–39-Year-Old Subjects				*Coefficients of Correlation with Age for Samples from 20–89-Year-Old Individuals*				
					Wet Tissue		*Tissue Nitrogen*		
	0–9 Years	*20–39 Years*	*40–59 Years*	*60–89 Years*	*r*	*t*‡	*r*	*t*	*N*
Hexokinase:									
Aorta	67	100	70	74	−0.21	1.49	−0.03	0.21	51
Pulmonary Artery	59	100	87	92	0.00	0.00	+0.06	0.53	53
Phosphoglucoisomerase:									
Aorta	79	100	89	87	−0.18	1.31	+0.05	0.36	55
Pulmonary Artery	72	100	89	85	−0.21	1.56	−0.11	0.79	55
Aldolase:									
Aorta	92	100	114	121	+0.19	1.72	+0.21	*1.98*	78*
Pulmonary Artery	90	100	94	106	+0.07	0.57	+0.08	0.65	69*
Enolase:									
Aorta	58	100	100	92	−0.12	0.94	+0.10	0.78	63
Pulmonary Artery	61	100	106	108	+0.05	0.36	+0.14	1.05	58
Lactic Dehydrogenase:									
Aorta	49	100	139	76					67**
Pulmonary Artery	75	100	129	94					67**
Aconitase:									
Aorta	143	100	97	99	−0.04	0.41	+0.11	1.12	104
Pulmonary Artery	—	100	87	88	−0.26	*2.18*	−0.14	1.14	66
Isocitric Dehydrogenase:									
Aorta	104	100	107	92	−0.04	0.29	+0.08	0.58	55
Pulmonary Artery	81	100	99	92	−0.05	0.34	+0.10	0.68	49

‡ $t = r\sqrt{\frac{n-2}{1-r^2}}$

* Coefficients of correlation calculated for samples from 20–69-year-old subjects.
** Because of the type of enzyme variation, the coefficients of correlation were not calculated.

TABLE I (*Continued*)

	Percentage Values of Fresh Arterial Tissue Expressed on the Basis of Data Recorded for 20–39-Year-Old Subjects				*Coefficients of Correlation with Age for Samples from 20–89-Year-Old Individuals*				
					Wet Tissue		*Tissue Nitrogen*		
	0–9 Years	*20–39 Years*	*40–59 Years*	*60–89 Years*	*r*	*t*‡	*r*	*t*	*N*
Fumarase:									
Aorta	126	100	73	62	−0.46	*4.97*	−0.29	*2.92*	94
Pulmonary Artery	—	100	69	56	−0.51	*5.60*	−0.35	*3.53*	91
Malic Dehydrogenase:									
Aorta	99	100	101	86	−0.21	1.50	−0.08	0.64	67
Pulmonary Artery	70	100	101	69	−0.26	*2.42*	−0.25	2.22	66
TPN-Malic Enzyme:									
Aorta	94	100	99	90	−0.05	0.36	−0.03	0.22	55
Pulmonary Artery	119	100	129	87					49**
Glyoxalase I:									
Aorta	121	100	92	81	−0.30	*2.65*	−0.07	0.59	73
Pulmonary Artery	103	100	80	66	−0.38	*3.33*	−0.31	*2.68*	69
Glycogen Phosphorylase:									
Aorta	111	100	90	68	−0.23	*2.15*	−0.18	1.67	84
Pulmonary Artery	—	100	95	91	−0.11	0.90	0.00	0.00	68
Phosphoglucomutase:									
Aorta	100	100	87	76	−0.35	*2.98*	−0.32	*2.70*	66
Pulmonary Artery	—	100	96	82	−0.25	1.86	−0.16	1.18	54
Glucose-6-P-Dehydrogenase:									
Aorta	33	100	95	86	−0.10	0.81	−0.08	0.64	67
Pulmonary Artery	33	100	95	85	−0.11	0.88	−0.04	0.32	65
6-P-Gluconate-Dehydrogenase:									
Aorta	123	100	104	101	+0.02	0.14	+0.07	0.48	50
Pulmonary Artery	85	100	116	107	+0.07	0.48	+0.14	0.98	50
Ribose-5-P-Isomerase:									
Aorta	60	100	124	92					58**
Pulmonary Artery	—	100	105	91	0.00	0.00	+0.03	0.21	51
Transketolase:									
Aorta	92	100	100	112	+0.13	0.85	+0.20	1.31	43
Pulmonary Artery	87	100	97	97	−0.03	0.17	+0.17	0.97	34

TABLE I (*Continued*)

	Percentage Values of Fresh Arterial Tissue Expressed on the Basis of Data Recorded for 20–39-Year-Old Subjects				*Coefficients of Correlation with Age for Samples from 20–89-Year-Old Individuals*				
					Wet Tissue		*Tissue Nitrogen*		
	0–9 Years	*20–39 Years*	*40–59 Years*	*60–89 Years*	*r*	*t*‡	*r*	*t*	*N*
Phosphomannose Isomerase:									
Aorta	98	100	101	98	−0.02	0.17	+0.09	0.78	80
Pulmonary Artery	—	100	88	86	−0.25	*1.98*	−0.13	1.00	61
Diaphorase:									
Aorta	64	100	83	73	−0.23	*2.37*	−0.18	1.82	100
Pulmonary Artery	75	100	94	93	−0.01	0.09	−0.04	0.38	98
Cytochrome C Reductase:									
Aorta	102	100	86	78	−0.20	*2.02*	−0.19	1.92	100
Pulmonary Artery	82	100	93	77	−0.16	1.59	−0.14	1.38	98
Beta-Hydroxyacyl DH:									
Aorta	27	100	88	77	−0.25	*2.37*	−0.09	0.86	91
Pulmonary Artery	40	100	95	—	−0.04	0.23	+0.12	0.69	34
Alpha-Hydroxybutyric DH:									
Aorta	74	100	60	62	−0.31	*2.20*	−0.04	0.27	47
Pulmonary Artery	72	100	74	66	−0.51	*2.64*	−0.32	1.58	23
Glutamic Dehydrogenase:									
Aorta	112	100	75	60	−0.28	*3.36*	−0.15	1.62	116
Pulmonary Artery	91	100	78	52	−0.34	*3.05*	−0.27	*2.35*	72
Glutathione Reductase:									
Aorta	79	100	110	109	+0.10	1.09	+0.21	*2.32*	118
Pulmonary Artery	78	100	99	91	−0.13	1.10	+0.11	0.93	73
Glutam. Oxalac. Transamin.:									
Aorta	58	100	91	90	−0.10	0.70	+0.06	0.42	51
Pulmonary Artery	57	100	91	97	−0.03	0.14	+0.20	0.94	23
Glutam. Pyruv. Transamin.:									
Aorta	65	100	87	92	−0.17	1.14	−0.04	0.27	46
Pulmonary Artery	—	100	81	67	−0.20	0.94	−0.08	0.36	24
Leucine Aminopeptidase:									
Aorta	110	100	95	85	−0.24	1.96	+0.07	0.55	65
Pulmonary Artery	88	100	88	78	−0.35	*3.30*	−0.20	1.60	63

TABLE I (*Continued*)

	Percentage Values of Fresh Arterial Tissue Expressed on the Basis of Data Recorded for 20–39-Year-Old Subjects				*Coefficients of Correlation with Age for Samples from 20–89-Year-Old Individuals*				
					Wet Tissue		*Tissue Nitrogen*		
	0–9 Years	*20–39 Years*	*40–59 Years*	*60–89 Years*	*r*	*t*‡	*r*	*t*	*N*
Cathepsin:									
Aorta	99	100	108	114	+0.16	1.42	+0.15	1.32	80
Pulmonary Artery	—	100	143	170	+0.16	1.33	+0.20	1.68	69
Total Proteolysis:									
Aorta	86	100	111	108	+0.18	1.63	+0.18	1.63	80
Pulmonary Artery	—	100	123	138	+0.31	*2.68*	+0.29	*2.50*	69
Thromboplastin:									
Aorta (Intima)	—	100	64	47	−0.34	1.72			28
Pulmonary Artery (Intima)	—	100	194	395	+0.38	2.05			25
Hexosamine Synthetase:									
Aorta	65	100	90	102	−0.06	0.32	+0.24	1.30	30
Pulmonary Artery	75	100	95	113	+0.07	0.26	+0.30	1.20	16
Adenylpyrophosphatase:									
Aorta	92	100	86	82	−0.22	1.78	0.00	0.00	63
Pulmonary Artery	78	100	90	75	−0.38	3.20	−0.13	1.02	63
Inorganic Pyrophosphatase:									
Aorta	79	100	87	83	−0.17	1.30	−0.06	0.44	58
Pulmonary Artery	58	100	95	80	−0.23	1.80	−0.21	1.64	60
Purine Nucl. Phosphorylase:									
Aorta	94	100	98	110	+0.09	0.89	+0.21	*2.10*	98
Pulmonary Artery	—	100	102	102	+0.02	0.18	+0.02	0.18	87
5-Nucleotidase:									
Aorta	38	100	119	115	+0.05	0.45	+0.16	1.44	82
Pulmonary Artery	71	100	165	178	+0.33	*2.97*	+0.27	*2.41*	74
Creatine Phosphokinase:									
Aorta	103	100	72	53	−0.40	*4.06*	−0.32	*3.12*	87
Pulmonary Artery	—	100	37	35	−0.53	*2.28*	−0.42	1.76	16
Phosphomonoesterase:									
Aorta	50	100	94	92	−0.11	0.85	−0.09	0.70	65
Pulmonary Artery	55	100	103	92	−0.06	0.47	+0.20	1.59	63

TABLE I (*Continued*)

	Percentage Values of Fresh Arterial Tissue Expressed on the Basis of Data Recorded for 20–39-Year-Old Subjects				*Coefficients of Correlation with Age for Samples from 20–89-Year-Old Individuals*				
					Wet Tissue		*Tissue Nitrogen*		
	0–9 Years	*20–39 Years*	*40–59 Years*	*60–89 Years*	*r*	*t*‡	*r*	*t*	*N*
Aliesterase:									
Aorta (Intima)	96	100	110	103	+0.06	0.59			100
Pulmonary Artery (Intima)	—	100	92	113	+0.18	1.06			36
Phenolsulfatase:									
Aorta	116	100	63	46	−0.42	*4.33*	−0.34	*3.39*	89
Pulmonary Artery	—	100	71	68	−0.27	*2.02*	0.00	0.00	54
Beta-Glucuronidase:									
Aorta	55	100	145	137	+0.31	*2.73*	+0.36	*3.22*	71*
Pulmonary Artery	—	100	176	173	+0.45	*2.72*	+0.43	*2.58*	31*
Coenzyme A:									
Aorta	169	100	139	110	+0.11	1.39	+0.20	1.91	90
Pulmonary Artery	—	100	114	78					31**
Total Riboflavin:									
Aorta	115	100	88	74	−0.42	*4.42*			93
Flavin Adenine Dinucleotide:									
Aorta	100	100	84	64	−0.41	*4.29*			93
Nicotinic Acid:									
Aorta	124	100	95	89	−0.18	1.37			58
Glutathione:									
Aorta	136	100	140	187	+0.38	*2.92*	+0.48	*3.87*	52
Pulmonary Artery	—	100	119	132	+0.29	1.36	+0.31	1.46	22
Pyridoxine:									
Aorta	87	100	108	110	+0.16	1.57	+0.13	1.28	95
Pulmonary Artery	—	100	98	98	−0.05	0.32	+0.05	0.32	44
Biotin:									
Aorta	58	100	109	115	+0.07	0.65	+0.29	*2.78*	85
Pulmonary Artery	—	100	110	115	+0.11	0.87	+0.23	1.88	63

rophosphatase, and leucine aminopeptidase, when activities were expressed on the basis of wet tissue weight, whereas the concentration of aldolase showed a tendency to increase. Of the enzymes predominantly located in the mitochondria, a decrement in activity with age was observed for fumarase, glutamic dehydrogenase, and beta-hydroxyacyl dehydrogenase. Markedly lower values have further been reported by Maier and Haimovici (1957) for succinic oxidase and cytochrome C oxidase in aortic tissue from old subjects; the decrease in activity of these two mitochondrial enzymes is probably significant from the point of view of cellular aging because of their association with energy production.

It is generally believed that beta-glucuronidase and cathepsin are located mainly in the lysosomes. The activities of both these enzymes increase notably with age. This observation may be of some importance since it has been proposed by Bourne (1956) that increase in hydrolytic enzyme activity is one of the fundamental changes taking place in aging cells. A decrease with age was observed for the microsome-located DPNH-cytochrome C reductase. It is of interest to note that two enzymes which have been described as being present to an appreciable extent in the nucleus, aldolase and 5-nucleotidase, showed increments in activity in connection with aging of the aortic tissue.

For most of the arterial enzymes studied, the alterations with age recorded for adult tissue samples were of the same pattern for the pulmonary artery as observed for the aorta. However, in several cases the extent of change was somewhat different.

In vitro investigations by Dyrbye (1959) have shown that the metabolism of sulfated mucopolysaccharides in human aortic tissue decreases considerably with age. A distinctly lower incorporation of methionine-S^{35} into aortas of old oxen than into arterial samples of young cattle was reported by Fontaine *et al.* (1960).

With regard to the coenzyme concentrations listed in Table I, the arterial tissue contents of total riboflavin and flavin adenine dinucleotide decreased markedly with age; in contrast to this, increase was exhibited by glutathione. It is assumed that riboflavin and flavin adenine dinucleotide occur largely in the mitochondria and glutathione in the nucleus. Studies performed by Kempf *et al.*

(1961) on bovine aortic tissue revealed a decrease in total adenylic nucleotides and ATP in old animals. On the basis of these findings it was suggested that one of the metabolic phenomena of aging is related to a diminution of energy transfer which might result in lower rates of protein and enzyme synthesis.

Although several of the age changes in enzyme activities of human arterial tissue are rather conspicuous, the factors responsible for such alterations have not been clearly disclosed. The observed enzymic decrements may to some extent be the result of changes in the composition of the arterial wall by replacement of functioning cells with fibrous elements. The decrease with age in the glycogen phosphorylase and creatine phosphokinase concentrations is probably associated with some atrophy of the smooth muscular tissue. When enzymes can be classified on the basis of their structure and chemical nature of active centers, an evaluation of the relationship between the observed activity changes and enzymic molecular composition should be made and the results presented in Table I may be of value for this purpose.

Considerable progress has been made in recent years concerning the role of nuclear DNA in controlling protein biosynthesis and literature evidence suggests that enzyme deficiency can be caused by mutation of structural and regulator genes. With regard to factors involved in enzyme induction and repression, the influence of hormones must be considered, and studies by the author (Kirk, 1964) have revealed significantly lower concentrations of four TPN-dependent enzymes in aortic and coronary artery tissue derived from adult women than from male subjects. The reduced levels of these enzymes may be associated with the lower susceptibility of premenopausal women than men to arteriosclerosis.

Even though much work has been completed on enzymic changes in human arterial tissue associated with aging, many additional investigations are required; for comparative purposes, similar systematic studies on animal tissues might also be desirable. When the intermediary metabolism of the arterial wall has been established in detail through determinations by the conventional homogenate procedures, enzymic assays by O. H. Lowry's methods on individual cells from tissue samples of young and old subjects are recommended. Research on enzymes in subcellular fractions of endothelial cells will be another approach for evaluation of the cellular aging process.

Possibilities for future research are very promising because of the recent enormous improvements in biochemical analytical techniques.

REFERENCES

Bertolini, A. M., Massari, N., and Quarto di Palo, F.: *Gerontologia. Aspetti Metabolica.* Milano, Fondazione Carlo Erba, 1962.

Bourne, G. H.: Physiological and cellular aspects of aging. *Nature, 178:*839, 1956.

Dixon, M., and Webb, E. C.: *Enzymes,* 2nd ed. New York, Academic Press, 1964.

Dyrbye, M. O.: Studies on the metabolism of the mucopolysaccharides of human arterial tissue by means of S^{35}, with special reference to changes related to age. *J. Gerontol., 14:*32, 1959.

Fontaine, R., Mandel, P., Pantesco, V., and Kempf, E.: Le métabolisme de la parois artérielle et ses variations au cours du vieillissement. *Strasbourg Medical, 9:*605, 1960.

Kempf, E., Fontaine, R., and Mandel, P.: Etude comparée des nucléotides libres, adényliques et uridyliques, des aortes bovidés jeunes et âgés. *C. R. Soc. Biol., 155:*623, 1961.

Kirk, J. E.: Intermediary metabolism of human arterial tissue and its changes with age and atherosclerosis. In *"Atherosclerosis and Its Origin",* M. Sandler and G. H. Bourne, eds. New York, Academic Press, 1963, pp. 67-117.

Kirk, J. E.: Comparison of enzyme activities of arterial samples from sexually mature men and women. *Clin. Chem., 10:*184, 1964.

Maier, N., and Haimovici, H.: Metabolism of arterial tissue. Oxidative capacity of intact arterial tissue. *Proc. Soc. Exp. Biol. Med., 95:*425, 1957.

Schneider, W. C.: Biochemical constitution of mammalian mitochondria. *J. Histochem. Cytochem., 1:*212, 1953.

Section IV
MODELS OF AGING

Chapter 14

SENESCENCE AND CULTURED CELLS*

LEONARD HAYFLICK

THE APPARENT indefinite multiplication of isolated vertebrate cells in tissue culture has often been cited as evidence for the thesis that senescence in higher animals is a phenomenon resulting from the effects of events at the supracellular level (Pearl, 1922; Bidder, 1925; Cowdry, 1952; Medawar, 1958; Maynard Smith, 1962; Comfort, 1964). The notion that isolated animal cells in culture are capable of unlimited proliferation has profoundly influenced thinking on many fundamental biological questions, not the least of which are theories of senescence. It will be the purpose of this essay to reexamine evidence for the view that cells grown *in vitro* are capable of indefinite multiplication and to challenge the common interpretation of those results.

THE MISCONCEPTION

It is Alexis Carrel to whom credit is given for observing that animal cells released from *in vivo* control mechanisms by *in vitro* cultivation, will perpetuate themselves indefinitely. This so-called "immortality" of cultured cells was based on a series of experiments purporting to show that fibroblasts derived from the heart of a chick embryo could be kept in an active state of division for an indeterminate period of time (Ebeling, 1913; Parker, 1961). Since, even with more modern and sophisticated cell culture techniques, actively dividing chick cells cannot be maintained much beyond one year, there is serious doubt that this common interpretation of Carrel's experiment is valid. An alternative explanation is that the method of preparation of chick embryo extract,

* These studies were supported (in part) by United States Public Health Service Career Development Award 5-K3-CA-5938 and Contract PH-43-62-157 from the National Cancer Institute.

used as a source of nutrients for his cultures and prepared daily under conditions easily permitting cell survival, contributed new, viable, embryonic cells to the chick heart strain at each feeding. Waves of mitotic activity were reported to be co-incidental with the periodic addition of chick embryo extract (Ebeling, 1913). The chick embryo has been, perhaps, the most popular source of cells for tissue cultures, yet no one has succeeded in confirming Carrel's studies. In spite of this, Carrel's conclusion that isolated vertebrate cells are capable of indefinite multiplication is correct—but for the wrong reasons.

A REAPPRAISAL

It is now known that normal or cancerous cells derived from almost all vertebrate (and some insect) tissue can be cultivated *in vitro* for various periods of time. Such cell populations divide for a finite number of generations and after cessation of mitotic activity the culture finally undergoes total degeneration. These events may span a period of days, weeks, or months but do not exceed one or two years. Cell populations first released from tissue by enzymatic or mechanical means and cultivated *in vitro* are called "primary cultures" (Fig. 1, Phase 1). If such a population is capable of further cell division, necessitating transfer to more culture vessels (Fig. 1, Phase 2), a serially passaged cell culture results which we have chosen to call a "cell strain" (Hayflick and Moorhead, 1961). Muliplication in long-term culture is less likely for fixed post-mitotic or highly differentiated parenchymal cells, consequently the kind of cell population most likely to divide for long periods of time *in vitro* are fibroblasts regardless of the tissue of origin. The ultimate cessation of cell division is followed by complete degeneration of the strain and is designated Phase 3 (Fig. 1).

Cell strains have three fundamental properties:

1) When derived from normal tissue, they possess the morphological, physiological, and immunological properties of normal cells during their *in vitro* life. When derived from tumor tissue they retain those properties.
2) They have the karyotype of the cells of the tissue of origin. For example, when derived from normal human tissue, cell

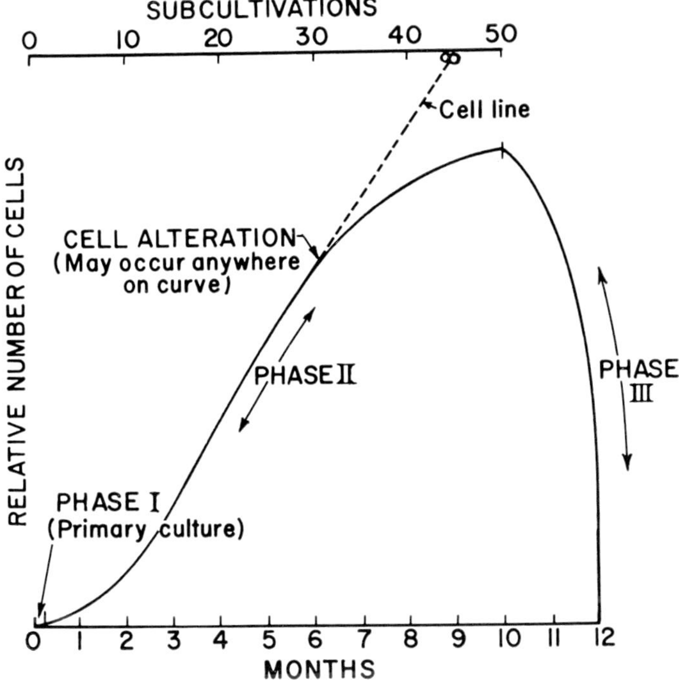

FIGURE 1. Diagrammatic representation of the theory of *in vitro* vertebrate cell proliferation. Phase 1, or the primary culture, terminates with the formation of the first confluent cell sheet. Phase 2 is characterized by more cell multiplication, necessitating repeated subcultivations. Cells in Phases 2 and 3 are termed "cell strains." Cell strains characteristically enter Phase 3 and are lost after a finite period of time. Conversely, a spontaneous alteration could occur at any point on the curve, giving rise to a "cell line" whose potential for further multiplication is infinite. However, thus far human diploid fibroblast strains have not been found to alter spontaneously. The abscissa indicates the number of cell passages (doublings) expected from human diploid cell strains of embryonic origin and, although the shape of the curve is identical for all cell strains, the passage numbers may vary.

strains have the diploid number of forty-six chromosomes. Female cells retain sex chromatin at interphase.

3) They have a limited potential for multiplication *in vitro* and undergo a finite number of cell doublings.

Thus the establishment of a cell strain is the most common consequence of animal tissue first cultivated *in vitro*. It is our contention that the regularly repopulated cell cultures of Carrel were of this type. Subsequently, Gey and Gey in 1936 and Earle in 1943 demonstrated the spontaneous occurrence of murine cells later found to be, unequivocally, capable of dividing for an indeterminate period of time. Since then, at least 225 cell populations with the extraordinary capacity to multiply *in vitro* indefinitely, have been spontaneously derived from different kinds of mammalian tissue (Hayflick and Moorhead, 1962). These cell populations previously designated "cell lines" (Hayflick and Moorhead, 1961) are often morphologically distinguishable from cell strain populations (Hayflick, 1961). The biological characteristics of cell lines had led us to the conclusion that regardless of the tissue of origin, whether normal or cancerous, all shared properties with cancer cells.

Thus, *cell lines* have these three fundamental properties:

1) When inoculated into suitable hosts the cells will multiply and often metastasize. Cells from human cell lines inoculated into terminal cancer patients will behave in this fashion (Southam, Moore and Rhoads, 1957). Most will grow when placed in the immunologically privileged site of the hamster cheek pouch (Handler and Foley, 1956; Foley and Handler, 1957,1958). Diploid cell strains will not multiply long in either environment (Hayflick and Moorhead, 1961).

2) They do not have the karyotype of the tissue (or strain) of origin and are usually heteroploid, aneuploid or, rarely, pseudodiploid. Most often they exhibit a distribution of chromosome numbers around a modal value which in the case of human cell lines is usually in the seventies. Sex chromatin is not retained in cell lines derived from female tissue.

3) Cell lines will, apparently, multiply indefinitely *in vitro*. Some have been in continuous cultivation in many laboratories longer than twenty years with a doubling time of twenty-four hours.

The relationship that cell lines bear to cell strains may be similar to the relationship that transplantable tumors bear to normal tissue. Cell strains and cell lines may be the *in vitro* counterparts of, respectively, normal cells and cancer cells *in vivo*. We can consider this relationship to be:

Heteroploid Cell Lines (*in vitro*)	:	Transplantable Tumors (*in vivo*)	=	Diploid Cell Strains (*in vitro*)	:	Normal Somatic Cells (*in vivo*)

1) Heteroploid	1) Diploid
2) Cancer cells (histological criteria)	2) Normal cells
3) Indefinite potential for division	3) Finite potential for division

Thus, the phenomenon of the alteration of a cell strain to a cell line is important because, in its simplest terms, it can be regarded as oncogenesis *in vitro*. Until recently, when cell lines were obtained from fish tissue (Wolf and Quimby, 1962), no non-mammalian cell lines had been authenticated. The spontaneous occurrence of a cell line is a rare event in the cultivation of most animal cell strains. The major exception to this generalization is the behavior of mouse cells, which when cultured *in vitro* have the unique property of almost always spontaneously altering from a cell strain to a cell line with the concomitant acquisition of the ability to multiply indefinitely (Rothfels, Kupelweiser and Parker, 1963; Todaro and Green, 1963). Since, after Carrel's studies, much of the early work in tissue culture was done with murine cells, it was "logical" to extrapolate the observations on chick and murine cells and conclude that all animal cells cultivated *in vitro* would, under the proper conditions, divide indefinitely. We contend that this generalization, without a critical qualification, is fallacious and that the normal somatic cells of these two species behave diametrically opposite when cultivated *in vitro*. Chick cells never become cell lines and mouse cells almost always do. The essential qualification to the generalization is that only cells acquiring malignant properties *in vitro*, are capable of unlimited division.

The *in vitro* behavior of normal somatic cells which is pivotal to the development of many theories of vertebrate aging, reveals that they do have a finite lifetime. There is some reason to believe that, even with the limited evidence available, a graded scale might be drawn representing the predisposition for alteration to a cell line by the cells of various animal species. Chick cells would lie at the base of the scale and mouse cells at the top with human cells positioned somewhere nearer the base. An explanation for these relationships is not known although it is intriguing to observe that old laboratory mice almost always die of cancer (Strong,

1935) and mouse cells when grown *in vitro* almost always acquire such properties.

It is important to stress that alterations occur fortuitously in cell cultures and under conditions that, until recently, could not be defined. The spontaneous alterations described in the literature (Hayflick and Moorhead, 1962) have emerged in many different kinds of culture environments. Conditions for reproducibly altering cell strains to cell lines, if known, would be a powerful tool for the study of the *in vitro* conversion of normal cells (strains) to cancer cells (lines). Recently, it was discovered that the infection of human diploid cell strains with the virus $S.V._{40}$ (Koprowski, Pontén, Jensen, Ravdin, Moorhead and Saksela, 1962; Shein and Enders, 1962) and diploid rodent strains with the polyoma virus could provide these conditions (Vogt and Dulbecco, 1960; Sachs and Medina, 1961).

THE IMPLICATIONS

However, of interest to us presently is that characteristic of diploid cell strains by which they are capable of only a limited number of doublings *in vitro,* and what relevance this observation may have to our understanding of the phenomena of senescence. It should now be clear that since heteroploid cell lines share properties with cancer cells, considerations of aging at the cellular level must be related to the behavior of normal diploid cell strains *in vitro* and not to heteroploid cell lines. In fact, any theory of aging must have as a corollary an explanation for the apparent escape from senescence by malignant cells both *in vitro* and *in vivo.*

On the basis, arguments marshalled against cellular theories of aging that are based on the myth of "immortal" cell cultures must be reevaluated since those cells that do proliferate indefinitely *in vitro* are abnormal and usually behave like malignant cells. Contrariwise, normal cells *in vitro* do have a finite life-span as do the animals from which such cells have been taken. There is no confirmed evidence that normal cells can be maintained in a state of active proliferation in cell culture for a period of time in excess of the specific age of the species from which the cells were obtained. It is our contention that *in vivo* vertebrate senescence phenomena at the level of the cell also occurs *in vitro* when the proper systems are compared.

In earlier work with human embryonic diploid cell strains derived from lung tissue we observed that after a period of active multiplication, generally less than one year, these cells demonstrated an increased doubling time (normally twenty-four hours), gradual cessation of mitotic activity, accumulation of cellular debris and, ultimately, total degeneration of the culture. This phenomenon, called Phase 3 (Fig. 1), has been a common observation by cell culturists using cells from many other types of tissue, and technical difficulties have usually been invoked to explain this event. We view this event as an innate characteristic of all normal cells grown *in vitro;* and we are certain that optimum conditions for the multiplication of many cell types do exist. The Phase 3 phenomenon in the course of the *in vitro* cultivation of human diploid cell strains derived from fetal lung tissue has been shown to occur after about fifty cell doublings. Diploid strains derived from other organs give essentially similar results. This event, now confirmed in many laboratories, is unrelated to media composition, presence of microorganisms, or the depletion of some non-replicating metabolic pool. Consequently, the hypothesis has been proposed that the finite lifetime of diploid cell strains *in vitro* may be the cellular expression of senescence so well known at the level of the whole animal (Hayflick and Moorhead, 1961; Hayflick, 1965).

Since diploid cell strains have a limited doubling potential *in vitro,* studies on any single strain would be severely limited were it not possible to preserve these cells at sub-zero temperatures for apparently indefinite periods of time. This maneuver allows for the construction of a number of interesting experiments. The reconstitution of frozen human fetal diploid cell strains has revealed that regardless of the doubling level reached by the population at the time it is preserved the *total* number of doublings that can be expected is about fifty including those made prior to and after preservation (Hayflick and Moorhead, 1961; Hayflick, 1965). Storage of human diploid cell strains merely arrests the cells at a particular doubling level but does not influence the total number of expected doublings. It has also been shown that the ability to double fifty times is probably a characteristic of each clonable cell in the population and that mixed populations of cells with different doubling potentials do not influence each other.

Of greater importance, perhaps, is the finding that diploid cell strains derived from the lungs of adult humans reach Phase 3 after about twenty doublings *in vitro* (Hayflick, 1965). Although cell strains from a number of young and old adults were studied, no precise correlation was found between the number of doublings *in vitro* and the chronological age of the donor. If such a correlation does exist, present methods of determining numbers of doublings are too imperfect to uncover the relationship. Nevertheless, it is clear that the doubling potential of embryonic human diploid cell strains is far greater than for those derived from adults. Human diploid fibroblast strains derived from adult tissues are, with the exception of doubling potential, biologically identical with those derived from embryos. Adult strains preserved at low temperatures can also be arrested at any doubling level, yet the total number of doublings possible is about twenty. A mechanism postulated to explain these phenomena depends upon an accumulation of a greater burden of heritable damage by adult cells before cultivation *in vitro* (Hayflick, 1965).

IN VIVO EVIDENCE

If the concept that the finite lifetime of normal cells *in vitro* is related to a potential finite lifetime of cells *in situ*, then it would be valuable to answer the question: Can normal somatic cells divide indefinitely under any conditions? Certainly, the best conditions would be those offered by an *in vivo* environment and the question could be answered by serial orthotopic transplantation of normal somatic tissue to new, young, inbred hosts each time the recipient approaches old-age. Under these conditions, do transplanted normal cells of age-chimeras proliferate indefinitely? Data from four different laboratories in which mammary tissue (DeOme, 1964), skin (Krohn, 1962) and hemopoietic cells (Ford, Micklem and Gray, 1959; Cudkowicz, Upton, Shearer and Hughes, 1964; Siminovitch, Till and McCulloch, 1964) were employed indicate that normal cells, serially transplanted to inbred hosts, do not survive indefinitely. Furthermore, the trauma of transplantation does not appear to influence the results (Krohn, 1962) and finally in heterochronic transplants survival time is related to the age of the grafted tissue (Krohn, 1962). It is well known that under similar conditions of tissue transplantation, cancer cell populations can be serially passed indefinitely (Stewart, Snell, Dunham and Schlyen, 1959). The implications may be that acquisition of potential for unlimited cell division or escape from senescent changes by mammalian cells *in vitro* or *in vivo* can only be achieved by cells which have acquired properties of cancer cells. Paradoxically this leads to the conclusion that in order for mammalian somatic cells to become biologically "immortal" they first must be induced to the neoplastic state either *in vivo* or *in vitro*, whereupon, they can then be subcultivated or transplanted indefinitely.

Although the karyotype of human diploid cell strains is very stable during periods of active proliferation (Phases 1 and 2), aneuploidy and other chromosome abberations do occur during Phase 3. In this connection, a relationship has been demonstrated between chromosome abberations of somatic cells *in vivo* and natural aging by scoring anaphase anomalies in regenerating mouse liver tissue. (Crowley and Curtis, 1963). Within each strain of mouse tested there was an age-correlated increase in anaphase and telophase abberations scored following partial hepatectomy. Of even greater interest are the observations that increased hypodiploid counts in the peripheral blood leucocytes of man are correlated with the chronologic age of the donor (Jacobs, Court Brown and Doll, 1961; Hamerton, Taylor, Angell and McGuire, 1965). There exists, therefore, *in vivo* evidence for age associated chromosomal anomalies that are also involved at the time of decreased proliferation of human diploid cells *in vitro* (Phase 3).

Appreciation of the finite doubling potential of *normal* cells *in vitro* has launched studies to compare the specific age of a vertebrate species and the number of cell doublings accrued by their cells when grown *in vitro*. In a general way, there seems to be some relationship since there is little doubt that the fibroblasts of man—the longest lived mammal—undergo more doublings than cell strains of a number of laboratory animals. It may be found that the differences in specific age of different vertebrate species may be reflected by the numbers of doublings of their unaltered normal cells when cultured *in vitro.*

The very low doubling potential of unaltered parenchymal cells *in vitro* is not an argument against the hypothesis that fibroblasts which undergo many more doublings *in vitro,* may senesce. Highly differentiated normal parenchymal cells which have a limited capacity to divide *in vivo* should not be expected to behave differently *in vitro.* Likewise those theories of aging that emphasize the critical importance of events occurring in non-dividing parenchymal cells are not in jeopardy as a result of acceptance of evidence that normal cells have a finite division potential. Justification for attributing senescence or other complex biological phenomena to a single causative event is probably unwarranted. It is wise to assume that in those animals where vigor declines with age, the responsible processes are multiple and to treat senescence as a sum of all these factors. It is probable also that at the cellular level different events lead to the aging of different cell types. Thus the life span of all fixed post-mitotic mammalian parenchymal cells may be limited as a result of "copying errors" leading to reduced molecular turnover and consequent impaired cell function. Non-dividing cells are also assumed to be programmed by a vulnerable DNA. The nuclei of fixed post-mitotic, non-dividing parenchymal cells are surely no less susceptible to damage than those of the stem cells of proliferating tissue.

PROTOZOA AND CULTURED CELLS COMPARED

The concept that normal dividing cells never have an opportunity to age because they periodically yield new daughter cells before age changes take place also bears reexamination. What is in question here is whether the product of a cell division is always a pair of daughter cells, each having the same age status. This notion makes the very important assumption that dividing cells yield daughters that are "separate but equal." There is little, if any, evidence that bears on this important point in mammalian cells and no factual data opposing the possibility that one daughter cell may receive one or more old organelles and the other only new organelles. To assume that each daughter mammalian cell is equivalent in age status may be untrue and cell culture may lead to an examination of this question.

Since populations of vertebrate cells in culture have an independent existence and can be manipulated like microorganisms it may be useful to compare certain aspects of the behavior of both. Studies with protozoa do not unequivocally demonstrate the "immortality" of unicellular organisms or that the outcome of a protozoan cell division is a pair of rejuvenated infant cells instead of a mother and daughter cell of different seniorities.

For example, it has been shown (Danielli and Muggleton, 1959) that amoebae will multiply indefinitely if kept on a food supply permitting logarithmic vegetative multiplication but, if kept on a limited food supply and then transferred to the optimum diet, they have a variable life span. This span of from thirty days to thirty weeks is dependent on the conditions of exposure to the deficient diet. Since it is likely that amoebae in the natural state do not always have an optimum food supply, their usual fate is probably one in which senescence occurs. A number of other investigators have also concluded that many clones of protozoa do not propagate asexually indefinitely. Such observations have been made with *Uroleptus* (Calkins, 1919) *Paramecium* (Sonneborn, 1938) and with an *Ascomycete* (Rizet, 1953). Other clones of protozoa apparently do reproduce asexually and indefinitely. The extensive studies of Jennings (1945) bear directly on this question and on clonal rejuvenation by conjugation. It was found that the viability of the progeny of *Paramecium bursaria* by conjugation varies greatly even when the conjugants are young and that a high proportion of ex-conjugants normally die. The rate appears to be highest in those clones that are most closely related. Fifty-three per cent of ex-conjugants die before undergoing five cell divisions and 30 per cent die without dividing at all. Conjugation produced non-viable clones, clones of limited survival and some vigorous clones apparently capable of unlimited asexual reproduction. It is suggested that it is from these latter clones that laboratory cultures are normally obtained. Jennings concludes that death is not a consequence of multicellularity and that it occurs on a vast scale in the protozoa "from causes which are intrinsic to the organism." He claims that "most if not all clones ultimately die if they do not undergo some form of sexual reproduction . . . Rejuvenation through sexual reproduction is a fact . . . yet conjugation produces, in addition to rejuvenated clones, vast numbers of weak, pathological or abnormal clones whose predestined fate is early death." He adds that some very vigorous clones may be produced "that may continue vegetatively for an indefinite period, without decline or death." Reference should be made to Comfort (1964) and Strehler (1962) for an exhaustive discussion of this subject.

It is, however, interesting to note that a similar kind of clonal variation occurs with the human diploid cell strains. Some isolated single embryonic cells give rise to progeny capable of about fifty doublings (Hayflick, 1965) and others yield colonies composed of varying numbers of cells or no clones at all (Merz and Hayflick, 1965). However, the uncloned or wild embryonic cell population always undergoes about fifty doublings. Perhaps of interest in this connection are reports of the exchange of genetic material by mammalian somatic cells *in vitro*. (Barski, Sorieul and Cornefert, 1960; Ephrussi, Scaletta, Stenchever and Yoshida, 1964).

FUTURE

On the basis of current evidence, the finite life-time of normal cells *in vitro* may not only be a model for aging in the whole organism, but indeed, might be the same phenomenon reduced to a lesser degree of complexity. A number of generally accepted age-associated phenomena found at the tissue or whole animal level lend themselves to reexamination at the level of the cultured cell. Quantitative studies such as those of Lefford (1964) clearly demonstrate that as age increases there is a concomitant prolongation of the latent period of fibroblast migration from chick heart explants *in vitro*. This confirms earlier studies (Carrel and Burrows, 1911; Cohn and Murray, 1925) demonstrating that the "growth rate" of emigrating fibroblasts from chick heart explants decreases with the age of the donor. The phenomenon has also been observed in explanted rat livers where it was concluded that the "growth capacity" is inversely proportional to the age of the animal (Glinos and Bartlett, 1951). Similar observations have been made *in vivo* where the time-lag in reaching the peak mitotic rate lengthens with age (Howes and Harvey, 1932). This age-associated parameter is now amenable to study with normal human cells *in vitro,* not only with explants or monolayers but also at the level of the individual cell or clone.

Since collagen is produced by human diploid cells (Hayflick and Moorhead, 1961), age related properties of this material obtained from embryonic and adult strains may be a useful area of inquiry. The contractility and thermal shrinkage of collagen, which varies with the age of rats (Verzár and Thoenen, 1960), might be compared at Phase 2 and 3. The current interest in the apparent age-accelerating effects of radiation may also be extended to include studies at the cell level where reduction in average life-span of animals exposed to ionizing radiation may have its parallel in cultured normal cells. Although the specific effect of sublethal doses of radiation on the time of occurrence of Phase 3 has not as yet been reported, studies have been made which show a definite effect of radiation on the replication of human diploid cell strains (Puck, Morkovin, Marcus and Cieciura, 1957; Norris and Hood, 1962).

The relatively recent resolution of two technical problems in the management of animal cell cultures should facilitate the design of a number of intriguing experiments bearing not only upon questions of the aging of individuals but of the evolution of the entire species. The ability to establish normal diploid cell strains from small skin (or other tissue) biopsies of any individual plus the capacity to preserve these cells at sub-zero temperatures has fascinating experimental possibilities. Our experience with human diploid cell strains stored in liquid nitrogen only extends over a period of four years, yet after this time at −190 C. there is no diminution in rate of division or doubling potential. If such cell populations are found to retain these properties after a lapse of decades, then it might be concluded that if non-dividing cells age they can only do so while being functionally competent. Alternatively, if it is found that their viability or doubling potential diminishes with storage then preservation of cells at −190 C., where molecular activity is biologically negligible, may not protect them from the age-accelerating effects of, for example, radiation.

Although the experimenter would not be present to capitalize on his foresight, it would be a simple task to deposit ampules of normal human and animal cells in a well protected capsule buried in the Antarctic with instructions for reconstitution. This might lead an investigator, generations hence, to compare, among other things, the evolutionary aspects of aging at the cellular level.

CONCLUSION

The purpose of this essay is not to develop another theory of aging but merely to reconsider, in light of newer knowledge, the question of the finite lifetime of cells cultured outside of the animal body and what bearing this should have on current hypotheses. It is now possible that the powerful technique of cell cultivation may be exploited in investigating problems of senescence. Once the myth of the unlimited proliferation of normal cells *in vitro* is laid to rest, more emphasis should be placed on the notion that senescence results from a greater expression of events at the cellular level than at the tissue, organ or organism level. That is not to say that senescence, as a multi-causal phenomenon, is in no way a consequence of deteriorative supracellular events.

REFERENCES

Barski, G., Sorieul, S., and Cornefert, F.: Production dans des cultures *in vitro* de deux souches cellulaires en association, de cellules de caractère "hybride". *C. R. Acad. Sci. (Paris), 251:*1825, 1960.

Bidder, G. P.: The mortality of plaice. *Nature (London), 115:*495, 1925.

Calkins, G. N.: *Uroleptus mobilis* Eng. II. Renewal of vitality through conjugation. *J. Exp. Zool., 29:*121, 1919.

Carrel, A., and Burrows, M. T.: On the physiochemical regulation of the growth of tissues. *J. Exp. Med., 13:*562, 1911.

Cohn, A. E., and Murray, H. A.: The negative acceleration of growth with age, as demonstrated by tissue culture. *J. Exp. Med., 42:*275, 1925.

Comfort, A.: *Ageing: the Biology of Senescence.* New York, Holt, Rinehart, and Winston, 1964.

Cowdry, E. V.: Aging of individual cells. In: *Cowdry's Problems of Aging.* (Lansing, A. I., ed.) Baltimore, Williams and Wilkins, 1952, pp. 50-88.

Crowley, C., and Curtis, H. J.: The development of somatic mutations in mice with age. *Proc. Nat. Acad. Sci. USA, 49:*626, 1963.

Cudkowicz, G., Upton, A. C., Shearer, G. M., and Hughes, W. L.: Lymphocyte content and proliferative capacity of serially transplanted mouse bone marrow. *Nature (London), 201:*165, 1964.

Danielli, J. F., and Muggleton, A.: Some alternative states of amoeba, with special reference to life-span. *Gerontologia (Basel), 3:*76, 1959.

DeOme, K. B.: cited in Hayflick, L., The limited *in vitro* lifetime of human diploid cell strains. *Exp. Cell Res., 37:*614, 1965.

Earle, W. R.: Production of malignancy *in vitro.* IV. The mouse fibroblast cultures and changes seen in the living cells. *J. Nat. Cancer Inst., 4:*165, 1943.

Ebeling, A. H.: The permanent life of connective tissue outside of the organism. *J. Exp. Med., 17:*273, 1913.

Ephrussi, B., Scaletta, L. J., Stenchever, M. A., and Yoshida, M. C.: Hybridization of somatic cells *in vitro.* In: *Cytogenetics of Cells in Culture.* (Harris, R. J. C., ed.) New York, Academic Press, 1964.

Foley, G. E., and Handler, A. H.: Differentiation of "normal" and neoplastic cells maintained in tissue culture by implantation into normal hamsters. *Proc. Soc. Exp. Biol. Med., 94:*661, 1957.

Foley, G. E., and Handler, A. H.: Tumorigenic activity of tissue cell cultures. *Ann. N.Y. Acad. Sci., 76:*506, 1958.

Ford, C. E., Micklem, H. S., and Gray, S. M.: Evidence of selective proliferation of reticular cell-clones in heavily irradiated mice. *Brit. J. Radiol., 32:*280, 1959.

Gey, G. O., and Gey, M. K.: The maintenance of human normal cells and tumor cells in continuous culture. *Amer. J. Cancer, 27:*45, 1936.

Glinos, A. D., and Bartlett, E. G.: The effect of regeneration on the growth potential *in vitro* of rat liver at different ages. *Cancer Res., 11:*164, 1951.

Hamerton, J. L., Taylor, A. I., Angell, R., and McGuire, V. M.: Chromosome investigations of a small isolated human population: chromosome abnormalities and distribution of chromosome counts according to age and sex among the population of Tristan da Cunha. *Nature (London), 206:*1232, 1965.

Handler, A. H., and Foley, G. E.: Growth of human epidermoid carcinomas (strains KB and HeLa) in hamsters from tissue culture inocula. *Pro. Soc. Exp. Biol. Med., 91:*237, 1956.

Hayflick, L.: The establishment of a line (WISH) of human amnion cells in continuous cultivation. *Exp. Cell. Res., 23:*14, 1961.

Hayflick, L.: The limited *in vitro* lifetime of human diploid cell strains. *Exp. Cell Res., 37:*614, 1965.

Hayflick, L., and Moorhead, P. S.: The serial cultivation of human diploid cell strains. *Exp. Cell Res., 25:*585, 1961.

Hayflick, L., and Moorhead, P. S.: Cell lines from non-neoplastic tissue. In: *Growth, Including Reproduction and Morphological Development.* (Altman, P. L., and Dittmer, D. S., ed.) Washington, Federation of American Societies for Experimental Biology, Biological Handbook Series, 1962.

Howes, E. L., and Harvey, S. C.: Age factor in velocity of growth of fibroblasts in the healing wound. *J. Exp. Med., 55:*577, 1932.

Jacobs, P. A., Court Brown, W. M., and Doll, R.: Distribution of human chromosome counts in relation to ageing. *Nature (London), 191:*1178, 1961.

Jennings, H. S.: *Paramecium bursaria:* life history. V. Some relations of external conditions, past or present, to ageing and to mortality of exconjugants, with summary of conclusions on age and death. *J. Exp. Zool., 99:*15, 1945.

Koprowski, H., Pontén, J. A., Jensen, F., Ravdin, R. G., Moorhead, P. S., and Saksela, E.: Transformation of cultures of human tissue infected with simian virus SV_{40}. *J. Cell Comp. Physiol., 59:*281, 1962.

Krohn, P. L.: Review lectures on senescence. II. Heterochronic transplantation in the study of ageing. *Proc. Roy. Soc. Med., 157:*128, 1962.

Lefford, F.: The effect of donor age on the emigration of cells from chick embryo explants *in vitro. Exp. Cell Res., 35:*557, 1964.

Maynard Smith, J.: Review lectures on senescence. I. The causes of ageing. *Proc. Roy. Soc. Med. 157:*115, 1962.

Medawar, P. B.: *The Uniqueness of the Individual.* New York, Basic Books Inc., 1958.

Merz, G., and Hayflick, L.: Unpublished observations, 1965.

Norris, G., and Hood, S. L.: Some problems in the culturing and radiation sensitivity of normal human cells. *Exp. Cell Res., 27:*48, 1962.

Parker, R. C.: *Methods of Tissue Culture.* New York, Hoeber Medical Division, Harper and Row, 1961.

Pearl, R.: *The Biology of Death.* Philadelphia, J. B. Lippincott Co., 1922.

Puck, T. T., Morkovin, D., Marcus, P. I., and CiecIura, S. J.: Action of x-rays on mammalian cells. II. Survival curves of cells from normal human tissues. *J. Exp. Med., 106:*485, 1957.

Rizet, G.: Sur l'impossibilité d'obtenir la multiplication végétative ininterrompue et illimitée de l'ascomycète, *Podospora anserina. C. R. Acad. Sci. (Paris), 237:*838, 1953.

Rothfels, K. H., Kupelwieser, E. B., and Parker, R. C.: Effects of x-irradiated feeder layers on mitotic activity and development of aneuploidy in mouse-embryo cells *in vitro.* In: *Canadian Cancer Conference,* Volume 5 (Begg, R. W., ed.) New York, Academic Press, 1963.

Sachs, L., and Medina, D.: *In vitro* transformation of normal cells by polyoma virus. *Nature (London), 189:*457, 1961.

Shein, H. M., and Enders, J. F.: Transformation induced by simian virus (SV_{40}) in human renal cell cultures. I. Morphology and growth characteristics. *Proc. Nat. Acad. Sci. USA, 48:*1164, 1962.

Siminovitch, L., Till, J. E., and McCulloch, E. A.: Decline in colony-forming ability of marrow cells subjected to serial transplantation into irradiated mice. *J. Cell Comp. Physiol., 64:*23, 1964.

Sonneborn, T. M.: The delayed occurrence and total omission of endomixis in selected lines of *Paramecium aurelia. Biol. Bull. Wood's Hole, 74:*76, 1938.

Southam, C. M., Moore, A. E., and Rhoads, C. P.: Homotransplantation of human cell lines. *Science, 125:*158, 1957.

Stewart, H. L., Snell, K. C., Dunham, L. J., and Schlyen, S. M.: *Transplantable and Transmissable Tumors of Animals.* Washington, Armed Forces Institute of Pathology, 1959.

Strehler, B. L.: *Time, Cells, and Aging.* New York, Academic Press, 1962.

Strong, L. C.: The establishment of C_3H inbred strain of mice for the study of spontaneous carcinoma of the mammary gland. *Genetics, 20:*856, 1935

Todaro, G. J., and Green, H.: Quantitative studies of the growth of mouse embryo cells in culture and their development into established lines. *J. Cell Biol., 17:*299, 1963.

VERZÁR, F., AND THOENEN, H.: Die Wirkung von Elektrolyten auf die thermische Kontraktion von Collagenfäden. *Gerontologia (Basel), 4:*112, 1960.

VOGT, M., AND DULBECCO, R.: Virus-cell interaction with a tumor producing virus. *Proc. Nat. Acad. Sci. USA, 46:*365, 1960.

WOLF, K., AND QUIMBY, M. C.: Established eurythermic line of fish cells *in vitro*. *Science, 135:*1065, 1962.

Chapter 15

PERSPECTIVES IN RESEARCH ON THE AGING OF INVERTEBRATES

B. L. STREHLER

INTRODUCTION

IT IS A PLEASURE AND AN HONOR to contribute some thoughts on prospective areas in research on the aging of invertebrates to this volume dedicated to Professor Fritz Verzár. Professor Verzár, during his fifteen years of intensive interest in aging, has become the benevolent elder statesman of the field, while maintaining and directing an imaginative and productive research activity in his Basel laboratory. A considerable portion of the groundswell of interest in, and research on the fundamental aspects of aging can be traced directly to his influence, and to his counterparts in other countries.

The invertebrates encompass a range of living forms, both in body structure and in mode of existence which far exceeds the variety of life we see among vertebrates. This plethora of different forms of life among the invertebrates furnishes both a potential boon and a potential pitfall for research in aging; for on the one hand it should be possible to find model systems among the various invertebrates suitable for testing almost any particular hypothesis of aging. On the other hand, once the applicability or nonrelevance of the hypothesis is established for a given invertebrate form, one still is left with the question of whether the phenomenon observed expresses itself in vertebrates, particularly in man, as well as in other invertebrate types.

From an abstract point of view, an understanding of the aging process in any form of life is equally as interesting as human aging; but it must be recognized that abstract information, while titillating the intellectual palate, is not the only motivation in aging research. Indeed, the most pressing motivation is probably a mixture of curiosity about human aging and the desire to modify and control to whatever extent is possible its effects on human life. Therefore, research on the nature of aging in various invertebrate forms may actually detract from our progress in understanding mammalian and, particularly, human aging; and may inject complexities or simplifications into our thinking that have little or no relevance to the aging of highly complex social vertebrates.

In looking at the aging phenomena in invertebrates, therefore, and in considering those projections of research which would have the likelihood of embracing phenomena occuring throughout the range of life, I have selected a few topics for a brief discussion which seem to me to be potentially useful in their implications for aging of vertebrates, and especially of man.

SOME SPECIFIC AREAS FOR FUTURE RESEARCH

The advantages of invertebrates as tools for aging research are similar to their advantage in other types of study; namely, that it is usually possible to find some form of life which has a property or structure of interest in some accessible or exaggerated form, so that experimental manipulations and their effects can more easily be correlated than in a multifactored system in which cause and effect may be associated only through complex intermediate steps. For example, the study of the electrical properties of axones has been greatly facilitated by using the giant axon of the squid whose dimensions are of sufficient magnitude to permit microinjection and the insertion of internal electrodes within the axoplasm; Drosophila salivary gland chromosomes, lamp brush chromosomes, and the Balbioni rings have afforded tools to cytologists and developmental biologists as well as to geneticists. In such cases, questions have been answered which could not have been, if mammalian cells had been the object of study.

The rule, then, for aging research in invertebrates, is to select an hypothesis and then to look for the form of life which has the characteristic to be tested in exaggerated form. What are the questions in the biology of aging that may be particularly susceptible to study in model invertebrate systems?

These questions among others, are discussed in categorical form below: 1) Is an indefinite life span feasible for multicellular organisms and, if so, what are the peculiarities and limitations of those systems exhibiting it? 2) Is there a genetic programming of aging and what are its main features? 3) To what extent can the functional capacity of cells and tissues during aging be modified by environmental factors, such as hormones, food supply, pH and temperature?

Category I: Indefinite Life Span

Among all higher animals, only the vertebrates of indeterminate size, such as the long-lived turtles, may possibly be capable of an indefinitely long life time.[1] Among invertebrates the best documented instances of indefinitely long life spans occurs among the anemones.[2] It has been assumed that in the former cases, the apparent indefiniteness of life span is due to the continual addition of new cells in animals of indeterminate size according to the general hypothesis expressed by Bidder;[3] and that in the case of the anemones which probably have a maximum size determined by the niche that they occupy and by food supply, that the indefinitely long life spans observed must be due to a continual replacement of all cell types at a rate sufficient to replenish any cells or other structures which undergo senescent change. It seems imperative to study in a comparative fashion the biochemistry, histology, histochemistry and physiology of these two forms of life, and to determine whether there is any peculiarity in the origin of cells that differentiates them from their very short-lived relatives within the same phylum. Despite the remarkably unique observations on the great life span of anemones, no one has made an intensive investigation of the obvious age-related biological parameters of these species of animals. An intensive study of the histochemistry and biochemistry of Campanularia and other short-lived hydrozoans, should also be undertaken, for in these two typical coelenterates we have examples of animals with very long life spans and very short life spans in which the general body plan and mode of structure and function determine these differences. Campanularia affords a unique opportunity to study the sudden death of an entire functioning individual, which can be induced by certain environmental factors, (Fig. 1 and Table I) such as a brief

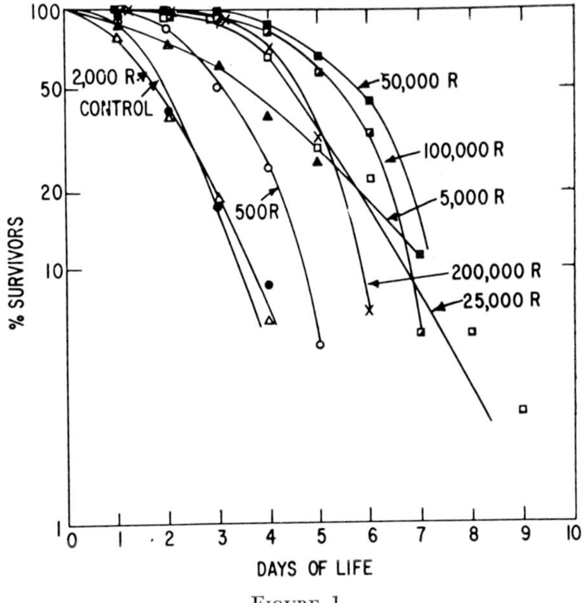

FIGURE 1

Log survivorship curves for *Campanularia flexuosa* hydranths after various exposures to x-rays.

Mean longevities ± σ_{mn}M's are:

● Controls — 2. 7 ± 0. 3 days (N = 23)
○ 500 r — 3. 6 ± 0.07 days (N = 81)
△ 2,000 r — 2.41 ± 0.07 days (N = 49)
▲ 5,000 r — 3.87 ± 0. 3 days (N = 15)
□ 25,000 r — 4.88 ± 0.25 days (N = 37)
■ 50,000 r — 6.11 ± 0. 4 days (N = 9)
◢ 100,000 r — 5.78 ± 0.17 days (N = 51)
× 200,000 r — 5.07 ± 0.22 days (N = 15)

TABLE I

ATP CONTENT OF CAMPANULARIA HYDRANTHO DURING DEVELOPMENT AND AGING

Stage	*ATP/Hydranth* ($g \times 10^{10}$)
Hydranth bud	15.0
Early differentiation	7.0
Complete differentiation but not extended	33.0
1 day old (young)	18.0
2–3 days old (middle-aged)	12.0
4–5 days old (old)	4.5

hypoxia, and according to Crowell, a brief exposure to a low temperature environment (4-10° C.).

Category II: Genetic Programing of Aging

The second general area in which the invertebrates may afford particularly useful experimental material is in the context of the general question, "To what extent does the genetic apparatus contain information which predetermines, as it were, the time of senescence and death?" In the clonal aging first observed in paramecia[4] and other protozoan species, and more recently reported for diploid human strains in cell culture,[5] there is implicit the idea that certain cells can undergo only a certain number of divisions following the process of fertilization or of autogamy, and that the mitotic machinery must then be revitalized through reoccurrence of fertilization. Fertilization is usually regarded as an evolutionary adaptation that assures a periodic resegregation of genetic material so that drastic changes in environment will not extinguish the line of animals or plants possessing it, and so that new variants may take over the niche, under altered environmental conditions. However, clonal aging in protozoa and possibly in mammalian cells, suggests that fertilization may have quite another function; namely, the reactivation of all of the genetic code that is necessary for continued existence. This hypothesis, it seems to me, is one of the most promising possibilities for exploring the general nature of aging; and it is only among the invertebrates that some of the fundamental questions implicit in this hypothesis can be tested rigorously. Since fertilization is such a general biological phenomenon and takes place by comparable mechanisms in all forms of life where it occurs, except possibly in bacteria, the study of the chemical changes occuring in the genetic material at the moment of fertilization and immediately following it, may be of prime significance in understanding clonal aging, and whatever implications it may have for aging in the mammalian system.

The following related ideas are implicit in some of the studies conducted by Dr. H. von Hahn, at Dr. Verzár's Institute in Basel.[6,7] Assuming that the process of development entails the selective activation and/or repression of different portions of the genome in different cell types, that the aged differentiated cell may overextend itself as far as the production of specific repressors is concerned, thus programming its own death as an unexpected extention of its own differentiation process, it would be desirable to determine the types of complexes associated with DNA, in animals, and in particular, in clones of cells obtained from animals of different ages, and in different stages of clonal aging. Dr. von Hahn has found an increase in certain histone components in thymus DNA chromatin with age,[8] and it would be highly instructive to determine whether there is a denudation of DNA in the chromosomes activated by the fertilization process.

Invertebrates may furnish the ideal material for testing this hypothesis, for certain of them produce very small eggs in very large numbers, and the isolation of DNA from an unfertilized egg containing only one set of chromosomes per potential individual, is no mean technological achievement and requires extremely large numbers of eggs. The colonial coelenterate, *Hydractinia echinata*[9] appears to be a highly suitable organism for such studies. These animals which live on the shells occupied by hermit crabs, and exist as male or female colonies, produce thousands of eggs per day, per colony, which can be released at the behest of the experimenter, by placing the individuals in the presence of light for a few minutes, after a few hours of darkness. We are currently engaged in devising means of culturing these animals and harvesting their eggs in large numbers to test some of the above possibilities.

Another type of biological clock has been suggested by Medvedev[10] as a factor in biological aging and involves the systematic exposure of one portion of the genetic apparatus after another to the messenger RNA synthesizing machinery. Medvedev has outlined this hypothesis in a recent publication.[10] The use of lamp brush chromosomes and other cytologically distinctive chromatin materials for such studies is an area that should not long be neglected. It is becoming increasingly apparent that the functional state of many organisms, including mammals, undergoes periodic fluctuations, sometimes diurnal, sometimes on a weekly or monthly basis. For example, the rate of cell replacement, or mitosis, is vastly greater at certain hours of the day than at other times. These fluctuations are no doubt under humoral or neural control and there seems a considerable likelihood that the same factors which control these circadian rhythms may also be altered during senescence.

Certain invertebrates show a very distinct periodicity or rhythm in their activities. These forms furnish excellent materials for studying circadian rhythms vs aging.

Finally, invertebrates, including the insect, *Habrobracon,* are ideally suited to test certain theories of individual aging involving the genetic apparatus.[11] The short life spans of worker bees as compared to the queen bee, the effects of royal jelly, the occurrence of parthenogenetic reproduction in various insects and the lack of

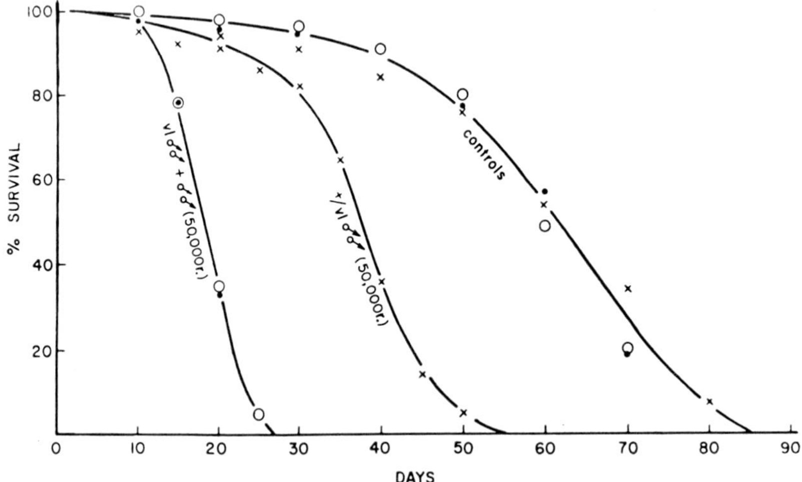

FIGURE 2. The effect of ploidy on survival of control and irradiated *Habrobracon*. × diploid males, • and ○, haploid males (from Clark[11]).

difference in life span demonstrated by Clark[11] in different ploidy classes of Habrobracon lines (Fig. 2), all are excellent examples of past and future prospects for testing specific genetic theories of aging.

Category III: Effect of Environmental Factors on Aging

Because many invertebrates can be cultured on defined chemical media or foods, and because they show remarkable responses to both nutritional and hormonal factors in growth, cell death and regeneration, they are highly adaptable as model systems in which the control of cell death, growth, differentiation and maturation can be modified. Microsurgical techniques for endocrine transplants in diptera, such as the fruitfly, and orthoptera, such as the roach, have been developed by Bodenstein,[12] and while the mechanism of action of the hormone ecdyson and others involved in the complex cycle of molting, growth and maturation, have not yet been worked out, it should not be an impossible task to push forward our understanding of the mode of action of these isolable substances with proper investment of interest, facilities, and talent.

Once again, the potentiality of using coelenterate material, which because of the general simplicity of its organization has a unique value in studies of regeneration, should not be overlooked. For example, what are the factors controlling polarity in regeneration and the nature of the substances or influences operating during the regeneration of hydranths of *Tubularia crocea*?

A second major environmental factor which can be studied to great advantage in certain invertebrates, both because of their short life span and simplified body structure, is the effect of temperature on the rate of senescence and death. Although temperature effects were among the first noted as having a striking influence on length of life, by Loeb and Northrop[13] at the beginning of this century, the mechanism by which low temperature slows down the rate of the aging process has not yet been settled. It appears clear that aging is not a result of thermal denaturation, but it is not certain whether the effect of low temperature is simply to slow down all processes, including aging, or whether there is a shift in the balance of synthetic and degradative processes as a function of temperature which somehow favors the long persistence of the individual. The firefly lantern, in which remarkable changes with age have recently been demonstrated,[14] is perhaps ideally suited as an object for specific histochemical and biochemical studies relating temperature and aging. A variety of changes occurs in the amounts of different chemical substances and enzymes in this organ as it ages. Figure 3 a and b, for example, illustrates the drastic decrease in RNA content which occurs during the aging of the firefly lantern. The level of this class of substances involved in protein synthesis falls both in the cytoplasm of the photogenic layer (*legend B*) and in the cells lining the tracheoles (*legend A*). A different, but equally striking change occurs in the level of glycogen stores in both the photogenic (*legend B*) and reflector layers (*legend C*) of this organ (see fig. 4 a and b) as well as in the protein and lipid stores of the photogenic layer (not shown). These large changes both in energy source and in the machinery for producing proteins, as well as the amount of functioning enzymes, furnishes an interesting model for senescence at the molecular level in which an array of related compounds and processes are implicated. The clarification of the origin and development of these changes is clearly susceptible to early attack.

It should be possible to differentiate the various hypotheses regarding synthesis and degradation, consumption of reserve materials, etc., by judicious application of modern quantitative histochemical techniques to this structure. In particular, the study of the changes in the efficiency and rate of ATP formation and mitochondrial oxidative phosphorylation under environmentally explicit conditions is feasible with this organism.

CONCLUSION

The foregoing essay attempts to set forth some of the areas in which exciting discoveries relating to the aging process may be un-

---

FIGURE 3 a-b illustrates the decrease of ribonucleic acid (RNA) with age in the photogenic and reflective layers as well as in the nuclei of the lantern of *Photinus pyralis*. RNA corresponds to darker areas (pyronine-methyl green method). Top, young; bottom, old. ×120.

A. Tracheoles are the tubular structures in the upper portion of each section.

B. Photogenic layer lies between the tracheoles.

C. The reflector layer lies immediately below the photogenic layer.

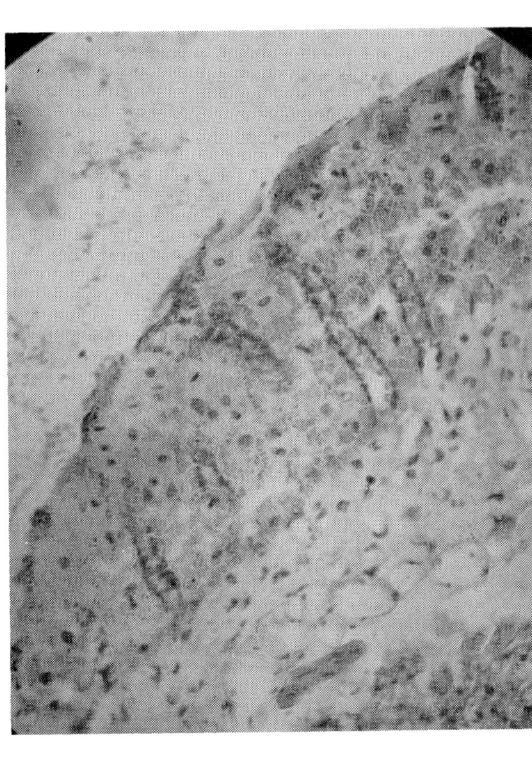

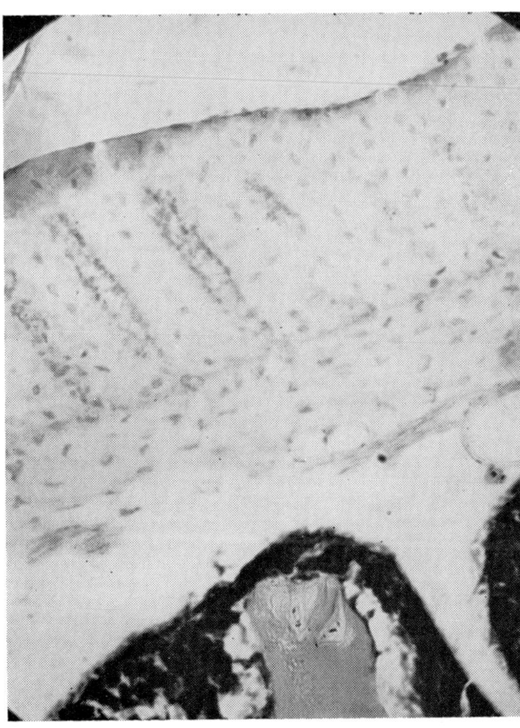

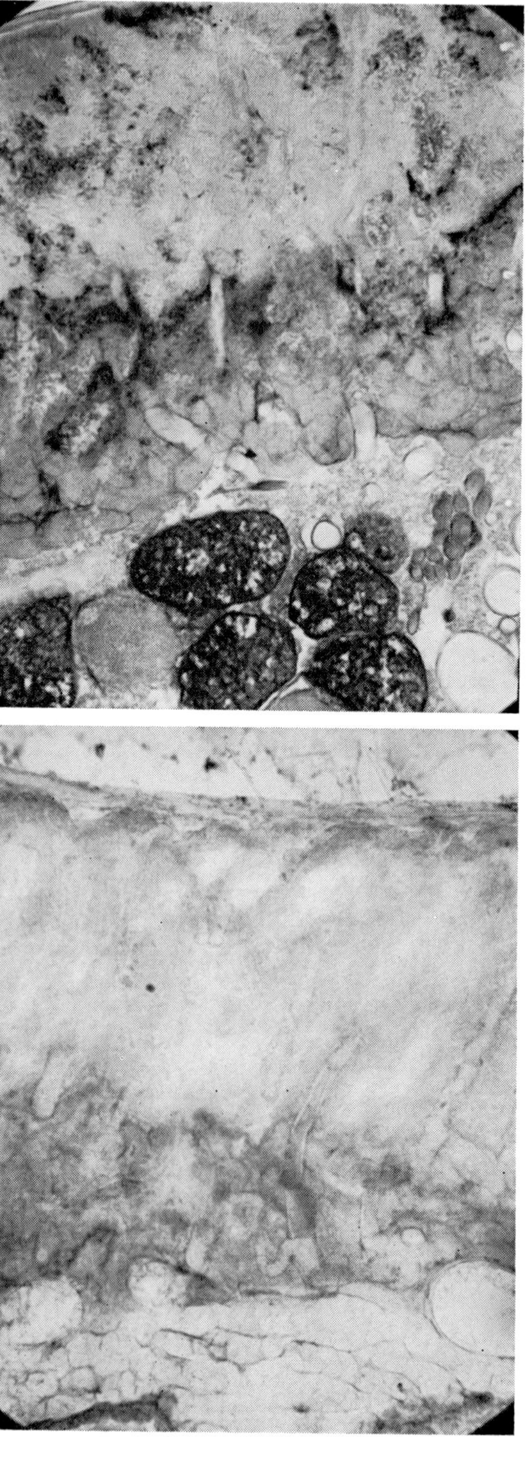

FIGURE 4 a-b shows the difference in glycogen conent in the young (top) and old (bottom) luminescent organs of the firefly *Photinus pyralis* as determined by the PAS reaction. In both the photogenic layer and the reflective layer, glycogen, which appears as the dark areas, decreases as the insect ages. ×120.

---

covered. The phenomena and problems enumerated are selected so as to have the greatest probability of being applicable to more complex metazoa, since they embrace processes common to all living things.

REFERENCES

1. STREHLER, B. L.: *Time, Cells, and Aging,* New York, Academic Press, 1962, 230 pp.
2. ASHWORTH, J. H., AND ANNANDALE, N.: Observation on some aged specimens of *Sagartia Troglodites* and on the duration of life in coelenterates. *Proc. Roy. Soc. Edinburgh, 25:*295, 1904.
3. BIDDER, G. P.: The mortality of plaice. *Nature, 115:*495, 1925.
4. MAUPAS, E.: Récheches experimentales sur la multiplication des infusoires ciliés. *Arch. Zool. exp. Gen., 6:*(2), 165, 1888.
5. HAYFLICK, L.: The limited *in vitro* lifetime of human diploid cell strains. *Exp. Cell Res., 37:*614, 1965.
6. HAHN, H. P. VON: The role of desoxyribonucleic acid (DNA) in the aging process. *Gerontologia, 8:*168, 1963.
7. HAHN, H. P. VON: Age-related alterations in the structure of DNA. II. The role of histones. *Gerontologia, 10:*174, 1964/65.
8. HAHN, H. P. VON: Analysis of histones from thymus of young and old bovines by gel filtration. *Gerontologia, 10:*107, 1964/65.
9. MINER, R. W.: *Field Book of Seashore Life,* New York, Putnam, 1960, 888 pp.
10. MEDVEDEV, Z. A.: The nucleic acids in development and aging, in *Advances in Gerontological Research.* B. L. Strehler, ed., 1964, Vol. I pp. 181-202.
11. CLARK, C. M.: Genetic factors associated with aging, in *Advances in Gerontological Research.* B. L. Strehler, ed., New York and London, Academic Press, 1964, Vol. I, pp. 207-252.
12. BODENSTEIN, D.: Le rôle des hormones dans la régeneration des organes des insects *Scientia, 53:*1, 1959.
13. LOEB, J., AND NORTHROP, J. H.: On the influence of food and temperature upon the duration of life. *J. Biol. Chem., 32:*(1), 103, 1917.
14. PRESS, G. D., RAYCHAUDHURI, A., AND STREHLER, B. L.: Histochemical changes in the firefly lantern during the aging process. *J. Geront., 21:*13, 1966.

Chapter 16

REGENERATION AND REJUVENATION OF INVERTEBRATES

L. HARANGHY AND A. BALÁZS

THE GREATEST SIGNIFICANCE of the connection between aging and regenerating ability lies in the fact that those species which are capable of a high degree of regeneration (or morphallaxis and somatic embryogeny) rejuvenate during the process, i.e., their tissue elements are restored to youth.

Among invertebrates we meet with various degrees of regenerating ability. In the phylum of protozoa and in the plasmodroms and ciliophores alike, we can find species incapable of cell regeneration and those which are capable in the highest degree. One of the first observations concerning this question dates back to Max Hartmann (1922), who kept *Amoeba proteus* alive for 130 days with daily amputations, whereas the individuals of this species normally divide every other day. Similar results were achieved with multicellular invertebrates such as *Stenostomum unicolor* and *S. leucops.* The opposite can be found in the more developed forms of the ciliates, whose regenerating ability is much smaller.

Here immediately a question arises on which only future research can throw light. Formerly the individual and clonal life spans in protozoa were not divided sharply. The amoeba type species of comparatively simple structure are undoubtedly capable of a high degree of regeneration, and this has a rejuvenating and life span lengthening effect. At the same time, it seems probable that such "intermitotic" creatures, in their life between two divisions, only reach a certain phase of maturity but do not age. However, those species in which this could be established (protozoa, for instance, as in Rudzinska's 1961 investigations) have a postreproductive period partly analogous to that of multicellular organisms and perish after involutional symptoms appear. They have—

at least in old age—a low level of regenerating ability. Accordingly the question is in which structure or mechanism are ability of aging and incapability of somatic embryogeny connected? Differentiation, which was frequently mentioned earlier, cannot be regarded as a causal factor, since numerous cases of highly differentiated cells are known in which regenerating ability is of a high degree.

A certain parallelism can be observed between the measure of regenerating ability and philogenetic development in the phylogeny of multicellular invertebrates. Thus, for example, there is no doubt that sponges, hydras and planarians regenerate better than molluscs or most insects. For all that, among the metagenetic forms of *Cnidarians,* the medusae or *Rotatoria* among worms can replace their lost body parts only in a small degree. On the other hand, comparatively highly developed snails such as *Asteroidea* and *Holothurioidea* regenerate excellently. Therefore, regenerating ability, evolutional level and aging are not in direct causal connection with each other.

Compared to the number of investigations performed on vertebrates, especially mammals, those which examine the connection between the ontogenetic state of development and regenerating ability by reliable methods are insignficant. The bulk of observations relate to comparison of embryos, sexually immature individuals or those having just reached sexual maturity. Among these (according to investigations performed on planarians by Tokin, 1961, and observations by Pai, 1928, on *Anguillula*) there is no doubt that regenerating ability of the organs decreases significantly during the course of growth. At the same time, according to our own investigations (Balázs, 1965), mortality as a result of amputations was higher in sexually immature planarians then in developed or old specimens. As to its effect on the fibroplasy of aging, the literature records divergent observations, as in the case of mammals (Bourlière, 1950; Bucher and Glinos, 1950; Comfort and Doljanski, 1958; du Noüy, 1936; Schulz and Doberauer, 1960, and other works). Pai (1928) established that in an advanced stage of involution *Anguillula* is incapable of both wound healing and cytoplasmic regeneration, and perishes as a result of the slightest amputation. Our own experience (Haranghy and Balázs, 1964) on *Dugesia lugubris,* however, reveals that concerning the eyes, accessory eyes, pharynx, sexual openings or body pigmentation, regeneration is neither quicker nor more thorough in young, sexually mature samples three to twelve months old than in old ones of three to four years.

In mitoses, however, the latent time for proliferation is somewhat longer (Lindh, 1959) and the initial growing speed of regenerating blastem is somewhat less in the old than in the young. At the same time, the aging of planarians undoubtedly proceeds at a more temperate speed and rhythm than that of eutel species (Balázs and Burg, 1962). This can probably be ascribed to the fact that a typical regeneration, reduction and heteromorphosis do not occur more frequently in old samples than in those of middle age, even following a repeated series of amputations (Haranghy and Balázs, 1964).

Further researches must reveal whether ontogenetic decrease of regenerating ability stands in direct connection with the aging type. It may be that both can be ascribed to a third factor.

In regard to the connection between regeneration and aging among invertebrates, the following research tasks arise:

1) Is the present day conception correct, that a high degree of regenerating ability (and perhaps the temperately aging type) depends in the first place on the fact that a great number of totipotent reserve cells are preserved in the respective group of animals, even in old age? The fact itself is indisputable; in *Dugesia lugubris,* for instance, we established that the number of neoblasts is approximately the same in old age as it is in young, sexually mature samples. Furthermore, it is necessary to establish which endogenous stimuli induce the embryonic type of cells to differentiate (e.g., in the case of eutel animals or mammals) and which intrinsic factors make it possible for well regenerating groups to avoid differentiation and preserve totipotence even in old age.

2) At present the question of whether the possibility of the reserve-cell's differentiation in all directions (its totipotence) is a necessary condition for a high degree of regenerating ability is a problem that remains to be solved. It is conceivable that it could be substituted for artificially by a greater number of not yet differentiated cells, capable only of differentiating in a deter-

mined direction. Numerous undifferentiated cells occur in higher organisms too, for instance, in the haemopoetic tissues of human beings. Their development, however, is limited to the mesenchymal direction (Haranghy, 1934). Rejuvenating effect can also be achieved in a lesser degree if we increase physiological regeneration by artificial means in old age. Such regeneration undoubtedly is diminished with age in certain cell types. Investigations performed on Lieberkühn crypts of mice by Fry, Lesher and Kohn (1962) an on human nails by Knobloch (1951) point to this.

3) Numerous investigations prove that the presence of totipotent cells, serving as material for reparative regeneration, is not sufficient for differentiation to replace all cells which perish in old age. For instance, from the posterior fragments of *Dendrocoelum* (Bácsy and Török, 1961) no head part developes, although wandering of neoblasts and blastema formation occurs in these cases too. The organizing, integrative factor is absolutely indispensable for regulating the mechanism. In the first place we know from investigations performed by Török (1958) on planarians that such an inductional role can be attributed to the neurons of the nervous system. According to Harms (1949) the nervous system is the primary factor; *Protula* was able to rejuvenate old individuals by grafting them with young heads. The question remains whether this function is only characteristic of well regenerating animals in old age or if the nervous system of an organism incapable of somatic embryogeny also preserves its regenerating ability.

4) It is by no means yet decided to what degree rejuvenation occurs as an effect of regeneration in the regenerate, and to what degree in the original starting body-part. Histological and biochemical investigations performed on higher organism prove that the regenerate is a biologically young, new formation. Verzár and Willenegger (1961), for instance, established that collagen occurring in the scars of old people is of youthful character because it contains a high percentage of labile collagen.

It is a very important fact that from investigations performed chiefly on invertebrates, the conclusion can be drawn that the larger the amputated body-part, the greater (within certain limits) the rejuvenation. And, which is even more siginficant, not only the regenerate but, as we know from the investigations performed on planarians by Brøndsted (1955), Lender (1950, 1956), Lindh (1959) and others, the original starting body-part also rejuvenates. Reorganization is not complete, since elements of the nervous system, sensory cells etc. remain intact and do not undergo a disintegrative process. The fact that in Sonneborn's (1930) classical investigations the individuals of clonal progeny regenerated from the head part of the *Stenostomum* supplemented from the posterior body-part can probably be attributed to this. Investigations on rejuvenation performed on *Dugesia lugubris,* based on quantitative, objective criteria (restoration of accessory eyes, ratio of fertility) established (Balázs, 1964) that rejuvenation of the original, starting body-part never means a complete return to its former state. Since heterocrony comes into being through biologically older, rejuvenated parts of the organs and/or cells, the question arises whether histological decomposition (which can undoubtedly be established) and reorganization really lead to lengthening of the life span.

In this connection it would be of decisive significance to investigate the life spans of regenerating organisms after amputations performed at different levels, by means of regular survival curves. Such an investigation could compare active life periods only. It would be unjustified to compare the period from amputation to complete regeneration with the corresponding time lapse in the life of the control. To our knowledge such experiments, meeting the requirements of up-to-date gerontology, have not been performed yet, either on vertebrates or invertebrates. The only exceptions are experiments performed on the vegtatively propagating animal groups. Hartmann (1922) proved on *Stenostomum* species, Beauchamp (1931) on *Fonticola vitta,* that the cycle of life between divisions can be prolonged many times. These types, however, generally lose their individuality before aging. Recently Hackett, Boss and Dijkman (1963) have achieved a life span prolonging effect on algae (*Acetabularia crenulata*) by a series of amputations.

5) Further investigations will have to determine whether totipotent cells, playing a decisive role in regeneration and at the same time in rejuvenation of the tissues are characteristic for a species or can be transplanted to other species. In this connection

Lindh's (1959) hetero-transplantation experiments between *Dugesia polychroa* and *Dugesia lugubris* are of great interest. In these he revealed that neoblasts of species with a different number of chromosomes can migrate into each other's body fragments following their parabiosis. The question remains whether in the case of taxonomically distant species the reserve cells are also non-specific.

6) At the present time it seems probable (but still has to be proved) that regeneration is not connected with the neoblasts and other totipotent cells, and thus is a molecular and not a cytological effect. Since it can be established just by planarians as proved by the McConnel school that the organic basis of association (or conditioned reflex formation) is not the neuron but a substance of macromolecular dimension in the neuron, the previously mentioned conception does not seem impossible. Its practical significance can be of the utmost importance not only in gerontology, but in traumatological, surgical and other connections as well.

7) In the golden age of experimental gerontological research at the beginning of the twentieth century, comparative investigations were relatively more widespread. Later on, one-sided human and mammalian investigations predominated in gerontology. The efforts of the International Gerontological Association and of numerous researchers, notably Verzár, introduced experimental quantitative measuring requirements in gerontology and furthered comparative research. Numerous procedures are being reevaluated and included in the field of gerontological investigations on the basis of many interesting data which have accumulated in the previous decades. These have resulted from investigations of disintegrational, decompositional, inductional and inhibiting factors (e.g., starvation occurring among *Turbellarians,* and histolysis appearing in the course of metamorphosis by insects in connection with histogenesis).

Decompositional factors are more widespread among invertebrates than among vertebrates. Besides amputation or wounding, certain signs indicate that in species capable of a high degree of somatic embryogeny, starvation also produces a similar effect. Thus, Child (1913, 1914) demonstrated that *Phagocata velata* rejuvenate by starvation and that undernourishment hinders aging and fragmentation. In the course of starvation the body volume of planarians decreases to 1/300 of normal. According to Hyman (1951) this can be attributed in the first place to degeneration of the tissue, which is significant in the mesenchyma, the gonads and the intestinal ducts; at the same time the nervous system, the epidermis and the muscles hardly alter. A high degree of decomposition is followed by quick regeneration (in case of regular nourishment) which exhibits an intermediate process analogous to reparative and physiological regeneration. According to Hyman (1951) the rejuvenating characteristics of starvation are proved by the shape of the oxygen-consumption curve. It must be mentioned that on the basis of other criteria, starvation often appears as an influence which hastens aging (Krumbiegel, 1929; Lindh, 1959; Comfort, 1964).

In a wider sense histolysis of the *Holometabola* insects is a special decomposing factor of invertebrates. Here the producing factor is of hormonal or more exactly neurohumoral character. Histogenesis, redifferentiation commencing in the second period of the pupal stage, starts from the so-called imaginal discs. Future researches will have to decide if moulting and pupation hormones bring about a disintegrational process similar to histolysis, followed by redifferentiation at a later period of imaginal life. It is a pity that the literature dealing largely with the metamorphosis of insects contains little data concerning imagines, although from the standpoint of gerontology they alone are of interest. Engelman's (1959) implantation experiments performed on *Leucophaea* and Novak's present work on *Pyrrhocoris* are very significant from the gerontological point of view. If it were possible to bring about on imaginal tissues, even if only partly, a process similar to pupal histolysis, we would approach the practical realization of a highly differentiated organism's rejuvenation. It is feasible to obtain a result producing histolysis on older imagoes without a regenerating, histogenetic course following.

8) The vegetatively propagating invertebrates reveal numerous phenomena in the course of reproduction which undoubtedly must be included in the sphere of regeneration and rejuvenation. Child (1913, 1914) has established that *Phagocata* show symptoms

of old age after reaching maturity: depigmentation and anorexia appear, a disintegrative process commences in the eyes, the pharynx and the head parts and eventually the animal fragments. This is followed by a regenerating phase in which each fragment encysts and new planarians grow, which are similar in every respect to the young animals emerging from the cocoons. This cycle is repeated under natural conditions for a long time without loss of vitality. This particular type of asexual reproduction is only one of a number of more or less divergent vegetative propagations which have been described in other species. In all of these, it is the basic principle which interests the gerontologist: what kind of organic, cytologic or molecular organization is necessary for old organisms, affected by endogenous or exogenous factors, to differentiate in such a manner that a rejuvenating redifferentiation will follow?

9) The literature of up-to-date gerontology mainly contains data relating to reparative, physiological regeneration, while the limits of compensating regeneration in old age by invertebrates are unknown. MacKay *et al* (1924) and Verzár (1955) made interesting statements on the compensatory hypertrophy of mammals. It would be important to ascertain how all this is manifested by invertebrates, e.g., in the *Ciona* syphon-regeneration among ascidians or in the hypertrophic leg and antenna regeneration of the *Asellus aquaticus.* There is no doubt, as perhaps the previously summarized data prove, that the connection between regeneration and aging can be studied especially well in invertebrates. One of the reasons for this is that more species with extreme regenerating ability are to be found, and these show the differences in a much more marked fashion that do vertebrates. The life span of invertebrates is usually much shorter and their regeneration much quicker than in vertebrates; thus, observing the conditions of survival following reorganization and constructing significant mortality curves is essentially easier. It seems probable that, as in the case of developmental mechanics around the beginning of the twentieth century, experimental gerontology will gain ground more and more in the course of years to come on eutel and well regenerating invertebrate species. In the pursuit of this aim Professor

Verzár's work is authoritative. Following his lead, we endeavour to supply data which will throw light on the biological basis of aging.

REFERENCES

Balázs, A.: Experimental investigations on the regenerative ability of planarians in old age. In Balázs, A., ed.: *Int. Conf. Geront.* Akadémiai Kaidó, Budapest, 1965, pp. 111-116.

Balázs, A.: Experimental analysis of aging and rejuvenation in planarians. In From Hansen, P., ed.: *Age with a Future.* Munksgaard, Copenhagen, 1964, pp. 155-158.

Balázs, A., and Burg, M.: Span of life and senescence of *Dugesia lugubris. Gerontologia, 6:*227, 1962.

Bácsy, E., and Török, L. J.: Contributions to the regenerative capacity of *Dendrocoelum lacteum. Acta Biol. Hung., 12:*313, 1961.

Beauchamp, P.: Races et nodes de reproduction chez la *Planaire fonticola* vitta. *C. R. Soc. Biol., 107:*1001, 1931.

Bourlière, F.: Sénescence et vitesse de cicatrisation chez la rat. *Rev. Med. Liege, 5:*669, 1950.

Brøndsted, H. V.: Planarian regeneration. *Biol. Rev., 30:*65, 1955.

Bucher, N. L. R., and Glinos, A.: The effects of age on regeneration of rat liver. *Cancer Res., 10:*324, 1950.

Child, C. M.: The asexual cycle of *Planaria velata* in relation to senescence and rejuvenescence. *Biol. Bull. Wood's Hole, 25:*181, 1913.

Child, C. M.: Asexual breeding and prevention of senescence in *Planaria velata. Biol. Bull. Wood's Hole, 26:*286, 1914.

Comfort, A.: *Aging; the Biology of Senescence.* Routledge and Kegan Paul, 1964.

Comfort, A., and Doljanski, F.: The relation of size and age to rate of tail regeneration in *Lebistes reticulatus. Gerontologia, 2:*266, 1959.

Du Noüy, P. L.: *Biological Time.* Methuen, London, 1936.

Engelmann, F.: Über die Wirkung implantierter Prothoraxdrüsen im adulten Weibchen von *Leucophaea maderae.* Blatteria. *Z. Vergl. Physiol., 41:*456, 1959.

Fry, R. J. M., Lesher, S., and Kohn, H. I.: Influence of age on the transit time of cells of the mouse intestinal epithelium. III. *Ileum. Labor. Invest., 11:*289, 1962.

Hackett, H. E., Boss, M. L., and Dijkman, M. J.: Regeneration and proportional life span extension of *Acetabularia crenulata* Lamouroux. *J. Geront., 18:*331, 1963.

Haranghy, L.: Deutung der Veränderungen der Milz bei Diphtherie auf Grund der Milzveränderungen nach Rizinvergiftung. *Zbl. Allg. Path., 60:*161, 1934.

Haranghy, L., and Balázs, A.: Aging and rejuvenation in planarians. *Exp. Geront., 1:*77, 1964.

Harms, J. W.: Altern und Somatod der Zellverbandstiere. *Z. Alternsforsch., 5:*73, 1949.

Hartmann, M.: Über den dauernden Ersatz der ungeschlechtlichen Fortpflanzung durch fortgesetzte Regenerationen. *Biol. Zbl., 42:*364, 1922.

Hyman, L. H.: *The Invertebrates, Vol. III.* McGraw Hill, London, 1951.

Knobloch, H.: Fingernagelwachstum und Alter. *Z. Alternsforsch. 5:*357, 1951.

Krumbiegel, I.: Untersuchungen über die Einwirkung der Fortpflanzung auf Altern und Lebensdauer der Insekten ausgeführt an Carabus and Drosophila. *Zool. Jahrb. Abt. Anat. Ontog., 51:*11, 1929.

LENDER, TH.: Demonstration du role organisateur du cervean dans la régénération des yeux de la planaire *Polycelis nigra* par la méthode des greffes. *C. R. Soc. Biol., 144:*1407, 1950.

LENDER, TH.: L'inhibition de la régénération du cerveau de la planaire *Polycelis nigra* et *Dugesia lugubris. Bull. Soc. Zool. Fr., 81:*192, 1956.

LINDH, N. O.: Heteroplastic transplantation of transversal body sections in flatworms. *Arkiv. Zool., 12:*183, 1959 .

MACKAY, E. M., MACKAY, L. L., AND ADDIS, T.: The degree of compensatory renal hypertrophy following unilateral nephrectomy. I. The influence of age. *J. Exp. Med., 56:*255, 1932.

PAI, S.: Die Phasen des Lebenszyklus der *Anguillula aceti* Ehr. und ihre experimentell—morphologische Beeinflussung. *Z. Wiss. Zool., 131:*293, 1928.

RUDZINSKA, M. A.: The use of a protozoan for studies on aging. II. The macronucleus in young and old organisms of *Tokophrya infusionum:* light and electron microscope observations. *J. Geront., 16:*326, 1961.

SCHULZ, F. H., AND DOBERAUER, W.: Regeneration und Alter. *Klin. Med., 15:*475, 1960.

SONNEBORN, T. M.: Genetic studies on *Stenostomum incandatum* n.sp.I. The nature and origin of differences in individuals formed during vegetative reproduction. *J. Exp. Zool., 57:*57, 1930.

TOKIN, B. P.: Regeneration and somatic embryogenese (in Hungarian). *Biológiai Közlemények, 9:*3, 1961.

TÖRÖK, L. J.: Experimental contributions to the regenerative capacity of *Dugesia (Euplanaria) lugubris.* O. Schm. *Acta Biol. Hung., 9:*79, 1958.

TÖRÖK, L. J., AND BALÁZS, A.: Histological and histochemical analysis of the nervous system and neoblasts of aged planarians. Lecture on the Internat. Geront. Conference, Budapest. 1962.

VERZÁR, F.: Compensatory hypertrophy of kidney and adrenal in the lifespan of rats. In *IIIrd Congress Int. Assoc. Gerontology, London, 1954.* Livingstone, London, 1955, p. 139.

VERZÁR, F., AND WILLENEGGER, H.: Aging of the collagen in skin and scars. *Schweiz. Med. Wschr., 91:*1234, 1961.

Chapter 17

MODELS OF AGING—INSECTS

MORRIS ROCKSTEIN

INTRODUCTION

WHEN DESCARTES observed, *Cogito, ergo sum,* he could well have added the corollary, *Cogito, ergo cognosco senescam moriarque,* or "I think, therefore I know that I shall grow old and die." That is by way of saying that in addition to the conscious realization of his existence, man, unlike other animals, is patently aware of the fact that a major consequence of his very existence is that he must grow old and ultimately pass from this earthly vale of tears. Such a realization of the predestined course of his life has not only evoked considerable speculation concerning man's post-mortal fate, but in the curious and the inquisitive, an interest as well in the nature of the aging process and its possible amelioration, if not its delay.

As a biologist, I think of the life history of all metazoon animals as being subdivisible into three clearly definable stages, *viz.,* 1) the period of embryonic development following fertilization of the ovum, 2) the trimester of life during which growth and maturation to mature adulthood occur and the latter part of which period is marked by a more or less equal matching of the animal's capacity to survive with the assaults and insults of the internal and external environment, and 3) finally, the stage during which a distinct, involutionary process is patently manifest and the ability of the organism to withstand the stresses and strains of the environment fail in a progressive and cumulative fashion as a function of time, ultimately to result in death. This final period we call *senescence.*

On several previous occasions, both in publications and in symposia, I have presented convincing evidence (Rockstein, 1958) that each of these stages, including the period of senescence, is genetically predetermined both as to course and duration for each, as well as the average, individual in a given strain or species, at the climactic moment when the spermatozoon and ovum meet—at fertilization.

Understandably, but unfortunately, the first two phases of life, mentioned above, have been the individual and combined objects of scientific (and speculative) scrutiny from the beginning of modern science, but it is only within the past two decades or so that there had been any really rational speculation and, more important, actual experimental attention paid to the entire process of aging and, more specifically, to senescence as a distinct attribute of living things. Indeed, the relatively young life of the Gerontological Society (founded in 1945) is cogent testimony to this relatively recent interest in gerontology as a genuine scientific discipline.

INSECTS AS EXPERIMENTAL ANIMALS IN THE STUDY OF AGING

For well over a decade, I have been concerned with establishing firm and reproducible criteria, especially biochemical ones, for the process of aging, particularly in structures known to exhibit time-related alterations of a degenerative nature, both as regards gross function and structure, as well as in intra- and sub-cellular components from mitochondria to enzymes to metabolites. As much by choice as by chance, I have pursued these studies with certain species of insects which, in my opinion at least, represent the *sine qua non* of experimental animals for basic studies of the process of aging for the following reasons.

Versatility

It is very likely that the actual number of insect species may eventually total two million in number. This tremendous success in the evolution of a peculiar form of life over a period of well over 350 million years has permitted a wide degree of diversification with respect to food habits, temperature preferences and distribution. Indeed, species of insects are known to occupy areas inhabited by virtually all other invertebrates and vertebrates, as well as some unique ecological situations in which no other animals can survive. This includes the hot springs of Yellowstone

Park with temperatures of 120° F., where immature larval forms of a common family of flies thrive and, by contrast, the snow line of the high Alps, where a primitive form of orthopteran insect, related to the common cricket and the common cockroach, is to be found. Although limited to fresh water, the air, the ground and subterranean habitats, one can even find, on the shores of the sea in small pools of tidal water trapped in crevices or rocks, clusters of a small springtail, the maritime collembolid. Even in the hot sand dunes of the desert, species of insects are known to exist and persist.

The ability of insects to feed on virtually every form of matter is indicative of the tremendous versatility which evolution has bestowed upon this most successful of all animal groups. Thus, Brues (1946) in his insect dietary, and Folsom and Wardle (1934) in their early work on insect ecology, both point with great reserve to the wide variation in dietary of insects in relation to their success, abundance and diversity on one hand, and their economic and medical importance, on the other. Thus, the herbivorous locusts, grasshoppers, crickets, chinch bugs, beetles, plant sucking insects like aphids and true bugs depend upon *plants* for their existence; predatory wasps, flies, mosquitoes, lice and even hymenopterous insects like ants depend upon other animals for their own existence. Indeed, it is a rare human who has not experienced the painful or unpleasant presence of a predatory, blood sucking insect like a mosquito or fly or, in some cases, head and body lice, which depend upon humans for their own survival. The tremendous versatility of insect food habits extends, as we well know, to their ability to feed on dead organic matter, as well as their deriving energy from inorganic sources. Thus, the termite, the wood-boring beetles and the larvae of scavenger flies make possible the return of the elements in dead organic material, whether it be of plant or animal origin, to a free form, to be utilized by plants once more in the synthesis of the basic nutrients of life.

All of this is by way of showing that insects, like higher mammals and even man himself, have adapted, through evolution, to ecological situations and dietary requirements similar if not identical to those of other higher animals including man, and that one might expect, similarly, their basic body structure and cell biology to be not dissimilar to that of man himself. Moreover, this tremendous versatility of insects makes them extremely useful if not unique as experimental animals, in permitting experimentation in all fields of biology, but especially in experimental gerontology itself.

Availability in Large Numbers

Unlike mammals, with small litters and a limited number of offspring during their lifetimes, insects as a group possess an unusually high reproductive potential. Such animals as the common house fly have an unbelievable potential for reproduction even when beginning with relatively small original, ancestral populations. Thus, it has been calculated (West, 1951) that a gravid female capable of producing four to six batches of about 100 to 150 eggs each could theoretically be responsible for as many as 325,923,200,000,000 offspring in one summer. In our own laboratories, we are able to produce many thousands of adult flies for studies on aging, exactly every two weeks, under controlled conditions of temperature and humidity. Even more striking than this is the fact that a queen honeybee, with a life span of approximately six years, can lay two to three thousand eggs a day at the height of the honey flow season and produce a summer colony with the strength of at least one hundred to two hundred thousand worker bees. Similarly, a termite queen, laying as many as six eggs per minute, has been known to produce a nest housing up to one and three-quarter million termites. Ant nests, likewise, have been known to contain as many as a quarter of a million individuals in the North American mound-building ant colonies. Finally, the formidable carnivorous driver ants in the American tropics unquestionably occur in numbers far exceeding ten million individuals per acre.

Short Life Span

More important to the gerontologist, however, is the fact that the life span of species of some insects is so short as to permit a number of replicate studies of various biological phenomena, with age as a parameter, in a single year. Thus, the house fly, with a longevity of not more than ten weeks at the very maximum (under optimal conditions) permits at the very minimum, three replicate, generation studies in one year and, by judicious overlapping of such studies, this can be increased by a number of times, within the limits of space and personnel available.

Size

Despite their relatively small size, insects can be readily studied either by the use of large numbers of animals, all descendants from single pairs of parents (or ancestors, at least) or by means of many microtechniques of a chemical or an electrical or other physical nature available today. Indeed, with the development of microelectronic instrumentation capable of high amplification, action potentials of insect nerve fibers have been the object of considerable recent extensive study. On the other hand, this characteristic of small size means that extremely large numbers of insects can be housed in animal quarters normally capable of accommodating only small numbers of mammals and at a cost relatively insignificant in comparison to that required for mammals.

Availability of Pure Strains

The development of pure strains of flies, bees and even beetles today, makes more certain and more reliable the observations and experimental results obtained in biological studies of such individuals. Indeed, Thomas Hunt Morgan and his colleagues recognized this particular attribute of the common "fruit fly," *Drosophila melanogaster,* in their pioneer work in genetics in the latter part of the first half of the century. As a specific example, this author has published life tables (Rockstein and Lieberman, 1959) for a highly inbred strain of the common house fly (NAIDM), which continue to be confirmed over a long-term study period on the physiology of aging in this common insect, just as long as the conditions of rearing and maintenance remain unchanged.

Manageability

Because insects are poikilothermous animals and therefore adjust their body activities to the external environmental temperature, insects, unlike mammals, permit ready manageability as regards their total life span, as well as the duration of individual stages of development and maturation. Thus, in the NAIDM strain of house fly employed in our laboratory, the house flies maintained at 82° F. and at a relative humidity of 45 to 50 per cent, under constant lighting conditions, go through a two-week to two-week generation cycle, with the peak emergence of thousands of adult flies every two weeks between Wednesday evening and the following Thursday afternoon. In this way, flies of known age, within very narrow ranges (of, for example, zero to five minutes of age), can be isolated and made available for aging studies.

Insects as Models of Aging

Accepting the fact that insects represent a highly advanced and successful group of animals, with many desirable features making them highly suited to gerontological research, one cannot underemphasize the comparative value of principles derived from such studies of insects, inasmuch as the past ten years or better have seen a tremendous expansion of biological, biochemical and biophysical studies of insects which reveal their anatomy, morphology, physiology and their basic cell biology and cell chemistry to be virtually identical with those of higher vertebrates, including man.

AGE-DEPENDENT SYSTEMS IN INSECTS

The very recent review by Clark and Rockstein (1964) has brought up-to-date the still fragmentary picture of the biology of aging in insects. What is particularly notable from this summary of the literature in the field is the relatively few individuals who have devoted a major portion of their research attention to this field of aging in insects (*viz.*, Ludwig, Maynard-Smith, Maurizio and Rockstein. See Clark and Rockstein, 1964).

Thus, one finds from the research to date on insect aging, that:

1) Insect life tables follow those obtained for other species, with survivorship curves varying from the rectangular to the intermediate to the diagonal curve, just as they do in mammals and other vertebrates. Moreover, in virtually all species studied, with the exception of some unusual strains, the female of each species consistently shows a dramatically longer mean and maximum life span than the male of the same species.

2) Age-related structural changes in insects parallel those obtained for higher animals. Thus, the depletion of nerve cells (Rockstein, 1950) in the brain of the honeybee follows the pattern almost identical with that reported for the human brain. Similarly, aging in motor ability has been found to be accompanied both by depletion in the nutrients in the flight muscle of winged insects as well as, more dramatically (Rockstein and Bhatnagar, 1965), by the decrease in number of the giant mitochondria, which serve as the chemical "powerhouses," as it were, for the energizing of flight ability. This is accompanied, in the adult male house fly particularly, by the failure of flight ability which is manifested in the abrading and ultimate, complete loss of wings, together with decline in activity in certain key enzyme systems before and during the actual loss of wings.

Whereas depletion phenomena, on the one hand, account for senescence in some insectan structures, accumulation phenomena, on the other hand, such as are seen in certain tissues of higher vertebrates (pigment granules), are also characteristic of certain insect species which have been studied. Thus, "age pigments" accumulate in the aging honeybee, as reported by Haydak (Clark and Rockstein, 1964). The accumulation of urates, especially, as a storage-excretion phenomenon in most species of insects may likewise be related to longevity (Clark and Rockstein, 1964).

3) Functional changes of a gross nature are often accompanied by demonstrable structural and intracellular chemical changes. Probably the most exciting if not challenging of all age-related physiological phenomena in insects is that of metachemogenesis, first described by this author (Rockstein, 1959a), which concerns the post-emergent changes of a maturation nature, both in the ability to fly, as well as in distinct structural (intracellular) and biochemical (enzyme) changes accompanying such maturing of flight ability. Corresponding to such changes, this author has likewise described structural and chemical changes accompanying the *senescence* of flight ability, especially in the house fly (Rockstein, 1959b, 1960; Clark and Rockstein, 1964; Rockstein and Bhatnagar, 1965).

4) Life span can be altered by increasing the temperature at which the insects are reared and maintained (which usually di-

minishes the life span, with some exceptions) (see Clark and Rockstein, 1964), or by lowering of temperature, by alteration in diet, by population density, by parental age and by exposure to radiation (Clark and Rockstein, 1964; Dauer, Bhatnagar and Rockstein, 1965; Bhatnagar, Rockstein and Dauer, 1965). The interesting, recent findings by Rockstein *et al.*, (1965) that house fly adult male longevity is *increased* by exposure of the very young pupae to extremely high dosages of x-rays compares favorably with similar findings for x-ray exposure of mammals.

GOALS AND CHALLENGES IN EXPERIMENTAL INSECT GERONTOLOY

As in the case of the entire field of experimental gerontology, important facts about aging do not *explain* the phenomenon, nor do they necessarily lead to the possible amelioration or delay in the aging process.

Nevertheless, if we are to consider the many challenges facing gerontologists today, at a time when the field is growing rapidly, but is still very young, it is obvious that there are a number of criteria which must be met in satisfying not only the outside critic, but also the investigator, himself, who is pursuing to the ultimate the explanation of this highly complex and still poorly understood phenomenon. Thus, one must first establish such primitive statistics as reliable maximum and mean life spans for each species, obtained under fixed conditions and preferably those approaching the natural environment of the animal concerned. The preparation of life tables and, therefore, day-to-day if not hour-to-hour records of longevity (or, if you will, survival) should likewise be obtained, again under carefully controlled conditions, for each species. The interpretation of these survival curves is another question in itself and probit analysis of such data should be employed, to be sure.

Experimentally, one might then attempt to alter the longevity data whether they be the mean life span, the maximum life span, or the shape of the survival curve. Should alteration in life span be successful in the case of each of a number of variables, then the duration of life and the time of death must be further related to specific structural and physiological changes, which can be truly considered age-dependent and not pathological in the more specific sense. This clearly implies a knowledge on the part of the gerontologist of what are truly *normal* "age-dependent changes," as opposed to "pathological" alterations, as well as those changes which are demonstrably the direct outcome of single or cumulative environmental influences, operating independently of the genetically programmed (aging) processes or perhaps in concert with age-related programmed deteriorative changes. This is indeed a weighty challenge which only the daring will attempt to face.

It is therefore obvious that the experimental gerontologist, whether he be concerned with plants, humans, bacteria or insects, is faced with objectives and concomitant challenges not unique or peculiar to that single area of biology which occupies that researcher's attention. Indeed, as in the case of any specialist in any field of biological science, whether it be microbiology or physiology or biochemistry, the gerontologist, employing time as a parameter in his experiments and observations, is concerned with the broader, as well as the more specific, still unsolved and unanswered questions facing contemporary science. How the common elements, making up the compounds of which elemental protoplasm itself is fabricated, are ultimately organized into a complex being which we call the living organism is probably the final question to be answered. Nevertheless, only through the clarification of the mode of expression of the hereditary material, beginning with the moment of union of the two parental gametes, and the inexorable, programmed expression of the determinants of heredity, in the step-by-step development of the primitive embryo, of the immature prenatal form, of the maturing young, and finally the involutionary-oriented senescent adult, can gerontologists themselves have a clear understanding of the nature of the aging process. This includes not only the direct and indirect influences of the genetic material itself, on the one hand, but also the actions of an intercellular nature of one developing structure upon another in producing the form and substance of each part of each individual and, therefore, the form of the total individual himself. Moreover, the still unanswered question of development and progressive changes with time in the secretion by endocrine structures within each particular developing and growing organism is equally applicable to the programmed time-dependent changes in endocrine secretions and their effects upon structure and function in the last trimester of existence (i.e., the slow downhill-directed period of life which we speak of as senescence) as it is to embryonic development and maturation.

Finally, the concept of aging as a species-evolved, specific biological attribute cannot be ignored and it is only the philosophical biologist, equipped with the basic facts accumulated by his fellow experimental gerontologists, who can theorize concerning the evolution of senescence as a property of complex living organisms, by which the members of each species are permitted, as it were, to reach that point in each of their life histories at which the perpetuation of the species is assured, through the participation of genetic factors which postponse the process of aging until such time as the reproductive potential of the average individual of that species can be realized and following which the action of a deleterious "gene" assumes ascendancy. Only natural selection can have enforced such a complex genetic mechanism, whereby favorable genetic factors are operating up to a particular point in the life history of the individual and following which, the factors of senescence assume a predominance.

Certainly, one can suggest that aging is a biological phenomenon which has undergone evolution and that the possession of a finite life span is indeed an essential feature of species survival and effective existence of the individual at each generation. Finally, one can say, unequivocally, that there is still no general theory of aging which can be applicable universally to a large or indeed even a significant range of different animal species. As Clark and Rockstein (1964) have stated, "The study of physiological aging has both the challenge and charm of any classical biological problem with both theoretical and practical implications." Only through the participation of more and more new workers in all areas of the biological and physical sciences can the expectation of the formulation of such an invulnerably sound theory be realized. The wealth of living material available to the experimental gerontologist in the form of the versatile insect should in part permit the making of major strides in the direction of clarifying some of the still poorly understood and even ill-defined characteristics of the aging process in general and senescence in particular, in all higher forms of life.

ACKNOWLEDGMENT

The research reported upon (by Rockstein and colleagues) in this chapter was supported in part by funds from NICHD Research Grant #HD 00571, from the U.S. Public Health Service.

REFERENCES

BHATNAGAR, P. L., ROCKSTEIN, M., AND DAUER, M.: X-irradiation of pupae of the house fly, *Musca domestica,* and adult survival. *Exp. Geront., 1:*149, 1965.

BRUES, C. T.: *Insect Dietary*. Cambridge, Harvard University Press, 1946.

CLARK, A., AND ROCKSTEIN, M.: Aging in insects. In: *Physiology of Insecta,* M. Rockstein, ed. New York, Academic Press, 1964.

DAUER, M., BHATNAGAR, P. L., AND ROCKSTEIN, M.: X-irradiation of pupae of the house fly, *Musca domestica,* L., and male survival. *J. Geront., 20:*219, 1965.

FOLSOM, J. W., AND WARDLE, R. A.: *Entomology—Its Ecological Aspects.* Philadelphia, Blakiston, 1934.

ROCKSTEIN, M.: The relation of cholinesterase activity to change in cell number with age in the brain of the adult worker honey bee. *J. Cell. Comp. Physiol., 35:*11, 1950.

ROCKSTEIN, M.: Heredity and longevity in the animal kingdom. *J. Geront., 13:* (Suppl. 2), 7, 1958.

ROCKSTEIN, M.: Metachemogenesis. Postemergence chemical maturation in holometabolous insects. *Smithsonian Inst. Misc. Collections, 137:*263, 1959a.

ROCKSTEIN, M.: Biology of aging in insects. *Ciba Foundation Colloquia on Aging, 5:*247, 1959b.

ROCKSTEIN, M., AND BHATNAGER, P. L.: Age changes in size and number of the giant mitochondria in the flight muscle of the common house fly, *(Musca domestica,* L.). *J. Insect Physiol., 11:*481, 1965.

ROCKSTEIN, M., BHATNAGAR, P. L., AND DAUER, M.: Adult emergence of the housefly, *Musca domestica,* from X-irradiated pupae. *Ann. Entom. Soc. Amer., 58:* 375, 1965.

ROCKSTEIN, M., AND LIEBERMAN, H. S.: A life table for the common house fly, *Musca domestica. Gerontologia, Basel, 3:*23, 1959.

WEST, L. S.: *The Housefly*. New York, Comstock Publ. Co., 1951.

Chapter 18

MAMMALS

A. COMFORT

THE ACTUARIAL AGING OF MAN, leaving aside his very much longer life span in relation to body size, is apparently typical of that found in large mammals of fixed adult size, and similar in form even to that of small mammals which grow for a large part of the life span (e.g., rats); it is probably similar in form to that of vertebrates generally.

It has been very hard to be certain of this similarity, because of the shortage of lifetime data for fully-adapted mammal populations. At the time of the foundation of the International Gerontological Association in 1950, the only complete mammalian—and indeed vertebrate—actuarial data available were for man and small rodents, chiefly laboratory rats and mice. This is because species and individuals which are genuinely kept throughout life, without culling, and with accurate individual identification and record, are very few. Recent years have seen the setting-up and partial completion of longitudinal studies, e.g., on beagles (Anderson and Hart, 1955), but the difficulty and tediousness of such work is evident. Cross-sectional methods have been applied to small samples, e.g., of dogs of various breeds (Comfort, 1960). They could be used also on mammals which can be aged by inspection of some cyclically-deposited structure (horn rings, cementum layers in seals, wax-plugs in cetacea, antler pedicels in caribou)[1] but only one study of this kind has produced a complete life table, that of Murie on wild Alaskan sheep (1944).

The limitations of zoo data, both in the poor survival of zoo animals and in the dubious identification of individuals kept together, have long been realised. So has the basic inaccuracy and

[1] References to work not nominally cited will be found in: Comfort, A. (1964) *Aging; the biology of senescence.* London, Routledge and Kegan Paul: N.Y., Rinehart.

arbitrariness of the standardised "life spans" assumed for different species in work such as that of Rubner (1908). To this day the tables of life spans in standard works of reference are based largely on folk-lore. Where such data must be used for theory-building, experience has shown that the maximum recorded age and the last-decile survival under life-table conditions are relatively little affected by all but the most adverse conditions. The longevities which they measure are those of relatively indestructible individuals, and remain rather constant for the species or strain.

This review will not give lists of observed longevities, which have been fully summarized elsewhere.[1] It seems more profitable to consider those correlations which have a more direct bearing on the nature of the age process—the most important being that with brain size. Attempts to correlate longevity with total lifetime metabolism continue, but the chief exceptions to the brain-body rule do not fit well into such a pattern. The relatively large brain-size of small cetacea seems to be connected with the possession of extra postural equipment, while the very long lives of bats for their size —connected by many authors with their partial poikilothermy (Bourlière, 1957)—is equally evident in tropical, non-hibernating species (Herreid, 1964). In these respects we are still in the situation described by Bacon—"Neither do those things which may seem concomitants give any furtherance of this Information (the greatness of their bodies, their time of bearing in the Womb, the Number of their young ones, the time of their growth, & and Rest) in regard that these things are intermixt—sometimes they concur, sometimes they sever." (*Historia Vitae et* Mortis)

Closer to the main stream of gerontological speculation are the attempts to correlate longevity with index of cephalization, since these have obvious connections both with the homeostatic reserve, which is impaired with aging, and with the question of fixed cell number. Studies of the effects of low-dose radiation have been chiefly important in focussing research on the need for longitudinal life studies of large mammals, but the direct application of results to the formulation of theories of natural aging still involves very large assumptions.

The outstanding problem of mammalian aging, when we come to explain the shape of the survival curve as seen in man, horse, dog, sheep, and rodents—the forms where it is now known or can be inferred—is probably that of deciding which of three systems plays the largest part in timing senescence: change in dividing cell quality ("faulty copying"), loss or damage among fixed cells, and colloidal change in molecules. This last includes both extracellular structural molecules (collagen) and the intracellular information store. Auxiliary theories which look for aging in increasing autoimmune diversity all start with one or other of these types of change. A purely neurogenic aging due to loss of brain channel number is also not ruled out, nor is the intermediate possibility of organ loss in structures such as renal tubules, where cells are replaceable but whole nephra are not. The hypotheses about molecular and cellular aging presented in other chapters could be very largely tested by inspection if enough mammalian data were available; for the time being they should at least not contradict the few data which we have.

Horse data from the *General Stud Book* of race-horses have made it possible to investigate survival curves in a large mammal both in general and in relation to parental age, parental longevity and coat-colour. The most important consequences of these studies for general gerontology are the Gompertzian shape of the total survival curve, which is a good fit with a prosperous human curve, reduced by a factor of just over 3; and the apparent absence of any detectable paternal age effect. Curves for thoroughbred mares from four years typically give a median of around twenty-two years and a limit of just over thirty. The probable upward limit of record in horses of this type is around forty. Roughly comparable figures for human populations would be 72, 105, 120. The attempt to find paternal age effects in man has been made, but is apt to be frustrated by correlations between the ages of spouses. In horses, where there is no such correlation, the offspring of old stallions (fillies only) show no disadvantage in lifespan compared with the fillies sired by the same stallions in youth.

Compared with horse studies on thoroughbreds and Arabians, which are unusually well documented, dog studies have proved extremely difficult, and apart from the uncompleted beagle work now in progress in Oregon they have been driven back to cross-sectional data for small samples of a few breeds. They are important, however, since intraspecific variation in body-size as a determinant of lifespan is not easy to study in mice, apart from exceptional strains such as *obese* animals. Breeders have not yet produced mice so different in stature that, like a wolfhound and a miniature chihuahua, one breed could swallow the other whole. Some horse data suggest an inverse relationship between body size and life-span, percherons being shorter-lived than small ponies. The life-span in dogs is known to vary from breed to breed, and to favour the small and medium breeds, partly because of the incidence of specific disease such as bone tumours and partly through differences in general vigour.

Differences in size between dog breeds are greater than in any other domestic mammal, and breed characters are stable, if not genotypically uniform. These size differences, at least in parenchymatous organs, represent differences in cell number, but not cell size (so that the bigger the dog, the greater the number of postzygotic divisions in the history of the average liver or gland cell). The same may well apply to neurones: Great Danes have been shown to have more posterior root fibres than terriers (Häggqvist, 1948) though actual cell counts on different cerebral regions would be a daunting undertaking.

Scanty data from small samples make it clear that the general veterinary impression is quite correct, and that large dogs are much shorter lived than small and medium breeds, the medians for pekinese, cocker spaniels, mastiffs and Irish wolfhounds being 10.5, 12.5, seven and seven years to the nearest half-year, and the highest sample records fifteen to twenty, sixteen, nine and fourteen years (an underestimate for spaniels, considering other data). There is therefore a real intra-breed disadvantage in large size. The nature of this, in terms of vigour loss, is not clear, but big breeds apparently owe some of their attributes to an allometric disturbance of the whole front end of the animal. As a result the pituitary in crosses is proportionate in size to the head rather than to the whole dog, with demoralizing consequences on the concertina-skinned basset-St. Bernard crosses which Stockard (1941) used to support some naïve arguments against miscegenation. Both incidence and earliness of bone tumour occurrence increase with size of dog. The most interesting comment from dog figures, however, is upon Sacher's (1959) theory of the relation between index of cephalization and life span in different mammalian species (Fig. 1, a, b). Dog breed differences fit quite well to Sacher's equation, with only slight changes of constant despite the paucity of data (see Table I).

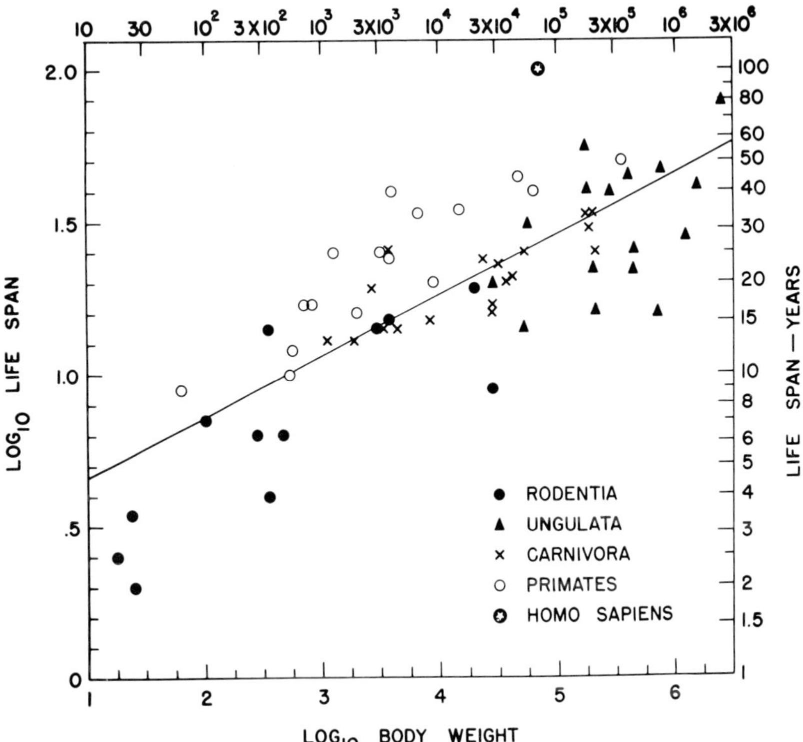

FIGURE 1a. Relation of lifespan to body weight for sixty-three species of mammals. Data plotted on double logarithmic grid. The symbols denote groups of species as follows: open circles—primates and lemurs; solid circles—rodents and insectivores; crosses—carnivores; solid triangles—ungulates and elephants; star in circular field—man. From Sacher (1959).

The significance of the equation itself is not clear, though hypotheses are possible: that small brain size itself correlates with relatively numerous postzygotic divisions in parenchymatous organs, and hence with "faulty copying" which is great in relation to the homeostasis obtaining in fixed cells; that large brains represent resourceful animals—*der Klugste am langsten lebt*—a theory of interest only in that it set off the comparative study of brain size and guided attention to the next possibility, i.e., that since aging is a dissolution of homeostasis and information, and the brain their main extranuclear organ, it may be in the brain rather than in the cellular information store that physiological "noise" accumulates.

$$x = 0 \cdot 636z - 0 \cdot 225y + 1 \cdot 035$$

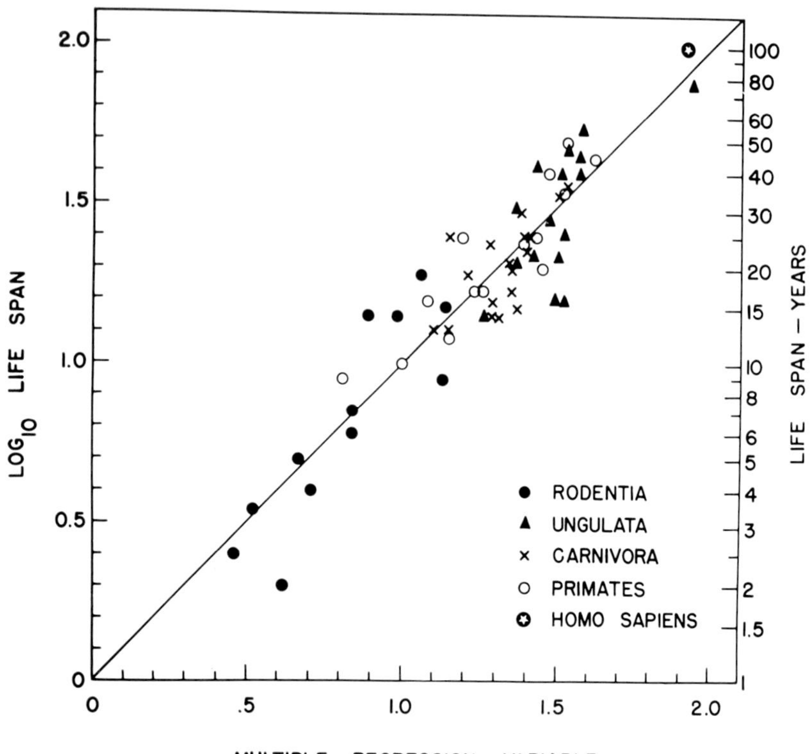

FIGURE 1b. Relation of life span to multiple regression variable defined by equation (*above*). Symbols as defined in legend to Figure 2. From Sacher (1959).

TABLE I

BRAIN WEIGHT, BODY WEIGHT, AND ASSUMED LIFE SPAN IN DOGS

Breed	*Body Wt (Kg) y*	*Brain Wt (Gm) z*	*log x_1*	*log x_2*	*log x°*	*x° (Years)*
Pekinese	5.6	58.7	1.40	1.28	1.30	20
Dachshund	8.2	70.9	1.33	1.20	1.28	19
Fox terrier	7.8	67.9	1.31	1.18	1.20	($\nless$16)
Mastiff	42.2	116.5	1.30	1.17	1.15	14
Leonberger	47.6	113.0	1.29	1.28	1.15	14
St. Bernard	47.0	113.7	1.34	1.20	1.15	14

$\log x_1 = 0.636 \log z - 0.225 \log y + 1.035$ (Sacher's equation; Sacher 1959).

$\log x_2 = 0.6 \log z - 0.23 \log y + 0.99$.

x° = observed or assumed life span.

Body and brain weights from Stephan (1954).

This might well be the Shavian or the Pavlovian view, and in man at least no psychiatrist with experience of the origin of bodily disorder in psychocerebral function would be surprised to find it true. More solid evidence comes, perhaps, from Jarvik's work (1963) suggesting that of all the indices of future life-expectation, rate of aging in psychological function is the sharpest tool. This is a chicken-and-egg situation, however, like that which relates continued interest, e.g. in science, sex or politics, to haleness in age: does the continuance depend on vigour, or produce it? Here lower animals, with a less active psycho-social life than our own, are probably better subjects for the general study of aging, even though Muhlbock (1957) has shown that the introduction of one young female increases the longevity of old bachelor mice, whom she grooms. Decline of channel number, loss of fixed postmitotics in the hypothalamic system, where so many other clocks are located, and a primary decline of brain-controlled homeostasis are not impossible mechanisms of mammalian aging *per se*.

A safer, because more diversified, investment is the notion of progressive loss in fixed cells generally. This, if true, would relate human and mammalian aging directly to what happens in subvertebrate animals which consist of fixed cells (insect imagoes, for instance). It cannot be related to the age-like changes induced by low-level radiation, because of the vast doses needed to affect longevity in animals consisting wholly of fixed cells, and there are as yet few counts or experiments to support it directly—the chief, perhaps, being Krohn's finding that the implanted ovary has an "age" independent of that of its host (Krohn, 1962). The alternative theory, which invokes somatic mutation and looks for faulty copying in dividing cells, seems mathematically unlikely if we consider it in terms of cell loss. It can be sophisticated to operate by way of some feedback effect (autoimmunity, change in some cells leading to inhibition of division in all, and the like) and has a measure of support from Hayflick's (1965) observation that somatic clones in culture appear to have definite life spans. More satisfactory, perhaps, would be some hybrid theory relating the longevity of end-point cells in a cell line to the fact of their having reached a certain degree of differentiation. Such lines may in fact end in "hidden" fixed postmitotics which, through some system of equilibrium or deficit of stem cells, are then not replaced. We find a hint of such an idea in the theories propounded in another connection by Osgood (1964).

Another feature shared by mammals and by other organisms of most types, from suctorians upward, is the fact that reduced caloric intake appears (in rodents at least) to delay senescence to the same extent that it delays development. The data here strongly support the idea that a decline in cell division or maturation, or both, is the operative factor, but "protection" of postmitotics, their information store or their lysosomes, cannot be ruled out from the observed pattern of behaviour in retarded mammals. In fact, the benefit observed from caloric restriction insufficient to arrest growth could be adduced as support for such a mechanism.

The concept of molecular aging, fully discussed in other contributions, with which the work of Prof. Verzár is now firmly linked, could possibly pre-empt some of these other models: if information-containing molecules deteriorate through cross-linkage, with an increase in the production of "nonsense" materials, whether enzymatic, antigenic or templates, then neurone loss, fixed cell loss generally, and increasing derangement of dividing cells might all result. I will leave the evidences in regard to the mammalian model to other authors in this volume.

From the other end of the subject, longevity differences between closely related mammalian species do not at the moment help us much in generating hypotheses, but should be fittable to the hypotheses we adopt. Thus there appears to be a sizeable difference in longevity between sheep and goats, and between *Peromyscus* and *Mus,* while *Mus bactrianus* is apparently longer-lived than *M. musculus:* If we knew more, we might make use of such differentiae.

Finally, from the standpoint of experimental medicine, the accessible points in the mammalian cycle where we might without injury modify it have not yet been located. Dietary means might be palliative in man, but are not likely to produce the effects seen in the rat, nor would these effects be desirable. Of the mammalian hormones affecting apparent "youth" of tissue constituents, somatotrophin and anabolic steroids look the best worth studying. Replacement therapies with other hormones, singly or together, have some remedial use but not much prospect as fundamental modifiers of the mammalian life span. The evolutionary side of the mammalian model is as obscure as it is in other organisms. Though aging represents an apparent exhaustion of homeostatic program through relaxation of the pressure of selection at high ages, the survival curve of small and large animals is similar, and the reserve of longevity over natural wild expectation, in mice and rats, for example, is large, though nothing like as large as in small birds. If the rate of noise-accumulation, whether in cells, molecules, brain or the system as a whole is tailored by evolution to fit the wild performance and the requirements of selection, we have still not hint of how precisely this comes about, nor why further increase in fertility or longevity is limited to produce the very stable statistical patterns which we now see in the different species.

REFERENCES

ANDERSON, A. C., AND HART, G. H.: Kennel construction and management in relation to longevity studies in the dog. *J. Amer. Vet. Med. Ass., 126*:366, 1955.

BOURLIÈRE, F.: The comparative biology of aging; a physiological approach. *CIBA Found. Colloq. Aging, 3*:20, 1957.

COMFORT, A.: Longevity and mortality in dogs of four breeds. *J. Geront., 15*:126, 1960.

HÄGGQVIST, G.: Nervenfaserkaliber bei Tieren verscheidener Grösse. *Anat. Anz., 96*:398, 1948.

HAYFLICK, L.: The limited *in vitro* lifetime of human diploid cell strains. *Exp. Cell. Res., 37*:614, 1965.

HERREID, C. F.: Bat longevity and metabolic rate. *Exp. Geront., 1*:1, 1964.

JARVIK, L. F., AND FALEK, A.: Intellectual stability and survival in the aged. *J. Geront., 18*:173, 1963.

KROHN, P. L.: Heterochronic transplantation in the study of aging. *Proc. Roy. Soc.* [*Biol.*], *157*:128, 1962.

MUHLBOCK, O.: Discussion. *CIBA Found. Colloq. Aging, 3*:117, 1957.

MURIE, A.: *The Wolves of Mt. McKinley*. Washington, U. S. Parks Service, 1944.

OSGOOD, E. E.: The etiology of leukemias, lymphomas and cancers. *Geriatrics, 19*: 208, 1964.

RUBNER, M.: Probleme des Wachtums und der Lebensdaner. *Mitt. Ges. inn. Med., Vienna, 7*:58, 1908.

SACHER, G.: Relation of life span to brain and body weight in mammals. *CIBA Colloq. Aging, 5*:115, 1959.

STEPHAN, H.: Die Anwendung der Snell-schen Formel $h = k^s \cdot p$ auf die Hirn-Korpergewichtsbeziehungen bei verscheidenen Hunderassen. *Zool. Anz., 153*:15, 1954.

STOCKARD, C. R.: The genetic and endocrine basis for differences in form and behavior. *Anat. Mem. Wistar Inst., 19*:1, 1941.

Section V

ENVIRONMENTAL FACTORS IN AGING

Chapter 19

THE POSSIBILITY OF INCREASED LONGEVITY BY THE CONTROL OF MUTATIONS*

H. J. CURTIS

IN THIS BRIEF EXPOSITION I should like to assess, in a general way, the current state of the science of gerontology, and to indulge in some rather uninhibited speculation on the general nature of the advances which I feel sure will be made in the field of aging in the next decade or two.

First, let me limit my field to a consideration of the biology of aging. In taking a sober look at the advances which have been made in this field in the past few decades, it appears to me that the view is rather disappointing. Most other sciences have made advances during this period too spectacular and well known to repeat here. Even the clinical and sociological branches of gerontology have made great strides. But with few exceptions, it has only been within the past very few years that biological gerontologists have stopped arguing the questions that have been debated without success for decades, and started to blaze new trails. Not long ago, biologists could not agree on a definition of aging, and were busy trying to find "the" cause of aging which would explain everything that has been called aging in all living organisms from a bacterium to man in one simple formula.

A measure of the failure of biologists to understand and thereby control the aging process is that the *maximum* human life span has remained unchanged throughout recorded history. During this time medical scientists have increased the *average* human life span dramatically. But it is apparent that the methods of modern medicine have gone about as far as it is possible to push them, and if we

* Research carried out at Brookhaven National Laboratory under the auspices of the U. S. Atomic Energy Commission.

are to achieve a significantly longer human life span a completely different approach must be taken. In this paper I should like to assess the possibility of doing this, and point out some possible avenues of approach to the problem.

THE CURRENT STATE OF THE PROBLEM

I think that by now most of us are willing to admit that what has been called aging in the different biological organisms is probably a completely different phenomenon in each form with very little basic resemblance between them. Thus, aging in paramecia, trees and man probably have virtually nothing in common from a basic biological point of view. I would then like to further limit my topic to aging in mammals.

Another great step forward was the final realization that aging in mammals is basically a cellular phenomenon, and that various signs and symptoms are referable to cellular malfunction and not to some vague failure of an over-all organization, even though the exact nature of the cellular deficiencies may be difficult to localize in all cases.

We are now starting to have some concept of the mechanisms within the cell which are responsible for the deleterious changes which take place with time. First, it is necessary to recognize two quite different general types of somatic cells in mammals. The first is the relatively undifferentiated cell resembling an embryonic cell but which may exist in animals throughout their lives. Such cells are those of the crypts of the intestinal tract. They continue active division throughout the life of the individual and their progeny differentiate into very specialized cells. At the other end of the spectrum are the highly differentiated cells which never divide once they are laid down. Such are the neurones of the central nervous system. Between these extremes there are all degrees of differentiation. Each cell type has a different part to play and enters the aging syndrome in a different way.

Consider first the undifferentiated cells. As far as we know they are virtually immortal. The crypt cells continue to function well until a vascular accident or death cuts off their food supply. If a mutation occurs in one of these cells, it is sloughed off and its place is taken by one of the adjacent normal cells in the same way that a suspension of bacteria keeps itself pure. But in this type of cell there is always the possibility of a mutation which will turn it into a cancer cell, which is certainly one of the prime manifestations of aging in the mammal.

On the other hand the nondividing cell cannot form a cancer, but it can and does undergo mutation which changes the functional capacity of the cell. Since these cells never undergo division, there is no opportunity to discard aberrant cells. The chromosomes of the cell nucleus are ultimately responsible for the functions of the cell, and if even a very small part of one chromosome is damaged (a mutation) it will cause a malfunction in one or more cell functions. This control is normally exerted by the production of specific enzymes which catalyze the reaction in question. So if a mutation occurs in a gene which synthesizes (indirectly) an enzyme essential to the life of the cell, the cell will eventually die. If the enzyme is not completely essential, it will probably at least be important enough to cause the cell to be deficient in some function. If enough cells in an organ become so altered, the entire organ becomes inefficient and this leads to the deficiency symptoms of senescence.

THE MUTATION THEORY

It then appears that a mutation in a somatic cell can cause cancer on the one hand and organ breakdown on the other. There are obviously all stages between these two extremes. This is the essence of the somatic mutation theory of aging, and it is apparent that, if true, it could account for many of the signs and symptoms of aging in the mammal. This is an attractive theory but it is by no means completely proven, and it might be well at this point to mention some of the pieces of evidence which argue in its favor.

1) There seems little doubt now that somatic cells do undergo mutation at a very high rate and do so whether or not they undergo division (Curtis, 1963). Further, in mice and presumably all mammals, mutations build up with age in the somatic cells until as many as 70 per cent of the liver cells for example, will have grossly abnormal chromosomes (Crowley and Curtis, 1963).

2) Ionizing radiation shortens the life span of mammals in a manner closely resembling that of aging, so the phenomenon is commonly referred to as radiation-induced aging. Radiation also

is a very potent mutagenic agent. The degree of acceleration of aging produced by various kinds and regimens of radiation is proportional to the number of mutations produced by that treatment (Curtis, 1963).

3) Pure strains of mice which have a short life span develop somatic mutations at a high rate, and those that are long lived develop mutations much more slowly (Crowley and Curtis, 1963).

4) The mutation hypothesis of cancer induction is too well known to need elucidation, and the more we find out about carcinogenesis the more it appears that mutation is at least one component of the process (Curtis, 1965).

5) The loss of parenchymal cells with age seems reasonably well substantiated (Shock, 1961). One of the consequences of mutation is certainly cell death, when the mutation eliminates a gene responsible for an essential cellular function.

6) At least some of the vascular disorders associated with aging may be due to mutations occurring in the intima of the vessels, leading either to an abnormal cholesterol metabolism or a breakdown of the integrity of the vessel (Werthessen, 1962).

7) The autoimmune diseases are rightfully receiving a good deal of attention today, and by far the most plausible explanation for the initiation of the reaction is a mutation (Walford, 1962).

It would then seem that there must be a cause and effect relation between somatic mutations and aging. This is not to say that all of the phenomena which are commonly associated with aging in the mammal are explicable in terms of deleterious mutations. But at least many of the "nonprogrammatic" aspects seem explicable in these terms, and if one is to make progress in the retardation of the basic aging process, this seems a reasonable place to begin.

THE CAUSE OF MUTATIONS

First, we must inquire what causes the mutations. Whereas no definite answer can be given to this question, at least we can point out several things which have been ruled out as causes. First, we find that the liver cells of the mouse continue to develop mutations as a function of age in spite of the fact that they do not undergo division during this time (Stevenson and Curtis, 1961). At one time it was felt that spontaneous mutations are due to errors of replication. This is a natural supposition, but these and other experiments show that most if not all spontaneous mutations are not due to this cause.

Next, it is well known that ionizing radiation can cause mutations in cells regardless of the stage of the cell cycle in which it is administered. Indeed, many of the facets of the mutation theory have been worked out on the basis of the finding that under a wide variety of conditions, the mutations produced by a given radiation treatment exactly parallel the shortening of the life span caused by that treatment. We know there is always with us a small amount of background radiation due to cosmic rays and to radioactive minerals in the earth. The intensity of this radition is well known. It varies somewhat from place to place but in all but an extremely few remote places the values are very small in comparison to values which are known to cause mutations or life shortening in mice. Indeed, from the known reactions to radiation it can be estimated that less than 0.1 per cent of the observed chromosome aberrations and life shortening in mice could be due to background radiation (Curtis and Crowley, 1963). It then seems safe to rule out this also as a cause of mutations and aging.

We are then driven to the conclusion that chromosomes are not very stable structures, and forces such as those of thermal agitation can cause a break in the structure. Whereas this statement is probably true, it is only part of the story. As we are learning more and more about the structure of chromosomes and DNA, we find there are forces at work to keep the system stabilized and to repair genetic damage in the cell. Thus, if a cell receives a dose of radiation which damages the chromosome structure, a large fraction of this damage can be repaired, especially if there is sufficient time allowed between the damage and the initiation of cell division (Curtis *et al.*, 1964). It now seems reasonably certain that these repair processes are brought about by reactions catalyzed by enzymes continually present in the cell. It is thus apparent that the state of the chromosomes of a cell is a balance between the forces tending to disrupt them and those attempting to repair them.

It should be noted that the repair mechanism cannot handle a large chromosome break, or it can be swamped if too many small breaks occur at once (Curtis and Tilley, 1965). Perhaps two small breaks occurring simultaneously very close together may constitute a large break which cannot be repaired. In any event we know that breaks do accumulate with age in the nondividing cells of the mammal, and there is quite good evidence to indicate that all cells that do not undergo division tend to accumulate mutations in spite of the presence of these repair mechanisms. Cells like the bone marrow cells which are continually undergoing division probably undergo mutation as readily as any other cells, but since a mutated cell has a selective disadvantage during cell division as compared to a normal cell, such an organ tends to cleanse itself of mutated cells.

But irrespective of whether or not it is a dividing or a nondividing cell, the basic problem with aging is to understand and control the mutation process.

THE CONTROL OF MUTATION

Such control has, in the past, been considered a virtually hopeless task. The spontaneous mutation rate for any given species was considered a fixed and unchangeable quantity. But today we know this is not true for many things, and in some situations we are acquiring the ability to control, to some extent, the spontaneous mutation rate. If this could be done for humans there is every reason to believe that the life span could be very appreciably extended. The work with lower forms gives us great hope that it may be possible some day to do this, and this seems to be the only real possibility for materially extending the life span beyond its present duration in western societies. The story is admittedly becoming rather speculative, but at least the conjecture starts with solid experimental data. There are three lines of evidence on which we can base our hopes.

1) In plants, both the spontaneous and the radiation induced mutation rate depend upon the light intensity, the temperature, the moisture content of the soil, the ionic balance in the nutrient medium, and, indeed on almost anything which affects cell growth (Steffensen, 1955). In addition, the chromosome stability of mammalian cells growing in tissue culture has been considerably

influenced by the ionic balance of the growth medium, and calcium seems to be the most important ion in this regard (Basrur and Baker, 1963). This effect has not yet been demonstrated in the mammal *in vivo,* but it seems safe to predict that it will be demonstrated before long although the magnitude of the effect cannot be predicted. As we learn more about the forces tending to stabilize chromosomes, it does not seem too optimistic to think that other ways will be found for achieving increased stability.

2) As indicated previously, specific mechanisms are present in all cells for the repair of genetic damage. This can be observed in mammalian liver cells as the repair of chromosome aberrations following radiation damage (Curtis *et al.,* 1964) and in germ cells as a decreased mutation rate when radiation is administered slowly as compared to rapid administration (Russell, 1963). There is at least some evidence to indicate that some of the permanent damage suffered by cells subjected to radiation is due to the fact that the repair processes become saturated. Since enzymatic deficiencies of other kinds in cells can be overcome by appropriate measures, there is ample reason to hope that such might be possible here also. If this could be accomplished it would certainly help to stabilize the chromosome structure and thus retard aging.

3) Genetic research has shown that in some if not all living systems there are mutator genes present in the genome of the cells of the organism. When a mutator gene is present in the dominant condition, the spontaneous mutation rate is greatly increased (Demerec, 1937). The exact nature of the action of the gene is not known, but it behaves as if it synthesizes a mutagenic chemical compound within the cell which then increases the "spontaneous" mutation rate of all genes. Such genes have never been demonstrated in mammals but it would be surprising if they were not present in some form. It may even be that in a mammal some cells actually secrete a mutagenic compound which is responsible for the very high mutation rate observed in mammalian cells. This would put into somewhat more concrete form the proposal, advanced quite seriously, that some gland must secrete a "death hormone" which is responsible for aging (Koshland, 1962). But this latter is in the realm of high speculation. In any event, assuming

mutator genes do in fact occur in mammals, it should be possible by appropriate means to overcome their effect, once we know how they function.

These three lines of evidence then form the very real hope for the future. It is clear that a number of forces are at work tending to disrupt the integrity of the chromosomes of mammalian cells and thus bring on aging. In order to extend the human life span, it will be necessary to combat these forces, just as the science of medicine has been busy for many years combatting other forms of disease.

If it is possible to alter the chromosome stability of plant cells, it should also be possible to do so for mammalian cells. Likewise, since it is possible to either counteract or augment various enzymatic processes which occur in mammalian cells, it should be possible eventually to augment the enzymatic processes in these cells responsible for chromosomal repair. And finally, it should eventually be possible to determine and control the genes within the mammalian cells which may be responsible for at least part of the molecular instability of these cells.

These are difficult assignments and will not be accomplished tomorrow. But I am convinced that if the maximum human life span is to be appreciably extended, it will be necessary to solve them, and I believe them to be soluble.

SUMMARY

A further extension of the human life span will require a radically different approach from that so far employed. Mutations in somatic cells are a major cause of aging, and it will be necessary to stabilize the chromosome structure of these cells if aging is to be retarded. The possibility that this may be achieved comes from three different lines of evidence. 1) Mutations are caused by an inherent chromosomal instability, but it is possible to increase artificially the chromosomal stability of some cells. 2) There are specific enzymatic processes within cells which repair chromosome damage, and it should be possible to augment these processes. 3) There is reason to believe that mammalian cells may contain genes which are partly responsible for the high mutation rates observed.

It is to be expected that future research will lead to a better understanding of these phenomena, which in turn, will lead to their control.

REFERENCES

BASRUR, V. A., AND BAKER, D. G.: Human chromosome breakage in low calcium cultures. *Lancet,–*:7290, 1106, 1963.

CROWLEY, C., AND CURTIS, H. J.: The development of somatic mutations in mice with age. *Proc. Nat. Acad. Sci. USA, 49*:626, 1963.

CURTIS, H. J.: Biological mechanisms underlying the aging process. *Science, 141*:688, 1963.

CURTIS, H. J.: Somatic mutations and carcinogenesis. *Cancer Res., 25*:1305, 1965.

CURTIS, H. J., AND CROWLEY, C.: Chromosome aberrations in liver cells in relation to the somatic mutation theory of aging. *Radiat. Res., 19*:337, 1963.

CURTIS, H. J., AND TILLEY, J.: The failure of chromosomal repair in mice following neutron irradiation. *Radiat. Res., 25*:12, 1965.

CURTIS, H. J., TILLEY, J., AND CROWLEY, C.: The elimination of chromosome aberrations by cell division. *Radiat. Res., 22*:730, 1964.

DEMEREC, M.: Frequency of spontaneous mutations in certain stocks of *Drosophila melanogaster. Genetics, 22*:468, 1937.

KOSHLAND, D. E., JR.: Catalysis in life and in the test tube. In: *Horizons in Biochemistry* (B. Pullman and M. Kasha, eds.), Academic Press, New York, 1962, pp. 265-283.

RUSSELL, W. L.: The effect of radiation dose rate and fractionation on mutation in mice. In: *Repair from Genetic Radiation* (F. H. Sobels, ed.), New York, Pergamon Press, 1963, pp. 205-217.

SHOCK, N. W.: Physiological aspects of aging in man. *Ann. Rev. Physiol., 23*:97, 1961.

STEFFENSEN, D.: Breakage of chromosomes in *Tradescantia* with a calcium deficiency. *Proc. Nat. Acad. Sci. USA, 41*:155, 1955.

STEVENSON, K. G., AND CURTIS, H. J.: Chromosomal aberrations in irradiated and nitrogen mustard treated mice. *Radiat. Res., 15*:774, 1961.

WALFORD, R. L.: Auto-immunity and aging. *J. Geront., 17*:281, 1962.

WERTHESSEN, N. T.: The site of the primary lesion in artherosclerosis. *Angiology, 13*:520, 1962.

Chapter 20

IS THERE A RELATIONSHIP BETWEEN AGING, THE SHORTENING OF LIFE-SPAN BY RADIATION AND THE INDUCTION OF SOMATIC MUTATIONS?

PETER ALEXANDER

WHEN FACED with a complex biological process, much can often be learned by modifying it in a deliberate and controllable manner. Hence the suggestion associated with the names of Henshaw (1957) and Failla (1958) that exposure to ionizing radiations accelerated aging appeared to offer a new approach in the search for the basic processes involved in aging. Wartime studies showed that rodents, that had been exposed to doses of ionizing radiation which were not fatal, did not make a complete recovery. Irreparable injury was revealed as a reduction in the length of expectation of life. One factor in the radiation induced shortening of life span was an increase in the incidence of malignant disease, but in addition there were pathologically undefined late effects that caused irradiated rats and mice to die on the average earlier than control groups. This observation was linked with the well-established fact that radiation is mutagenic and the hypothesis was put forward that "physiologic and radiologic aging are consequences of somatic mutation followed by genetic transition." Two years after this idea had been presented in the open literature, Szilard (1959) concluded that the occurrence of point mutations involving individual genes was quantitatively not capable of explaining aging in mice, but postulated instead that aging was the result of a series of somatic mutations which rendered all the genes in a whole chromosome ineffective. Again radiation was claimed to mimic aging. Probably because of its simplicity and universality, the somatic mutation idea, both in its original form and in various modifications, continues to receive a great deal of attention and has the support of one of the foremost biologists of our time (Burnet, 1965).

In this paper I propose to summarize data which I believe show that for mice:

1) The phenomenon of radiation-induced life span shortening is substantially different from normal aging.

2) Mutagenic chemicals which are not cytotoxic do not shorten life span.

Taken together these observations lead to the concept that somatic mutations are not an important factor for either normal aging or radiation-induced life span shortening in mice and presumably other mammals.[1]

To avoid misunderstanding it must be stressed that to deny an important role to the induction of somatic mutations in bringing about aging does not question that genetics constitute an important aspect of gerontology. The duration of maximum attainable life is an inherited property and both in man and in insects the rate of onset of senile deterioration has been demonstrated to be gene controlled (Rockstein, 1958).

SOMATIC MUTATIONS AND THE DEFINITION OF AGING

The term somatic mutation is generally used to describe alterations in the genome which are reflected phenotypically in the daughter cells after division. In connection with the problem of aging this term has also been invoked for changes in the genome of post-mitotic cells which become manifest functionally without an intervening mitosis. As far as I know, there is no evidence that this type of genetically determined damage can occur, but the concepts of molecular biology according to which synthesis of messenger RNA occur on the DNA suggests that it is feasible. The frequency of spontaneous mutations in dividing somatic cells has been determined in a number of cases and is of the same order as mutations in germ cells (Burnet, 1965). Consequently there is every reason to believe that the total number of such mutations present in the cells of the body will increase with time (i.e., as the animal gets older). Such an accumulation must on the whole be harmful and the progressive increase with age of cancer and leukaemia, as well as of auto-immune diseases, has been interpreted in

[1] The conclusion that somatic mutations are not responsible for aging in insects has been reached by several workers (*e.g.*, Lamb and Maynard Smith, 1964).

this way. The question which we have to ask ourselves is not whether somatic mutations do or do not cause aging, but whether they are a major factor in producing those processes of physiological deterioration which we know as aging.

The answers may well be different for different animals and may depend also on the criteria chosen for measuring the rate of aging. The experimental gerontologist has been forced by experimental difficulties to use as a measure of aging, one of the consequences of aging, namely, the average life span. The process of aging leads in an accident-free environment to a limitation of life span, but, as other factors also exert an influence, length of life is not a good measure for the rate of aging. At best the relationship between time of death and aging is very indirect and in certain animals there may be no correlation at all. The average life span of different strains of mice varies widely but in general the short-lived strains have a high—and genetically determined—incidence of malignant disease which kills prior to senescence and there is no evidence to indicate that the true rate of aging varies. Treatments which delay the development of leukaemia will increase average life span in mice with a high spontaneous incidence of this disease, but such procedures—which incidentally include whole body radiation—are not a "cure for aging" although such statements have been made and constitute the basis for the claim that some chemicals with antioxidant properties retard aging (Harman, 1957).

In the last six years, Curtis (1963) has attempted to measure the rate of somatic mutation in mice and claims to have found close correlations with aging. I am skeptical of the interpretations of the results, which I do not believe constitute experimental proof for the somatic mutation hypothesis. The test used as a measure for somatic mutations involves destroying 65 per cent of the liver with a large dose of carbon tetrachloride; the remaining cells in the liver are thereby stimulated into division and three days later many mitoses occur. The animal is then killed and the cells of the liver examined for abnormal chromosomes. The rate of chromosome abnormalities is assumed—without any direct evidence—to be proportional to the number of somatic mutations present in the animal. The number of chromosome abnormalities was shown to increase linearly in the first twelve months of life but then levels off; this by itself provides no evidence for a causal relationship especially since there is no increase at later times when aging becomes apparent. The critical experiment (Crowley and Curtis, 1963) is that the number of chromosome abnormalities is greater in mice with a short natural life span (i.e., 395 days) than in those that have the more normal life expectancy of 600 days. If these life spans were a measure of the rate of aging this would be an impressive correlation. Unfortunately there is no evidence that the short lived mice aged rapidly since they were females from a strain with a very high incidence of mammary cancer. They died from malignant disease before they ever had a chance to get old! In human beings (Jacobs *et al.*, 1963) the proportion of cells with an abnormal karyotype increases with age, but the abnormality is confined to the sex chromosomes. Though an interesting observation, this provides no support for the thesis of Curtis.

The most cogent reason for considering the somatic mutation hypothesis relies on radiation causing an acceleration of aging. The very reasonable presumption, on which Failla and Henshaw based their original idea, that radiation induces not only germ, but also somatic mutations has since been experimentally verified. Also Albert (1958) showed that potential chromosome lesions could remain latent for many months so that when mitosis was stimulated months after irradiation the cells of the liver still showed increased chromosome abnormalities. If, therefore, somatic mutations are an important cause of aging, radiation must accelerate aging. The converse however is not necessarily true since the cytogenetic effects of radiation are not of course the only biological lesions introduced by ionizing radiations and the possibility has to be borne in mind that radiation-induced life span shortening may not be due to damage of the genome. While experiments with irradiation cannot prove the correctness of the somatic mutation hypothesis, failure of radiation to promote aging would appear to eliminate it.

COMPARISON OF LIFE SPAN SHORTENING BY RADIATION WITH NORMAL AGING

Aging is the sum of a number of physiological changes—to some extent independent of one another—which lead to impairment of function, a lowering of adaptation, a greater susceptibility to certain pathologies such as cancer and ultimately to death. The end effect of senescence is to impose an upper limit on the expectation of life, but the force of mortality is not a measure of the rate of senescence. The absurdity of claiming that a treatment accelerates aging because it increases the force of mortality is obvious if one considers human beings. Cigarette smoking causes a contraction in the time axis of the normal survival curve but as the increased mortality rate is due principally to the induction of two diseases—lung cancer and chronic bronchitis, which are almost wholly absent in non-smokers—no one would claim that life span shortening by smoking is an acceleration of aging. The occurrence of these diseases is not merely brought forward in time, but they are induced *de novo* by smoking.

The symptoms of aging are not the pathologies, but the physiological deterioration of brain, muscle and kidney as well as the changes in the extracellular connective tissue. The latter of course is the principal cosmetic factor of aging. While the physiological changes of aging are readily apparent, their measurement in experimental animals has, in general, not been attempted and the criterion for acceleration of aging by irradiation has been largely limited to studies of life span and pathologies. This limitation does not apply to man and there is a great deal of experience from the survivors of Hiroshima and Nagasaki. The Atomic Bomb Casualty Commission made a very detailed comparison, (Hollingworth, *et al.*, 1962) involving many thousands of people, between survivors who were known from their immediate symptoms to have sustained a large dose of radiation and a closely matched unirradiated population. Many strongly age related physiological factors were studied including blood pressure, vital capacity, gastric and heart function, immunological capacity, skin elasticity, time of onset of grey hair and blunting of sensory organs. The latter in particular with accurately quantitated in relationship to age. Not a single test revealed differences between the control and the irradiated population and there was no indication that the irradiated group behaved in any respect as if they were older than their chronological age (i.e., no evidence for an aging effect due to a high dose of radiation).

In experimental animals deterioration of physiological functions are much more difficult to measure and only a very few age-related responses have so far been used to look for an aging effect produced by doses of whole body radiation which reduces average life span in a marked way. Verzár (1956) demonstrated a most striking correlation between age and the force of thermic contraction of the tendons of the rat tail. Radiation of young CBA mice with 1100r of x-rays given in four exposures separated by one month shortened their average life span from 760 days to 400 days, but did not alter the rate of "aging" of the tail tendons as measured by the Verzár test (Alexander and Connell, 1960). Lisco *et al.* (1958) found that the latent period for the induction of epithelioma with carcinogenic hydrocarbons varied with age but that whole body irradiation did not affect the age dependence. Fertility changes in female mice after non-lethal irradiation which leads to life span shortening follow a pattern which is quite different from that observed normally and the radiation effect in no way mimics aging (Russell and Oakberg, 1963).

AGE AND RADIATION ASSOCIATED PATHOLOGIES

Another way to test if radiation affects aging is to compare the pathologies of irradiated and normal animals. Logically this is not a very satisfactory approach since the onset of pathologies is not a direct consequence of aging. However, this hypothesis would be strengthened if the time-course of the various diseases was advanced to the same extent and by a factor comparable to that of life span shortening. Very extensive investigations (Upton *et al.*, 1960; and Lindop and Rotblat, 1961) led to the suggestion that radiation moved the clock forward, but these data relied on a classification of *the* cause of death. Not only is this notoriously difficult to establish in old animals[2] but necropsy studies cannot provide data for the rate of progression of the various diseases. For this reason we have attempted to follow the onset and incidence of disease by killing groups of ten mice at monthly intervals and sub-

[2] In our experiments with CBA mice (Connell and Alexander, unpublished) we attempted a similar approach but felt ourselves quite unable to reach any definite conclusion from necropsy studies since the animals that had died often had many different pathological changes, especially kidney lesions.

jecting them to a histopathological examination of selected organs. We have confined ourselves to irradiation with 1100r in four doses. After the last irradiation the animals were divided into groups designated to be killed at specified dates. On the basis of our earlier data the size of the groups was adjusted to allow for intercurrent deaths so that at the specified times there should always be ten animals alive in each group.

At the present time we have not been able to analyse in detail the large amount of material available, but the salient features are clear (a preliminary report has been published, Alexander and Connell, 1963a). The most striking fact is that even very old mice (e.g., more than two and one-half years) when killed while still fit have remarkably few pathologies and are almost indistinguishable from young animals. The initial object of the experiment, which was to compare the rate of onset of the disease conditions seen post-mortem in animals that had died or become moribund, could not be achieved. The striking pathologies seen in the latter animals must have set in rather rapidly prior to death because they were absent when mice were killed while they were still fit. This is particularly evident with the kidney lesions; pronounced tubular degeneration, necrosis and abscesses, which are such a striking feature in animals that had died, were not observed in serial killing. Some relatively minor changes were seen to increase progressively with age but in no case were these accelerated by irradiation; amongst these were amyloid infiltration of the heart, malpigian corpuscles in the spleen becoming less distinct, enlargement and infiltration by blood of the mesenteric nodes, calcium and deposits in the kidney tubules and later in the glomerulus region followed in old age by amyloid deposits.

The most convincing evidence based on age-associated pathologies against the concept that radiation ages, comes from investigations on the development of various neoplastic conditions. The CBA mice have a high spontaneous incidence of benign hepatoma but the time of appearance of the benign hepatomas is exactly the same in the irradiated as in the control population (Connell and Alexander, 1959; Alexander and Connell, 1963a). Lung tumours would suggest the opposite; radiation has no significant influence on the incidence of these tumours, but they appear earlier. It could be argued from this example that radiation had speeded up the "internal clock" of the animal about twice in agreement with the observed life-span shortening; in other words radiation accelerates aging.

The appearance of cataracts illustrates another type of response. Radiation reduced the latent period, but also increased the total incidence. The situation is even more complex since the cataracts in the irradiated group were morphologically quite different from senile cataracts. It might therefore be more correct to look upon radiation as bringing about a new late somatic change which is quite absent in the unirradiated population. Mole (1958) and Upton *et al.* (1964) recorded an even more striking example of radiation producing new late diseases. Using strains of mice in which leukaemia is very rare they found, following irradiation, a very high incidence in old mice.

We conclude that comparisons of the pathologies at the time of death cannot be used to establish if radiation advances the onset of age associated diseases. The limited data from serial killing fails completely to support this concept and in our investigation all the conceivable variables were seen.

1) The time-course and incidence are completely unaffected by 1100r in spite of the fact that the disease seems to be related to age;

2) The latent period is unaffected but the incidence is increased;

3) The latent period is shortened and the total incidence is increased;

4) The latent period is shortened but the total incidence remains unaltered.

If radiation were to induce a process akin to normal aging then most of the major pathologies should fall into the last category. There is yet another possible variant, namely that radiation delays or prevents certain diseases. An example has not been observed by us but has been seen in strains of mice having a high spontaneous leukaemia incidence (Mole, 1958).

INDUCTION OF SOMATIC MUTATIONS WITH CHEMICAL AGENTS

The theory that the principle reaction at the subcellular level responsible for aging is the occurrence of somatic mutations can also be tested by studying the effect of mutation producing chemical substances on life span. If they have no effect then this disproves the hypothesis; if they shorten life span then it remains to be established whether this is a true acceleration of aging.

Bifunctional alkylating agents are highly mutagenic to all forms of life including mice. We (Alexander and Connell, 1960) found that two substances belonging to this group (Myleran® and Chlorambucil) brought about a shortening of life-span in a way akin to irradiation and this finding has been extended to other members of this group by Upton *et al.* (1963) and Dunjie (1964). There is no reason for ascribing the capacity of these substances to shorten life span to their mutagenic activity since all the polyfunctional alkylating agents have a large spectrum of biological activities and, in particular, are highly cytotoxic to dividing cells, a property to which they owe their role in the chemotherapy of cancer. The monofunctional alkylating agents and, in particular, ethyl methane sulphonate (EMS: $C_2H_5.O.SO_2.CH_3$) are much more suitable for testing the somatic mutation hypothesis since they are highly mutagenic at dose levels where they show no cytotoxicity. EMS has been shown to produce mutations in drosphila, neurospora, barley, bacteria and bacteriophage (Alexander and Connell, 1963b) and recently Bateman (1963) showed that it produced mutations in mice at a dose level of 50 mg/kg. But EMS even when given at very high doses in mice does not produce any detectable life-span shortening.

While we have no direct data showing the relative number of somatic mutations produced in the mouse by the various chemicals, figures are available (see Table I) for the production of sex-linked recessive lethal mutations in *Drosphila.* If, for purposes of comparison, we equate mice with *Drosphila* then the EMS treatment used in the mice (i.e., as shown in Table I) provokes very many more mutations than do the treatments with x-rays, Myleran and Chlorambucil. The extrapolation from germ mutations in the fruit-fly to somatic mutations in the mouse involves many uncertainties, but the difference in the observed mutation yield in *Drosphila* between EMS and the other treatments is so sufficiently great that one can feel confident that the same relative order is maintained. On a weight basis these chemicals do not differ very greatly in mutagenicity; in mice the EMS treatment is likely to be much

TABLE I

COMPARISON OF MUTAGENIC AND LIFE-SPAN SHORTENING ACTIVITY OF X-RAYS BIFUNCTIONAL ALKYLATING AGENTS AND ETHYL METHANE SULPHONATE

Treatment†	*Average life-span*‡	*% animals at death with neoplasia other than hepatoma*	*Estimate of mutagenic action in Drosophila at comparable doses (% sex linked recessive lethals)***
None	762	23	—
3×300r+200r; total 1,100r of X-rays	404	38	3.1
3×25 mg/kg myleran; total 75 mg/kg	593	24	0.4
3×20 mg/kg chlorambucil; total 60 mg/kg	491	36	0.7
3×200 mg/kg ethyl methane sulphonate; total 600 mg/kg	693*	94	10.1
Second series (unpublished results)			
None	795	28	
3×200 mg/kg ethyl methane sulphonate; total 600 mg	805	92	

† The radiation and the chemicals were administered to 11-14-week-old animals at three weekly intervals. The doses given were approximately one half of the acute LD_{50} dose and in the fractions scheme used did not give rise to a significant number of early deaths.

‡ Time when 50% of the mice were dead.

* Most of the animals in this series were killed when they reached a moribund state to assist pathological study. The true life-span of the animals that had received ethyl methane sulphonate is therefore longer and approximates more closely to that of the controls.

** The basis of this estimate is described by Alexander and Connell (1963b).

more mutagenic than the others because this substance could be administered at much higher doses.

Biochemical investigations have shown that EMS is rapidly distributed throughout all the organs in the body and there is no reason to believe that its failure to shorten life-span is due to the fact that it does not reach a particular group of cells. It is noteworthy that EMS is carcinogenic but it produces its cancers too late to bring about a detectable alteration in the average length of life. If the reasonable assumption is made (Burnet, 1965) that there is a close parallelism between the induction of germ and somatic mutations then these results indicate that raising the somatic mutation rate many times above the normal does not affect life span. Such a conclusion would appear to be irreconcilable with the concept that the accumulation of somatic mutations throughout life causes aging.

THE CAUSES OF RADIATION-INDUCED SHORTENING OF LIFE-SPAN

The experiments with EMS also suggest that the induction of mutations is not responsible for the life-span shortening produced by irradiation[3] or by the cytotoxic polyfunctional alkylating substances. The principal characteristic of these two classes of agents is that they act predominantly on cells capable of division; early pathological effects of radiation occur in those tissues where cell turnover is rapid (e.g., bone-marrow and intestinal mucosa) but there is also damage in such organs as the liver and the kidney, but this is usually delayed because the cells divide only infrequently. Radiation damage both in the long and short term is concentrated in organs capable of regeneration, yet it is precisely these organs that show least progressive deterioration with age. In old animals the liver and the haemopoietic system retain both their physiological function and capacity for regeneration and cell production; skin from old animals grows normally on transplantation (Krohn, 1962). Hypertrophy or regeneration of the liver, kidney and thyroid gland has been demonstrated to remain permanently impaired after exposure to ionizing radiation (Bacq and Alexander, 1961) and damage to organs and tissues, where cell division is infrequent but none the less necessary, seems to provide a reasonable explanation for life span shortening by radiation. Casarett (1963) has drawn particular attention to the epithelial lining of blood vessels in this connection.

[3] This deduction cannot necessarily be extended to other systems and the effect of ionizing radiations on life-span in insects may have a genetic origin, especially since the effect only sets in at much higher doses than for mice. In insects cell division only occurs in the brain and testes and massive cell death following irradiation is unlikely. Life-span shortening in insects may therefore only be seen when the dose is sufficiently high for an effect of radiation other than cell death to come into play.

AGING AND THE DEATH OF POST-MITOTIC CELLS

Except at supra-lethal doses, radiation does not kill highly differential cells such as muscle or nerve which are incapable in the adult of undergoing mitosis. Yet as Shock (review, 1964) has pointed out it is the death of such cells—cells whose loss cannot be made good by division—which is most closely allied to the physiological manifestation of aging. On this interpretation one would not expect there to be a close correlation between the limitation of attainable life span due to aging and life span shortening by irradiation. To understand the underlying processes of aging we must determine the causes of death of post-mitotic cells. What are the relative contributions of "clinkering up" with age pigments (Strehler, 1962), the formation of crosslinks as suggested by Bjorksten (1962) or the changes in elasticity of the collagen matrix? This is an area of almost complete ignorance and one which requires a great deal of basic experimentation that will in the initial stages be far removed from the phenomenon of aging. Death of cells cannot be considered only at the level of individual cells since interactions between organs (i.e., host factors) are likely to be involved; autoimmune reactions may become more prevalent with age and thereby contribute to the death of post-mitotic cells. On the other hand several studies show a progressive impairment of the immune mechanism with age and current ideas suggest that such a change may be mediated through cell death in the thymus (Miller, 1965).

The data available at the present time are quite insufficient to decide whether the changes in the immune system with age are a cause or a consequence of the death of irreplacable cells. Immunology would appear to be one of the most fruitful areas for research in mammalian gerontology especially as it may provide the link with cancer. In recent years (Alexander, 1965) evidence has been accumulating which shows that immunological factors oppose the growth of primary cancers and that the development of tumours requires that the immune response is overwhelmed, bypassed or eliminated. In man, the biological force of cancer—as measured by the age specific death rate—increases rapidly and progressively with age and it is tempting to look for a correlation with a possible effect of senescence on the capacity to mount primary immunological reactions.

ACKNOWLEDGMENT

This investigation has been supported by grants to the Chester Beatty Research Institute (Institute of Cancer Research: Royal Cancer Hospital) from the Medical Research Council and the British Empire Cancer Campaign for Research, and by the Public Health Service Research Grant No. CA-03188-08 from the National Cancer Institute, U.S. Public Health Service.

REFERENCES

ALBERT, M. D.: X-irradiation induced mitotic abnormalities in mouse liver regenerating after CCl_4 injury. *J. Nat. Cancer Inst., 20:*309, 1958.

ALEXANDER, P.: Immunological reactions of the host against primary tumours. In: *Scientific Basis of Surgery,* W. T. Irwin, ed., London, Churchill, 1965.

ALEXANDER, P., AND CONNELL, D. I.: Shortening of life-span of mice by irradiation with X-rays and treatment with radiomimetic chemicals. *Radiat. Res., 12:*38, 1960.

ALEXANDER, P., AND CONNELL, D. I.: Differences between radiation induced life-span shortening in mice and normal aging as revealed by serial killing. In: *Cellular Basis and Aetiology of Late Somatic Effects of Ionizing Radiations,* R. J. C. Harris, ed., New York, Academic Press, 1963a.

ALEXANDER, P., AND CONNELL, D. I.: The failure of the potent mutagenic chemical ethyl methane sulphonate to shorten the life-span of mice. In: *Cellular Basis and Aetiology of Late Somatic Effects of Ionizing Radiations,* R. J. C. Harris, ed., New York, Academic Press, 1963b.

BACQ, Z. M., AND ALEXANDER P.: *Fundamentals of Radiobiology,* Oxford, Pergamon, 1961.

BATEMAN, A. J.: Methyl methane sulphonate as a mutagen. *Brit. Empire Cancer Campaign Report, 41:*521, 1963.

BJORKSTEN, J.: Aging: present status of our chemical knowledge. *J. Amer. Geriat. Soc., 10:*125, 1962.

BURNET, M. J.: Somatic mutation of chronic disease. *Brit. Med. J.,* Feb. 6th:337, 1965.

CASARETT, G. W.: Concept and criteria of radiologic aging. In: *Cellular Basis and Aetiology of Late Somatic Effects of Ionizing Radiations,* R. J. C. Harris, ed., New York, Academic Press, p. 189, 1963.

CONNELL, D. I., AND ALEXANDER, P.: The incidence of hepatomas in irradiated and non-irradiated CBA male mice as a criterion of aging. *Gerontologia (Basel), 3:*153, 1959.

CROWLEY, C., AND CURTIS, H. J.: The development of somatic mutations in mice with age. *Proc. Nat. Acad. Sci. USA, 49:*626, 1963.

CURTIS, H. J.: Biological mechanisms underlying the aging process. *Science, 141:*686, 1963.

DUNJIE, A.: Shortening of the span of life of rats by Myleran. *Nature (London), 203*:887, 1964.

FAILLA, G.: Mutation theory of aging. *Ann. N. Y. Acad. Sci., 71*:1124, 1958.

HARMAN, D.: Prolongation of the normal life span by radiation protective chemicals. *J. Geront., 12*:257, 1957.

HENSHAW, P. S.: Genetic transition as a determinant of physiologic and radiologic aging and other conditions. *Radiology, 69*:30, 1957.

HOLLINGWORTH, J. W., BEBE, G. W., ISHIDA, M., AND BRILL, A. B.: Medical findings on atomic bomb survivors. The uses of vital and health statistics for genetic and radiation studies. p. 77, publ. United Nations, 1962.

JACOBS, P. A., BRUNTON, M., COURT BROWN, W. M., DOLL, R., AND GOLDSTEIN, H.: Change of human chromosome count distribution with age: Evidence for a sex difference. *Nature (London), 197*:1080, 1963.

KROHN, P. L.: Heterochronic transplantation in the study of aging. *Proc. Roy. Soc.* (series B), *157*:128, 1962.

LAMB, M. J., AND MAYNARD SMITH, J.: Radiation and aging in insects. *Exp. Geront., 1*:11, 1964.

LINDOP, P. J., AND ROTBLAT, J.: Long-term effects of a single whole body exposure of mice to ionizing radiations. *Proc. Roy Soc.* [*Biol.*], *B154*:332, 1961.

LISCO, H., DUCOFF, H. S., AND BASERGA, R.: Effect of radiation on latent period of chemical carcinogenesis. *Bull. Hopkins Hosp., 103*:101, 1958.

MILLER, J. F. A. P.: Function of the thymus in immunity. In: *Scientific Basis of Surgery,* W. T. Irwin, ed., London, Churchill, 1965.

MOLE, R. H.: The development of leukaemia in irradiated animals. *Brit. Med. Bull., 14*:(No. 2) 174, 1958.

ROCKSTEIN, M.: Heredity and longevity in the animal kingdom. *J. Geront., 13*:Suppl. 2, 7, 1958.

RUSSELL, W. L., AND OAKBERG, E. F.: Effects of irradiations on fertility in female mice. In: *Cellular Basis and Aetiology of Late Somatic Effects of Ionizing Radiations,* R. J. C. Harris, ed., New York, Academic Press, p. 229, 1963.

SHOCK, N. W.: Intrinsic factors in aging. In: *Age with a Future,* P. From Hansen, ed., Copenhagen, Munksgaard, 1964, p. 13.

STREHLER, B. L.: *Time, Cells and Aging.* New York, Academic Press, 1962.

SZILARD, L.: On the nature of the aging process. *Proc. Nat. Acad. Sci. USA, 45*:30, 1959.

UPTON, A. C., FURTH, J., CHRISTENBERRY, K. W., BENEDICT, W. H., AND MOSHMAN, J.: Some late effects in mice of ionizing radiation from an experimental nuclear detonation. *Cancer Res., 20*:(Suppl.), 1, 1960.

UPTON, A. C., JENKINS, V. K., AND CONKLIN, J. W.: Myeloid leukaemia in the mouse. *Ann. N. Y. Acad. Sci., 114*:189, 1964.

UPTON, A. C., KASTENBAUM, M. A., AND CONKLIN, J. W.: Age specific death rates of mice exposed to ionizing radiation and to radiomimetic agents. In: *Cellular Basis and Aetiology of Late Somatic effects of Ionizing Radiations,* R. J. C. Harris, ed., New York, Academic Press, 1963, p. 285.

VERZÁR, F.: Das Altern des Kollagens. *Helv. Physiol. Pharmacol. Acta, 14*:207, 1956.

Chapter 21

NUTRITION AS A FACTOR IN AGING

DANIELA SCHLETTWEIN-GSELL

SINCE THE BEGINNING OF MEDICINE, nutrition has been considered one of the most important factors in aging. Much has been whispered about the rejuvenating force of some magic potions. Witchcraft was usually necessary for their preparation, and gold, which in its ultimate alchemistic purity was equivalent to the elixir of life, and the philosopher's stone were the most frequent ingredients. Frankincense, pearls, rosemary oil, the heart-bone of deer and viper flesh often appeared in these formulae.

In more recent times it has been fashionable to imitate food habits of populations reported to have a great number of old men in good form. The best known example is Metchnikoff (1907) who popularized yoghurt, the sour-milk drink of the Bulgarians, and not long ago a tourists' guide to the mountains of Savoy announced that this part of France was the home of especially old men because families mainly lived on bread and wine. More cheerful advice can be found on a Colombian stamp of 1958 which shows the picture of a purported 167-year-old citizen and says: "Don't worry, drink lots of coffee and smoke a good cigar." Even to-day certain substances have not entirely lost their magic power: gold is added to strengthening liqueurs (*Danziger Goldwasser*), wine is called the "milk of the old men" and few foods have been spread by dietitians with more enthusiasm than yoghurt.

Compared to this wide-spread belief in the effect of nutrition on the aging process, little is known about recommended dietary allowances in old age; less about the influence of the quantity of nutrition on aging and practically nothing about the influence of the quality of nutrition.

Recommended dietary allowances are usually considered to be the same for old subjects as for younger adults with the exception of calorie intake which is adapted to changes in physical activity.

Experimental studies on absorption from the intestine on minimum requirements, retention, serum level and excretion in old age have been carried out for many nutrients, but no significant differences between young and old subjects could be shown. Discordant results have been explained as consequences of the often poor clinical state of the elderly subjects. Two factors which are of basic importance in the evaluation of these experiments, adaptation capacity and previous intake, however, are different in young and old age.

Adaptation capacity has been shown to be different in old age with respect to several environmental factors such as temperature, oxygen pressure etc., but there have been practically no studies on the adaptation capacity to food intake in old age. Adaptation is the reason that an animal tends to drift into an equilibrium whatever the intake is, provided it is constant. Usually the point, rather arbitrarily chosen, at which adaptation becomes very slow is called the minimum requirement. Experiments are often of too short duration to take adaptation capacity into account. This is especially true for experiments on old subjects. Closely related to the problem of adaptation is the influence which the prior level of intake exerts on the nutritional requirements. Young animals on a high nutritional intake and suddenly deprived of a specific nutrient excrete at first larger amounts than if they had previously been on a low intake (Ashworth, 1933). This aspect again has not been systematically considered in experiments with old subjects although in the case of old age this may be of special importance since the intake of a whole life-time is involved.

Present dietetic prescriptions for old persons—frequent as they are—mainly have the intention of adapting quantity and quality of the diet to the involutional processes of the aging body and to the socio-economic situation of old persons. Specific recommendations are included to prevent certain old age diseases: calorie reduction is suggested to prevent obesity, fat reduction to prevent arteriosclerosis. Relative or absolute increase of protein and minerals is recommended as a protection against infections, osteoporosis and anemia. High intakes of vitamins are believed to have general stimulating effects. None of these prescriptions is concerned with aging *per se.*

Some of the present theories on aging discuss the influence of the quantity of nutrition on the aging process.

McCay's startling results on rats fed a restricted diet have initiated a great number of experiments on the relation between life-span and quantity of nutrition. McCay (1939) raised immature rats on a diet containing all the essential nutritional elements but lacking sufficient calories to promote growth and maturation. He was able to keep the immature rats in a state of immaturity for periods up to 900 days, and was able to reinitiate growth in these retarded animals by the simple expedient of raising the caloric intake to an adequate level. These animals lived as much as 200 days longer than the controls. Collagen also ages less rapidly in these animals (Chvapil and Hruza, 1959). Similar experiments have been conducted on widely different species which seem to confirm McCay's discovery: Rockstein and Lieberman (1959) showed the effect of under-feeding on the life-span of the house-fly; Rudzinska (1962) described similar observations on *Tokophrya infusorum* and Danielli and Muggleton (1959) on the amoeba.

These experiments have been interpreted in different ways. Most authors basically agree that they support the theory that higher energy expenditure shortens life, since a strictly limited daily diet must result in a lower expenditure of energy.

There are, however, other possible factors involved in these results: rats kept under laboratory conditions probably overeat because they lack physical activity. Domestication or loss of instinct results in the storage of more reserves of fat than are advantageous to the organism. Some experiments have been started to test this view (Holeckova and Chvapil, 1965).

Most interesting results have been presented by Ross (1961), who fed qualitatively different diets to rats. Life-span was highest on a diet rich in sucrose and low in casein and it was found that animals fed this diet *ad libitum* had a ten to twenty per cent lower caloric intake than animals fed the other diets. Besides these experiments very little is known about possible influences of qualitative nutritional factors on aging.

A recent Swedish publication stresses the importance of folic acid (Nyström, 1964). Earlier studies on nutritional imbalances had shown, that life-span of rats is increased, if methionine or to a lesser degree if lysine is added to the diet (Lang, 1957). If these amino acids were added to the diet through several generations, a high percentage of the females were sterile in the fourth and fifth generation. It had never been shown whether this increase in life span reflects differences in the aging process, but if an excessive amount of methionine was added to the diet, there was a marked inhibition of growth which, according to investigations by Klavins and Peacocke (1964) appears to be due to a combination of a reduced total food intake and a toxic effect produced by the methionine.

Studies on methionine supplements to the diet are especially interesting in the light of recent findings of Tuttle, *et al.* (1965) who observed a higher minimum requirement of methionine in old than young men. Oeriu and Tanase (1963) on the other hand reports an increase of free amino acids in the tissues of aging rats (and men) which can be changed in ways characteristic for young adults by administering cysteine, the demethylated form of methionine. In Oeriu's opinion changes in the metabolic balance of cysteine and cystine which regulates the activity of several enzymes are responsible for the aging process. Oeriu's theories have never been compared with the dietary studies on methionine although certain parallels are obvious.

Other qualitative factors could influence the aging process as well: Björksten (1962) has emphasized the analogy between gelatine overtanned by formaldehyde and senescent tissue and has suggested that senescence is the result of *in vivo* tanning by cross-linking agents such as free radicals, aldehydes etc. normally present in the tissue. In his opinion nutritional intake would influence the effect of cross-linking agents via the quantity of nutrition: the greater the rate of metabolism the more cross-linking agents might be produced.

Furthermore it is possible that certain food-stuffs produce more cross-linking agents than others. Foods contain tanning substances in different quantities. A very high content is characteristic for tea. The influence of massive doses of tea throughout life-time is at present being studied in Verzár's laboratory. The diet normally consumed by men or laboratory animals has, however, never been investigated from this point of view.

It is also possible, that differences in the preparation of food result in different metabolic by-products: the effect of milk should be compared if given in the form of fresh milk or in the form of cheese; vegetables and fruit compared if consumed raw or boiled; meat if boiled or fried, etc. It is possible that some of the beneficial "secrets" of the different cuisines (e.g., of the Chinese food) may be discovered by such studies.

The toxic effect of metabolic by-products of food has always been emphasized by those authors who thought that aging is caused by auto-intoxication. Korenchevsky (1961) was a champion of this theory. Fisher (1956) has calculated that if the diet normally given to rats contains sufficient amounts of all essential amino acids, then tyrosine, phenylalanine and tryptophan are present in amounts which exceed the toxic limit for some animals. Similar imbalances are probably present in many diets consumed by humans and may be mainly caused by socio-economic conditions. Preparation of the meal and order of the menu may also be an important factor for such imbalances.

Studies on the effect of nutrition in germ-free animals will be of special value to clarify the importance of toxic substances produced by micro-organisms normally present in the intestinal tract which had been accused by Metchnikoff (1907) as auto-intoxicating factors.

Leopold (1960) has shown that in soybeans and spinach plants the ripening of fruit or flowers is associated with the development of some lethal condition in the plant and removal of the ripening parts averts or at least delays the lethality. The nature of the lethal effect of one plant part upon another is not known. Vegetables consumed by animals or men often consist of those parts of the plants in which the lethal factor seems to be present (as removal of these parts averts the effect). It would seem most interesting to investigate possible effects of these factors on the consumers.

Further effects of nutrition are indicated by the findings of Selye (1962) on calciphylaxis. Calciphylaxis is a condition of induced hypersensitivity in which tissues respond to appropriate challenging agents with a precipitous local or systemic calcification. Some experimental calciphylactic reactions resemble known clinical diseases of men or animals such as progeria, arteriosclerosis, senile osteoporosis, etc. Sensitizers used for inducing hypersensitivity are, among others, DHT, vitamin D_2 and vitamin D_3. Challengers are, among others, metalic compounds, tissue extracts and egg constituents. Both, substances used as sensitizers and as challengers, are thus present in the conventional diets of men and animals. It is possible that reactions similar to experimental calciphylactic reactions are continuously produced by substances taken with the diet.

The order in which nutrients are offered would seem to be of great importance for this phenomenon. Changes in food habits at different times of life, order of food availability during the day and even the composition of food during a single meal might be of interest.

Nutritional research is extremely difficult to conduct in men where individual habits, socio-economic status and adaptation complicate the evaluation of the findings. Extensive nutritional studies have been done on conventional laboratory animals and to a lesser degree on fish. Studies on the sensitizing effect of certain nutrients as well as experiments on the tanning effect of food would seem easier to conduct in animals with a less varied nutrition such as invertebrates than in man. Even micro-organisms which have been of great help in earlier investigations on amino acid imbalance might be used in the study of the effects of nutrition on aging. From all these points of view it thus seems probable that nutrition is very important among the extrinsic factors influencing the aging process.

REFERENCES

Ashworth, U. S., and Brody, S.: A study of the age changes and other factors which may influence the basal or endogenous nitrogen metabolism. *Univ. Missouri Agr. Exp. Sta. Res. Bull.*, Nos. 189, 190 and 191, 1933.

Björksten, J.: Aging: present status of our chemical knowledge. *J. Amer. Geriat. Soc., 10*:125, 1962.

Chvapil, M., and Hruza, Z.: The influence of aging and undernutrition on chemical contractility and relaxation of collagen fibres in rats. *Gerontologia (Basel), 3*:241, 1959.

Danielli, J. F., and Muggleton, A.: Some alternative states of amoeba with special reference to life span. *Gerontologia (Basel), 3*:76, 1959.

Fisher, R. B.: Possible toxic effects of amino-acids in normal diets. In: Verzár, F. (ed.), *Symposium über experimentelle Alternsforschung*. Basel, Birkhäuser, 225, 1956.

Holeckova, E., and Chvapil, M.: The effect of intermittent feeding and fasting and of domestication on biological age in the rat. *Gerontologia (Basel), 11:* 96, 1965.

Klavins, I. V., and Peacocke, I. L.: Pathology of amino-acid excess. *Brit. J. Exp. Path., 45:*533, 1964.

Korenchevsky, V.: *Physiological and Pathological Aging.* Basel, S. Karger, 1961.

Lang, K.: *Biochemie der Ernährung.* Darmstadt, Steinkopff, 1957.

Leopold, A. C.: Senescence of plants and plant organs. In: Strehler, B. (ed.), *The Biology of Aging.* Washington, Amer. Inst. Biol. Science, 207, 1960.

McCay, C. M., Maynard, L. A., Sperling, G., and Barnes, L. L.: Retarded growth life span, ultimate body size and age changes in albino rat after feeding diets restricted in calories. *J. Nutr., 18:*1, 1939.

Metchnikoff, E.: *The Prolongation of Life.* London, Heinemann, 1907.

Nyström, B.: A theory on aging. *Svensk. Läkarticln, 61:*1078, 1964.

Oeriu, S. and Tanase, I.: Biochemische Aspekte der Alterungsprozesse. *Z. Alternsforsch., 17:*35, 1963.

Rockstein, M., and Liebermann, H. M.: A life table for the common house fly. *Gerontologia (Basel), 3:*23, 1959.

Ross, M. H.: Length of life and nutrition in the rat. *J. Nutr., 75:*197, 1961.

Rudzinska, M.: The use of a protozoon for studies on aging. *Gerontologia (Basel), 6:*206, 1962.

Selye, H.: *Calciphylaxis.* Chicago, The University of Chicago Press, 1962.

Tuttle, S. G., Bassett, S. H., Griffith, W. H., Mulcare, D. B., and Swendseid, M. E.: Further observations on the amino-acid requirements of older men. *Amer. J. Clin. Nutr., 16:*225, 1965.

Chapter 22

AGING AND ENVIRONMENT

RALPH W. BRAUER

In writing a note for a volume celebrating Professor Verzár it seems in order to recall that he has been prominent among the great biologists who during the first half of this century established a pattern of study of physiology in which experiment and observation were forever alternating with philosophical questioning of the meaning of the data gleaned. His work clearly has been that of one who loved to observe, and for whom no observation, no experiment was complete until it had been scrutinized, and winnowed by speculation, and thus made to yield the seeds for further and ever more incisive study. This spirit, it seems to me, is peculiarly essential in the field of gerontology, and it thus seems far more than an accident that for many years now F. Verzár has been among the foremost contributors to the study of aging and senescence. That mixture of curiosity, delight in thinking out conclusions, and humility in testing and reevaluating these in turn, so prominently his, is sorely needed in the exploration of the interplay of time and environment in molding the aging of the individual.

Gerontology, it would seem, has in recent years outgrown an early, almost scholastic tendency for seeking a single common cause for a supposedly single basic process of "aging." Senescence now is recognized as a phenomenon characterized by the progressive accumulation of changes in various organ systems, at various rates, each contributing in its measure to reduce the vitality of the individual, to increase his vulnerability, and thus to produce the peculiar shape of the life table characteristic of so many species in relatively sheltered environments.

Such a phenomenon invites a pragmatic approach, and in the hands of the medical profession this has found its logical expression in the "critical organ system" approach which in recent years has shed much light in particular upon the changes in the cardiopulmonary system in the aged. Among the general conclusions derived from this body of work, one singularly pertinent to the present discussion is the striking degree to which the time course and even the clinical character of the pattern of changes in the cardiovascular and respiratory systems are amenable to modification by a host of environmental factors. Nutrition, emotional stress, exercise, altitude, atmosphere pollution or purity, are only a few of the most important of these modifying factors. Widely different patterns of change thus appear in, let us say, senescent Grison farmers and New York stock brokers, as groups or as individuals. Senescence in such groups with divergent environmental and occupational histories can no longer be validly described by any single parameter. The relative simplicity of a roughly common form of life table thus serves to conceal a very real and highly significant diversity of aging patterns.

To reveal these, and to render them in turn amenable to quantitative study and comparison requires a wholly different descriptive apparatus. Professor Verzár's studies on connective tissue aging represent an excellent example of the search for and the characterization of what may be referred to as "calendar functions," parameters which allow the description of the time course of change in a particular organ system in a quantifiable manner, or conversely, which can be used to define the lapse of biological time with regard to that organ system, independently of actual physical time. The relation to the latter now becomes meaningful only if the conditions under which the subject lived were properly defined. It would seem that the use of multiple functions of this type, on the same groups of individuals, could provide a meaningful basis for description and for analysis or comparison of the patterns of aging between groups differing widely in their environmental histories. The procedure might be to select one or a few specific calendar functions to define a functional biological time scale, and plot other parameters against this scale. Such a diagram would reveal qualitative differences in aging patterns by divergence of the lines representing any particular parameter for each of the groups being compared; similarity of aging patterns, even if absolute rates were to differ between the groups, would be reflected in identical, or at least in parallel lines on such a calendar function diagram.

Thermodynamically speaking, living systems are of necessity open systems: they are inconceivable without an environment with which they must interact continuously. The lapse of time thus inescapably becomes equivalent for any living individual to the accumulation of an ever lengthening history composed of the environments experienced and the interactions which have taken place with each. Do these experiences pass by like shadows on a stone wall, leaving no trace behind? Or does each leave behind imprints that do not wholly vanish but rather accumulate in the memory of a man, or in a well kept chronicle? How important is this "biological memory" in the life of the individual? Could one conceivably even go to the extreme of considering whether to a biological system the lapse of time is expressed as the sum of these accumulating experiences, and whether these in turn represent in a way the only meaningful measure of "elapsed time"?

It seems curious that gerontologists as a group have shown very little interest in the experimental study of biological time. A rich source of experimental and conceptual stimulation would seem to lie in the body of work slowly accumulating under the hands of those interested in diurnal and longer biological rhythms. As yet, there is no answer to the question whether individuals "age" by days, by minutes, or by their own time as a function of the accumulation of events and interactions in their individual lives. The fact that in adult vertebrates the diurnal cycle can be lengthened or shortened only to a very limited extent (10 or 15 per cent) by manipulation of time cues such as light and darkness has been interpreted as pointing to one or several "endogenous oscillating systems" with circadian periods, i.e., periods near twenty-four hours, as the master time keepers. Ontological studies suggest that these time keepers do not appear until rather late in embryonic life, and supersede other, shorter period rhythms. Even in the adult, circadian rhythms can eventually be disrupted by depriving the individual of time-giving stimuli for extended periods. No data are as yet available on the effects of such manipulations on the onset of senescence. Yet here would seem to lie one area of extraordinary theoretical interest to gerontologists; a key to some of the questions raised above, and a worthy extension of earlier work on the manipulation of biological time by hibernation, by temperature changes, or by nutrition.

Regardless of the outcome of such studies on the existence or lack of an absolute biological clock related to physical time, the content of the time elapsed, in terms of environments and experiences sustained, seems bound to affect the course and especially the patterns of aging. An analysis of a wide variety of environmental stresses has revealed that, wherever they have been looked for, residual effects of such stresses have been detected. Conditions as varied as chronic altitude exposure and repeated caisson experiences, ionizing radiation exposure and environmental noise levels in relation to auditory acuity, local cold exposure and marginal nutritional deficiencies fall into a common pattern; in each case there is a relatively marked prompt or early response, which for the most part is rather promptly reversed, but which leaves behind a residual change, usually small in magnitude, but detectable by suitable techniques and experimental designs. The levels of "stress" used to produce these effects usually exceed the amplitude of normal environmental fluctuations by a fair margin. Yet, there are indications that this is by no means an invariable requirement, and that minute changes often repeated might accumulate to detection threshold levels as effectively as the levels of stress residues due to fewer but larger perturbations.

Unfortunately, data available on this subject are limited by the character of the effects pertinent to the present discussion: In general, the residue represents small and relatively inconspicuous effects by the side of the far more marked changes elicited promptly, and reversed nearly as promptly. Thus, experimental study of these residual effects requires a rather special design, incorporating relatively sensitive and selective detection methods, extended observation periods, careful control of conditions under which test populations are reared and maintained, and more sensitive statistical control than is customary for studies of direct effects.

On the whole, animal experimentation in this field has proved most difficult. Not merely the relatively large numbers of subjects required and the costly holding periods, but in particular the rigid requirements for environmental control more often than not involving parallel cohorts in more than one closely controlled environment, have discouraged any broad attack upon these problems. In thinking about perspectives in gerontology, it seems well to recognize this fact at the same time as the great importance of further efforts in this direction. In an age when control, and hence selection of the environment is coming within the reach of an increasing segment of the populations of many nations, an understanding of the subtle ways in which environment can influence population quality is more than a mere scientific desideratum. Beyond question, judgments in this connection will be made and will eventually mould public policy. It would be well if they were informed by scientific understanding, even if the decisions will ultimately involve ethical and social value judgments not properly within the scope of scientific inquiry. If large scale facilities are needed in gerontology, here surely is one destination for them, and a national institute pattern might prove the one practicable way to meet this need.

Human biology studies in the same area cannot hope to afford a means of analyzing cause and effect relations in this field. They might, however, provide an excellent means for assessing the relative importance of one or another factor, and for uncovering phenomena worthy of more incisive study. One question in particular remains to be assessed. While many specific perturbations have been shown to leave residual effects, it is not clear to what extent the normal stresses of everyday life exceed the threshold where they, too, leave residues. It has been pointed out above that life of necessity involves interaction of the living animal with its environment. Attempts to study nearly stimulus-free, neutral environments by and large have shown these to be extraordinarily stressful to man. Clearly some balance between challenge and accommodation is as essential to the survival of the individual as of the species. Where this balance is optimal; where the threshold lies for the production of irreversible changes, and the eventual consequences of such changes cannot be predicted *a priori*. Studies on human populations would be highly desirable. Some of the experimental data now available do indeed suggest effects of the kind under discussion at levels of stress well within the limits of what is normally encountered in a modern industrial civilization. Finding a suitable population base for studies of this kind is apt to prove far from easy. One group that looks fairly promising may be briefly described as an example. Indian populations in the Andean highlands of Peru have been subjected to considerable social and economic pressure for a long time. Within the last fifty to seventy years, socio-political conditions of these groups have improved somewhat, and in particular have restored to them a measure of mobility. This has resulted in emigration from the highlands areas. One of the streams of emigrants has flowed toward the Eastern Andean slopes and the upper reaches of the Amazon and its tributaries. Often the migration pattern has been one in which emigrants from a particular community have moved jointly, and established a new community at lower levels, while the present communities persisted in the highlands. A recent trip by the author and Dr. Berendsohn of Lima revealed, along an 1800 mile stretch of the Andes, a series of such "paired" communities where close relatives often lived in widely different environments. This distribution affords as close an approach to a controlled laboratory experiment involving human populations as seems feasible in a non-totalitarian society. Since in many cases the migration can be dated forty or fifty years ago, the potential for gerontological studies seems real. This is especially true since surface appearances support the view that important differences in the appearance of old people of similar age can be detected between such pairs of closely related communities.

Some comment may finally be in order here to relate the concepts advanced above to other formulations of the basic phenomena of senescence. It is surely not pretended that the ideas presented have superseded or must supersede formulations in which aging is conceived of, so to speak, as a consequence of original sin, an inherent weakness to which the flesh is heir. In focussing upon the environment in which aging takes place and upon the interaction of living systems with their environments, one does not in any way escape the verities of death in all higher organisms; one has merely shifted the focus to an area that has tended to be neglected by gerontologists and taken cognizance of some of the inviting experimental and theoretical opportunities inherent in this particular manner of viewing the phenomena. In particular, it should be noted that the views here expressed do not conflict in any way with the impressive array of data concerning the eminent role of genetic factors in controlling aging processes. Surely, it is now well understood that in early development genetic factors do not determine structure as such, but rather the processes that lead step by step to the final structure; processes which function only if given the right microenvironment at the right time. The final structure of a functioning organism thus is a historical product in which genetic control and environmental factors cooperate, and which is predictable merely because the range of the succession of environments is limited, and once initiated, is partly determined each time by the preceding steps. There is no reason for assuming that this kind of interplay ceases at maturity. However, in the adult the sequence of external environments, and to a smaller measure of internal microenvironments, is no longer predetermined as uniquely as it is in the developing embryo. The questions that remain are properly those of mechanisms, and of the range of variability producing significant effects as against the range compatible with survival. Genetic effects in this view would modify the responses to a given environmental challenge, the degree to which changes become irreversible, and the degree to which residues would influence subsequent responses. There is much in modern genetics that would make such a view an appealing interpretation of the role of inheritance in aging.

The present essay thus presents an attempt to project a picture of aging as growing out of the interaction of the individual living system with the series of environments to which it is exposed as an inescapable consequence of the very act of living. It is suggested that this line of reasoning invites gerontologists to a number of fields of experimentation they have hitherto not cultivated to any major extent. Considerations of biological rhythms, of irreversible residues of specific stresses, and description of patterns of aging in populations living in different environments by calendar function diagrams, promise to yield new organized knowledge which should justify these speculations even if in time it would serve to prove these concepts inaccurate. At present, however, it is contended that the picture here presented, as far as it goes, is not only an invitation to future work but also serves to integrate a large proportion of the available data.

(Data and references documenting more fully many of the points alluded to in this paper will be found in "Irreversible Effects of Environmental Stress," by the present author, constituting Chapter 17 of *The Physiology of Human Survival,* Otto Edholm and A. L. Bacharach, editors, Academic Press, London, 1965.)

Chapter 23

GERMFREE ANIMALS IN THE STUDY OF MICROBIAL EFFECTS ON AGING

H. A. GORDON

THE ROLE which microbial flora plays in the aging of higher organisms is essentially unknown. Some of its effects which are commonly observed in conventional animal populations are acute and chronic inflammations which flare up or persist in the course of life. In experimental work, these episodes represent a source of error that is seemingly inherent in all conventional animal colonies. Unable as we are to control these gross effects of the flora, we have been even less successful in pinpointing long range flora actions that may modify aging from the molecular to the organismic level.

In order to circumvent the difficulties that originate from the experimental animal's coexistence with the uncontrolled, variable and biologically active flora, various approaches may be used: 1) By insemination of innocuous micro-organisms early in life and by maintaining the animals in clean quarters and on sterilized diets, one may obtain a colony of animals that is free from specific pathogenic microorganisms. To our knowledge, the value of this approach has not yet been fully tested for work on aging. 2) For regimentation of the existing flora in conventional animals, some mode of control (e.g., antibiotic treatment) may be used. This approach, in itself, is inadequate for basic work on aging, because it entangles us even more in the complexities of the "host–microbial contaminant–controlling agent" relationships. 3) The purist's approach is to start out with an animal that is delivered at birth free from the flora and then maintain it either in this state, or after insemination with known contaminants, in comparison to conventional controls. This type of experimentation will not only give us microbially standardized animals (to which, at best, the first two possibilities are limited), but it will also offer a tool to differentiate between the effects of microbial and non-microbial factors on aging phenomena. In other words, it will permit a critical study of host-flora relationships and work on any experimental variable that might be selected for inquiry, undisturbed by the ubiquitous flora. This approach, which in essence, is an extension of the microbiologist's pure culture concept to all biologic forms, is the basis of the so called gnotobiotic experiment.* Since this type of work represents a relatively new area, the present chapter, concentrating on host-flora relationships, will review briefly its background and basic findings, in addition to the application and speculation on the use of gnotobiotic animals in aging studies.

HISTORICAL ASPECTS

The history of research with germfree animals is a fascinating chapter of experimental biology. We seldom witness as clear and early definition of the concepts, given by distinguished authors, followed by well planned and enthusiastically pursued experimental approaches, and repeated failures on formidable technical difficulties, as is the case in our area. Main trends in biologic thinking, including the aspect of aging, kept clashing on these issues without finding resolution until, perhaps, very recent times. And all this is recorded in publications that to date number less than a few dozen.

The discoveries of microbial pathogenicity of the mid-nineteenth century were necessarily followed by queries concerning the so called normal microbial associates of the host. It is in this area that the need for germfree studies was outlined for the first time. The recognition that, after birth, astronomical numbers of seemingly non-pathogenic microorganisms invade various cavities of the body and remain there in intimate association until death,

* The field of gnotobiotics (Reyniers *et al.*, 1949) includes the study of plants and animals that are maintained either free, or live in association with known microbial associates. The word "germfree" (or its synonym "axenic"), accordingly, designates the microbe-free form of gnotobiotic life. At this writing the germfree animal may be defined as a host reared in the absence of demonstrable living bacterial, mycological, protozoan and macroparasitic associates according to the test procedures routinely employed. Rickettsiae and virus have not been studied sufficiently to be included in the above statement.

suggested that these associates, most likely, affect the life of the host in some fashion. The idea of using microbially sterile animals for the elucidation of flora effects on the host originated with Pasteur (1885). Duclaux (1885), one of his associates, carried out the first germfree experiment by sprouting peas and beans in sterile conditions. In this, it seems, the previous work of Boussingault (1838) on plants grown in nutritionally sterile soils, which eventually led to the discovery of nitrogen fixation, served as an analogy. Though Pasteur and his group did not continue work in this area, his thoughts influenced greatly its development in the successive years. From the available sources (see also Schottelius, 1908) we may attempt to reconstruct briefly his trend of ideas as follows: All existing higher organisms (i.e., which survived the course of phylogenesis) live in intimate association with their microbial flora. In view of this, and in the sense of a positive evolution, we must postulate (and expect) the development of some form of synergism between the host and its normal contaminants. Therefore, if we prevent this association, as is the case in the germfree experiment, life (or at any rate normal life) might become impossible.

The ideas of Pasteur were first challenged by Nencki (1886) on theoretical grounds. In view of the role which intestinal bacteria play in the production of aromatic and other allegedly toxic substances, he rejected the possibility of host-flora synergism in animals. This concept was later elaborated by Metchnikoff (1903) in considerable detail. To him the normal flora represented primarily a "fighting antagonist."

In order to supply experimental evidence to this controversy, the first germfree animal experiments were run. Technically, these were almost impeccable, yet nutritionally they had to be failures on account of the inadequate heat-sterilized diets fed to the animals. Nuttal and Thierfelder (1895-97), in an attempt to support Nencki, reared a germfree guinea pig; Schottelius (1899-1913), aligning with Pasteur, hatched germfree chickens. Others followed. At the time of World War I, with no conclusive evidence in view, germfree experimentation came to a practical standstill. In the course of this early work, the aspect of aging versus normal flora was repeatedly mentioned, directly and by implication. For the time being, however, all had to remain in the realm of speculation, because the practical prerequisite, the successful rearing of germfree animals over generations, was still decades away. Yet we owe the groundwork of our edifice to this era.

In the early thirties interest was renewed and two groups of workers undertook the problem of making germfree animals a modern investigative tool: one at the University of Notre Dame in the United States (Reyniers, 1932; Reyniers *et al.*, 1946-1960), the other at the University of Lund in Sweden (Glimstedt, 1932; Gustafsson, 1946). The crucial event, the birth of germfree offspring from germfree parent animals took place some twenty years later. Shortly after, in 1958, the first (and to date, the only) aging colony of germfree rats and mice was started at Notre Dame. This work, largely preliminary, was concluded in 1963. The presently offered data on aging rest on the observations of this work (Gordon, Bruckner-Kardoss and Wostmann, 1964). The writer and his collaborators are deeply grateful to Professor Verzár who in word (1960) and deed was the prime catalyst of this project.

GERMFREE ANIMALS IN COMPARISON TO CONVENTIONAL CONTROLS*

General Characteristics

The germfree state, observed in a number of animal species, does not impart any special, readily visible characteristics. Germfree rats and mice grow fairly well and generally maintain their normal body weight throughout life. The conventional controls fed the same sterilized diet compare favorably to the germfree and to other conventional animals kept on unsterilized practical ration. Signs of pronounced nonspecific stress are missing in these animals.

Status of Body Defenses

A great deal of work done on germfree animals during the past decade concentrated on their defensive apparatus. In this area most data concur that germfree animals display a singular underdevelopment in their cellular and humoral defensive elements.

* Several review articles have been written on this subject; particularly pertinent in the present context are those of Gordon (1960), Mickelsen (1962) and Luckey (1963).

Against this bland germfree background, the normal conventional animals appear to be in a state of remarkable defensive stimulation. Thus, workers in the germfree field commonly speak of a "mild inflammation" that the flora in normal life imparts to microbially exposed organs. Among those primarily involved are the digestive and respiratory tracts, and probably the skin. The evidence on which this conclusion rests is as follows: reduced wet weight and elevated dry matter per cent in the exposed organs of germfree animals; reduced contingent of RE elements, and in some instances, of the connective tissue framework; the lymph nodes involved in draining these areas are considerably smaller and show reduced cellularity; regional blood flow of these organs, including the animal's cardiac output, is also reduced; serum proteins that are commonly associated with body defenses are substantially lower in germfree animals. The reduced defensive potential plausibly portrays the reduced defensive requirements in these animals; otherwise, they appear well adapted to their environment. When challenged by insemination of a normal flora inoculum, it was found that these animals will promptly muster adequate responses within a few weeks of adaptation (Wagner, 1959).

With progress of age, the defensive underdevelopment of germfree rats and mice (and for that matter the mild inflammation of the conventional controls) shows little change from the post-weaning period to the beginning of old age. The involved lymphoid organs indicate an early increase and later decline in weight that is observed both in germfree and conventional animals. These statements naturally do not refer to the frank inflammatory episodes that occasionally develop in conventional animals in the course of life. The functional consequences of the absent flora stimulation and of the needlessness to maintain active defenses in exposed organs of the germfree animal are largely unexplored. The histologic picture of the intestinal mucosa and of the pulmonary alveolar wall, taken as examples to show that these membranes are uncluttered by the customary mass of RE elements and framework tissue, indicate that in the germfree state they are reduced to non-defensive functional essentials. It might be considered, that these conditions of germfree life are conducive to functional relief (or improvement) of the involved membranes. An illustration for this is the increased arteriovenous oxygen difference that was calculated for germfree rats (from reduced cardiac output and from essentially unchanged metabolic rate). This might indicate enhanced passage of oxygen across the alveolar wall. Another suggestive observation in this general area is of the lower values of cholesterol found in the wall of the aorta in older germfree animals. This may permit the speculation that in conventional animals the greater accumulation of cholesterol in the arterial wall is due to the summation of direct or indirect minor lesions which are caused by episodes of microbial penetration during the life time (Wostmann, 1963).

Anomalies of Germfree Life

In addition to signs indicating relief from the "defensive burden," certain departures from physiologic normality were known to exist in germfree animals. Among these, the oldest observation is the paradoxical enlarged cecum which continues to be one of the main unsolved problems of germfree life. In 1896, Nuttal and Thierfelder, observing their week old germfree guinea pigs, wrote: ". . . der Blinddarm war stark aufgetrieben und mit brauner, käsig, geronnener Flüssigkeit schwappend gefüllt." Cecal enlargement (seen mainly in rodents) was found to develop in germfree animals during the lactation period (Wostmann and Bruckner-Kardoss, 1959) and to progress during their entire life span. In animals maintained on practical type diets the cecal contents average six to tenfold that of the normal values; in extreme cases ceca weighing 20-25 per cent of the animal's bodyweight have been observed. The ceca of germfree animals reared on semi-synthetic diets are smaller. The cecal contents are liquid and practically isotonic with blood, contrasting the mostly thick, hypertonic contents of normal animals. The wall of the cecum is paper-thin and its musculature shows reduced tonus. Though considerable water reabsorption takes place from the lower bowel, the voided feces of germfree animals are more moist than controls. Signs of hemoconcentration that are observed occasionally in these animals have been linked to the loss of liquid via the lower bowel. The indication that hemoconcentration is waning in cecectomized animals suggests that there is basis for this speculation.

The composition of germfree intestinal contents are different from those of conventional animals in other details also. They have a faint, not unpleasant caramel odor; indole and skatole were absent. The levels of digestive enzymes are elevated (Borgström *et al.*, 1959). Appreciable amounts of bilirubin were found in the feces of germfree rats, while there was no urobilin in urine and feces of these animals (Gustafsson and Swenander-Lanke, 1960). Labeled bile acids administered to germfree rats were recovered quantitatively from the supernatant of ultracentrifuged cecal contents. In conventional controls approximately one third of the label was found in the sediment (Gustafsson *et al.*, 1957). Recently, in the contents of the lower bowel of germfree rats and mice bioactive substances were found in great excess over conventional controls (Gordon, 1965). One of these agents, acting in minute quantities on a variety of smooth muscle preparations *in vitro* and *in vivo*, has been identified as a congener of hypotensive peptides. The cecum of a germfree rat or mouse may contain over fifty times the amount of this agent than is found in conventional control ceca.

Another, still unidentified substance, which could be separated by chromatography from the musculoactive agent, exerts toxic effects (and is ultimately lethal) on parenteral administration in germfree or conventional recipient animals. Of this substance, a germfree mouse may hold in its cecum over five times the LD_{50} (in reference to ip injected 20 g mice), while cecal contents of conventional control mice are relatively nontoxic. The demonstration of such potent agents in a germfree intestinal content came as a surprise and caused speculation that they may be involved in maintaining the anomalies of the germfree lower bowel. The possibility that this assumption might be correct was recently suggested by the following experiment. In germfree rats which were orally monocontaminated with *Salmonella typhimurium*, transient cecal reduction occurred. Under these circumstances the size of the cecum and the concentration of the musculoactive agent in the cecal contents showed a marked parallelism (Wiseman and Gordon, 1965). Thus our concept of germfree cecal enlargement is changing. Originally it was suspected that it is caused mainly by the lack of microbial pressor activity on the intestinal musculature. In view of the recent findings, we must consider the action of accumulated depressor substances. These substances appear to be normal metabolic products of the host, which in normal life are inactivated by the flora.

Little is known about the fate and effects of the anomalies of germfree life with advancing age. The cecal enlargement clearly progresses from young to older age (demonstrated in mice). Preliminary data indicate a parallel increment in the concentration of the musculoactive agent in the ceca of germfree mice. Liver cholesterol, which is always higher in germfree than in conventional animals (rats), shows a gradual increment with age. It is suspected that involved in this change is the elevated level of soluble bile acids found in the lower bowel of germfree animals which, being available for reabsorption, serves as a greater "cholesterol precursor pool."

Lesions at Natural Death; Life Tables

Observations derived from a colony of approximately 200 germfree mice and the same number of conventional controls which were maintained on sterilized rations and were held to natural death, indicated the following trends. The prevalent lesion observed at death among the germfree mice was associated with the enlarged cecum of these animals. Most frequently it appeared that the muscle tonus became reduced to the point that propulsive movements were severely impaired or came to a complete standstill. The gastrointestinal tract was greatly distended and filled to a maximum in its entire length. Occasionally, intestinal volvuli were observed, mostly at the ileo-cecal-colic junction. In the conventional control mice inflammatory lesions of the lungs and of the abdominal organs were predominant. The incidence of tumors seemed to be fairly similar in both groups. The mean age reached by the mice in this colony was as follows (means and standard deviations are given in months): Germfree males 24.2 ± 5.6, females 22.7 ± 4.7; conventional males 15.9 ± 3.4, females 17.2 ± 3.9. In another colony of conventional mice which were fed non-sterilized rations, these values were approximately 2 months longer than those given for conventional mice receiving the sterilized diet. Accordingly, germfree mice indicated a higher mean age than any of the conventional controls. Germfree males showed similar, or even higher age at death than germfree females. Among the conventional controls this condition was reversed.

COMMENTS, CONCLUSIONS AND PROSPECTS

The study of host-contaminant relationships is a relatively neglected area in work on aging. This was indicated at the last International Congress of Gerontology in Copenhagen (1963) where among the papers presented only two dealt with studies on the microbial variable. It appears that the cause of this is not the absence of problems, but the lack of available control and testing techniques in this area. Presently, gnotobiotic experimentation promises to supply the needed critical tool. Though many details yet await elaboration, the germfree-rearing techniques, diets and animals appear adequate for long range studies. After the initial difficulties had been overcome, it became evident that the problems encountered in this type of work are far less formidable than was originally anticipated.

The gnotobiotic approach is truly of fundamental importance in work on aging: it cuts across virtually all areas of concentration by permitting study without microbial interference and by allowing precise evaluation of microbial contribution to the host. In the words of the enthusiast, it is an untapped experimental cornucopia. This, unquestionably, is true. However, one must not lose sight of the fact, that the germfree animal is not only a host *minus* germs, but also an animal *minus* responses to germs, *plus* an accumulation of active metabolites of the host. This fact must be woven into all consideration and work in this area.

In the light of the scanty available results which concentrate mainly on flora-effects, it seems that one part of the host's lifetime experience with its flora is detrimental. This is indicated by the impairment of exposed biologic membranes, by the repetitive occurrence of inflammatory episodes and by the shorter survival time of conventional animals in comparison to their germfree counterparts. Under these circumstances it is hardly surprising to find that those animals which are naturally better equipped to combat infections will lose their advantage in germfree life. Thus, the female's known greater resistance to infections may explain the similarity in survival between males and females in the germfree colony. Another group of flora effects is clearly advantageous for the host's life. Actually, without these effects, normal life does not seem to be possible. In this context it is indicated that the host left to its own resources is not entirely self-contained. Apparently, in its normal metabolic pathways it is producing an excess of harmful substances that need to be inactivated in order to ensure physiologic normality of the body. In germfree animals the development of the resulting malfunctions is slow and non-spectacular. Yet, they are conspicuous enough and worsen with the progress of age. Terminally, they appear as a major factor (if not the major factor) in the animal's downfall. Thus, we can view antagonistic and synergistic effects as a dual function of the flora.

At this point, the following question poses itself. Does the flora exert its detrimental and advantageous effects in its entirety or is it conceivable that the different roles are played by different elements of the flora? To this question of considerable importance there is no answer as yet. In view of the fact that the resultant effect of the total flora is not purely additive, and as commonly known, intra-flora antagonisms and synergisms exist, the task of pinpointing microbial associates that are detrimental or advantageous for the host (if there be such separate entities) within the flora's ecologic framework appears a formidable one. Two approaches present themselves as possible pathways for exploring this issue. One is the trial and error method based on the study of the effects of arbitrarily selected microbial contaminants on the host, in known mono-, di- and poly-associations. This approach promises to fill endless numbers of progress reports.

The other, slightly more adventurous possibility includes antibiotic treated control animals as a procedural aid. Feeding antibiotics at low levels to conventional animals has been shown to render them qualitatively germfree-like, in some instances. Under these circumstances the mild inflammatory processes of exposed organs (mainly the intestine) subside. Comparing the intestinal flora of these antibiotic-treated animals to that of untreated controls, one may be able to identify missing microbes in the former group which, in turn, may be responsible for maintaining the mild inflammation in the latter group. This approach has also the advantage that it permits one to identify the implicated microbes, inseminate them into germfree controls and observe what their effect on the host is as monocontaminants. Moreover, another group of these monocontaminated animals can be treated with the same antibiotic and be tested later as controls for the evanescence of defensive stimulation. Finally, by the same approach, antibiotic treated germfree controls may offer information about the direct effects of various antibiotics on the host, when these are fed at nutritional levels. In short term experiments, the value of this approach has already been proven (Gordon *et al.*, 1957). Depending on the outcome of these experiments we may learn that detrimental and indispensible microbes are, or are not, the same group. If the latter applies, then our intestinal synergists are comparable (of course, not in function but in terms of importance) to the microbial symbionts which assimilate nitrogen on the roots of leguminous plants.

The problem of influencing (mainly reducing) the concentration of the accumulated bioactive substances in the gut lumen of germfree animals is another important issue. Germfree animals with low, conventional levels of these substances in their gastrointestinal tract and other implicated areas (and therefore hopefully void of the germfree anomalies) may be better experimental models in our area than their presently available counterparts endowed with the "germfree megacecum." One already tested and somewhat drastic approach consists in removing surgically the cecum early in life (no successive dilatation develops in the ileocecal or other areas), reducing thereby premanently to a minimum the originally large cecal pool in these animals (Gordon *et al.*, 1965). In this context the anticipation is evident that cecectomized germfree animals will fare even better in an aging colony than the unoperated germfree controls. Another possibility for reducing the concentration of bioactive substances in gut contents may be by way of food additives. Thus, it was indicated that, e.g., weak cationic exchange resins may be useful in reducing the concentration of the musculoactive agent in cecal contents of germfree animals.

In case this work will point in the future to specific elements of the flora that need to be eliminated or preserved, the problem of practicing rational flora control arises in larger populations, including humans. For all practical purposes our association with a flora will continue and therefore all possible approaches to this question will have to be adapted to this inescapable condition. The oral seeding of desirable flora elements early in life, followed up by re-seeding, which will entrench themselves and prevent invasion of detrimental elements, is an old and probably feasible approach. The other possibility is by instituting an antibiotic regimen which aims at the exclusion of detrimental elements. In animal nutrition, as well known, this is the basis for the elimination of growth depressing microorganisms (Coates *et al.*, 1951). With insufficient knowledge in the area for long range administration, and with the menace of developing thereby resistant microbial strains, we seem to be rather far from this approach. Yet we are reminded that in certain animal populations the natural diet contains antibiotic agents which act on the intestinal flora but have no ill effects on the host (some antarctic animals described by Sieburth, 1961).

In conclusion, it appears that two opposing thoughts concerning the role of the microbial flora on the host, Pasteur's and Metchnikoff's, may be resolved in the sense that both were partially right.

REFERENCES

Borgström, B., Dahlqvist, A., Gustafsson, B., Lundh, G., and Malmquist, J.: Trypsin, invertase and amylase content of feces of germfree rats. *Proc. Soc. Exp. Biol. Med., 102:*154, 1959.

Boussingault, J. B.: Recherches chimiques sur la végétation, entreprises dans le but si les plantes prennent de l'azote à l'atmosphère. *C. R. Acad. Sci. (Paris), 6:*102, 1838.

Coates, M. E., Dickinson, C. D., Harrison, G. F., Kon, S. K., Cummins, S. H., and Cuthbertson, W. F. J.: Mode of action of antibiotics in stimulating growth of chicks. *Nature (London), 168:*332, 1951.

Duclaux, E.: Sur la germenation dans un sol riche en matières organiques, mais exempt de microbes. *C. R. Acad. Sci. (Paris), 100:*66, 1885.

Glimstedt, G.: Das Leben ohne Bakterien. Sterile Aufziehung von Meerschweinchen. *Anat. Anz.,* Ergänz-heft, *75:*79, 1932.

Gordon, H. A.: The germfree animal. Its use in the study of "physiologic" effects of the normal microbial flora on the animal host. *Amer. J. Dig. Dis., 5:*841, 1960.

Gordon, H. A.: Demonstration of a bioactive substance in caecal contents of germfree animals. *Nature (London), 205:*571, 1965.

Gordon, H. A., Wagner, M., and Wostmann, B. S.: Studies on conventional and germfree chickens treated orally with antibiotics. Antibiotics Annual, 1957-58, p. 248. H. Welch (Ed.), N. Y. Antibiotica, Inc.

Gordon, H. A., Bruckner-Kardoss, E., and Wostmann, B. S.: Aging studies in colonies of germfree and conventional animals. In *Age with a Future* (Proceedings of the 6th International Congress of Gerontology, Copenhagen, 1963), Munksgaard, Copenhagen, 1964, p. 220.

GORDON, H. A., BRUCKNER-KARDOSS, E., STALEY, T. E., WAGNER, M., AND WOSTMANN, B. S.: Characteristics of the germfree rat. *Acta. Anat. (Basel),* 1965, in press.

GUSTAFSSON, B.: Några erfarenheter från bakterierfri uppfödning av råttor. *Nord. Med., 32:*2665, 1946.

GUSTAFSSON, B., BERGSTRÖM, S., LINDSTEDT, S., AND NORMAN, A.: Turnover and nature of fecal bile acids in germfree and infected rats fed cholic acid-24-14C. *Proc. Soc. Exp. Biol. Med., 94:*467, 1957.

GUSTAFSSON, B., AND SWENANDER-LANKE, L.: Bilirubin and urobilins in germfree, ex-germfree and conventional rats. *J. Exp. Med., 112:*975, 1960.

LUCKEY, T. D.: *Germfree Life and Gnotobiology.* New York, Academic Press, 1963.

METCHNIKOFF, E.: Les microbes intestinaux. *Bull. Inst. Pasteur, 7:*215 and 265, 1903.

MICKELSEN, O.: Nutrition, germfree animal research. *Ann. Rev. Biochem., 31:*515, 1962.

NENCKI, M.: Bemerkungen zu einer Bemerkung Pasteur's. *Arch. Exp. Path. Pharmakol., 20:*385, 1886.

NUTTAL, G. H. F., AND THIERFELDER, H.: Thierisches Leben ohne Bakterien im Verdauungskanal. *Z. Physiol. Chem., 21:*109, 1895. II. *Ibid., 22:*62, 1896. III. *Ibid., 23:*231, 1897.

PASTEUR, L.: Observations relatives a la note . . . de M. Duclaux. *C. R. Acad. Sci. (Paris), 100:*68, 1885.

REYNIERS, J. A.: The use of germfree guinea pigs in bacteriology. *Proc. Indiana Acad. Sci., 42:*35, 1932.

REYNIERS, J. A., TREXLER, P. C., ERVIN, R. F., WAGNER, M., LUCKEY, T. D., AND GORDON, H. A.: The need for a unified terminology in germfree life studies. *Lobund Reports, University of Notre Dame Press, Notre Dame, Indiana, 2:*151, 1949.

REYNIERS, J. A., TREXLER, P. C., ERVIN, R. F., WAGNER, M., LUCKEY, T. D., AND GORDON, H. A.: Work published in Lobund Reports I, 1946; II, 1949; III, 1960; Notre Dame University Press, Notre Dame, Indiana.

SCHOTTELIUS, M.: Die Bedeutung der Darmbakterien für die Ernährung. *Arch. Hyg., 34:*210, 1899. II. *Ibid., 42:*48, 1902. III. *Ibid., 67:*177, 1908. IV. *Ibid., 79:*289, 1913.

SIEBURTH, J. M.: Antibiotic properties of acrylic acid, a factor in the gastro-intestinal antibiosis of polar marine animals. *J. Bact., 82:*72, 1961.

VERZÁR, F.: Editorial. *Gerontologia (Basel), 3:*104, 1960.

WAGNER, M.: Serologic aspects of germfree life. *Ann. N. Y. Acad. Sci., 78:*261, 1959.

WISEMAN, R. F., AND GORDON, H. A.: Reduced levels of a bioactive substance in the caecal content of gnotobiotic rats monoassociated with *Salmonella typhimurium. Nature (London), 205:*572, 1965.

WOSTMANN, B. S.: Intestinal microflora and cholesterol catabolism. *Proc. Indiana Acad. Sci., 73:*83, 1963.

WOSTMANN, B. S., AND BRUCKNER-KARDOSS, E.: Development of cecal distension in germfree baby rats. *Amer. J. Physiol., 197:*1345, 1959.

Section VI

THEORIES OF AGING

Chapter 24

AGING: A COROLLARY OF DEVELOPMENT

PAUL WEISS

PREAMBLE

THIS ESSAY is written in full realization of its inadequacy. Yet a request to contribute to a volume commemorating the eightieth birthday of a friend committed to the study of gerontology, whose very youthfulness belies the stigma of the aging process, could not be declined simply for lack of qualification. A commentary by one who has never studied specifically the later part of the life span may seem presumptuous. Yet, it may not be wholly unwarranted to try to raise the sights from specific factual data to the broad overall perspective of biological processes in general from which they must be viewed and rated. And viewed from that perspective, the *aging* process, so called, appears but as a conveniently, but arbitrarily, delineated aspect of the process of *development*. The purpose of the following brief essay, therefore, is to place it back into that context.

Development consists of a continuous succession of processes of change and transformation, going on incessantly in uninterrupted sequences throughout the life span of an individual from egg until death. True, the rate of change varies markedly for different periods, and from tissue to tissue, and the *average* of these kinetics taken over the body as a whole can be said, in general, to decline with time. However, those changes of kinetics which strike the superficial observer or the self-observing subject as sudden and abrupt, reveal themselves on closer inspection as continuous and gradual, without the sharpness of demarcation which our conventional terminology seems to denote.

In this light the aging process appears as an integral facet of the continuous progress of development of an organism. It cannot be dealt with as if it were a separate and separable encumbrance, superimposed upon the ordinary processes of life—a sort of extraneous contamination, like a bacterial infection, that could be stripped off film-like once it has formed, or hopefully, be totally averted. Aging is not only with Minot (1908) the price we pay for our developmental differentiation: it *is* differentiation. On these grounds, I have given it at least "honorable mention" in my text on *Principles of Development* (1939, pp. 27-35), and nothing discovered in the quarter of a century and more since has weakened the argument.

A BRIEF SYNOPSIS OF DEVELOPMENT

The more we learn about development, the harder it becomes to compress its essence into a brief essay. The following synopsis, therefore, is crude and sketchy. Its main objective is to give concrete meaning to the loose term "differentiation," the substance of which is the source of "aging."

The egg, as the link between successive generations, reflects this role in its dual constitution: as both a highly specialized cell of the somatically differentiated maternal gonad and the germinal primordium of the new offspring. It carries over, accordingly, two sets of properties. One is the set of chromosomes containing the genome, now identified with specifically arrayed sequences of nucleotide pairs in strands of DNA, which at fertilization are combined with the paternal genome. The other set is the map of cytoplasmic organization which the egg derives directly from its residence in the ovary. Although this cytoplasmic pattern has often been eclipsed by monopolistic attention to the genome, it is important to restore it to its determinant role as a primordial framework of organization with which the genome is bound to interact. Its firm physical bearings lie presumably in a surface mosaic in the egg cortex, in which fields of different chemical composition and physical constitution are mapped out in typical configuration. During the subsequent cleavage of the egg by cell division, the various blastomeres thus receive disparate portions of this surface mosaic while all of them receive nuclei possessing the same full genic complement. As a result, nuclei that are erstwhile equivalent and interchangeable come to lie, from the very first, in different cytoplasmic environments. This sets the stage for *differential* nucleo-cytoplasmic interactions in different regions of the germ. Each cell genome thus is exposed from the very start to a system of different conditions arrayed in a specific pattern which is as much a part of the basic blueprint of the new organism as is the orderly array of genes. In further consequence, the interactions between the two systems yield different products and diverse effects in the different regions of the germ.

The evidence that the genome as such remains throughout life essentially identical in all cells of an organism (except for sporadic somatic mutations) is compelling. Yet, despite this essential constancy of their genic content, cell lines diverge progressively in the development of higher organisms. It is this process of diversification—"differentiation" in the strict sense—which is basic to our understanding of aging, as follows.

The brilliant progress of molecular cytogenetics, resting heavily on microbial evidence, has led to the concept of a direct transcription and subsequent translation of the DNA code, through various RNA intermediates, to the orderly sequence of amino acids in the synthesis of cell proteins. Since in bacteria the generative and somatic cell is one and the same, bacteria obviously cannot furnish a model for the puzzling problem of differentiation in higher forms. For in the latter, a great diversity of qualitatively different cell types emerge during ontogeny. Just how many, is indefinite. The only sure fact is that estimates based on morphological criteria vastly underrate the real magnitude. For a realistic perspective, the reader may be referred to an earlier summary account (Weiss, 1953). A sharp distinction must be made between the differentiation of an individual cell ("cytodifferentiation") and the differentiation among cell *strains*. Cytodifferentiation refers to the elaboration by a given cell, mostly the terminal descendant of a cell line, of specialized characters or products by which we have come to identify that cell as belonging to a given type; such critical products are, for instance, myofibrils, secretions, blood pigments, antibodies, pigment granules, and so forth. *Strain* differentiation, by contrast, denotes the splitting of the progeny of cells of common origin into branch lines of different "potencies," that is, restricted repertories of performance and production faculties differing qualitatively from branch to branch. The fact that the branch lines are capable of passing on their differentials, once established, to their descendants indefinitely even in a common indifferent environment (e.g., in tissue culture) proves that strain differentiation connotes some indelible change which can be propagated through many cell generations without attenuation.

Admittedly, we still miss the key to the explanation of either cytodifferentiation or strain differentiation, although the former is beginning to yield. In each cell, only a selected fraction of the full complement of genes which it contains is supposed to be active in a given instant, the rest being effectively blocked (the blocking effect recently ascribed to histones). This evidently presupposes a rather well-structured *extragenic* machinery to do the proper "activating" and "blocking." Such a view is perhaps conceivable as long as one focuses on a single *individual* cell in cytodifferentiation. But its extension to *strain* differentiation presents difficulties. Consider that a thyroid cell can either grow and divide, giving rise to another thyroid cell, or alternatively switch to manufacturing thyroxin and colloid. The same extragenic models (or "templates," as I have termed them) would therefore at one time have to induce the genomes to fashion more of their own kind needed for further self perpetuation of that special cell line while at another time, they would have to trigger the machinery for the synthesis of a special product. It seems that cytoplasmic RNA units are somehow involved in the extragenic template systems, but if so, one must postulate that they come in as many distinct molecular forms as there are self-perpetuating types of differentiation. The immense diversity of differentiations seems to militate against explanations of differentiation in terms of somatic mutation or of induced enzyme synthesis.

To put it candidly, the detailed mechanisms of differentiation are still wholly conjectural. Nevertheless, some general rules which bear on the aging problem have emerged. They can be summarized roughly as follows.

1) The Egg Mosaic

For brevity, we lump all intracellular, but extragenic, matter into a single compartment. The primary topographic pattern of cytoplasmic egg districts, outlined above, places the equal genomes of cleavage nuclei into preformed unequal intracellular environments. The ensuing "epigenetic" interactions between each genome and its local environment elaborate these primordial differences. Thus, from the very start, the genome is a captive of its intracellular environment. Both are in "cross talk": the various environments "demand" and each genome "responds" with a matching answer provided for in its "code," thus altering its own intracellular environment. Where this process is slow relative to the rate of cell division, a multitude of cells of comparable constitution–identical genomes in identical environments–arise. The subsequent, strictly "epigenetic," differentiation among their progeny, however, poses a new problem.

2) Epigenetic Differentiation

The answer lies in the group dynamics of the cell population, which creates secondary inequalities among the erstwhile equal members of a group. As the extragenic *intra*cellular environment determines the genic response, so the *extra*cellular environment, in turn, affects the intracellular system in various degrees of specificity. For any given cell, all other cells are part of the "extracellular environment." The interactions between contiguous cells (by contact) or distant cells (through diffusing products) thus introduce a new major diversifying principle. When interactions between two cell types, though in theory mutual, are conspicuously unilateral, they are often referred to as "inductions."

3) Nature of Cell Interactions

The kinds and modes of operation of cell interactions are too varied to submit to any common formula (Weiss, 1963). They may involve transfer of substances, electric polarization, mechanical deformations, osmotic or pH changes, activation or stoppage of movements or of energy delivery, redistribution of cell content, and above all, such specific changes in the *intracellular* environment as may evoke an altered response from the genome.

4) Progressive Dichotomous Differentiation

Schematically, therefore, if we designate the genome as **G**, its intracellular environment as I, and the extracellular environment (e.g., a cell of another type) as E, the following chain of events takes place:

$$I_1 \rightarrow G \rightarrow I_1;\ E \rightarrow I_1 \rightarrow I_2;\ I_2 \rightarrow G \rightarrow I_3;\ E \rightarrow I_3 \rightarrow I_4;\ I_4 \rightarrow G \rightarrow I_5;\ \text{etc.}$$

Note that E and G can communicate with each other only indirectly through the mediation of I, in which G lies entrapped. If, in addition, we let E go through a series of modifications E′, E″, E‴, · · · , we gain a realistic, if diagrammatic picture of differentiation as a stepwise process of progressive diversification inasmuch as the internal changes in one cell create a changed external environment for its neighbors. The stabilization of self-perpetuating cell types $I_n \rightarrow G \rightarrow I_n \rightarrow G \rightarrow I_n$ · · · , mentioned earlier, further complicates the picture.

This mode of development contains several potential sources of aberrations. 1) G in a particular cell line may suffer a somatic mutation to G′; the whole descendant cell generations will then show altered behavior. 2) The process $I_1 \rightarrow I_2$ might deviate to $I_1 \rightarrow I_2'$, leaving two possibilities: a) $I_2' \rightarrow G \rightarrow I_3$ (the genome failing to discriminate between I_2 and I_2' as if $I_2 \sim I_2'$); the error would then remain confined to the affected single individual cell without entailing lasting effects on the descendants. b) $I_2' \rightarrow G \rightarrow I_3'$; consequently, $I_3' — G \rightarrow I_3' \rightarrow G \rightarrow I_3'$, etc.; the error would thus be perpetuated throughout subsequent cell generations. c) $E \rightarrow I_3' \rightarrow I_4'$; this would in general aggravate the deviation. d) $E \rightarrow I_3' \rightarrow I_4''$, where $I_4'' \sim I_4$; this would correct the error and bring the cell line back on the track. Net error relevant to strain differentiation thus is the sum of self-perpetuating deviations of positive and negative signs. Since the probability of each positive deviation being offset by one of opposite sign is very low, errors of types (b) and (c) are apt to become compounded as cells continue to proliferate.

5) *Developmental Variance*

The outlined sequential origin of terminal "characters" of the body through numerous seriated interactions, in each of which the genome functions as reactor, but never as an autocratic actor, rules out any concept of the developmental course as following rigidly and microprecisely laid out linear tracks. In contrast to the high degree of precision in the specific array and reproductive duplication of the genes, the extragenic system, with which they must continuously interact, is far more variable due to the random fluctuations of both the outer and inner environments. Consequently, the respective interactions and their results are equally variable. Development thus becomes a probabilistic, rather than micro-deterministic, phenomenon. The range of variability—the margin for error—is held within tolerable bounds a) by the evolutionary eradication of non-viable excesses; b) by stabilizing dynamic devices of cells and organ systems, such as the regulatory functions of the nervous system, of hormones, of "homeostatic" mechanisms, of growth correlations, and so forth; and c), above all, by the composite network character of living systems, as follows.

6) Network Dynamics

Development does not proceed as a bundle of separate linear single-tracked courses. Rather, the program of development calls for many secondary linkages and cooperative interactions between cells (and products) of diverse origins and different prior histories. As developmental diversification increases, so does the number and intricacy of interdependencies. But the outlined variations of erstwhile independent component courses and kinetics also become compounded as time goes on. Thus, while mutual dependence grows, the probability of the actual occurrence of the scheduled linkages declines. This would seriously jeopardize development, were it not for the provision in the developmental program of *multiple pathways* converging toward common unified results. Instead of linear deterministic chain reactions, we discover a multidimensional network system of dynamic interactions, intricately

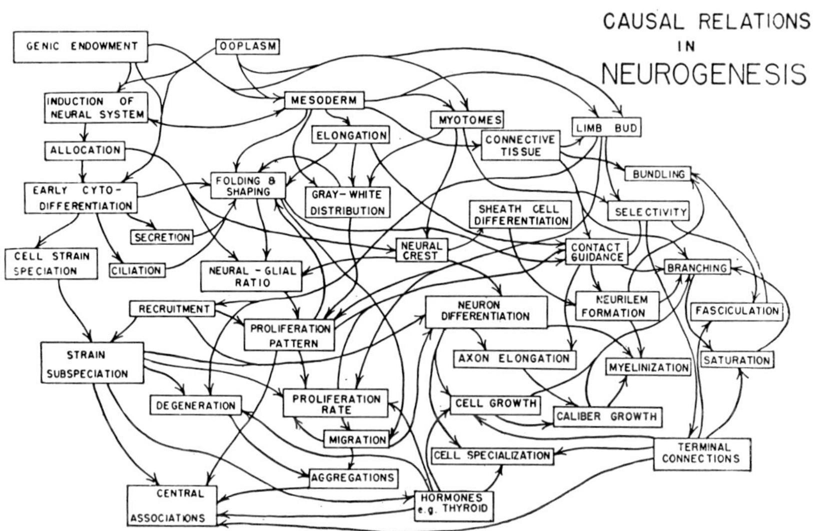

FIGURE 1

branched and anastomosed. As illustration, I reproduce in Figure 1 from an earlier publication (Weiss, 1955) the network of dynamic interactions and dependencies involved in the development of the nervous system. Every arrow represents an activity for which a physical or chemical effect upon another branch has been experimentally demonstrated. For intracellular events likewise, the linear chain reaction concept must be replaced by network theory, as is clearly reflected, for instance, in the diagram by Nicholson (1963) showing the net of alternative pathways in an intracellular metabolic system (Fig. 2). The point is that such networks endow the respective systems with high degrees of elasticity; if any one branch line lags or fails, the remaining bypasses can still produce a viable. if slightly modified, result.

7) Commentary

All the preceding principles from (2) to (6) continue to operate throughout life, even though with increasing restrictions. The programming of the different courses of differentiation leads to the terminal variety of tissues with radically different properties, each continuing to grow, to react and to produce according to its own type and rate. Many cells remain in pre-terminal "bipotential" conditions, in which they can either reproduce more cells of their own kind or transform by cytodifferentiation into sterile workers of shorter or longer life expectancies. Times from reproduction to death vary from a few days (e.g., intestinal mucosa) to weeks (e.g., epidermis; blood elements) to years (e.g., bone cells). Other cell types grow continuously without dividing (e.g., neurons, which burn and discharge what they grow). None of them truly rest. And as they keep being exposed to the fluctuations of the internal and external milieu, the harmony of their dynamic and material interdependency relations continues to be subject to the danger of disruption by excessive deviations from the range of tolerable divergence.

AGING

There is nothing in this picture of development to suggest any abrupt discontinuity, whether initiation or cessation, from which one could date the onset of "aging." *Growth* goes on steadily. Its

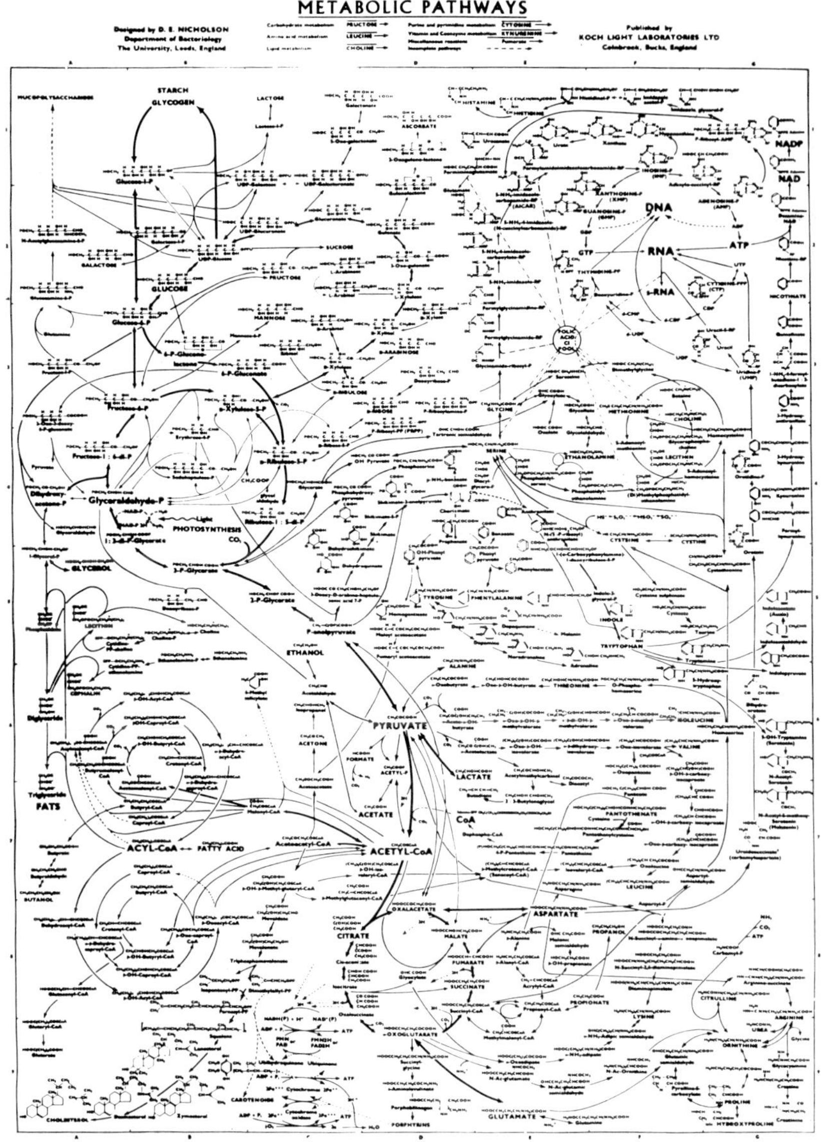
METABOLIC PATHWAYS
Designed by D. E. NICHOLSON
Department of Bacteriology
The University, Leeds, England
Published by
KOCH LIGHT LABORATORIES LTD
Colnbrook, Bucks, England
STARCH
GLYCOGEN
LACTOSE
GLUCOSE
DNA
RNA
ATP
NADP
NAD
ETHANOL
PYRUVATE
LACTATE
ACETYL-CoA
ACYL-CoA
FATS
CITRATE
ASPARTATE
GLUTAMATE

FIGURE 2

rate declines gradually but not necessarily because the reproductive units become less efficient, but chiefly because differentiation progressively reduces the generative compartments of cells and tissues by conversion into products (e.g., fibers) (Weiss and Kavanau, 1957). Conversely, *cell degeneration* and *cell death* are by no means peculiar of older ages; they occur extensively in embryonic stages (Glücksmann, 1951). Progressive changes in *composition and physical properties* of tissues, particularly of the more inert extracellular components, (e.g., the fiber-to-ground substance ratio in tissue matrices) are likewise traceable to early life. So, really all the *elemental* attributes of what in later life one is accustomed to consider as the aging syndrome, are common attributes of the entire developmental process. It is correct, therefore, though commonplace, to describe aging in terms of common language, as simply a function of age. But then, what is aging in terms of developmental biology?

To summarize the answer, let us turn back to the seven criteria of differentiation enumerated in the preceding section. In (4) I have pointed to the sources and the compounding of errors, as life —i.e., development—proceeds. Each body component thus accumulates its own unique history of deviations. These of themselves need not be detrimental to the organism as a whole. What really troubles the organism is rather the increasing disharmony of *mutual relations* among the various component activities, a loss of integration. As pointed out in (6), numerous component processes must constantly cooperate for conjoint effects, and like a team of horses, some slow, some fast, hitched to a carriage, they are held in check by control reins as hinted at in (5,b). Now, if the same horses were to be released, they would disperse according to their speeds, as in a race and cease to act as a team. The same happens in the body if either the component processes get too far out of step or the checking devices lose their hold on them. The independent variance of the components discussed under (5) tends to have just such an effect. It cumulatively magnifies what were initially innocuous discordances (e.g., of timing or chemical specificity) to that critical degree of discrepancy where the erstwhile conjugated components will cease to mesh. The coordinating systems, as body parts, must share this fate. If, following our earlier analogy, we compare the system of interdependent component processes to an elastic network, more and more meshes will thus be strained beyond the stress limit and snap. More and more of the alternate bypasses formerly available to vicariate and compensate for lost interaction pathways will thereby be put out of commission. This then is the crux of the phenomenon which manifests itself to introspection, observation and measurement alike as *decline of plasticity, adaptability and efficiency* with age.

Aging, in biological perspective, therefore, must be regarded as basically a matter of disturbed normal *relations;* and not as a product of *"agents,"* such as "aging factors," "aging substances," "metabolic slags," etc., as it has at times been pictured. The latter misconception would not only, with Ponce de Leon, cruelly mislead public thinking, but misguide research. In my opinion, research on the biology of aging will always be auxiliary to research in *developmental biology* in general. Since time magnifies the effects of critical disturbances of interactive relations, the study of the aged will favor the discovery of such relations; this then will stimulate and guide the backtracking of those relations through their prior life history, when their ever present fluctuations and distortions had not yet become grossly disruptive, hence were accepted as "normal." Our dismally deficient knowledge of "normal" development, aggravated by our ready acceptance of words as substitutes for knowledge, might well receive as much enrichment through the tracing back of change from old to young as through the customary tracing forward from the egg.

Regardless of which end he chooses to proceed from, the searcher will be disappointed if he looks naively for "single causes" and strictly "deterministic" models. As development is a *probabilistic network of multifactoral dynamics,* so is aging. Szilard (1959) has correctly recognized the probabilistic nature of the aging process, although his specific model, derived from microbial concepts, is far too monotonic—indeed, too fatalistic—to fit the highly diversified developmental dynamics of metazoan organisms, including man. For unpreventable though the statistical deterioration of individual cell lines be, the network character of their interrelations enables the higher organism to stem impending disintegration within limits by appropriate compensatory and substitutive counter measures. To keep the latter faculties in training by practice throughout life is therefore the biologist's rational design for living: if aging is inevitable, we can at least retard its pace.

REFERENCES

GLÜCKSMANN, A.: Cell deaths in normal vertebrate ontogeny. *Biol. Rev., 26*:59, 1951.

MINOT, C. S.: *The Problem of Age, Growth, and Death.* New York and London, Putnam, 1908.

NICHOLSON, D. E.: Metabolic pathways. Colnbrook, England, 1963.

SZILARD, L.: On the nature of the aging process. *Proc. Nat. Acad. Sci., USA, 45*:30, 1959.

WEISS, P.: *Principles of Development.* New York, Holt, 1939.

WEISS, P.: Nervous system (neurogenesis), Eds. B. H. Willier, Paul Weiss, and Viktor Hamburger. In: *Analysis of Development.* Philadelphia, Saunders, 1955, pp. 346-401.

WEISS, P.: Cell interactions, In: *Proc. Fifth Canad. Cancer Conf.*, New York, Academic Press, 1963.

WEISS, P., AND KAVANAU, L.: A model of growth and growth control in mathematical terms. *J. Gen. Physiol., 41*:1, 1957.

Chapter 25

AUTOBIOTICS AND SENESCENCE

ALBERT SZENT-GYÖRGYI

CONTRIBUTORS to this volume have a dual reason for writing: the fact that they have to say something about gerontology, *and* their high esteem or friendship for Professor Verzár. Of these two I have only the latter, but, also, an additional one: gratitude. Without Professor Verzár's help I would not be a scientist today. During the years following the first world war my personal difficulties seemed insurmountable, and I prepared to go to the tropics searching the services of some government. If, instead, I landed at the University of Leiden, Holland, this was due to Professor Verzár's support. So, I do not want to be left out where homage can be paid to him.

Searching for an excuse to do so I find in my notes that inoculated cancer (Krebs 2 ascites as solid tumor) grows faster in young than in old animals. This may have been generally known before and can be illustrated by the following figures:

Weight of the tumor in 14 days in 4-week's-old mice	4823 mg
Weight of the tumor in 4-month's-old mice	2735 mg
Weight of the tumor in mice older than one year	542 mg

Alexis Carrel had similar results in his extensive studies on regeneration and was led to the conclusion that the rate of regeneration is a function of age.

What has led me to the above experiment was the study of certain substances, apparently involved in the regulation of cell behavior, substances, produced by the cells themselves. One of them, which we called "retine," seems to favor the physical state of the cell which corresponds to rest and thus inhibits proliferation. The other, "promine," was found to favor the physical state in which the dividing cell finds itself, and thus promotes proliferation. If retine is administered to a young mouse the tumor will grow slower. If promine is administered to an older mouse it makes the tumor grow faster. Retine and promine can thus wipe out the difference between young and old, at least as looked at from the narrow angle of this experiment. It seems likely that the rate of regeneration will show the same relations.

Till reliable and sensitive methods for the estimation of retine and promine are available little can be said about the concentration of these substances in different tissues at various ages; one can only make guesses and speculate. It is an experimental fact that retine and promine can mutually compensate each other's action on the rate of growth of cancer. So in a resting state the cell may contain a high concentration of promine if there is an equivalent quantity of retine present. It seems likely to me that in the young we will find a relatively high concentration of both substances, while in the old they may be present at low concentration. To have a strong regulation, both substances might be needed in relatively high concentration and the trend for malignancy in old age may be connected to low absolute value of the retine/promine quotient and the consequent failure of regulation. The fast growth of malignant tumors in the young may have something to do with the possibility of a high promine concentration.

Senescence is a very complex phenomenon but it is not impossible that the retine and promine concentration may have something to do with it, and that some of its symptoms may be influenced by the administration of these substances, once these are available in quantity.

The writer believes that retine and promine are but examples of a group of regulatory substances which have been hitherto greatly overlooked, which substances may be involved in more complex mechanisms and are produced by the cells themselves on the physical state and function of which they have a decisive influence. When talking of "regulation" one mostly thinks, in the first place, of hormones, produced by specific glands, or of the nervous system. This cellular level of the cell's own regulation has hitherto not received the attention it deserves and has been neglected by research.

Another member of this group of substances has been found,

lately, by Johnsson and Hegyeli in the writer's laboratory. This substance has a definite influence in cancer cells on the trend for organization to a tissue, and may be responsible, possibly, for "contact inhibition."

The research on this line is a most difficult one, partly owing to the low concentration of these substances, and partly to the complexity of their chemistry and functional relations. All the same, work in this direction seems to be promising and the present perfected methods of isolation may compensate for the difficulties. It is not impossible that senescence has an intimate relation to these mechanisms and their regulators which I called, tentatively, "autobiotics," being produced by the cells themselves on which they act.

Urine contains these substances in relatively high concentration, be this a leak or part of the regulation. Whatever the case may be, this could be important for two reasons. Firstly, because urine can serve advantageously as a starting material in the preparation and later identification of these substances and it can be hoped that, once satisfactorily identified, they all may be prepared also from tissues. But the content of these substances in urine could become important also because the urine may reflect the conditions within the body and thus may allow us to correlate the nature and quantity of these substances with biological and pathological conditions, one of which may be senescence. To get an insight into these relations, quantitative micromethods of estimation will have to be developed.

Indications have been obtained lately that retine and promine contain, as active groups, methylglyoxal derivatives. Since methylglyoxal interacts with SH there may be a link between these substances and the system of SH groups which, in their fixed form, seem to play an important role in catalytic activity, cell division and possibly, also, in deciding the physical state of the "protoplasm" by inducing association of macromolecules through the formation of disulphide groups, or their dissociation by reduction of S-S to SH. So this line of research may lead, in time, to a better understanding of the interrelation of various at present unconnected biological systems, which may also have relations to the problems of gerontology.

Chapter 26

ABNUTZUNGSTHEORIE*

GEORGE A. SACHER

INTRODUCTION

IN THE INTRODUCTION to his monograph on aging, Comfort comments (1964, p. 9):

> In almost any other important biological field than that of senescence, it is possible to present the main theories historically, and to show a steady progression from a large number of speculative, to one or two highly probable, main hypotheses. In the case of senescence this cannot profitably be done. . . . It is a striking feature of these theories (of senescence) that they show little or no historical development; they can much more readily be summarized as a catalogue than as a process of developing scientific awareness.

This appraisal is a clear statement of the views of many gerontologists including the present author. A distinctive quality of Comfort's discussion however is his vehement depreciation (*op. cit.,* p. 11) of the "wear-and-tear" theory, or *Abnutzungstheorie.*

Abnutzungstheorie clearly falls into the class of theories that "show little or no historical development." For half a century the theory has hovered in the limbo of ideas that are neither accepted nor denied. Since the issues involved lie at the very foundations of gerontology, continued failure to resolve them can jeopardize the integrity of the discipline. This essay examines some features of this history, and attempts to define the place of *Abnutzungstheorie,* not as an all-embracing "fundamentalist theory (to) explain all senescence" but rather as a constitutive part of a larger synthesis of knowledge about biological aging in nature. An important aspect of the subject, that dealing with the dependence on temperature

* Work supported by the United States Atomic Energy Commission.

of the rate of living, is not treated here, because a paper on the subject will appear soon (Sacher, 1966).

WEISMANN

In 1882, A. Weismann published his monograph, *Über die Dauer des Lebens,* which developed the implications for gerontology of his distinction between the potentially immortal germ plasm and its hapless transitory vehicle, the soma. He postulated that the organism has the primary function of propagating its germ plasm by sexual reproduction, and that natural selection operates to maximize the integrated utility of the organism for performance of that role. The reproductive capacity decreases with age, so that the lifetime reproductive utility of an organism reaches a maximum value and then declines with increasing age. It can even take on negative values as the sterile organism remains alive to compete with its progeny for food and territory. Weismann postulated that senescence evolved under natural selection as a means for terminating life before this phase occurs.

One criticism that has been made of Weismann's theory is that it employs circular reasoning. Comfort remarks that "this argument both assumes what it sets out to explain, that the survival of an individual decreases with increasing age, and denies its own premise, by suggesting that worn-out individuals threaten the existence of the young."

These objections arise not from an essential flaw in Weismann's argument, but rather from his unfortunate tendency to carry into his technical terminology ambiguous, emotionally colored words and phrases taken from everyday language. The perpetuation of such obsolete, imprecise terms in the literature is one reason for the stultification of gerontological theorizing that Comfort justifiably deplores. Hence the discussion here is of the "Weismannian" or "Neo-Weismannian" position rather than of Weismann's strict words.

A crucial point in the Weismannian theory is that both the germ plasm and the soma undergo aging in the organism. The complete pattern of reproductive behavior depends on the integrity of both germ plasm and soma, whereas the capability for somatic survival depends primarily on the soma and only secondarily on the germinal tissue. Hence individuals can be "worn-out" in respect to their reproductive utility and still be strong and wily enough to compete successfully with their immature or fecund descendants. Such a condition is evidently dysgenic, and the next step in the Weismannian argument is the postulate that the operation of natural selection leads to the evolution of life-termination mechanisms which tend to bring about an optimum relationship between somatic survival and reproductive utility.

At this point it becomes necessary to distinguish two senses of the term *aging* that are implicit in Weismann's theory.

First, there is *aging as an ineluctable accompaniment of the living state of matter*. Every living organism, with an internal *milieu* defined by its phenotype and environment, is characterized by a rate of degradation of its fundamental molecular units which is the irreducible minimum for the given *milieu* in that : a) it is a result of unavoidable random physicochemical microevents rather than of genetically directed mutational and involutional processes; and b) it maintains its characteristic stationary level in the presence of the full complement of preventive and reparative processes available to the phenotype. This will be called *obligate aging*. There is no present basis for assessing the relative magnitude of obligate aging rates in different molecular structures or in different tissues. One allowable statement is that for each kind of molecule or structure in each tissue, the amount of obligate aging is less than or equal to the amount of manifest senescent change.

The second component of aging consists of *all genetically actuated degradative or retrogressive processes that contribute to an increased determinateness* of the life termination process*. All additional properties or interactions with other phenotype characters such as growth pattern, etc., are incidental rather than essential characteristics, since they vary with circumstances. This genetically determined component of aging will be called *instrumental aging*.

The fundamental hypothesis of the Weismannian theory is that:

* Determinateness of the distribution of survival times may be defined as $D = \mu_1^2 / \mu_2$, where μ_1 and μ_2 are the first and second moments respectively. It ranges from 1, for a sharp spike distribution down to 0 for all distributions with infinite variance and finite mean.

a) instrumental aging is necessarily present in all metazoa, and b) it is adaptive because it evolves under positive selection pressures. The selective value of instrumental aging can be expressed in objective and quantitative terms. It brings about a truncation of the survival curve in such a manner that the average number of progeny reared per unit of habitat consumed is a maximum.* This is the reproductive utility of the individual and is a measure of the reproductive fitness of the population as it is affected by the age-fertility function and the survivorship curve.

The imputation of circularity in Weismann's argument can now be seen to be groundless. Obligate and instrumental aging, although they have a common name and, undoubtedly, a common material basis, are nevertheless profoundly different in their causal conditions. Also they almost certainly differ in pattern. After all, if random aging processes always spontaneously produced patterns of germinal and somatic aging such that reproductive utility was maximized, there would be no need to postulate instrumental aging. The utter improbability of such an outcome is of itself sufficient justification for postulating instrumental aging, granted that obligate aging exists.

Instrumental aging as defined here is a more inclusive concept than *programmed aging* as defined by Medawar (1957) and Comfort (1964). The latter term is properly applicable to the case of specific identifiable life termination mechanisms. Instances of such are the mortality processes in Saturniid moths which have been investigated by A. D. Blest (1960, 1963; Sacher, 1965a). The alternative, called "running out of programme" is regarded by Medawar and Comfort as a progressive loss of genetic control over the life processes of the organism which occurs because of the accumulation, unopposed by natural selection, of deleterious mutations that are expressed after the end of the reproductive span.

The phenotypic pattern of aging in mammals is certainly well described as a running out of program, but it needs to be realized that this is not necessarily evidence of failure of selection pressure to operate on deleterious alleles; it is in fact more plausibly viewed as an instrumental aging process under the control of the

* The author is aware that this definition is deficient in generality and exactness, but the deficiences are not of an important kind for this discussion.

genotype since most aging processes have identifiable beginnings early in life. Thus running out of genetic program is a case of instrumental aging if the parameters of the running-out process are genetically controlled and subject to modification by natural selection.

The denial of programmed aging by Medawar and Comfort is linked in their reasoning with a denial of obligate aging as a necessary physical limitation on the living state of matter. They offer in effect the contrary thesis that aging did not exist originally and it did not evolve—it just happened! The demonstrations of ways in which it *might* have happened—*vide* Medawar (1957) and Williams (1957)—are remarkably ingenious, but they hardly provide a solid evolutionary basis for the scientific study of the universal phenomenon of senescence. Selection for post-reproductive characters can in any event be accomplished by classical mechanisms of population genetics, along lines laid out by Haldane (1932) in his discussion of selection for traits of altruism and criminality.

RUBNER AND FRIEDENTHAL

Comparative investigation of the longevity and senescence patterns of mammals and birds leads to the conclusion that in these forms *natural selection has operated to evolve phenotypes with progressively lower rates of obligate aging.* The viviparous mammals are an extraordinarily favorable group in which to study this process. Here is a subclass* that has a monophyletic origin and contains about 4000 living species ranging in size from 2.5 to 100,000,000 grams. Yet the constancy of internal *milieu* that is assured by their constant body temperature has resulted in a high degree of uniformity of biochemical and physiological mechanisms throughout the subclass despite a tremendous variety of external adaptations.

The first biologist after Buffon to draw a significant inference about aging from the comparative study of mammals was Max Rubner. He showed in 1908 that the total energy expenditure per gram of tissue during adult life is roughly constant for five species

* Subclass Theria (Parker and Haswell), which comprises marsupial and placental mammals.

of domestic animals ranging from cat to cow. Rubner estimated the mean energy expenditure per gram per adult lifetime to be 192 kilocalories (kcal) for these five species, while for man, on the basis of a sixty-year adult lifetime, the estimate was 726 kcal. This observation suggests that there is an invariant rate of obligate aging in at least three orders of subhuman mammals, when this rate is measured not in units of time but in units of energy dissipation. It is also indicated that the human species has achieved a breakthrough, in that a human being can get three times more use out of his soma than a dog or horse can, if use is measured by energy output.

Rubner's observations raise some interesting questions and surmises. The discrepancy between man and the other mammals should have been especially disturbing to experimental gerontologists in view of the heavy reliance they must have on small, short-lived species. The historical record nevertheless does not show that Rubner's findings were extended, or even checked, between 1908 and 1959, although they were duly catalogued in several reviews during that time.

Curiously, a clue to the explanation of the discrepancy in lifetime energy dissipations between man and other mammals was given only two years later, in 1910, when H. Friedenthal published a paper pointing out that there are numerous large disparities in length of life between like-sized mammalian species. He assembled data on life spans and indices of cephalization* for eleven families of mammals and was able to conclude by inspection of these data that "Der Klügste lebt am längsten." A similar conclusion was drawn about the life spans of birds. Friedenthal's data were woefully weak, and his interpretations were developed around the preoccupations with energy metabolism which characterized that period. Nevertheless his assessment of the relationship between life span, brain weight and body weight was found to be correct after a lag of fifty years (Sacher, 1959).

Friedenthal's remarkable intuitions 55 years ago should have pointed the way to a major synthesis in gerontology, but they were almost entirely forgotten, and were unknown to me when my paper

* The definition of index of cephalization he used was Snell's original formula: I. of C. = (brain wt) / (body wt)$^{2/3}$.

on the subject appeared in 1959. The cephalization factor accounted for the discrepancy that Rubner had found between man and other mammals and led toward the generalization that length of life in mammals is quantitatively dependent on the rate of energy dissipation and on the functional capacity of the brain.

My statistical analysis of the relation of mammalian life span to brain weight and body weight (1959, 1965a) has put these relations on a quantitative basis, so that it will be possible in coming years to make a confident beginning on the experimental investigation of the implications of these empirical limiting relations (Sacher, 1965b).

Examination of the relation of lifespan to energy metabolism and brain size in the context of the Weismannian position that manifest senescence is preponderantly under the control of natural selection leads to a new outlook, namely that natural selection has operated on the mammalian phenotype to bring about independently in a number of orders an evolution toward greater longevity. This has been accomplished in two ways: by increase in body size with appropriate allometric increase in brain size (i.e., with constant index of cephalization), or by increase in index of cephalization. In the former case the lifetime energy dissipation remains approximately constant, so there is no real decrease in the rate of obligate aging per calorie expended (Sacher, 1959). This kind of allometric increase of body size seemingly requires only minor genetic change, since there are families and genera of mammals within which one finds a tenfold variation of body size together with a nearly constant index of cephalization. Evolution toward higher index of cephalization presumably requires much more extensive remodelling of the genotype, since large changes in the index of cephalization occur only at the family level or above (Sacher, 1965a).

The lifespan of *Homo sapiens* is about twice that of the higher anthropoids, which in turn have lifespans about 50 per cent greater than those of like-size nonprimates. The paleontological record indicates that the gap between the anthropoids and the other mammals with respect to brain size has been stable for tens of millions of years, but that the great leap in cephalization of genus *Homo* took place within the past two million years, after some ten million years of preparatory evolution toward bipedalism, the tool-using hand, etc. (Pilbeam and Simons, 1965).

There is no escaping the inference that the increase in the human lifespan also occurred in the past few million years, *pari passu* with the increase in brain size. It then becomes overwhelmingly probable that the increase in human lifespan is due to the increase in size of the brain and the concomitant increase in its capability for regulation of the *milieu intérieur* both directly and also indirectly through control of the external environment.

CONCLUSION

In a sense *Abnutzungstheorie* has already attained its objective by validating a fundamental hypothesis about the evolution of longevity and senescence and thereby providing a proved basis and direction for research on life prolongation. The conduct of that research is the proper responsibility of others: the disciplines of psychology, behavioral physiology, neurophysiology, behavioral embryology and genetics have new roles. However, these disciplines cannot function autonomously: they can only work with and through the morphological, cellular and molecular sciences. The only hope for the emergence of a science of the *living* and aging individual lies in the development of an equal partnership between the molecular and the behavioral sciences.

The problem they must solve is straightforward but profoundly difficult: to provide within the ontogeny of the developing individual a set of conditions, through nutrition, behavioral conditioning, provision of prosthetic sensory and memory devices, controlled environments, etc., that will be the equivalent of some hundreds of grams of additional brain capacity and several hundred millenia of brain evolution.

In the long run, of course, the goal is the development of a better brain through genetic selection. There unquestionably is variance in the efficiency of brains at constant size, so that some early improvement in brain performance should be possible with little average increase in brain size. This is important since some genetic remodelling of the female pelvic girdle would be necessary before there could be any appreciable increase in brain weight.

Medawar and Comfort, in their attack on Weismannism and

Abnutzungstheorie, convey the implication that adherence to such views stems from outmoded theological or metaphysical attitudes. Yet Medawar's view of sensescence has its own links to our theological past, for it offers us a Garden of pristine ageless perfection and a subsequent mutational Fall.

It is at least arguable that the concept of life as inherently finite is better founded in post-Darwinian biology and physics, especially since there is abundant evidence that the great accomplishment of mammalian evolution has been to transcend that finitude by the evolution of progressively longer life. Since the main, if not the sole instrument of this increase in longevity has been the nervous system, and since the mammalian nervous system has remarkable unity of structure, so that all facets of function increase together, it follows that throughout mammalian evolution longer life has also been a qualitatively better life. With this assurance, the prospect of moving toward deliberate eugenic selection for human longevity becomes less frightening.

As a program of social action, the approach to life prolongation through ontogenetic conditioning and genetic selection for better nervous systems is worth considering, from the standpoints of ethics and of technical feasibility, as an alternative to the programs of molecular engineering, organ transplantation, etc., that are now offered as the only course. J. Lederberg has suggested *euphenics* as a generic name for these latter approaches (1963). This is a felicitous term, but it is symptomatic of our time that in his inventory of possible euphenic procedures Lederberg overlooked the behavioral approach. Since the brain is in an essential sense the organ of longevity, and since it is by design a highly accessible and modifiable structure, there is reason to be hopeful for a program of *behavioral euphenics* that seeks to extend life by improving the ability of the organism to sense and control its own states (Sacher, 1965b).

REFERENCES

Blest, A. D.: The evolution, ontogeny and quantitative control of the settling movements of some New World Saturniid moths, with some comments on distance communication by honey-bees. *Behaviour, 16:*188, 1960.

Blest, A. D.: Longevity, palatability, and natural selection in five species of New World Saturniid moth. *Nature (London), 197:*1183, 1963.

COMFORT, A.: *Aging: The Biology of Senescence,* 2nd ed. New York, Holt, Rinehart and Winston, 1964.

FRIEDENTHAL, H.: Ueber die Giltigkeit des Massenwirkung fuer den Energieumsatz der lebendigen Substanz. *Zbl. Physiol., 24*:321, 1910.

HALDANE, J. B. S.: *The Causes of Evolution.* London, Longmans Green, 1932.

LEDERBERG, J.: Molecular biology, eugenics and euphenics. *Nature (London), 198:* 428, 1963.

MEDAWAR, P. B.: Old age and natural death *and* An unsolved problem of biology. In: *The Uniqueness of the Individual.* London. Methuen, 1957.

PILBEAM, L. R., AND SIMONS, E. L.: Some problems of hominid classification. *Amer. Sci., 53*:237, 1965.

RUBNER, M.: Probleme des Wachstums und der Lebensdauer. *Mitt. Ges. inn. Med., Wien, 7*:58, 1908.

SACHER, G. A.: Relation of life span to brain and body weight in mammals. In: *Fifth CIBA Foundation Colloquium on Aging.* Wolstenholme, G. E. W. and O'Connor, M. (eds.), p. 115. London, Churchill, 1959.

SACHER, G. A.: Some theoretical approaches: stochastic, system-theoretic, and molecular models. In: *Aging and Levels of Biological Organization.* Brues, A. M. and Sacher, G. A. (eds.). Chicago and London, University of Chicago Press, 1965a, p. 266.

SACHER, G. A.: On longevity regarded as an organized behavior: The role of brain structure. In: *Contributions to the Psychobiology of Aging.* Kastenbaum, R. (ed.), New York, Springer Publ. Co., p. 99, 1965b.

SACHER, G. A.: The complementarity between development and aging: Experimental and theoretical considerations. New York Academy of Sciences *Conference on Interdisciplinary Perspectives of Time.* Fischer, R. and Sollberger, A. (eds.). (In press), 1966.

WEISMANN, A.: *Ueber die Dauer des Lebens.* Jena, G. Fischer, 1882.

WEISMANN, A.: *Essays Upon Heredity and Kindred Biological Problems.* London, Oxford University Press, 1891.

W'LLIAMS, G. C.: Pleiotropy, natural selection and the evolution of senescence. *Evolution, 11*:398, 1957.

Chapter 27

ERROR THEORIES OF AGING

ZHORES A. MEDVEDEV

THE COMPLEX STUDY of aging of multicellular systems is actually the investigation of all biological characteristics of composition, structure and function in time and at all levels of organization. It is evident therefore that the appearance of any new line of research in biology, physiology, genetics, biochemistry etc. may lead to a corresponding development in gerontology. Naturally the tremendous success observed during the last decade in the study of biochemical and molecular-genetic basis of life phenomena was accompanied by simultaneous broadening of already existing lines of investigations in gerontology, by the formation of ideas on molecular aspects of aging, on the genetic programming of aging, accumulation of somatic mutations as the basis for aging etc. And, as in previous years, the study of aging of morphological, anatomical, physiological, functional and biochemical systems was concentrated primarily in the investigation of changes of these systems in aging. The new task which has appeared in gerontological research at present is the study of changes related to aging at the level of macromolecules, genetic informational systems, RNA and DNA replications, chromosomes, cytoplasmic organelles, the coordination of reactions in biochemical cycles, etc. Thus, theoretical analysis of the mechanisms of aging now deals with this level of organization.

The discovery of molecular-genetic regulated systems of heredity, morphogenesis, differentiation and coordination of various processes led to the attempts to find the mechanisms regulating the process of aging at this level. This broadening of gerontological investigation into molecular-biological and molecular-genetic aspects has led to the appearance of a number of theories which consider aging as the process of error accumulation during the reproduction of genetic structures.

In the analysis of different forms of variability of macromolecular structures like proteins and nucleic acids the possibility of errors in their reproduction seems to be the primary source of stable cumulative changes which spread later to all levels of organization of a living system. Under these circumstances the large body of experimental data on the mechanism and specificity of molecular changes after induced genetic and spontaneous mutations, radiobiological effects, pathological states, errors in synthesis etc. can be used as a ready base to estimate the possible forms of variability of these structures in time.

EVOLUTION OF THE THEORIES OF ERRORS OF REPRODUCTION

Early ideas concerning the macromolecular reproduction of errors as the cause of aging were quite one-sided and were proposed to explain some data on structural protein changes during aging. At that time the importance of the specific order of amino acids in protein molecules was not realized, genetic determination of this sequence was not known and therefore no arguments about the possibility of progressive significant changes in amino acid composition of individual proteins could be put forward. Since, for instance, it was known that aging is accompanied by the increase in the resistance of total tissue proteins towards proteolytic enzymes the corresponding hypotheses concerning the role of errors in protein synthesis suggested the exchange of protease-labile bonds in protein for stable bonds, the accumulation of optical antipodes of naturally-occurring substances in biopolymers, accumulation of cyclic compounds and diketopiperazines etc. These hypotheses, however, were not supported later by experimental data.

However, during the next period the general progress in our knowledge of the nature of molecular variability caused by irradiation, on the mechanism of mutations in gametes and somatic cells, on the mechanism of nucleic acid and protein synthesis led to new hypotheses on the relation between aging and error accumulation in reproduction of macromolecules. The critical analysis of these hypotheses was made recently by several authors (Medvedev, 1961; 1963; 1964; Strehler, 1962; Oeriu, 1964; Nagornii *et al.*,1963) It is important to emphasize the evident tendency in these works to broaden the problem of "errors" and to differentiate various types of errors in the total picture of changes related to aging. It became evident that any error in the reproduction of macromolecules and especially an error in DNA synthesis in somatic cells would change the genetic information and would be evident in subsequent replications. This sequence of events could be an elementary aspect of cell aging. At the same time it was understood that any other stable form of structure in tissues (collagen, elastin, nucleoproteins, complex pigments) is able to a certain degree to accumulate autonomously molecular changes leading to inactivation of living systems. Evident relations between mutations of cells and DNA alterations permitted at this period an analogy between aging and accumulation of mutations in somatic cells (Szilard, 1959; Failla, 1960; Curtis, 1963, 1964).

However the term "mutation" is only a description of cytological and genetic results of errors in DNA replication. Aging as a complex process, may reflect not only errors in DNA reproduction but also errors in RNA synthesis, errors in protein synthesis, in the formation of complexes, errors in macromolecular interactions (collagen fibrils, for instance) and even the "mistakes" during enzymatic reactions if more or less stable consequences of these errors exist or if casual disturbance of a reaction led to a number of mistakes in other processes.

In this connection anomalous enzymes or other proteins resulting from errors in the functioning of ribosomes, transfer or messenger RNA (with non-altered DNA) during its functioning might induce a series of new mistakes whose effect might be much longer than the lifespan of the anomalous protein molecule (especially of those enzymes which participate in the synthesis of proteins or nucleic acids or play regulatory roles). In this sense the theory of elementary reactions in understanding aging is more broad than the theory of somatic mutations (genetically important errors). But the extremely broad character of this theory is a drawback since in total consideration of molecular variability related to aging all possible errors and their consequences are included and this makes it difficult to study experimentally the molecular aspects of aging and the development of methods to regulate this process. The present tendency is therefore to identify the relative ontogenetical importance of different types of molecular variability, to calculate their frequency, elucidate the nature and relative "productivity" of those internal and external factors which are principal inductors of molecular variability and to delineate the internal mechanisms of correction of mistakes and elimination of damaged molecules and structures. Besides there is a tendency to seek the regulation system for induction and reduction of errors as a specific kind of regulating system which determines the processes of morphogenesis and species specificity of the lifespan. In the immediate future these tendencies will undoubtedly lead to important results in the analysis of causes of aging and its regulation.

FACTORS RESPONSIBLE FOR MOLECULAR ERRORS AND MOLECULAR VARIABILITY

The broad study of molecular variability not only in relation to aging but also in connection with problems of cancerogenesis, radiation injury, chemical mutagenesis, metabolism pathology etc. led to discovery of hundreds of factors and substances whose influence on biological structures leads to local molecular changes and errors. Many of these factors in various forms and with various frequency can act on any normal biological process and cause different distortions. Some of these factors act selectively on nucleic acids (nucleotide analogs), other on proteins (amino acid analogs). A number of factors (free radicals, radiation, microthermal concentrations, etc.) can damage any structure or compound. These factors can be classified on the basis of their nature (physical, chemical, physical-chemical, etc.), their origin (endogeneous, exogeneous), site of action (chromosomes, cytoplasm, intercellular structures, nucleic acids, proteins) or some other characteristics (Medvedev, 1961, 1963). But the relative significance of each type of factor in the total variability of a tissue still is obscure.

This direction of research—the elucidation of the specific share of various natural endogeneous and exogeneous in modifying molecular alterations is the task for the immediate future. So far some attempts to estimate the "share" of certain specific factors in the total sum of changes related to aging were made for radiation (Strehler, 1959, 1962; Curtis, 1963; Casarett, 1964) by comparing the total chronic irradiation under normal conditions (irradiation due to naturally occurring isotopes and cosmic radiation) with the decrease of lifespan and number of somatic mutation following controlled external irradiation. These comparisons did not offer evidence that the natural external and internal radiation play a significant role in the induction of accumulated changes in cellular aging but they may play a role in aging processes for systems with prolonged lifespan. Other possible general modifiers of macromolecules are so-called free radicals formed in cells after irradiation and microthermal release of the energy of chemical reactions and spontaneous errors of chemical reactions. The background of endogeneously formed free radicals may be registered by electron spin resonance. Hence in different tissues a certain background of molecular variability due to free radicals should be observed (the mutagenic effect of free radicals is a well known fact).

An attempt to determine the specific share of damage caused by free radicals in the total of alterations related to aging was made by Harman (1960, 1961, 1962) using "quenching" of free radicals especially under conditions of increased level of radiation. The author reported an increase in the lifespan in two strains of mice after administration of compounds capable of reacting quickly with free radicals.

Among spontaneous and induced chemical injuries those caused by the administration of nucleotide analogs are of special importance. The formation of nucleotide analogs in small amounts as a result of a certain level of errors in cycles of normal biosynthesis of nucleotides is possible principally in side reactions as well as in small deviations of different phases of transformation of precursors. Thus far 18-20 so-called unusual minor nucleotides with unknown function have already been found in DNA and RNA of mammals. Some of them are undoubtedly the result of certain errors in the synthesis of nucleotides. No doubt the total number of these analogs will increase as new methods of investigation are developed to permit their identification. It is possible to check this hypothesis by comparing the level of different minor nucleotides in RNA and DNA for instance in bacteria which possess the normal cycles of nucleotide biosynthesis (grown on minimal medium) in strains to which pure nucleotides are added (which lead to feedback inhibition of nucleotide synthesis) and in mutant strains unable to synthesize nucleotides. An analogous approach to the study of the role of minor bases is also suitable and of potential use in the study of cellular clones of mammals.

In the study of changes in fibrillar proteins related to aging (collagen and elastin) such form of molecular variability as cross-linking can be also evaluated quantitatively at present (Sinex, 1964).

For any factor of variability there exist many chemical, physical and biological antifactors which decrease the concentration of injuries (similar to radio-protective and antimutagenic substances). Some antifactors have appeared in the course of evolution (pigments which protect against ultraviolet radiation). Many factors of endogenous type are probably not yet known and the total picture of injury is, of course, a result of changing equilibration of modifying and stabilizing factors. Broad experiments in this field should be carried out. All we know at present and what can be used for theoretical analysis are the results of a few isolated experiments.

BASIC FORMS OF MOLECULAR ERRORS; THEIR RELATIVE FREQUENCY AND STABILITY

The problem of the relative significance of different kinds of errors in reproduction and renewal of various structures in the total picture of variability related to aging is of the same importance as the question of the comparative role of modifing factors. Speaking of molecular structures first one may state that errors in DNA replication are most stable. These errors are the basis for genetic and somatic mutations. Under normal conditions errors in the synthesis of polymers are characterised by certain "background" values. Thus for DNA replication error frequency is found to be 1×10^{-8} per base (Szilard, 1959). The genetic code being triplet it gives 3×10^{-8} per codon if the structural cistron includes 300 codons the number of "errors" per cistron will be 1×10^{-5}. This figure does not differ significantly from the experimentally observed frequency of mutation of individual genes in gametes (which is equal to 1×10^{-5} to 1×10^{-6} per generation).

At the same time stable genetic mutations of somatic cells occur much more often than in germ cells since meiosis, spermo- and ovogenesis and fertilization are powerful factors for the selection of "normal" genomes: the experimentally observed frequency of genetic mutations reflects only that part of mutations which came through this filter. If the frequency of mutations in somatic cells is 1×10^{-4} to 1×10^{-5} mutations per gene it is evident that during active synthesis for instance of 1×10^{3} types of protein per cell, one out of 10-100 mitoses will lead to genetic mutation of protein structure. However the genome of mammals includes not less than 1×10^{5} of structural cistrons a considerable fraction of which is repressed in individual cells. Hence considering the whole genome, practically every mitosis and every DNA replication (in nonproliferating cells) is accompanied by a mutation.

Synthesis of messenger RNA is probably characterized by the same level of errors transferred from genome into proteins. However, taking into account the short life-time of RNA molecules and the ability to act as a template in protein synthesis several times, the total sum of these errors seems to be higher than in the DNA but these errors are not transferred to cell offspring. A number of authors have stressed the importance of errors in RNA synthesis for the process of aging (Medvedev, 1961; Wulff *et al.*, 1962).

Even more probable are errors occurring in the process of protein synthesis as a result of misreading of genetic information; errors in interaction of amino-acids and activating enzymes; activating enzymes and transfer RNA; ribosome functioning etc.

A theoretical analysis of the problem of error level in protein synthesis was made recently by Orgel (1963). Orgel concludes that the probability of an amino acid replacement for another amino acid due to "non-perfectness" of "recognition" systems, though different for different pairs cannot be less than 1×10^{-4} for similar pairs (for example, valine and isoleucine). The experimental study of error frequency in protein synthesis (ovalbumine synthesis) carried by Loftfield (1963) has demonstrated that replacement of isoleucine by valine or leucine occurs with a frequency not more than once in 3000 times. In addition preliminary results of this investigation suggest that confusion between leucine and phenilalanine is also very rare. If one takes into consideration, however, that polypeptide chains are made up of twenty different amino acid residues one can assume that the total number of possible errors of such kind is rather significant and probably not less than 1-10 per cent of protein molecules possess different single substitution errors.

The electrophoretic and chromatographic extraction or recrystallization of proteins may remove not only impurities but trace fractions of proteins in which random amino-acid errors have occurred. Additionally the determination of protein composition and amino-acid sequences connected with the procedures where traces of amino-acids are in wrong positions, especially if they are random, cannot be recorded.

It was commonly thought that spontaneous errors in protein synthesis were temporary and not cumulative, since protein turnover permanently eliminated both functional and nonfunctional molecules. Orgel (1963), however, has shown theoretically that in the case of spontaneous nongenetic errors of protein synthesis the accumulation of errors was also possible and could lead to failure if some system for the elimination of defective molecules did not exist.

Error accumulation is related to the occurrence of erroneous amino-acid-S-RNA synthesis, RNA and DNA polymerases, ribosome proteins and other enzymes and proteins responsible for macromolecular syntheses. The defective proteins in this case lead to the increase of the level of errors and the process becomes progressive.

This possibility becomes especially obvious if one realizes the importance of configurational specificity of proteins and the role of so-called allosteric proteins and allosteric effects (Monod *et al.*, 1963).

One can suggest that among the populations of protein molecules of the cell, possessing, for example, two abnormal structural genes (*X* and *Y*), not only the populations of totally abnormal proteins (in homozygotes with respect to abnormal genes) and of half abnormal (heterozygotes) proteins *X* and *Y*, are present but only among hundreds of other genetically "normal" proteins. There would also be some contamination by randomly abnormal molecules and the level of such contamination has a tendency to increase with age.

If one realizes this tendency at the tissue level it becomes clear that both types of errors (somatic mutations and non-genetic errors of protein synthesis) are indistinguishable because the somatic mutations are also random. The randomness of any errors (genetic and non-genetic) in space and in time makes extremely difficult the study of the pattern and spectrum of these errors with respect to age and even to prove their real existence.

In addition to the mutations of the structural genes as we have emphasized (Medvedev, 1963, 1964), the mutations of gene-regulators and errors of synthesis of regulator proteins may have special importance in aging. In such an event the coordination of repressed and active genes and the maintenence of cell specialization may be partially distorted.

It is quite obvious that in considering the question of which of the factors and forms of molecular variability makes the greatest contribution to the total sum of molecular and subcellular damage and errors we must also take account of the equally important one of which *molecular-genetic or functional systems are most sensitive to the action of these errors.*

The material concerned with morphogenesis which we have already discussed gives us reason to suppose statistically, that it is a disturbance of the molecular-genetic control of the maintenance of some particular type of specialization which is the most frequent result of the action of any factor causing intracellular damage. In any specialized cell only a very small part of the general stock of genes is "active," The majority of the genes are specifically repressed. If we assume, for example, that free radicals or spontaneous errors in replication do not have a selective effect in damaging selectively those genes which are "active," then the probability of damage to repressed genes, and to systems involved in the synthesis of repressors and inductors will, statistically, be far greater than the "incidence" of damage to active genes. For this reason the conversion of certain repressed genes to the active state as a result of damage to the repressors must, statistically, occur more often than damage to genes actively synthesizing messenger RNAs, which would lead, for example to the production by them of anomalous proteins of some sort. As a result of these occurrences there must develop self-perpetuating, random, unprogrammed, "loud" micro-disturbances of specialized cells which are the equivalent of somatic mutations. Morphogenesis, which had stopped when sexual maturity was reached, is, as it were, prolonged but occurs slowly and chaotically and is directed towards the creation of disharmony.

As result of mutationally produced inconsistencies in genetic regulation, not only the pattern of proteins typical for differentiated cells but also the relative normal rates of the synthesis of different proteins may be altered (appearance of hyper- or hypofunctions and incorrectness of biochemical coordination at the cellular level).

The main difficulty in the experimental study of the spectrum, pattern, sequence, frequency and other characteristics of errors is undoubtedly related to their almost endless heterogeneity and diversity and with the existence of many possible levels of disorder (disorder among amino-acid residues in proteins, among the mixture of different protein populations, within the genome, among different cellular organelles, among the cells of a given tissue or organ and asynchrony of events in all the above structures). Therefore the effective investigation of these errors is possible only when one can separate the elementary events and factors (single cells, cell organelles, single protein synthesizing systems). There are almost no suitable biochemical approachs now for the exploration of *random* molecular alterations during aging of somatic cells. There exist only certain cytological methods: the calculation of the increase of the number and types of chromosomal aberrations, the increase of heteroploid cells with aging etc. which reflect comparatively significant magnitudes of molecular alterations.

SYSTEMS FOR THE CORRECTION AND ELIMINATION OF MOLECULAR AND GENETIC ERRORS IN SOMATIC CELLS

If any error in metabolism, synthesis of proteins, RNA or DNA were conserved in the course of time with exactly the same low rate as their rate of occurrence, a continuously increasing accumulation of errors would be observed and the maintenance of life in complex systems would become impossible. Under such conditions natural selection would affect ontogenesis not only by means of selection at the level of molecular replication precision (with an increase in number of genes, relative frequency of certain gene mutations per unit time often decreases), but also by altering the efficiency of elimination of damaged structures.

Elimination of molecular lesions may be seen most clearly in the removal of a high percentage of genetically abnormal cells from a population of rapidly dividing cells. Elimination processes of this kind have been studied in detail in numerous investigations dealing with postradiation recovery of tissues (for example by measuring the number of chromosome abnormalities induced by radiation remaining at various times after exposure). In the course of several reproductions following nonlethal irradiation, the number of aberrant cells approaches almost the normal level, though it does not reach it exactly. A somewhat increased level of abnormalities may be observed even a few years after irradiation. It is noteworthy that the rate of selection of normal cells after mutagenic treatment is not the same in different tissues.

It seems that due to effective selection the decrease in lifespan of chronically irradiated individuals is caused rather by damage of tissues normally having stable cell composition, as Curtis has calculated (1963, 1964), than by damage of sensitive tissues capable of rapid replacement of cells in their populations.

However, in tissues having stable cell composition postradiation recovery, although it is less rapid, also takes place. Consequently, in the latter case the elimination of lesions may also occur and not only through lethality of damaged cells, but also by means of complete or partial regenerative or functional replacement of lethally damaged cells. Recovery may proceed at both chromosome (reunion of broken ends) and genome (polyploidization) levels. For instance, diploid cells may, obviously, accommodate more mutations than a haploid cell can, the same is true for tetraploid cells compared to diploid ones, octoploid cells compared to tetraploid ones and so on. Thus, gradual but significant accumulation of polyploid cells in almost all the organs (Falzone *et al.*, 1962; Hoffman *et al.*, 1961. Brodsky, 1964) may be interpreted as a process of functional regeneration. Elimination of stable anomalies in protein composition of cells may apparently be achieved through the altered antigenic properties of such cells.

Furthermore, the formation of tissues with a stable cellular composition (non turning over) during morphogenesis may serve, as a means of compensating for the accumulation of molecular lesions. Although mitosis is a mechanism for eliminating genetic lesions it possesses a correspondingly greater sensitivity to the level of lesions. Thus, the cells which have lost their ability to divide, e.g., nervous or muscular cells, may endure significantly greater doses of damaging agents (radiations, mutagens) than the cells of actively renewing tissues do, e.g., bone marrow, intestinal epithelium.

It seems likely that multiple mechanisms for eliminating or blocking the effects of anomalous proteins exist at the molecular level as well. However, our knowledge of the nature of these mechanisms preventing the rapid accumulation of errors is far too limited. Practically no experimental research on this subject has yet been carried out although appropriate experiments tracing the fate of labeled anomalous proteins and nucleic acids in a population of normal macromolecules are presently quite feasible through current experimental techniques. We should mention a single study by Setlow and Carrier (1964) on bacterial systems in which a molecular mechanism correcting the errors induced by UV in DNA has been found (formation of thymine dimers). This mechanism is related to a distinct locus (Howard-Flanders *et al.*, 1962). It is also noteworthy that in heterozygotes for many genetic protein anomalies, e.g., for the synthesis of numerous abnormal hemoglobines, the proportion of normal to abnormal synthesis almost never approaches the theoretically expected ratio of 1:1. Normal hemoglobine always predominates. The same is observed in heterozygotes for several enzymatic abnormalities. Investigations on the nature of factors inhibiting anomalous synthesis is, undoubtedly, one of the most important problems in molecular gerontology.

MECHANISMS GOVERNING THE OCCURRENCE OF ERRORS

The existence of genetic control over the lifespan, the rate and forms of aging, terms (tablo) of morphogenetic stages and period of reproduction leads naturally to the idea that special molecular mechanisms for this control exist. There is a large group of species in which the death of the individual is determined not by the slow process of wearing out, but by some rapid morphogenetic process following sexual multiplication. Such types of ontogenesis are especially frequent in the plant world.

Such a relationship between the sexual process and death also exists in many insects, lower animals etc. Even in higher animals many authors recognize a correlation between the rate of sexual maturing and the lifespan. In many cases, there is no doubt of the connection between sexual reproduction and the death of the individual; for the onset of sexual maturity and the sexual process or the process of multiplication (the formation of seeds, eggs etc.) leads to the "incorporation" of a supplementary morphogenetic process which leads to death.

In both the animal and the plant kingdom increasing complexity and size of the individual has led to an increase in the complexity of the reproductive process. In such cases the survival of a line has selected against the ability to reproduce a large number of offspring in a single act of reproduction and selected for the ability to carry out several reproductive acts one after another. In many animals there has arisen the need to feed, protect and train the offspring until they become sexually mature. A new and prolonged phase of maturity has arisen in ontogenesis; it separates the attainment of sexual maturity from death by a long period of time which is very different in different species. Such species-specific aging also suggests an active genetic control of aging through a particular genetic system giving rise to involutionary processes. It is still not clear what the molecular nature of this control is. Earlier we suggested, (Medvedev, 1961, 1963) in the first place, that the "incorporation" of aging might be related to a loosening of nuclear control over RNA synthesis, which may be related to the increase of lifespan of messenger RNA molecules in specialized differentiated cells and the autonomous accumulation of errors in such "stable RNA." The lifespan of other forms of RNA in specialized cells is also increased.

Furthermore, we suggested that there might exist within cells special error generators, that is to say, genes which control the synthesis of minute amounts of the so-called "unusual" minor nucleotides which are found as contaminants among the principle nucleotides of RNA and DNA. We consider it possible that there may be a genetically controlled endogenous production of some of such compounds acting on RNA and DNA as a special slow mutagenic brake, that injects disharmony into the coordination of individual biochemical processes.

Finally, it is very probable that, after the completion of the morphogenetic programme, when, in the course of aging, random "incorporation" of certain genetic loci occurs, which changes the character of the biochemical specialization of the cells in a direction away from the normal, that this very process of "incorporation" may also be part of the programme of the genetic system. In other words, we propose that so-called somatic mutations leading to the accumulation of disharmony with increasing age may be a functional (selected) process in its own right, different from mutation of the reproductive cells which has a contrasting evolutionary significance.

For some microoganisms, plants and animals special *mutability genes* have been discovered and in some cases localized on the genetic map. It is possible that similar genes exist and act in somatic cells also, and determine one or another rate of error accumulation. The study of the influence of single gene alterations on the lifespan of mammals has recently been started (Casarett, 1964), as has been the breeding of inbred strains of mice with different lifespans.

But it is possible that genes or operons will be identified at some future time, as a result of this line of exploration, whose selective mutation, repression or induction may lead to a significant increase in life span through the decrease of the error frequency in living systems.

REFERENCES

BRODSKY, V. JA.: Somatic polyploidy as the form of physiological regeneration of organ's structures in ontogenesis of vertebrates. *Zh. Obschch. Biol., 25*:39, 1964.

CASARETT, G. W.: Similarities and contrasts between radiation and time pathology. *Adv. Geront. Res., 1*:109, 1964.

CURTIS, H. J.: Biological mechanisms underlying the aging process. *Science., 141*:686, 1963.

CURTIS, H. J.: Cellular processes involved in aging. *Fed. Proc., 23*:662, 1964.

Failla, G.: The aging process and somatic mutations. In: B. L. Strehler (ed.), *The Biology of Aging*. Washington. Amer. Inst. Biol. Sci., 1960, pp. 170-175.

Falzone, J. A., Barrows, C., and Yiengst, M.: Fractionation of rat liver nuclei into diploid and tetraploid DNA classes by continuous density gradient sedimentation. *Exp. Cell Res., 26*:556, 1962.

Harman, D.: The free radical theory of aging; the effects of age on serum mercaptan levels. *J. Gerontol., 15*:38, 1960.

Harman, D.: Prolongation of normal lifespan and inhibition of spontaneous cancer by antioxidants. *J. Geront., 16*:247, 1961.

Harman, D.: Role of free radicals in mutation, cancer, aging, and the maintenance of life. *Radiat. Res., 16*:753, 1962.

Hoffman, J., Huang, Ch. Y., and Post, J.: Aging and nuclear DNA. *J. Geront., 16*:389, 1961.

Howard-Flanders, P., Boyce, R. P., Simson, E., and Theriot, L.: A genetic locus in *E. coli* K12 that controls the reactivation of UV-photoproducts associated with thymine in DNA. *Proc. Nat. Acad. Sci. U.S., 48*:2109, 1962.

Loftfield, R. B.: The frequency of errors in protein biosynthesis. *Biochem. J., 89*:82, 1963.

Medvedev, Zh. A.: Aging of organism at the molecular level. *Usp. Sovr. Biol., 51*: 299, 1961.

Medvedev, Zh. A.: *Biosynthesis of Proteins and Problems of Ontogenesis.* Moscow, Medical Publish. House, 1963.

Medvedev, Zh. A.: The nucleic acids in the development and aging. *Adv. Geront. Res., 1*:181, 1964.

Monod, J., Changeux, J. P., and Jacob, F.: Allosteric proteins and cellular control systems, *J. Molec. Biol., 6*:306, 1963.

Nagornii, A. V., Nikitin, V. N., and Bulankin, I. N.: *Problem of Aging and Longevity*. Moscow, Medical Publish. House, 1963.

Oeriu, S.: Proteins in development and senescence. *Adv. Geront. Res., 1*:23, 1964.

Orgel, L. E.: The maintenance of the accuracy of protein synthesis and its relevance to aging. *Proc. Nat. Acad. Sci. U.S., 49*:517, 1963.

Setlow, R. B., and Carrier, W. L.: The disappearance of thymine dimers from DNA: an error-correcting mechanism. *Proc. Nat. Acad. Sci., U.S., 51*:226, 1964.

Sinex, F. M.: Cross-linkage and aging. *Adv. in Geront. Res., 1*:165, 1964.

Strehler, B. L.: Origin and comparison of the effects of time and high-energy radiations on living systems. *Quart. Rev. Biol., 34*:117, 1959.

Strehler, B. L.: *Time, Cells, and Aging.* New York, Academic Press, 1962.

Szilard, L.: On the nature of the aging process. *Proc. Nat. Acad. Sci. U.S., 45*:30, 1959.

Wulff, V. J., Quastler, H., and Sherman, F. G.: An hypothesis concerning RNA metabolism and aging. *Proc. Nat. Acad. Sci. U.S., 48*:1373, 1962.

Chapter 28

AUTO-IMMUNITY THEORIES*

ROY L. WALFORD AND GARY M. TROUP

THE AUTO-IMMUNE CONCEPT of aging postulates that increasing immunogenetic diversification or a pathogenetically analogous process involving one or many cell systems of the body causes aging. It is presumed that antigenic change, gain, deletion or other factors result in loss of the ability to recognize "self," and/or in the gain of antigens which are not of the nature of "self" (Walford, 1964; Blumenthal and Berns, 1964). Three different possible types of age-related alteration could have the effect of disturbed "self"-recognition. Gene deletion affecting immunologically competent cells (lymphocytes) of the body might result in reaction of these cells against the body, in short in a form of transplantation disease. Change away from "self" in the antigenic factors of nonlymphoid cells would result in these altered cells being recognized as foreign by the normal immune system of the body. Finally, a failure in the homeostatic mechanisms controlling tolerance might result in self-destructive immunologic activity without actual antigenic change in body cells. Any of these three types of alteration could set up immunological processes within the body of the nature of auto-immunity.

Two points should be emphasized about immunologic theories: 1) aging is assumed to result from reactions between cells rather than from reactions occurring primarily within individual cells; 2) immunologic diversification (such as that due to somatic mutation) would not necessarily lead to "loss of vitality" of the diversifying cells. The large number of different blood group iso-antigens on human erythrocytes serve no demonstrable function. Mutation from one to another would not lead to a deleterious biochemical change within the altered cell, although the cell might

* Supported by research grant HD-00534 of the National Institutes of Health.

well be eliminated following production of iso-antibodies against it by other cells.

Immunologic theories of aging are more or less directly susceptible to experimentation with already established technics. This is certainly a practical advantage over certain highly abstract approaches, which, like Greek science, depend mostly upon the overweight of philosophical beauty. It is also true that immunological processes can to some extent be controlled by available therapeutic procedures. This is likewise an advantage. Several types of pertinent experiments may be cited. The procedure of parabiosis sets the immunologic systems of two different animals in opposition. If the animals are chosen so that the genetic difference between them is not great, they will remain in parabiosis throughout the major portion of their life spans. A continuous low-grade immunologic battle between the partners may therefore ensue. Under these conditions parabiosis can be considered as a "model" for one of the immune processes perhaps concerned with aging. In hamsters (Walford and Hildemann, 1964) parabiosis with only minor immunogenetic difference between the partners accelerates the development of the major "disease of aging" in this species, i.e., amyloidosis. Rats surviving a long time in parabiosis demonstrate a marked shift in the age incidence of neoplasia towards a chronologically younger age (Hall, *et al.*, 1953). On the other hand, in long term parabiotic mice no change in rate of aging or disease patterns has been observed (Walford, Mansur and Sjaarda, unpublished observations), perhaps due to the tendency of mice to become tolerant or immunologically paralyzed across weak histocompatibility loci. Injection of newborn mice with lymphoid cells of a slightly different immunogenetic nature than the recipient animals constitutes another variety of pertinent immunologic experiment. This procedure leads to a considerable shortening of the mean survival of the injected mice as compared to controls, and to a shift towards a younger age in the incidence of lymphomas (Walford and Hildemann, 1965).

A large number of drugs are known to be relatively effective in suppressing the immune response, including humoral and/or homograft immunity. Drugs valuable in the treatment of auto-immune states, or in potentiating the survival of organ homografts, might have a positive effect on vertebrate life span if such life span is indeed influenced in a major way by self-destructive immunologic mechanisms. In our own laboratory C3H test mice, fed the immunosuppressive drug Imuran on a daily basis beginning in late adulthood, have shown a median survival time of one hundred and three weeks, as compared to a median survival time for control mice of ninety-four weeks. This experiment is still in progress with various drug levels. No other investigations are on record concerning the influence of immunosuppressive drugs upon life span.

Consideration of the possible effects of immune mechanisms on aging suggests a number of areas requiring further study. To take the simplest example, not a great deal is known about "normal" changes in the immune system with advancing years. A thorough review of morphologic changes in the system was accomplished some years ago by Andrew (1952). However, since that time it has become quite clear that the lymphoid organs cannot be considered as more or less one unit. So-called "peripheral" and "central" immunologic systems exist and are quite distinct in function. The central system consists of the thymus, the bursa of Fabricius in fowls, and probably the appendix. The peripheral lymphoid system consists of the spleen, lymph nodes and other areas of reticuloendothelial cell accumulation. With such orientation in mind, one can already find evidence from the literature that these two systems undergo age-related changes at different rates. The thymus involutes rather early in life, whereas the highest ratio of splenic weight to body weight occurs in late adulthood (the fiftieth to sixtieth year in the human). While there is not in fact much alteration with age in the body's ability to respond to exogenous stimuli by formation of iso-antibodies, there is indeed a remarkable increase of auto-antibodies in old, supposedly healthy people. The combined incidence is well over 25 per cent in the older population. This information may be garnered from the control data of those investigators currently studying the various recognized auto-immune diseases. These important findings are a by-product of investigation of known auto-immune diseases. It is quite possible that search for other antibodies of an auto-immune nature, but not obviously associated with clinically recognizable and popular diseases, would be fruitful. For example, naturally occurring antibodies to collagen have been found in normal human serum, but no attempt has been made as yet to demonstrate an age-specific incidence (Maurer, 1954).

Of critical need for auto-immune as well as somatic mutation theories of aging is the development of methods for measuring spontaneous somatic mutation rates. This will probably entail the delineation of minor cell populations by immunologic means. An attempt in this direction with the human ABO blood group system was made by Atwood (1961). Anti-A antibody was added to human group A blood and the cells were allowed to agglutinate and sediment. Continuous treatment of the small number of supernatant cells by this method led to the final recovery of a population constituting about 0.1 per cent of the original cells. The minor population lacked the A antigen and was of blood group O specificity. These cells might be expected to have arisen from group O erythroblastic predecessors and to represent an immunogenetically diverse population. There was no increase in their percentage with age, according to Atwood's data, but the oldest individual examined was only forty-nine. The assumption apparently made by Atwood (1961), as well as later by Burch (1963), that spontaneous somatic mutation should follow a linear relationship with age, cannot be accepted as valid until proven by direct measurement. If the mutation rate with age were of an exponential nature, Atwood's failure to find an increased percentage of immunologically diverse cells at age forty-nine would be understandable. The progressive development of chromosomal abnormalities in hepatic cells with age can be visualized as a kind of somatic mutation (Curtis, 1963), but technics for assessing less gross abnormalities, including especially abnormalities of an antigenic nature, require development.

A third area for future development concerns the effects of immunological reactions on biochemical processes. Very few pertinent direct experiments on this subject have been done. However, there is some evidence that proteins after combination with antibodies are rendered less susceptible to enzymic degradation (Stelos and Pressman, 1962). It is a well known fact of aging that the proteins from older animals are less susceptible to enzymic degradation than proteins from young animals.

The several "models" being used by us to investigate the immune theory of aging are concerned with transplantation disease mechanisms. Such mechanisms are involved both in the experiment of parabiosis and in the injection of newborn animals with immunologically competent cells of a different strain than the recipient. Despite the fact that so-called runt disease, secondary disease or transplantation disease in the injected newborn, and acute parabiotic rejection in adults are obvious biochemical catastrophies, practically no chemical studies of these phenomena have been undertaken. This is clearly another field meriting intensive investigation.

Concern with auto-immune concepts of aging necessitates consideration of the phylogeny of the immune response. Invertebrates are not regarded as having immunologic cell systems, as such systems are usually visualized in functional terms, and invertebrate aging cannot therefore be explained by auto-immune theories as currently formulated. Studies are in progress in several laboratories to find definitive evidence of immune processes, if such exist, in invertebrates. The critical factor requiring demonstration is anamnesis or immunological memory. Cooper has recently observed first- and second-set rejection of cuticle xenografts in earthworms, thus fulfilling the criterion of anamnesis for an immune response in this genus. Also, Tyler's auto-immune concept of cell structure merits thought in terms of the immunology of invertebrates (Tyler, 1946). Finally, cells which have nothing to do with immunologic response *per se* (for example, renal tubular cells) may upon disassociation *in vitro* reassociate to form in part their original relationship. Normal cells in tissue culture do not overgrow one another. These and similar phenomena, while not explicable in classical terms of immunity, nevertheless entail some type of self-recognition. It is easier to envision this recognition in quasi-immunologic than in biochemical terms. Such an approach may be able to include invertebrates in the concept of immunologic aging. There is a strong tendency among biologists to divide the great kingdom of animals very glibly into vertebrates and invertebrates. This division is valid descriptively but not necessarily functionally. If man were an echinoderm, the division would be into echinoderms and inechinoderms. The failure thus far to demonstrate immune-like processes in some lower animals cannot be generalized to all invertebrate phyla. Studies in this area are at a very early stage

It may be predicted that geriatricians in the future will be more concerned than at present with auto-immune "diseases of aging." From this category we would exclude most of the so-called "collagen" diseases such as systemic lupus, rheumatoid arthritis, dermatomyocitis, scleroderma and others. These on the whole are not "diseases of aging." They tend to have a peak incidence in mid-adult life. Comfort (1963) has suggested that the greater prevalence of these diseases in females mitigates against an auto-immune concept of aging because females live longer than males. However, if one restricts oneself to actual "diseases of aging" and inquires into auto-immune processes, or into diseases which might feasibly be of an auto-immune nature, one encounters primary and senile amyloidosis, diabetes, polyarteritis, temporal arteritis, certain forms of hemolytic anemia and perhaps chronic thyroiditis. All of these except the last are more common in males than in females. Furthermore, they have a rather high incidence in older individuals. Amyloidosis occurs in over 80 per cent of old humans and in a wide variety of other vertebrates (Walford and Lee, 1965). Maturity onset diabetes displays in some statistics an incidence of 10 to 20 per cent in the older population (Wilkerson and Krall, 1947). Idiopathic hemolytic anemia of the cold antibody type has an increasing frequency with age and appears to be slightly more common in males than in females. The auto-immune hemolytic anemia occurring with adulthood and age in NZB mice has its highest incidence in males (Holmes and Burnet, 1963). Most of the putative auto-immune "diseases of aging" are thus found more commonly in males than in females and occur not only in man but in other species. They are, as a group, far more common than the classical auto-immune diseases. It is thus of crucial importance to decide whether these various diseases are truly of an auto-immune nature. The immune status of the collagen diseases is supported by demonstration of circulating humoral antibodies in most of them. This has not been accomplished for amyloidosis nor for the majority of the other age-related diseases under discussion. Nevertheless, evidence thoroughly reviewed by MacKay and Burnet (1963) may permit one to include these provisionally among auto-immune entities.

In summary one may predict that future work in the immunology of aging will direct researchers somewhat away from the heavy biochemical preoccupation that has heretofore characterized this field. Adequate methods for detecting spontaneous somatic mutation rates will be worked out. A number of direct immunologic experiments calculated to influence the aging process will be undertaken and studied. Investigations of the effect of immunological reactions on biochemical processes and upon protein structure, of the chemical mechanisms involved in transplantation disease, and of the possible types of immune responses in lower organisms will provide basic data of crucial importance in evaluating autoimmune theories of aging.

In the summer of 1962 and in the company of W. H. Hildemann, one of us (RW) undertook a field expedition to South America. Live specimens of annual fish were collected in order to establish a colony at the University of California. This genus of fish has one of the shortest life spans of any higher vertebrate and is being used in studying some of the problems outlined in the present manuscript. During the expedition Hildemann noted that insects, particularly mosquitoes, were rare in ponds where annual fish abounded. This observation, plus the fact that annual fish can survive in temporary waters (their eggs remain viable in dried-up mud until the advent of seasonal rains), led to the suggestion (Hildemann and Walford, 1963) that these insectivorous fish might be ideal agents for the biologic control of insect populations in impermanent tropical waters. The proposal is currently under field trial by the World Health Organization and by Dr. Ernest Bay at the Riverside Campus of the University of California. This personal story plus the above several predictions and suggestions for further work in the immunology of aging and related phenomena illustrate that preoccupation with generalizing biologic hypotheses may take unexpected and in themselves fruitful turns. Theory is often most rewarding in the questions it causes one to ask.

REFERENCES

ANDREW, W.: Lymphatic tissue. *Cowdry's Problems of Aging,* 3rd ed. (ed. Lansing, A. I.), Baltimore, Williams and Wilkins, 1952.

ATWOOD, K. C., AND PEPPER, F. J.: Erythrocyte automosaicism in some persons of known genotype. *Science, 134:*2100, 1961.

BLUMENTHAL, H. T., AND BERNS, A. W.: Autoimmunity in aging. *Advances in Gerontological Research* (ed. Strehler, B. L.), New York, Academic Press, 1964, Vol. 1, pp. 289-342.

BURCH, P. R. J.: Autoimmunity: some etiological aspects. *Lancet, 1:*1253, 1963.

COMFORT, A.: Mutation, autoimmunity, and aging. *Lancet, II:*138, 1963.

CURTIS, H. J.: Biological mechanisms underlying the aging process. *Science, 141:*686, 1963.

HALL, C. E., HALL, O., AND CUNNINGHAM, A. W. B.: Spontaneous neoplasia in female parabiotic rats. *Texas Rep. Biol. Med., 11:*449, 1953.

HILDEMANN, W. H., AND WALFORD, R. L.: Annual fish—promising species as biological control agents. *J. Trop. Med. Hyg., 66:*163, 1963.

HOLMES, M. C., AND BURNET, F. M.: The natural history of auto-immune disease in NZB mice. *Ann. Intern. Med., 59:*265, 1963.

MACKAY, I. R., AND BURNET, F. M.: *Autoimmune Diseases.* Springfield, Thomas, 1963.

MAURER, P.: Antigenicity of oxypolygelatin and gelatin in man. *J. Exp. Med., 100:* 497, 1954.

STELOS, P., AND PRESSMAN, D.: Papain digestion of antigen-antibody precipitates. *J. Biol. Chem., 237:*3679, 1962.

TYLER, A.: An auto-antibody concept of cell structure, growth and differentiation. *Growth 10: (Suppl.),* 7, 1946.

WALFORD, R. L.: Further considerations towards an immunologic theory of aging. *Exp. Geront., 1:*67, 1964.

WALFORD, R. L., AND HILDEMANN, W. H.: Chronic and subacute parabiotic reaction in the Syrian hamster: significance with regard to transplantation immunology, experimental amyloidosis, and an immunologic theory of aging. *Transplantation, 2:*87, 1964.

WALFORD, R. L., AND HILDEMANN, W. H.: Life span and lymphoma incidence in mice injected at birth across a weak histocompatibility locus. *Amer. J. Path. 47:*713, 1965.

WALFORD, R. L., AND LEE, L.: Amyloidosis and the process of aging. *Fourth Internat. Symp. Immunopath.,* Monte Carlo, Feb. 1965 (in press).

WILKERSON, H. L. C., AND KRALL, L. P.: Diabetes in a New England town. A study of 3,516 persons in Oxford, Mass. *JAMA, 135:*209, 1947.

Chapter 29

BEHAVIOUR AND AGE: PROBLEMS AND THEORIES

A. T. WELFORD

If we leave aside the researches of pioneers such as Quetelet and Galton, the psychological study of ageing contains three clearly identifiable interests, each coupled with a characteristic methodology and manner of thinking. The first of these was originally concerned with the potentialities of older people for employment. W. R. Miles and his co-workers at Stanford University during the depression of the 1920s were moved by the difficulties of those unemployed in later middle life and asked themselves what kind of work was suitable for older people (Miles, 1965). Their researches continued for only a few years before the team was disbanded, but the problem was taken up again in 1946 by the Nuffield Unit for Research into Problems of Ageing, working at Cambridge University, and later by others in Britain, under the spur of a labour shortage which it was hoped might be mitigated by encouraging older people to remain at work instead of retiring. Both Miles's group and the British workers realised that, if their problem was to be solved, it would be necessary to discover and understand the fundamental changes of capacity that come with age. They therefore regarded their studies as falling within the field of human biology and concerned not so much with *old* age or with senility, as with processes of *ageing* throughout the whole span of normal adult life.

The second type of psychological gerontology deals with the clinical problem of differentiating normal effects of old age from various forms of mental pathology. Its aim is not so much a fundamental understanding of age changes as an accurate measurement of their effects, and it is less concerned with precise definition of what is measured than with the differentiation of one individual from another. A taxonomy of mental functions sometimes appears as a by-product and can be a valuable aid to thought although it depends somewhat upon the tests used. Combined indices based on a number of tests have been produced as a means of expressing overall "functional age" (Halstead *et al.*, 1963), although the variety of age effects and the different rates at which they proceed makes the meaning of such indices questionable.

The third application of psychology to gerontology has been in the social field. The increasing number of old people in the population has raised serious problems of their care and role in society. Psychological studies have therefore been made of personality traits, attitudes, values and roles played in relation to age, all of which are relevant to the design of facilities for old people in the community and of care for them in homes.

These three lines of work run parallel to broad divisions of general psychological study and interest—the first to experimental and physiological psychology, the second to clinical psychology and psychometrics, and the third to social psychology. Their diversity is reflected in the intermediate position that psychology commonly occupies between biology, medicine and social studies in universities, in research sponsoring schemes and, nearer home, in the International Association of Gerontology.

During the last few years these lines, especially the first and second, have tended to converge, and it is perhaps significant that J. E. Birren, to whom much of this coming together has been due, had experience as an experimental psychologist before going to the U. S. National Institute of Mental Health as head of the Section on Aging. Certainly collaboration between those working in these two fields promises to be fruitful by joining the experimentalist's interest in the detailed mechanism of behaviour with the clinician's viewing of age in the perspective of other organic and functional conditions.

THE DEVELOPMENT OF THEORY REGARDING AGE CHANGES IN BEHAVIOUR

In the 1940s theoretical issues over changes of behaviour with age followed the lines of those traditional in psychology. The question was debated as to whether age effects in peripheral structures—sense organs, muscles and joints—provided a sufficient explanation of trends in performance or whether central brain mechanisms were also involved. Alternatively it was questioned whether age differences of behaviour were due to biological changes in the organism or to the effects of environment and experience. The usual presumption was that any fall of performance among older people was due either to organic failure of their peripheral mechanisms, or to their interests having changed over the years or to their being "out of practice" for experimental tasks resembling those of school.

Probably the most important achievement of post-war research in psychological gerontology is that the traditional presuppositions have been reversed, so that central changes have come to be recognised as of principal importance, and have been linked plausibly with physical changes found to occur with age in the brain either directly (Welford, 1965a) or via likely metabolic changes (McFarland, 1963). This is not to say that peripheral mechanisms and experience are unimportant, but we need to think of peripheral and central, organic and experiential factors as all operating simultaneously and inextricably interwoven. Any given behaviour cannot, therefore, be *wholly* attributed to any one factor, although in particular circumstances one or another may *set limits* to performance. For example, as Weale (1965) has pointed out, age changes in pupil size and eye media can largely account for certain visual threshold phenomena, but they have only a small effect on perceptual changes clear of threshold, which are due mainly to central factors.

The 1940s marked the beginning of a rapid development of psychological theory owing to wartime contacts between psychologists and engineers over the design of service equipment. In particular, ideas were elaborated of man as a self-regulating servomechanism, analogies were drawn between human behaviour and computer operations, and mathematical "models" were formulated, notably that of "information theory" dealing with perception and choice in terms of the resolution of uncertainty. The experimental studies of ageing undertaken at that time were well in touch with these activities and contributed to them. As a result, broadly expressed theories of age effects, such as that the difficulty of older people in learning is due to lowered "plasticity," came to be replaced by more detailed and predictive hypotheses.

Most of these hypotheses deal with particular areas of facts and are, like their counterparts in general experimental psychology, limited in scope. They have been outlined elsewhere (Welford 1958, 1962a, 1964a, 1965a) and there is no need to go over them again here. Probably the one which comes nearest to being a "grand theory" capable of linking together findings from widely different areas is that originally proposed by Crossman and Szafran (1956) and developed by Gregory (1959). These authors suggested that age produces a lowering of the signal-to-noise ratio in the nervous system and brain, the noise being "neural noise" due to random spontaneous neural activity. The central effects of signals are conceived as having to be accumulated until they are distinguishable from the background noise. If they are strong they will be quickly and reliably distinguished, but if they are weak, or if the background noise level is high, performance will be slowed or errors will occur, speed and accuracy being complementary.

A lowering of signal level or rise of neural noise would clearly account for the slowing of performance, which is one of the most characteristic age changes. They would also affect other types of performance: for example, short-term memory is commonly regarded as carried in the form of activity in certain brain circuits which spans the period of retention. These dynamic traces tend to be broken up slowly over a period of time and much more rapidly by other activity involving a shift of attention. Any lowering of signal-to-noise ratio would weaken the traces and make them more liable to disruption. Short-term memory appears to be an important factor in many problem-solving and other intellectual tasks, so that any impairment of it would have widespread effects on performance.

The various age changes in the brain, including the loss of some cells and diminished functioning of others, as well as changes in sense organs, would obviously tend to lower signal levels in the sense of reducing the frequencies of nerve impulses produced by any given level of external stimulation, or from one part of the brain to another. At the same time longer after-effects of previous stimulation (Mundy-Castle 1953, 1962, Axelrod 1963) and increased arousal which may, as we shall mention later, occur in an attempt to compensate for loss of sensitivity, would tend to increase the level of neural noise (Welford, 1965a).

FUTURE LINES OF RESEARCH

Despite the progress which has so far been made, the formulation and testing of theories to account for changes of behaviour with age are in their early stages. Of the many opportunities offered by the present state of gerontological and general psychological research considered together, six appear to be especially promising:

1) Application of Decision Theory

The treatment of sensory thresholds has been transformed in recent years by the use of mathematical "decision theory" (Tanner and Swets, 1954; Swets *et al.*, 1961). Signals are assumed to be received against a background of random noise, either external noise, or internal neural noise, the intensity of which varies from moment to moment. The subject's task is to decide whether at any given moment a signal is present; or, in other words, whether his observation falls within the distribution of signal-plus-noise or of noise alone. If these two distributions overlap, some errors are inevitable and the best the subject can do is to establish a cutoff point, treating anything above this as signal and anything below it as noise. The cutoff point and the signal-to-noise ratio (and hence the average noise level) can be calculated from the errors made over a series of observations, provided certain assumptions are made about the noise distribution. Also if judgments are made at different levels of confidence, a series of cutoff points corresponding to these levels can be calculated.

The model is simple and powerful, and has a wide range of potential applications in experimental psychology, in relation not only to sensory thresholds but to many other types of judgment as well. For studies of ageing it offers a means of testing the signal-to-noise ratio theory much more thoroughly than has been done hitherto. It also offers a means of discovering how far the slowing of performance and apparent raising of thresholds in older people are due to genuine loss of sensitivity, and how far to increased caution leading to more rigorous criteria for acceptance of stimuli as signals.

2) Short-term Retention

We have already noted that short-term retention seems to enter into a number of complex performances, enabling events and actions over a period of time to be co-ordinated. There are indications that several different types of storage are involved, operating on different time-scales from a fraction of a second up to a few minutes, but so far most studies in relation to age have been confined to the retention of digits or similar material over a few seconds (for a brief review see Welford, 1964a).

There is a need in the study both of ageing and of human performance in general to consider other types of short-term storage of data. A beginning has been made by Broadbent and Heron (1962) who studied in relation to age the retention of simple instructions which changed from time to time during a continuous task. It would be desirable to go on from simple to more complex tasks, considering the complexity of programme that can be maintained, the degree of variation in a repetitive task that can be accommodated without a programme breaking down, and the problems that arise when frequent changes of programme are required.

Another type of short-term retention seems to be the basis of the perceptual frameworks combining visual, auditory, kinaesthetic and tactual data, all integrated over periods of time, in terms of which orientation is maintained. It is well known that such frameworks may be impaired in senility and some other pathological conditions, but there is little knowledge beyond a few exploratory studies of how they are built and maintained and the extent to which they change in the normal course of ageing (Szafran, 1958). Still less is known of the formation of conceptual frameworks or "mental models" such as are employed by operators of chemical and other remote-controlled plants to envisage a process they are controlling but cannot directly see, or by scientists and others who have to combine abstract data from various sources into a coherent scheme.

3) Recovery of Data from Long-term Memory

Although knowledge obviously tends to increase with age, older people may have difficulty in recovering data from memory when required for use (Birren, 1955; Wallace, 1956; Hurwitz and Allison, 1965). The question has been raised, although not yet fully answered, of whether the mere accumulation of data in memory makes recovery more difficult, or whether the "recovery mechanism" changes with age (Welford, 1958; Birren, 1964). The process of recovery can be made easier if the subject can form expectations about what will be required, based on experience of the same or similar situations on previous occasions. The further question is thus raised of how far older people are able to gain and use knowledge about the probabilities of recurrent events (Griew, 1962). A considerable volume of research has been done in recent years on the recognition of words under difficult conditions such as noise or masking by other words: such experiments provide a convenient means of studying certain aspects of data recovery and could well be used with old subjects in addition to the young adults normally employed.

4) The Process of Thinking

Despite a long succession of often brilliant pioneering studies, there is little systematic understanding of thinking as a psychological process. The modern treatment of thinking can be traced to a chapter by Craik (1943) in which he sets out an approach which is epitomized in the following statement:

> My hypothesis . . . is that thought models, or parallels, reality—that its essential feature is not "the mind," "the self," "sense-data," nor propositions but symbolism, and that this symbolism is largely of the same kind as that which is familiar to us in mechanical devices which aid thought and calculation (Craik, 1943 p. 57).

Many processes are obviously involved: selection of data from what is presented, classification, short-term storage, the building of conceptual models, decision and checking. Yet all these seem to represent ancillary operations or results of thinking rather than the central core of the process whereby data are co-ordinated and reorganised. This crucial stage in thinking seems largely to have eluded study: we need to know what "calculations" or "computations" can be handled by the brain, how more complex ones are broken down and how capacity for carrying out such operations is affected by the way data are presented and by various conditions affecting the subject. Some important attempts in this direction have been made: for example Bartlett (1958) and his co-workers have studied thinking as analogous to complex sensory-motor skills involving a series of component processes which have to be ordered and co-ordinated towards a final end result; Bruner *et al.* (1956) have studied in detail the strategies used by subjects in selecting and ordering the series of steps required to categorize material; Dienes and Jeeves (1965) have done the same for comprehending the structure of mathematical groups. These authors would, however, be the first to agree that there is much still to be done both in the way of new research and, perhaps, by pulling together work already done but scattered under labels other than "thinking." Again the incorporation of age as a variable in any further research could be valuable both to gerontology and to experimental and clinical psychology in general.

5) Arousal

The study of arousal effects has been one of the most significant lines of research during recent years in the borderland between psychology and physiology. The effects are held to result from diffuse impulses coming from the brain stem to the cortex which partially depolarise the cells there, rendering them more easily fired, so that the cortex becomes more sensitive and responsive than it would otherwise be. The intensity of the stream of impulses rises with any sensory stimulation to which the subject is not habituated, and as a result of effort or stress. The effects are correlated with various forms of autonomic activity, and these are commonly used as indices of arousal. If the level of arousal rises very high, performance, especially at complex tasks, tends to be impaired. Many reasons for this have been advanced: probably the simplest is that some of the cells in the cortex actually begin to fire, making the system "noisy" and lowering its capacity by rendering refractory some cells that would otherwise be available for carrying signals (Welford, 1962b; 1965b).

Pioneering studies by Shmavonian (Shmavonian and Busse, 1963; Shmavonian *et al.*, 1965) have shown that the relationships between arousal and age are complex: in some ways older subjects seem less, and in some ways more easily aroused than younger. Further research could be rewarding in showing the extent to which changes of effort and of reactions to stress are characteristic of age. It could also throw light on the important question of how far chronic stress, say in middle life, has cumulative and irreversible effects on reactivity to stress during later life.

6) A New Approach to Social Behaviour

Although much remains to be done to elucidate the basic mechanisms of human capacity and the ways they change with age, there is perhaps an even wider field of opportunity in the application of experimental and physiological psychology to social problems. Social psychology has in the past tended to have its own terms, concepts and standards. The time seems ripe to try to bridge the gap between it and more biologically based areas of the subject, seeking to understand social behaviour in terms of individual characteristics *plus* principles of interaction between individuals that these characteristics imply. A possible lead is contained in an important recent advance in the application of psychology to the operation of industrial and other equipment. Man and the machinery he uses have come to be treated together as parts of a single *system*, and it has been recognized that the behaviour of the various parts depends upon the system as a whole and upon its objectives. Research on human skills and capacities has yielded a wealth of essentially biological knowledge on the characteristics of the human parts of such systems, and studies within the field of control engineering have provided means of describing and understanding the behaviour of complex systems as wholes.

These developments open up a new approach to many social problems when one realizes that there are obvious similarities in the relationships between man and machine and between one person and others. Just as a man may have to understand readings on instruments, use these as a basis for control actions and then observe and react to the effects of his actions, so there is a constant interplay of information and action between persons. In both cases there will be restrictions on what can be achieved due to limited capacities in the various links in the system. In both, the behaviour of the system as a whole may be substantially affected by any change in the characteristics of the human link, such as may occur with age.

The systems approach provides a possible model for several changes of behaviour with age and serves to emphasize the difficulty of separating individual and social effects. Suppose, for example, that as certain capacities fall with age an individual attempts to hold achievement constant. He may increase his level of effort to such an extent as eventually to cause chronic stress—as shown by some older men whose jobs "get on top of them;" alternatively he may seek to supplement his capacities by recruiting those of others and become demanding and dependent. He may, of course, on the other hand fail to maintain achievement, reducing the level and range of his activity and saving current decision by increased reliance on routine.

Some possible results of age changes considered in these terms have been discussed elsewhere (Welford, 1964b) but there is clearly very much more to be done. Let us take only one example, that of what must now be one of the major social problems of the civilized world—the problem of so-called "loneliness" in old age. Complaints of loneliness obviously imply a failure to maintain social contacts in the face of conditions which make their achievement difficult. In some cases physical incapacity may cause isolation. Commonly, however, complaints come from people with little or no serious physical disability but a seemingly unrealistic demand for attention, who are unwilling to take the obvious steps to secure human contacts: in short the problem is not loneliness but *unsociability*. This might sometimes be due to an age change in the brain affecting personality, but the trouble often appears to be of long standing. Its origin must be a matter of speculation, but it could perhaps arise from one or both of two causes. First, those who complain of loneliness may never have developed their social skills, so that friendship is for them a harder task than it is for most. The enforced social contacts of work and family life have prevented the lack of skill becoming apparent until retirement or when children leave home, so that the difficulty, although present from early years, is not revealed until old age. Secondly, past experience may have set standards of attention which others are unable to maintain. Several studies and observations have suggested that extreme experiences of pleasure, fear or other strong feelings can have a permanent effect on a subject's expectations, so that an intense experience of success or pleasure can set a standard such that the person concerned is unlikely ever to be fully satisfied again. Anyone who has given himself to creative activities will have experienced something of this in his work. There are, perhaps, some experiences such as, for a woman, the profound satisfactions of bearing and rearing children, that colour a much wider sector of life.

PSYCHOLOGY AS A BIOLOGICAL SCIENCE

The nature and causes of loneliness in old age may seem a far cry from experimental and physiological psychology, and hardly an appropriate topic for inclusion in a tribute to a great physiological gerontologist. Yet there is no fundamental discontinuity between the problems of social and biological gerontology. Social problems are essentially the result of biological organisms facing their environment, human as well as material, and the nature and means of solving these problems must ultimately depend on factors of human biology within the individuals concerned which imply patterns of interaction between one individual and another.

The present divisions of psychology stem from the historical fact that, in order to make progress, it has been necessary to determine laws governing social behaviour and clinical conditions without attempting to tie them back into detailed biological mechanisms, in just the same way as psychology has had to study the behaviour of the whole organism before being able to relate it to detailed physiological functions. Unification of the various branches of psychology is proceeding, and it may be hoped that the next few years will see a clear recognition that human behaviour in all its aspects must come within the field of human biological science. Such a union could bring precision and a theoretical background into some areas where they are now lacking, and would broaden the present perspectives of experimental psychology. In this process, psychological gerontology, because of its common problems with the older biological disciplines, with clinical medicine and with social studies, seems well placed to make a leading contribution.

REFERENCES

AXELROD, S.: Cognitive tasks in several modalities. In *Processes of Aging,* R. H. Williams, C. Tibbitts and Wilma Donahue, eds., Atherton Press, New York, Vol. I, 1963.

BARTLETT, F. C.: *Thinking, an Experimental and Social Study.* London, Allen and Unwin, 1958.

BIRREN, J. E.: Age changes in speed of simple responses and perception and their significance for complex behavior. In: *Old Age in the Modern World,* Edinburgh, Livingstone, 1955.

BIRREN, J. E.: The psychology of aging in relation to development. In: *Relations of Development and Aging,* J. E. Birren, ed., Springfield, Thomas, 1964.

BROADBENT, D. E., AND HERON, A.: Effects of a subsidiary task on performance involving immediate memory by younger and older men. *Brit. J. Psychol., 53:*189, 1962.

BRUNER, J. S., GOODNOW, JACQUELINE J., AND AUSTIN, G. A.: *A Study of Thinking.* New York, Wiley, 1956.

CRAIK, K. J. W.: *The Nature of Explanation.* Cambridge Univ. Press, 1943.

CROSSMAN, E. R. F. W., AND SZAFRAN, J.: Changes with age in the speed of information intake and discrimination. *Experientia, Suppl. 4:*128, 1956.

DIENES, Z. P., AND JEEVES, M. A.: *Thinking in Structures,* London, Hutchinson, 1965.

GREGORY, R. L.: Increase in "neurological noise" as a factor in aging. In: *Proc. IV Cong. Int. Ass. Geront., Merano 1957, 1:*314, 1959.

GRIEW, S.: The learning of statistical structure: a preliminary study in relation to age. In: *Aging Around the World: Social and Psychological Aspects of Aging.* C. Tibbitts and W. Donahue, eds., New York, Columbia Univ. Press, Vol. 1, 1962.

HALSTEAD, W. C., MERRYMAN, PAT, AND KLIEN, BERTHA: The Halstead Index and differential aging. In: *Processes of Aging,* R. H. Williams, C. Tibbitts and Wilma Donahue, eds., New York, Atherton Press, Vol. I, 1963.

HURWITZ, L. J., AND ALLISON, R. S.: Factors influencing performance in psychological testing of the aged. In: *Behavior, Aging and the Nervous System,* A. T. Welford and J. E. Birren, eds., Springfield, Thomas, 1965.

MCFARLAND, R. A.: Experimental evidence of the relationship between aging and oxygen want: in search of a theory of aging. *Ergonomics, 6:*339, 1963.

MILES, W. R.: The Stanford University studies of later maturity. In: *Behaviour, Aging and the Nervous System,* A. T. Welford and J. E. Birren, eds., Springfield, Thomas, 1965.

MUNDY-CASTLE, A. C.: An analysis of central responses to photic stimulation in normal adults. *Electroenceph. Clin. Neurophysiol., 5:*1, 1953.

MUNDY-CASTLE, A. C.: Central excitability in the aged. In: *Aging Around the World: Medical and Clinical Aspects of Aging,* H. T. Blumenthal, ed., New York, Columbia Univ. Press, Vol. 4, 1962.

SHMAVONIAN, B. M., AND BUSSE, E. W.: Psychophysiological techniques in the study of the aged. In: *Processes of Aging,* R. H. Williams, C. Tibbitts and Wilma Donahue, eds., New York, Atherton Press, Vol. I, 1963.

SHMAVONIAN, B. M., YARMAT, A. J., AND COHEN, S. I.: Relationships between the autonomic nervous system and central nervous system in age differences in behavior. In: *Behavior, Aging and the Nervous System,* A. T. Welford and J. E. Birren, eds., Springfield, Thomas, 1965.

SWETS, J. A., TANNER, W. P., AND BIRDSALL, T. G.: Decision processes in perception. *Psychol. Rev., 68:*301, 1961.

SZAFRAN, J.: (1958) Cited by Welford, A. T. (1958).

TANNER, W. P., AND SWETS, J. A.: A decision-making theory of visual detection. *Psychol. Rev., 61:*401, 1954.

WALLACE, JEAN G.: Some studies of perception in relation to age. *Brit. J. Psychol., 47:*283, 1956.

WEALE, R. A.: On the eye. In: *Behavior, Aging and the Nervous System,* A. T. Welford and J. E. Birren, eds., Springfield, Thomas, 1965.

WELFORD, A. T.: *Aging and Human Skill.* Oxford Univ. Press for the Nuffield Foundation, 1958.

WELFORD, A. T.: On changes of performance with age. *Lancet,* Feb. 17, pp. 335-339, 1962a.

WELFORD, A. T: Arousal, channel-capacity and decision. *Nature (London), 194:*365, 1962b.

WELFORD, A. T.: Experimental psychology in the study of aging. *Brit. Med. Bull., 20:*65, 1964a.

WELFORD, A. T.: Aging and personality: age changes in basic psychological capacities. In: *Age with a Future,* P. From Hansen, ed., Copenhagen, Munksgaard, 1964b.

WELFORD, A. T.: Performance, biological mechanisms and age: a theoretical sketch. In: *Behavior, Aging and the Nervous System,* A. T. Welford and J. E. Birren, eds., Springfield, Thomas, 1965a.

WELFORD, A. T.: Stress and achievement. *Aust. J. Psychol. 17:*1, 1965b.

Section VII

THE FUTURE

Chapter 30

THE FUTURE FOR AGING RESEARCH*

HANS SELYE

WHEN I received the editor's request to write an article for this jubilee volume in honor of Professor Fritz Verzár, I was both pleased and horrified: pleased because this invitation gave me a most welcome opportunity to express my admiration and affection for an old friend who has become the respected dean of contemporary gerontology, but horrified because I doubted that I shall have anything to say that would be worthy of such an occasion. My anguish approached a state of panic when I realized that the topic assigned to me was "The Future for Aging Research," the concluding chapter of the "Festschrift"! Still, having been given many months to prepare myself for this assignment—by experimentation, meditation and the perusal of the manuscripts submitted by my colleagues—I though that some prophetic inspiration was bound to come in due time. Let me state quite frankly at the outset that this hope did not materialize. My extensive lucubrations about the manifold problems of aging have succeeded only in bringing back to me the wisdom of Faust (Goethe, Transl. 1949) who, having been faced with a situation not wholly unlike the one in which I find myself, was merely driven to exclaim:

"Alas! I have explored
Philosophy, and Law, and Medicine,
And over deep Divinity have pored;
Studying with ardent and laborious zeal;
And here I am at last, a very fool,
With useless learning cursed,
No wiser than at first!"

* The original experiments which form the basis of this review were performed with the assistance of The Medical Research Council of Canada and The John A. Hartford Foundation.

But then, as I know Professor Verzár, it may not displease him to hear this theme developed as it relates to the problems of gerontology.

Is There a Fountain of Youth?

It seems to have been silently assumed, since time immemorial, that the phenomena of aging must have a specific cause and that consequently, if we could discover what this is, it should be possible to stop the clock and perhaps even to turn it back.

Do we have any evidence for this kind of reasoning? Few people would feel encouraged to look for the cause of time and to seek for a prophylactic measure that might stop the influence of the ages upon the inanimate universe around us. What justification do we have to feel differently about the effect of age upon living matter? Could it not be that in both inanimate and living systems, aging is essentially an ineluctable manifestation of that kind of the entropy that affects all matter? This possibility should by no means discourage the gerontologist but only give a more realistic direction to his efforts. It seems rather unscientific to look for the "Fountain of Youth" until we have some reason to believe that such exists. By setting our aims too high, nothing can be gained and much can be lost, for we invite disillusionment when the solution of so many problems of the aged is clearly within reach.

It is primarily about these attainable aims, the projects which to my mind hold the greatest promise, that I should like to speak here. But first let me illustrate by a few examples why the hope for finding *the* theoretic explanation and *the* prevention or cure of aging strikes me as being devoid of any foundation. You may be for or against the "wear and tear" or *Abnützung* theory of aging in the sense in which it has been so masterfully propounded in an earlier chapter of this "Festschrift" (Sacher, Chapt. 26), but there can be little doubt that under constant use with the passing of time every construct, living or inanimate, wears out or, if you wish, "ages." This is true of human beings, insects, automobiles, civilizations, volcanoes and tornadoes alike but there is no reason to believe that all these wear out for the same reason or that any one prophylactic agent could keep them all young and vigorous. We

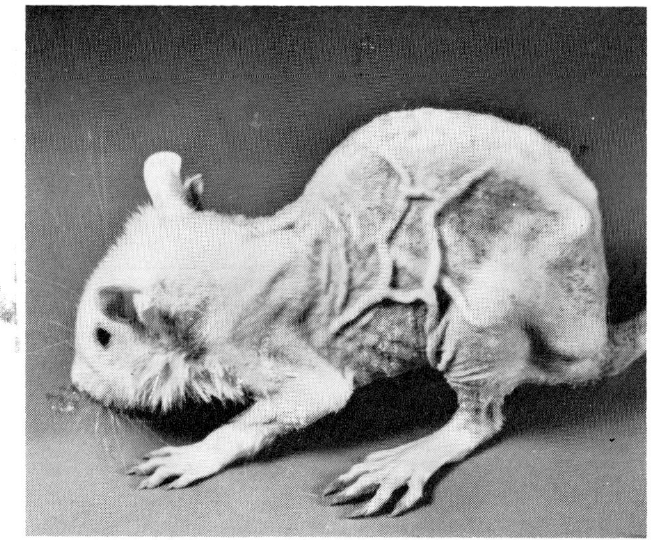

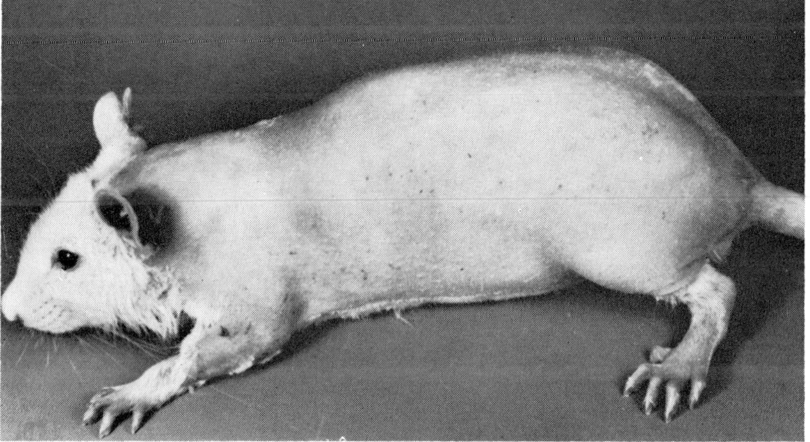

FIGURE 1. *Prevention of the DHT intoxication by Fe-Dex. Top:* General appearance of a rat treated with DHT. Marked hyposis. Pelvic bones and ribs visible through wrinkled, inelastic skin. *Bottom:* Rat of essentially normal appearance after treatment with DHT Fe-Dex. Both these rats were shaved for better visualization of the body.

posure to a variety of stressors (e.g., forced muscular exercise, cold, trauma). Here, we are evidently dealing with a pluricausal disease manifestation, since neither the humoral conditioning nor exposure to stress can produce similar cardiac lesions by themselves.

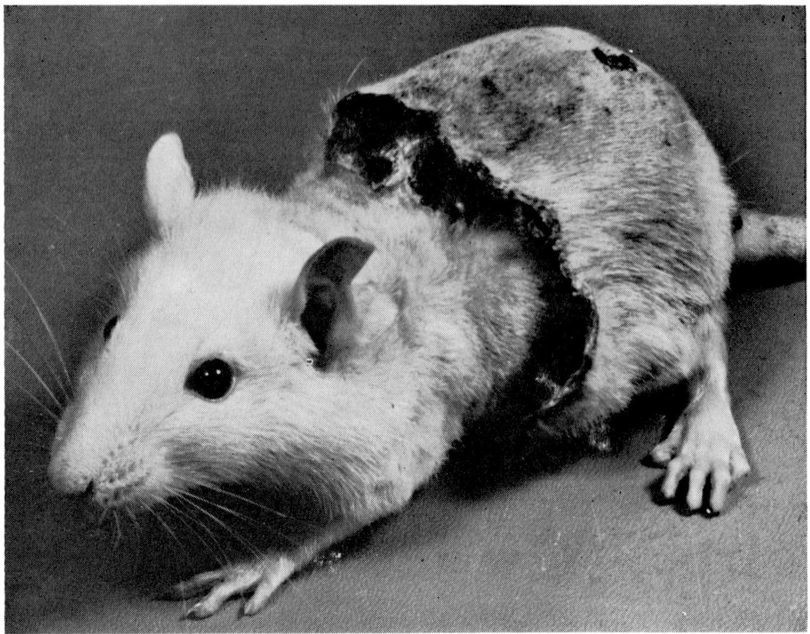

FIGURE 2. *Rat three weeks after sensitization with DHT followed by challenge with egg white.* The petrified old skin is almost fully detached and ready to be cast off. Both the old and the new skin are hair bearing. Curiously, the animal does not appear to be particularly damaged by this extensive molt.

Using this model, my associates and I (Selye, 1961) could show that:

1) These cardiac necroses are particularly severe in animals whose coronary arteries have undergone widespread calcification as a consequence of pretreatment with vitamin-D derivatives. (It will be recalled that in senile rats, the coronary arteries develop calcification, not atheromatosis.)

2) These cardiac necroses are not preceded, though they are often followed, by thrombosis of the vessels in the affected area. This change is particularly common in arteries damaged by calcification. Thus, it became evident that cardiac necrosis is not necessarily a consequence, but may be a cause of vascular occlusion.

3) Treatment with KCl or $MgCl_2$ just before exposure to stress can prevent these cardiac necroses.

4) Gradual adaptation to stressors (e.g., forced muscular exercise, cold) likewise protects against the induction of cardiac necrosis by subsequent humoral conditioning and renewed exposure to stress. Indeed, inurement to one stressor protects the trained animal against the production of cardiac necrosis, not only by the same, but even by unrelated stressors. Hence, here we are not merely dealing with specific adaptation to one agent (which would then lose its stressor effect), but the induction of a kind of tolerance to stress itself, no matter how produced.

Numerous observations on man support the concept of some causal relationship between stress and cardiac necrosis (Selye, 1961; Köhler, 1964; Heyden-Stucky, 1965), hence basic research on the underlying mechanisms would appear to hold the promise of clinically applicable results. The success of this approach depends upon the availability of suitable models of disease, and while that which we have here outlined has served a certain purpose, it is undoubtedly capable of further perfection and exploitation.

Calciphylaxis and the Progeria-like Syndrome

Calciphylaxis is a biological response through which the organism can selectively send large amounts of calcium salts to certain organs and cause their complete petrification. It depends upon two steps: sensitization by pretreatment with some calcifying agents, such as vitamin D_2-derivatives or parathyroid extract, followed by challenge with any one of many compounds among which metals and mast-cell dischargers are particularly efficacious.

On the other hand, prolonged pretreatment with minute doses of challengers can elicit a kind of "inverse calciphylaxis" which offers protection against soft-tissue calcification otherwise induced by diverse means. It has long been known that derangements in calcium metabolism, particularly the loss of bone minerals (osteoporosis) and the concurrent abnormal deposition of calcium in soft tissues (arteries, periarticular tissues, crystalline lens) are common in old people. It seemed of interest, therefore, to explore the possibility of gaining further information concerning this relationship by the use of the newly acquired knowledge in the field of calciphylaxis (Selye, 1962).

It was found that a condition reminiscent of progeria can be induced in rats by prolonged treatment with comparatively small doses of vitamin-D derivatives, particularly dihydrotachysterol. Animals so treated exhibit an extreme catabolism with wrinkling of the skin, loss of hair, generalized arterial calcification, involution of the musculature and sex organs, a greatly reduced life span and other manifestations reminiscent of progeria (Selye *et al.*, 1963; Tuchweber *et al.*, 1963).

Using this experimental model, it could be shown that:

1) Inverse calciphylaxis induced by chronic pretreatment with small doses of various challengers (e.g., iron compounds) can completely protect the rat against the progeria-like syndrome. This treatment prevents not only the pathologic deposition of calcium in soft tissues, but also the associated organ changes that are not accompanied by any demonstrable calcification (e.g., catabolism, cutaneous lesions, involution of the sex organs).

2) A variety of anabolic steroids, which normally exert no obvious effect upon calcium metabolism, prevent not only the catabolism but also the soft-tissue calcifications of the progeria-like syndrome otherwise induced by chronic vitamin-D overdosage.

Here, we appear to have a model which might lend itself to the objective study of at least one salient manifestation of aging: the disturbance in mineral metabolism.

None of the investigations just outlined can pretend to deal with the process of aging itself. Yet, they do furnish us with tools for the quantitative analysis of certain morbid changes which are common in aged individuals.

Conclusion and Outlook

Throughout the centuries it has been assumed as self-evident that aging has a specific cause and that consequently we might discover what this is and perhaps find ways to block it. The primary purpose of this brief survey was to emphasize that actually we have no justification for such an assumption. As far as I know, no one has ever suggested that maturation, the process of growing up, has any one specific cause. Undoubtedly, the hormones regulating growth and sexual development, as well as numerous dietary, nervous and other factors, play decisive roles here. Yet, we have no reason to suspect that a unified theory of "the growing-up process" could be formulated or that in this respect the clock could be turned back by some panacea which would interfere with all the relevant biologic reactions. In a period of basic research which has produced so many miracles from penicillin to interplanetary travel, optimism is understandable; far be it from me to discourage the exercise of unlimited imagination. What I have said is not intended to dissuade creative minds from continuing their search for an all-embracing theory which might lead to the prophylaxis or even the cure of the aging process itself. My purpose was only to point out that, at present, we have no objective basis for suspecting that such endeavors could be fruitful, while we do have many reliable techniques (and good reasons to assume that even better ones could be developed) for the study of individual morbid lesions which decrease life expectancy.

The basic question is really whether the spring in life's clock can or cannot be rewound after birth. To this question, I have no answer, but it seems to me that with the means now available, much more can be done to protect the spring and prolong its usefulness than to wind it up again.

REFERENCES

GOETHE, J. W.: *Faust.* (Translation by J. Anster.) London, The Oxford University Press, 1949.

HEYDEN-STUCKY, S.: Myokardinfarkt und psychischer Stress. *Schweiz. Med. Wschr., 95:*1045, 1965.

HUTCHINSON, M. K.: Physiological stress and aging. In: *A Report on the Fourteenth Annual Southern Conference on Gerontology.* Gainesville, University of Florida Press, 1965.

KÖHLER, J. A.: Über die moderne Therapie des Herzinfarktes. *Fortschr. Med., 82:*544, 1964.

SELYE, H.: *Stress.* Montreal, Acta Inc., Med. Publ., 1950.

SELYE, H.: *The Pluricausal Cardiopathies.* Springfield, Thomas, 1961.

SELYE, H.: *Calciphylaxis.* Chicago, The University of Chicago Press, 1962.

SELYE, H., STREBEL, R., AND MIKULAJ, L.: A progeria-like syndrome produced by dihydrotachysterol and its prevention by methyltestosterone and ferric dextran. *J. Amer. Geriat. Soc., 11:*1, 1963.

TUCHWEBER, B., GABBIANI, G., AND SELYE, H.: Effect of vitamin E and methyltestosterone upon the progeria-like syndrome produced by dihydrotachysterol. *Amer. J. Clin. Nutr., 13:*238, 1963.

NAME AND AUTHOR INDEX

(*Italicized* numbers indicate reference citations.)

Y

Z

SUBJECT INDEX

D

F

G

H

I

K

L

R

U

V

W

X

Y

QP
86
.S5